"Your friend if ever you had one" – The Letters of Sylvia Beach to James Joyce

European Joyce Studies

General Editor

Geert Lernout (*University of Antwerp*)

Editorial Board

Scarlett Baron (*University College London*)
Kasia Bazarnik (*Jagiellonian University*)
Valérie Bénéjam (*University of Nantes*)
Teresa Caneda (*University of Vigo*)
Ronan Crowley (*University of Antwerp*)
Anne Fogarty (*University College Dublin*)
Onno Kosters (*Utrecht University*)
John McCourt (*University of Macerata*)
Erika Mihálycsa (*Babes-Bolyai University*)
Fritz Senn (*Zürich James Joyce Foundation*)
Amanda Sigler (*University of Virginia*)
Sam Slote (*Trinity College Dublin*)
Dirk Vanderbeke (*Friedrich Schiller University of Jena*)
Dirk Van Hulle (*University of Oxford*)

Founded by

Christine van Boheemen-Saaf, in association with Fritz Senn

VOLUME 31

The titles published in this series are listed at *brill.com/ejs*

FIGURE 1   Sylvia Beach in the 1920s
PHOTOGRAPHER UNKNOWN. COURTESY OF SPECIAL COLLECTIONS,
PRINCETON UNIVERSITY

"Your friend if ever you had one" – The Letters of Sylvia Beach to James Joyce

Edited by

Ruth Frehner
Ursula Zeller

BRILL
RODOPI

LEIDEN | BOSTON

With the generous support of the Irish Embassy in Berne

Ambasáid na hÉireann | An Eilvéis
Embassy of Ireland | Switzerland

Cover illustration: collage by Ursula Zeller and Ruth Frehner. Letters and cards of Sylvia Beach: Sylvia Beach Estate, Fred Dennis; courtesy of Zürich James Joyce Foundation. Shadow Figures of Sylvia Beach and James Joyce: Courtesy of Sylvia Beach Papers, C0108, Manuscripts Division, Department of Special Collections, Princeton University Library.

Library of Congress Cataloging-in-Publication Data

Names: Beach, Sylvia, author. | Frehner, Ruth, editor. | Zeller, Ursula, editor.
Title: "Your friend if ever you had one" : the letters of Sylvia Beach to James Joyce /
    edited by Ruth Frehner, Ursula Zeller.
Other titles: Letters of Sylvia Beach to James Joyce
Description: Leiden ; Boston : Brill Rodopi, [2021] | Series: European Joyce studies,
    0923–9855 ; volume 31 | Includes bibliographical references and index.
Identifiers: LCCN 2021015530 (print) | LCCN 2021015531 (ebook) | ISBN
    9789004427037 (hardback ; acid-free paper) | ISBN 9789004427044 (ebook)
Subjects: LCSH: Beach, Sylvia—Correspondence. | Joyce, James,
    1882–1941—Correspondence. | Joyce, James, 1882–1941 Ulysses. | Léon, Paul L. (Paul Léopoldovitch),
    1893–1942?—Correspondence. | Publishers and publishing—France—Correspondence. |
    Booksellers and bookselling—France—Correspondence. | LCGFT: Personal correspondence.
Classification: LCC Z305.B33 A3 2021 (print) | LCC Z305.B33 (ebook) | DDC 070.50944—dc23
LC record available at https://lccn.loc.gov/2021015530
LC ebook record available at https://lccn.loc.gov/2021015531

Typeface for the Latin, Greek, and Cyrillic scripts: "Brill". See and download: brill.com/brill-typeface.

ISSN 0923-9855
ISBN 978-90-04-42703-7 (hardback)
ISBN 978-90-04-42704-4 (e-book)

Copyright 2021 by Koninklijke Brill NV, Leiden, The Netherlands.
Koninklijke Brill NV incorporates the imprints Brill, Brill Nijhoff, Brill Hotei, Brill Schöningh, Brill Fink, Brill mentis, Vandenhoeck & Ruprecht, Böhlau Verlag and V&R Unipress.
All rights reserved. No part of this publication may be reproduced, translated, stored in a retrieval system, or transmitted in any form or by any means, electronic, mechanical, photocopying, recording or otherwise, without prior written permission from the publisher. Requests for re-use and/or translations must be addressed to Koninklijke Brill NV via brill.com or copyright.com.

This book is printed on acid-free paper and produced in a sustainable manner.

in memoriam Hans E. Jahnke

Contents

Acknowledgements   XI
"Who is Sylvia? What is She?"   XIII
Editors' Introduction   XV
Letters 1921-1939   XXVII
List of Figures   XXXIII

The Letters of Sylvia Beach to James Joyce or Paul Léon 1921-1939

Introduction to the 1920s   3
    Ruth Frehner

Letters 1921-1929   17

Introduction to the 1930s   124
    Ursula Zeller

Letters 1930-1939   142

Appendix A: Chronology of Major Events 1917-1941   275
Appendix B: Survey of Correspondence between Sylvia Beach and James Joyce or Paul Léon   282
Appendix C: Survey of Correspondence re *Frankfurter Zeitung* Affair   305
Appendix D: Joyce's Book Orders through Sylvia Beach   309
Appendix E: Currencies: Historical Values and Their Equivalent in 2020   311
Bibliography   313
Index   322

Acknowledgements

The person to whom we owe our greatest thanks is no longer with us. Hans E. Jahnke, Giorgio Joyce's stepson, has been overwhelmingly generous to the Zürich James Joyce Foundation in donating all Joyce papers in his possession to our institute, the Beach letters being one of the core parts. On his visits to Zurich, where he had spent many a childhood year with his mother Asta and his new father, he also became a good friend to us, whose unique, waggish sense of humour we still miss.

Beach's family has been generous to us, too. We are grateful to her nephew Fred Dennis, executor of the Beach Estate, who promptly gave us green light, granting us permission to publish all documents.

While Hans Jahnke and Fred Dennis made this book project possible in the first place, we could enjoy the help of a number of people along the way towards the edition.

On our research visit to Buffalo, Michael Basinksi, former director of the Special Collections at Buffalo University, proved a generous and supportive host. In his successor James Maynard we found an equally kind and most helpful colleague, who provided us with further details on documents we were working with. We are also grateful to Assistant Curator Alison Fraser, who took care of further email queries.

At Princeton University, Don Skemer, Curator of Manuscripts, and his staff welcomed us for a full week and indefatigably attended to special requests. AnnaLee Pauls promptly and reliably supplied us with copies of central items in the Beach Papers, while Brianna Cregle kindly arranged for photographic material.

Catherine Fahy, whose catalogue of the Joyce-Paul Léon Papers in the National Library of Ireland was an indispensable tool for the 1930s correspondence, is to be thanked also for kindly transcribing some of the Beach to Joyce letters for us. More recently, Nora Thornton from the NLI staff has been very obliging, too, and attended to our further requests even before the reopening after the corona lockdown – and irrespective of regular office hours, at that.

Jean M. Cannon of the Harry Ransom Center in Texas, helped clarify a context by checking some letters for us in the William A. Bradley archives.

Many a friend and colleague from the global Joyce family needs to be thanked for sharing their expertise with us:

Luca Crispi kindly added extra footnotes, as it were, to his most useful essay on *Ulysses* in the marketplace. Sam Slote was more than once our port of call for information on genetic issues concerning "Work in Progress" and

Finnegans Wake. Eishiro Ito of Iwate Prefectural University most generously shared with us his knowledge on the early Japanese translations of *Ulysses*, both providing us with important details and adding to the broader picture of Joyce's reception in Japan. Carmelo Medina Casado devoted some precious time of his Buffalo research stay to our edition and looked up some details on an early draft of Issy's alphabet, while Cinzia Valenti, former ZJJF scholar, helped clarify some nuances in the Italian translation of an occasional poem for Ezra Pound. Andreas Weigel kindly shared his knowledge of Marcel Ray's involvement with *Exiles*.

We are further grateful to our good friend Harald Beck and to John Simpson, former Chief Editor of the OED, for their detective skills in identifying Michael Joyce and in finding his daughter Louise McConnell, who also provided us with useful information. We could moreover profit from John's knowledge of the historical postal system in Britain.

At Brill Rodopi, Masja Horn, acquisitions manager, has coordinated our project with great competence and kindness, and always with a sympathetic ear ... We are very fortunate that Geert Lernout, a long-time friend, has accompanied the book. Sincerest thanks for his advice and his careful copy-editing.

And not least, our warm *Merci!* goes to our team colleagues at the Zürich James Joyce Foundation. Fritz Senn, ZJJF director, was an inspiring presence, and it took us only three steps to next door to tap a lifetime's Joycean expertise. Silke Stebler typed up some materials for us and otherwise supported us with her unfailing cheerfulness. Frances Ilmberger joined us in processing the Jahnke papers and occasionally acted as book messenger between the English Department and the ZJJF. We also wish to thank the Foundation's Board of Trustees for their general support and encouragement.

At a crucial phase in our project, our good colleagues Gabriela Stöckli and Florence Widmer of Translation House Looren, Switzerland, offered us a 1-week retreat at their inspiring residential workplace (Alpine panorama included).

At home, Hans-Ulrich Kull and Hugo Ramnek were immensely helpful over years by their very forbearance (the skipped movie nights! The missed hiking weekends!...), as well as their interest in our work and in the story of Joyce and his enterprising publisher.

And finally, but importantly, the Irish Embassy in Berne has generously supported this book project. Our sincere thanks to Ambassador Eamon Hickey, with whom we have enjoyed various collaborations in matters Joycean.

"Who is Sylvia? What is She?"

She was a bookseller who cared less for books than for the men who wrote them – whence the title of her shop – and less for the writers who had written than for those who might.

    ARCHIBALD MCLEISH

• • •

I was very shy when I first went into the bookshop and I did not have enough money on me to join the rental library. She told me I could pay the deposit any time I had the money and made me out a card and said I could take as many books as I wished. There was no reason for her to trust me. She did not know me and the address I had given her could not have been a poorer one. But she was delightful and charming and welcoming.

    ERNEST HEMINGWAY

• • •

Sylvia had a vigorous clear mind, an excellent memory, a tremendous respect for books as civilizing objects and was really a remarkable librarian. ... Her little Shakespeare bookshop, which had become an incalculably large radiating center of literary influence and illumination over which she modestly presided, as small in her person as in her premises. ... Where she did not escape the publisher's fate was as the beast of burden struggling beneath the crushing load of a singular author's genius and egotisms, heavy as stones or marble in the case of the Dubliner Joyce.

    That *Ulysses* became the sort of book it is is largely due to her, for it was she in this, her one publishing venture, who decided to allow Joyce an indefinite right to correct his proofs. It was in the exercise of this right that the peculiarities of Joyce's prose reached their novel flowering.

    JANET FLANNER

• • •

Enterprise to her was a sporting proposition. ... Under the appearance of unassuming simplicity, acute judgements were made, and the relentless generosity acted in silence beyond argument or polemic, ... identifying her self-interest with the well-being of what she admired. The struggle for personal and individual values against bigness and commercialism has only begun. ... The influence and the force of her example begins to be felt. Her career, her life, was not a lesson: it had the style of a work of art.
>   LESLIE KATZ

"Enjoyer". C'est le mot qui venait le plus souvent à la bouche de Sylvia, et qui rend le mieux compte de son état d'enthousiasme perpetuel. Sylvia faisait hautement savoir lorsqu'elle enjoyait quelque chose. S'agissant de quelqu'un, enjoyer signifiait accueillir avec joie, faire fête.
>   MAURICE SAILLET
>   "Mots et Locutions de Sylvia"

All she ever did was to make me a present of the ten best years of her life.
>   JAMES JOYCE

Editors' Introduction

1 "The Silviest Beach of Beaches"

Sylvia Beach (1887-1962) was not the first woman to promote and support James Joyce – Margaret Anderson and Jane Heap of *The Little Review* as well as Harriet Weaver of *The Egoist* had been there before her. However, with her great courage, her perseverance, her enthusiasm, her generosity and – as it turned out – her entrepreneurial flair, it was she who gave the world Joyce's hitherto unpublishable *Ulysses*. For help and advice she could count on her companion Adrienne Monnier, whose bookshop and lending library "La Maison des Amis des Livres" had been Sylvia Beach's inspiration for her own enterprise "Shakespeare and Company". Not even a full year after early Spring 1921 when she and Joyce had decided to publish *Ulysses* under her imprint, the first two copies were handed over to Sylvia Beach at the Gare de Lyon when the early morning train arrived from Dijon on 2nd February 1922, Joyce's 40th birthday. A new era was to begin: by the end of May 1930, when the 11th edition had come out, 28,000 copies of *Ulysses* had been printed.

From that moment she would not only take care of the sales of *Ulysses* that provided a steady income to both of them, even though granted him very generous royalties at 25%, but she also helped Joyce with his post-*Ulysses* project – his *Work in Progress*, that was published in 1939 as *Finnegans Wake*. The latter was also meant to earn him an income by having fragments published, and Beach went out of her way to engage publishers of the various small presses that flourished in Paris for deluxe editions. This meant that she also worked as his literary agent, apart from being his money lender.

Being fluent in French, she moved with ease in the Paris circles, and she could open doors for Joyce to the French literary and cultural world. Her bookshop did not only attract patrons among the Americans that had come to Paris after the First World War, such as Ezra Pound, Gertrude Stein, Ernest Hemingway, Robert McAlmon ... it was also a centre for French writers like Valery Larbaud – who became the godfather of Sylvia Beach's shop – André Gide, Léon-Paul Fargue, Jules Romains, to name just a few. Her circle of friends also included musicians like Erik Satie or George Antheil. "Shakespeare and Company" was an immensely rich cosmos of its own, of which Beach's biographer, Noel Riley Fitch, conveys a vivid picture.

As publishers, both Beach and Monnier were exceptional: they did not have the ample financial resources (either through marriage or inheritance) enjoyed by many owners of the small presses in Paris.[1] They had to earn a living with their bookshops, although both did have some support from their parents – mostly, as Fitch points out, because both Beach and Monnier had "only" sisters but no brothers. But this, at least in Monnier's case, was above all money to get started.

Beach had earned some money of her own, but a major part came from her mother, who "believed in daughters having careers" and for whom "a bookstore was after her own heart", whereas her father would have preferred to have his daughters around him (Fitch, pp. 38 and 40). Eventually, Beach would make substantial profits from her *Ulysses* sales. At the same time, however, on top of paying all the printing and administrative costs for Joyce's novel, as well as his uniquely generous royalties, she paid "advances" for Joyce's private expenses, that were hardly ever returned.

After her 11th edition was sold out – at a time when relations between Beach and Joyce had become difficult – she came to realise that she no longer had the physical and emotional strength to launch another edition. By that time Joyce had found someone else, his friend Paul Léon, who was increasingly to replace her as Joyce's assistant and administrator. From 1932 he would also act as his personal consultant and legal adviser.

The present edition will also document this transition that took place in 1932-33 – no doubt a painful period for Sylvia Beach – as it includes all extant letters she wrote to her successor Paul Léon. Having kept *Ulysses* in print for 10 years, she would not be able to enjoy the fruits of her labour when the American edition came out in 1934, after the court case had been won. It sold more copies in the first two months than she ever did with her 11 editions.

When in 1936 Beach toyed with the idea of closing her bookshop, it was her French circle of friends that rescued the shop for a while. Then the end came in 1941, when the Nazis threatened to confiscate the "Shakespeare and Company" stocks. She rescued them to a top-floor flat above her store. The books survived. The bookshop did not.

1.1   *The Story of the Letters*

In 2006 the Zürich James Joyce Foundation received a generous gift from Professor Hans E. Jahnke (1943-2010), the son of Asta Osterwalder Joyce, second

---

[1] Examples are Nancy Cunard (*Hours Press*), Harry and Caresse Crosby (*Black Sun Press*), Robert McAlmon (*Contact Edition*), his office address being 12, Rue de L'Odéon – Beach's bookshop. Another one was William Bird who had the *Three Mountains Press* (Fitch, p. 154f. and Pearson, p.2f.).

wife of Joyce's son Giorgio. The donation consisted of personal books as well as medical, legal and various other documents of the Joyce family. The most extraordinary documents are note sheets and manuscripts, and many letters from James Joyce to Giorgio and family. Moreover, there were letters to James Joyce, most notably from the French literary critic Louis Gillet and – Sylvia Beach.[2] The items in question were originally part of Giorgio's estate, some of which Asta inherited after his death in 1976.

The above is the continuation of a story that takes us back to the 1940s when Joyce's wife Nora gave Maria Jolas a trunk with family papers into custody – most likely papers left behind when in 1939 the Joyces moved out of Paris. And it became a story of discovery that William Brockman disclosed at the end of the 1990s in the *Journal of Modern Literature*[3] in an article on Richard Ellmann's ways of gaining access to Joyce's papers and his use of them in the 1950s and 1960s while writing his biography and editing the volumes II and III of Joyce's letters.

Of particular interest is Ellmann's 1981 letter to Maria Jolas about what both of them used to refer to as the "famous trunk":

> If it hadn't been for the famous trunk, and your decision that I should see its contents with or without other authorization, I should hardly have had the courage to press on with my biography. It enabled me to speak to Stanislaus and others from a position of strength.
> quoted in BROCKMAN 1998/99, p. 258f.

Tracing the history and the contents of this trunk, Brockman concludes that Ellmann and Jolas acted with utmost circumspection, letting no-one outside the Joyce family know of its existence, not least for motives of being the first to lay hands on the treasure. They were "concerned that, were Giorgio or Stephen Joyce to come into possession of the papers in the trunk, they would sell or destroy them or at least make them unavailable" (Brockman, p. 259). Ellmann took extensive notes when he was able to examine them in 1953. According to his notes, the bulk of papers were letters written to Joyce during the 1920s and 30s. Among the writers were Sylvia Beach, Louis Gillet, Stuart Gilbert, Adrienne Monnier, Frank Budgen, Paul Léon, the law firm Monro Saw, John Rodker, Harriet Shaw Weaver, John Quinn. But there were also family letters:

---

2   See website of the Zürich James Joyce Foundation, http://www.joycefoundation.ch/jahnke-bequest-2 for a list of contents.
3   What follows is based on Brockman's account.

Lucia, Stanislaus, Giorgio, as well as summaries of letters from doctors about Lucia's problems.

In February 1955 Jolas wrote to Ellmann that she was tired of the responsibility as a keeper of these papers, and she travelled to Zurich – against Ellmann's advice to keep them as long as possible – and convinced Giorgio that he should take possession of the trunk, which he seems to have done. Thus the papers were no longer available for research, and Joyce's letters to Sylvia Beach (mostly held at Buffalo) were published in 1987 without their counterparts. They would have made some of his letters to her more intelligible.

It is ironic that the papers may briefly have been in Zurich in the fifties – long before the local Joyce Foundation was established. "In 1984," as Ellmann wrote to Jolas, "as a result of a settlement between Stephen Joyce and the heirs of George Joyce's second wife, Stephen Joyce was given possession of the 'famous' trunk" (Brockman, p. 262).

Some 20 years later it turned out that Ellmann's 1984 news was not the end of the story, when Stephen Joyce's stepbrother Hans Jahnke bequeathed his share in the contents of the "famous trunk" to the Zürich James Joyce Foundation. Ellmann's notes, however, were extremely useful: for one thing, he listed correspondents and documents that correlate with the contents of the Jahnke Bequest: letters from Beach and Gillet, family letters, medical documents about Lucia. The piece of evidence, however, is one of Sylvia Beach's letters. On 29 April 1927 she severely and memorably rebuked Joyce for telling her "cock and bull stories" instead of "owning up to spending too much money" – a letter that Brockman, probably for its unusual frankness, cited in his article.

Beach's letters to Joyce close a gap in epistolary scholarship. Together with those from Joyce to Beach they reveal something of a relationship which, for the disparateness of the material, both falls short of and yet goes beyond Beach's own account in her memoirs *Shakespeare and Company*, inasmuch as the letters in our book offer a glance into the prosaic world of everyday matters that were a substantial part of their relationship. On rare occasions, as in April 1927, they also allow a glimpse of her state of mind, which Beach would later suppress in the published version of her memoirs. The patient and ever obliging woman had, it seems for the first time, reached her limits. More was to come.

1.2   Scope of This Edition

The core of this collection of letters are those of Sylvia Beach to James Joyce from the Jahnke Bequest at the Zürich James Joyce Foundation. During our research we also located some unpublished letters, statements of accounts or messages from Beach to Joyce at the National Library of Ireland and at Buffalo which are here published for the first time.

Beach's twenty letters to Paul Léon, mostly written in the years 1932-1933, are held at these two repositories (with many of the NLI originals as carbon copies at Buffalo). To these we could add an unusually early letter from the Jahnke Bequest, dating from 25 August 1930: this may well be the first extant letter of the Beach-Léon correspondence. These letters poignantly continue – though via the intermediary Léon – the story of Beach's relationship to Joyce, at the same time that they document its lasting damage.

With the exception of one letter, all of the documents were addressed to Joyce or Léon, and while the great majority was written by Beach, six of them were written by her assistants on her behalf. As to the exception: it is a letter to Nora Joyce in September 1931 – very different in tone and therefore well worth including here.

Whereas 303 letters, postcards and telegrams from Joyce or Léon[4] could be located, only 146 documents from Beach to Joyce or Léon have been found. Of these, 131 documents are published for the first time, fourteen were published in Walsh's *Letters of Sylvia Beach* (2010) and one in Banta and Silverman's *James Joyce's Letters to Sylvia Beach* (1987, Appendix C). But in both publications annotations about the Joycean context had been kept to a minimum.

For copyright reasons it was not possible to publish a letters edition of the complete extant exchange of letters between the two protagonists. To give at least an idea of the epistolary corpus, the present volume provides a detailed survey of their correspondence as well as a visualization of their exchange in Appendix B. The survey also traces the movements of the correspondents: she mostly in Paris, except for summer breaks in the Haute-Savoie or at Rocfoin, he in many Paris flats and hotels or in eye clinics, and out and about, often at expensive hotels in French and Belgian seaside resorts or – a prolonged stay in 1931 – living in a flat in London in order to get married.

Beach's letters also allow us to determine more precisely some of the approximate dates in *James Joyce's Letters to Sylvia Beach*, particularly in August-September 1931.

---

4 This includes twenty-three unpublished cards to Beach (from 1921-1938) mostly for her birthday, Easter or Christmas, and eleven notes/cards without date (all at Buffalo); four of the latter were published in *JJtoSB*.

XX   EDITORS' INTRODUCTION

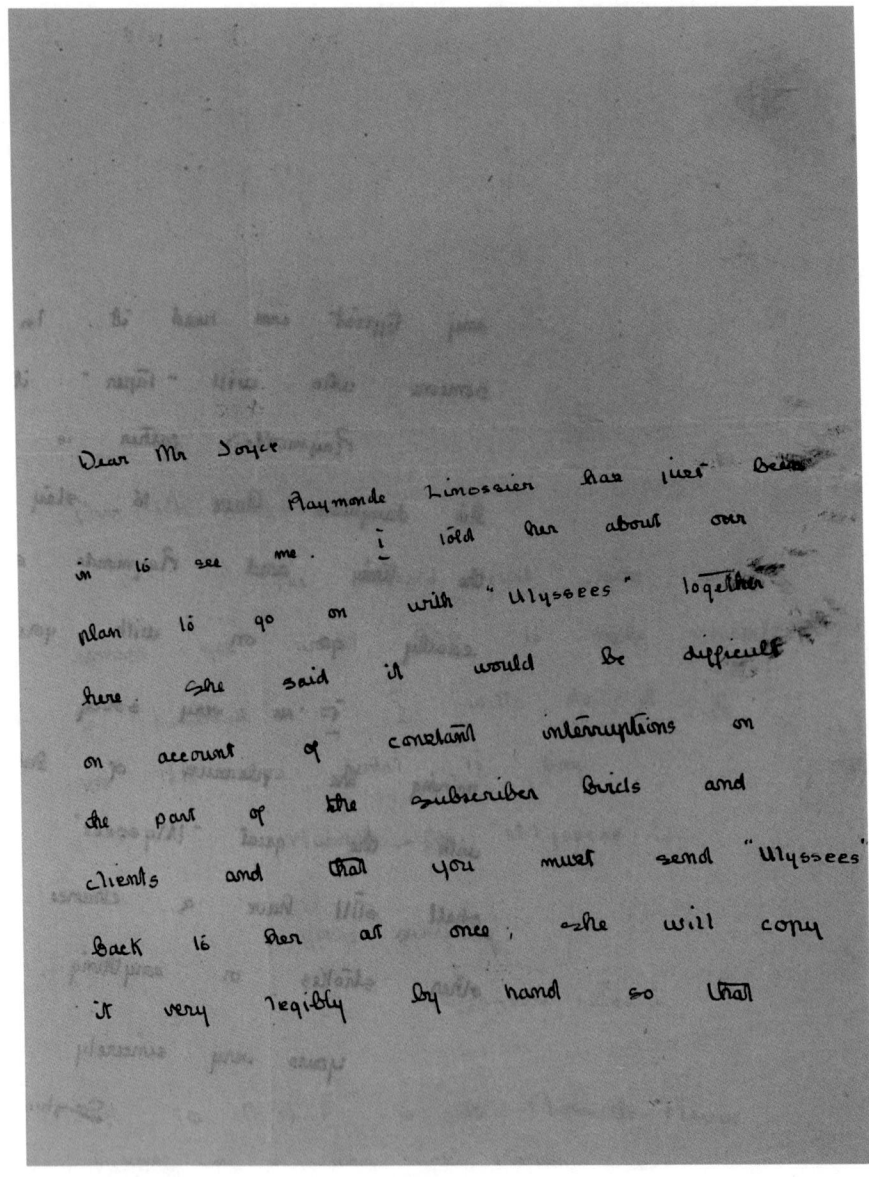

FIGURE 2   Letter of 16 February 1921
            © SYLVIA BEACH ESTATE

1.3   *Lacunae*

> Most of the letters I got from Joyce were, of course, written during my summer holidays or in the course of his own travels. And of course he always demanded replies by "tomorrow", "by express", "by return of post". As a rule, he would be in need of funds, and when I was away, he usually managed to get something through Myrsine, who was left in charge of Shakespeare and Company. As she well knew, whether anything was left in his account or not, we had to look after the author of Ulysses.
>
> *Sha&Co*, p. 196

In many cases, the letters from Beach to Joyce are conspicuously missing, above all in the 1920s, when the Joyces lived at a hotel in Paris (between September 1923 and the beginning of July 1924), or in periods when he was being treated for his eye-illnesses. Most notable is that there are no extant letters in three periods when Joyce was travelling and was himself a frequent letter writer, as in July-August 1925, in May-June 1927 and in the spring of 1928. In the early 1930s, however, the picture is somewhat different: the exchange of letters is extremely dense, above all over the period from the end of April 1931 to late September when the Joyces were in London, and also in 1932 and 1933, when Beach wrote her 'letters to Joyce' – wherever he was – mainly to Paul Léon, who preserved them. After 1933, letters grew very rare, indeed there is none from either in 1934 – except a birthday and a Christmas card from Joyce to her (Buffalo). The last such card dates from 1938.

The apparent lacunae in the 1920s might reflect that with Joyce's constant changes of address, it may have been more difficult for him to keep all his correspondence together. As to the gaps in her letters in periods when both were in Paris, we can only assume that correspondence was not really necessary since matters could be discussed in person. As letters from him to her were mostly in the form of a request that she complied with, she could tell him what she had done on his frequent visits to her bookshop.

1.4   *Repositories of Original Letters*

Of the present edition's 145 documents by (or on behalf of) Sylvia Beach to James Joyce or Paul Léon, 108 are part of the Hans E. Jahnke Bequest at the Zürich James Joyce Foundation.

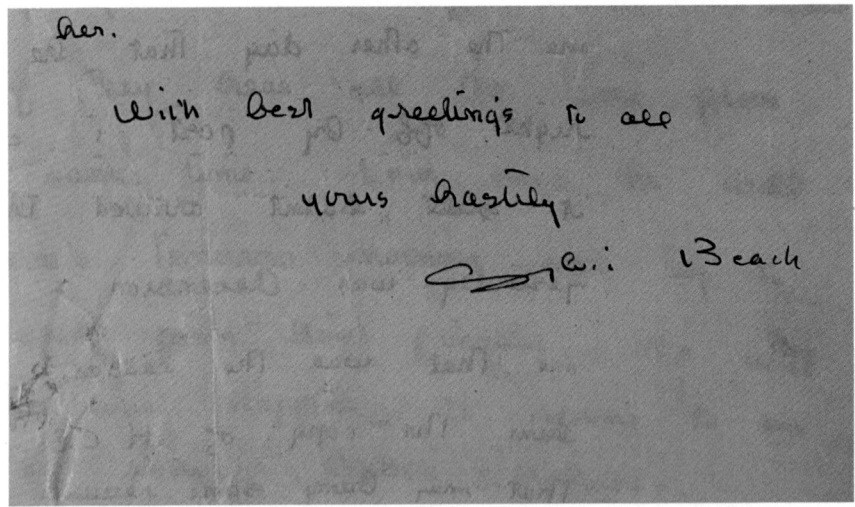

FIGURE 3   Letter of 15 May 1931
© SYLVIA BEACH ESTATE

The remaining 37 documents are in the following collections: at the National Library of Ireland there are 21; many of these are available as copies at Buffalo. 15 additional documents are only at Buffalo, and 1 letter is at Princeton.

1.5   *Material Quality of the Letters*

Beach wrote most of her letters in ink on Shakespeare & Company stationery. Her handwriting is very neat, her lines are at least double spaced and straight – she probably put a sheet of ruled paper under her stationery – with generous margins on the left. Her signature, sometimes with a slight upward slant, is often the only thing that departs from the straight line, with the exception of the postscripts. These are sometimes written diagonally to fill a corner, or fitted into the margins, or even next to Shakespeare's head at the top.

Considering her more than full working days, it is unusual that her handwriting suggests a slow writer: her letters are carefully written – crafted almost: her letters m, n and u are easily distinguishable, the *m*s and *n*s often with a kind of kink before the actual letter. She also makes extraordinarily wide spaces between words, which interrupts the flow of the hand considerably. Also, there are relatively few slips of the pen.

1.6 *Editorial Procedures*

1.6.1 Spellings

Letters are in many ways a mirror of the writer's personality and therefore we have kept editorial intrusions to a minimum. Beach was one of the few expats who had a very good knowledge of the French language and literature and made her closest adult friends among the French (Fitch, p. 99f.). So it is quite natural that some French spellings would creep into her writing, e.g. "enveloppe", or "november" (small case as in French), or the amalgamized spelling for Brussels which becomes "Brussells", reflecting the French double -l- of "Bruxelles". Idiosyncratic spellings have been preserved, and we have also refrained from using an indicator such as "sic" or have only used it when confusion might result. The letters are presented as *clear copy*: if Beach corrected her spelling during writing, only her corrected version is included, if she deleted a word and replaced it with another, only the replacement is shown. Apart from obvious slips of the pen, which have been corrected, there are no silent emendations.

1.6.2 Place Names

Whenever Joyce was not in Paris, he either provided Beach with his address for her correspondence, or his address could be inferred from his letter to her as he almost invariably used the hotel stationery provided. Hence the place name in an address is usually spelled in French or Dutch whenever he wrote her from his holidays there, whereas in the editorial text English is used. In the case of Ostende (French spelling) the English spelling "Ostend" in our editorial text is not an erroneous omission.

1.6.3 Underlinings

Beach is not consistent in her underscoring of work titles, they are therefore rendered as she wrote them, and likewise other underscores are shown as written.

1.6.4 Currencies

The currencies most frequently occurring in the letters are the (old) French franc, the British pound and the US dollar, occasionally the German Reichsmark is mentioned or the Japanese Yen. It is notoriously difficult to give today's value of a certain amount of money so far back in time, and because the period of 1920-1940 saw a lot of turbulence at the currency markets, we opted for a table giving today's (2020) purchasing power of the French franc, the pound and the dollar for the years 1921-1940. Thus at least an approximation of the present value of an amount mentioned in the letters can be determined. (Appendix E).

1.7 *Presentation of Letters*

Following the letter, there is a bibliographical note, with the following information:

1   *Material description*
2   *Dating*
3   *Irregular layout of the letter*

For any part of the letter (a passage from the main body of the text, an addition or postscript) deviating from standard layout, its actual position is described in the bibliographical note. There is one exception to this: 15 May 1929, where a more intrusive transcription suggested itself.

4   *Mention of enclosures*
5   *Addressee's address*

1.7.1 Languages Other Than English

Translations (mostly of short messages in French) are the editors' unless a published translation is available.

1.7.2 Annotations

Apart from the glossing of names or places etc., the annotations will provide the necessary context for understanding the letters and are also geared toward opening up paths for future research, with references to the vast archival resources of Joycean scholarship.

The letters from 1921-1930 have been annotated by Ruth Frehner, whereas Ursula Zeller has taken care of the letters from 1931-1939.

1.7.3 Identifications of Persons

First footnotes include notes about his/her biography; when a person's name occurs repeatedly throughout the letters, we will provide the back reference to the first note, followed by information pertinent to the immediate context of the letter. Identifications are not given for Joyce's immediate family: Nora, Giorgio, Lucia.

1.7.4 References to Unpublished Material

They provide the name of the repository and its relevant collection, and if deemed necessary, also the manuscript identification. However, where there is a comprehensive online catalogue, we have refrained from providing the manuscript ID: in recent years, major collections (Buffalo, and above all Princeton) have re-arranged / re-catalogued their holdings.

1.7.5 Abbreviations for Material Description of Documents

ADS	autograph document signed
ALI	autograph letter, signed with initials
ALS	autograph letter signed
AN	autograph note
ANI	autograph note, signed with initials
APCI	autograph postcard signed with initials (with or without picture; picture to be described in material description)
APCS	autograph postcard signed (with or without picture; picture to be described in material description)
TD	typed document
TDI	typed document, signed with initials
TDS	typed document signed
TDTS	typed document, type-signed
TG	telegram
TL	typed letter (original)
TLC	typed letter copy
TLCC	a carbon copy of a typed original
TLS	typed letter, signed
TLTS	typed letter, type-signed
TLTSC	typed letter, type-signed, copy
TLTSCC	typed letter, type signed, carbon copy

1.7.6 Citations for Location (Repositories) of Manuscripts

Buffalo	Rare & Special Books, James Joyce Collection, University at Buffalo, The State University of New York MS of Joyce's works are given with call number: e.g. Buffalo VI.I.41
Cornell	Wyndham Lewis Collection Division of Rare and Manuscript Collections, Cornell University Library, Ithaca N.Y.
NLI Léon	National Library of Ireland, The James Joyce – Paul Léon Papers
Princeton	Sylvia Beach Papers, C0108, Manuscripts Division, Department of Rare Books and Special Collections, Princeton University Library
Texas	University of Texas at Austin, Harry Ransom Humanities Research Center: William A. Bradley, Literary Agency.
ZJJF Jahnke	Zürich James Joyce Foundation, Hans E. Jahnke Bequest

1.7.7 List of Abbreviations for Reference Works Most Frequently Referred to

JJtoSB (for letter quotes); Banta and Silverman (for quotes from their text)	*James Joyce's Letters to Sylvia Beach, 1921-1940*. Ed. Melissa Banta and Oscar A. Silverman. Bloomington and Indianapolis: Indiana University Press, 1988.
Letters I-III	Joyce, James. *Letters of James Joyce*. Vol. I, ed. Stuart Gilbert. New York: Viking Press, 1957; reissued with corrections 1966. Vols. II and III, ed. Richard Ellmann. New York: Viking Press, 1964.
SL	Joyce, James. *Selected Letters of James Joyce*. Ed. Richard Ellmann. New York: Viking Press, 1966.
JJII	Ellmann, Richard. *James Joyce*. New York: Oxford Univ. Press, 1982.
JJA (+*vol. no*)	*The James Joyce Archive*, ed. Michael Groden et al. New York and London: Garland Publishing, 1977-79.
Fahy	Fahy, Catherine. *The James Joyce – Paul Léon Papers at the National Library of Ireland*. Dublin: National Library of Ireland, 1992.
Sha&Co	Beach, Sylvia. *Shakespeare and Company*. New York: Harcourt, Brace, 1959.
Slo + Ca	Slocum, John J. and Herbert Cahoon. *A Bibliography of James Joyce*. London: Rupert Hart-Davis, 1957.
JJAtoZ	Fargnoli, Nicholas A. and Michael P. Gillespie. *James Joyce A to Z. The Essential Reference to the Life and Work*. New York: Fact on File, 1995.
Our Exagmination	Beckett, Samuel et al. *Our Exagmination Round His Factification for Incamination of Work in Progress*. Paris: Shakespeare and Co., 1929.

Quotations from Joyce's works are given as follows:

ULYSSES *U* + episode and line number	Joyce, James. *Ulysses*, ed. Hans Walter Gabler et al. New York and London: Garland Publishing / Bodley Head 1984, 1986. In paperback by Garland, Random House and Bodley Head by Penguin between 1986 and 1992.
FINNEGANS WAKE *FW* + page and line number	James Joyce. *Finnegans Wake*. London: Faber & Faber, and New York: Viking Press, 1939 (identical pagination).

Letters 1921-1939

1921

3 January	Beach to Joyce	17
16 February	Beach to Joyce	18
22 February	Beach to Joyce	19
7 April	Beach to Joyce	20
n.d. [10 April]	Cyprian Beach pp Sylvia Beach to Joyce	22
28 June	Beach to Joyce	23
n.d. [between 10 June and 27 July]	Beach to Joyce	26

1922

27 July	Statement of accounts	27
n.d. [on or after 12 August]	Statement of accounts	31

1923

26 June	Beach to Joyce	32
29 June	Beach to Joyce	34
27 July	Beach to Joyce	36

1924

12 June	Beach to Joyce	38
n.d. [after 14 June, before 22 July]	Beach to Joyce	39
23 June [?1924]	Beach to Joyce	41
1 July	Beach to Joyce	42
11 July	Beach to Joyce	43
16 July	Beach to Joyce	45
22 July	Beach to Joyce	48
24 July	Beach to Joyce	51

29 July	Beach to Joyce	54
1 August	Beach to Joyce	56
7 August, pc	Beach to Joyce	58
8 August	Beach to Joyce	60
14 August	Beach to Joyce	61
n.d. [20(?) November 1924]	Beach to Joyce	64

1925

29 January	Beach to Joyce	66
14 March	Beach to Joyce	67
30 March, pc	Beach to Joyce	68

1926

[16 February] Mardi Gras	Beach to Joyce	69
22 May	Beach to Joyce	70
13 July	Beach to Joyce	71
n.d. [ca. 10 August]	Beach to Joyce	72
12 August	Beach to Joyce	74
19 August, pc	Myrsine Moschos pp Sylvia Beach to Joyce	76
n.d. [c. 28 August]	Beach to Joyce	78
September 1	Beach to Joyce	80
September 9	Beach to Joyce	82
September 10, telegram	Beach to Joyce	84
September 10, letter	Beach to Joyce	85
n.d. [before 16 September], pc	Beach to Joyce	86
16 September	Beach to Joyce	87
28 September	Beach to Joyce	89
29 September	Beach to Joyce	92
22 October	Beach to Joyce	94
25 October	Beach to Joyce	95
26 October	Beach to Joyce	96
2 November	Beach to Joyce	97
5 November	Beach to Joyce	99
24 November	Beach to Joyce	100

24 November	Statement of accounts	102
29 November	Beach to Joyce	103
n.d. Monday [?early December]	Beach to Joyce	104
17 December	Beach to Joyce	105

1927

29 January	Beach to Joyce	106
12 April	Beach to Joyce	107
29 April	Beach to Joyce	109
11 August, pc	Beach to Joyce	110
5 December	Statement of accounts	111

1928

30 July, pc	Beach to Joyce	112
10 August, pc	Beach to Joyce	114
n.d. [before 14 August], pc	Beach to Joyce	115
18 August	Beach to Joyce	116

1929

15 May	Beach to Joyce	120
6 August, pc	Beach to Joyce	122
n.d. [c. 1928-29]	Lists of works for *Work in Progress* anthology	123

1930

24 June	Statement of accounts	142
12 August, pc	Beach to Joyce	143
25 August	Beach to Paul Léon	145
9 December	Memorandum of Agreement	147
n.d. [?late 1930]	List of English articles on Joyce	149

1931

25 April	Beach to Joyce	151
27 April	Beach to Joyce	153
1 May	Beach to Joyce	154
2 May	Beach to Joyce	159
2 May	Beach to Joyce	160
9 May	Beach to Joyce	161
12 May	Beach to Joyce	164
15 May	Beach to Joyce	166
27 May	Beach to Joyce	167
29 May	Beach to Joyce	170
2 June, pc	Beach to Joyce	172
5 June	Beach to Joyce	173
6 June	Beach to Joyce	175
10 June	Beach to Joyce	179
13 June	Beach to Joyce	180
19 June	Beach to Joyce	183
1 July, pc	Beach to Joyce	184
8 July	Myrsine Moschos pp Sylvia Beach to Joyce	186
July 12	Beach to Joyce	189
15 July, letter	Beach to Joyce	190
15 July, telegram	Beach to Joyce	192
n.d. [c. 16 July 1931]	Beach to Joyce	193
17 July	Beach to Joyce	194
21 July	Beach to Joyce	197
6 August	Beach to Joyce	200
11 August	Beach to Joyce	205
13 August (1)	Beach to Joyce	209
13 August (2)	Beach to Joyce	211
17 August	Beach to Joyce	212
21 August	Beach to Joyce	214
22 August	Beach to Joyce	216
26 August	Beach to Joyce	219
27 August	Beach to Joyce	221
28 August	Beach to Joyce	224
1 September	Beach to Joyce	226
5 September	Beach to Joyce	228

14 September	Beach to Nora [Barnacle] Joyce	231
28 September	Beach to Joyce	232
10 November	Beach to Joyce	233

1932

2 February	Beach to Joyce	234
4 February	Beach to Paul Léon	235
9 February	Beach to Paul Léon	238
15 April	Statement of accounts	239
11 May	Beach to Joyce	240
8 August	Jean Henley pp Sylvia Beach to Joyce	241
18 August	Beach to Paul Léon	242
30 August	Beach to Paul Léon	243
31 August	Beach to Paul Léon	244
31 August, enclosure	Statement of accounts	245
24 September	Beach to Paul Léon	246
28 September	Beach to Joyce	247
28 September	Beach to Paul Léon	248
4 October	Beach to Joyce	249
24 October	Beach to Joyce	250
2 November	Beach to Joyce	252
8 November	Beach to Paul Léon	253
15 November	Beach to Paul Léon	254
28 November	Beach to Paul Léon	255

1933

February [?]	Beach to Joyce	256
3 March	Beach to Paul Léon	257
20 March	Beach to Paul Léon	258
31 March	Beach to Paul Léon	259
14 April	Beach to Joyce	260
8 May	Beach to Joyce	261
22 June	Beach to Paul Léon	262
1 July	Beach to Paul Léon	263

7 August	Jane van Meter pp Sylvia Beach to Joyce via Paul Léon	264
9 December	Beach to Joyce	265

1935

16 March	Beach to Joyce	266
13 September 193[?]5, pc	Beach to Paul Léon	267
5 December	Beach to Joyce	268

1936

28 February	Beach to Joyce	271
3 August	Margaret H. Newitt pp Sylvia Beach to Paul Léon	272
3 August, enclosure	Royalties Receipt	272

1937

2 July, pc	Invitation card for celebration of journal *Life and Letters*	273

1939

6 March	Beach to Paul Léon	274

Figures

1. Sylvia Beach in the 1920s   iv
2. Letter of 16 February 1921   xx
3. Letter of 15 May 1931   xxii
4. Joyce and Beach at 8, rue Dupuytren, 1921   21
5. Beach's first statement of accounts   29
6. Postcard of 7 August 1924   59
7. Adrienne Monnier's cottage at Les Déserts, Haute Savoie   75
8. Sylvia Beach at Les Déserts, undated   113
9. Postcard of 12 August 1930   143
10. Letter of 1 May 1931, with Adrienne Monnier's postscript   156
11. Letter of 6 June 1931   176
12. Sylvia Beach and Adrienne Monnier at the desk in "Shakespeare & Co", undated   182
13. Summer at Rocfoin: Adrienne Monnier, Madame Monnier, Sylvia Beach, James Joyce and M. Monnier, ca. 1928   188
14. Telegram of 15 July 1931   191
15. Letter of 6 August 1931   203
16. "Vielleicht ein Traum": a short story published under Joyce's name. *Frankfurter Zeitung*, 19 July 1931   204
17. James Joyce and Paul Léon, 1934   237
18. Letter of 5 December 1935, Beach's new stationery   270
19. Sylvia Beach at her bookshop, undated   275

*The Letters of Sylvia Beach
to James Joyce or Paul Léon 1921-1939*

∴

Introduction to the 1920s

Ruth Frehner

The very first pictures we have of Sylvia Beach and James Joyce show them in 1920 in the doorway of "Shakespeare and Company", Sylvia Beach's bookshop at 8, rue Dupuytren, before she moved her shop to 12, rue de l'Odéon in July 1921.

The door to her shop is right at the centre, with Joyce standing – sheltered – on the threshold in a relaxed pose, leaning with his right shoulder against the doorframe, his right leg crossed over his left, his right hand lightly propped up on a slim walking stick, his left in his trouser pocket: a bit dandyish, with his light-coloured shoes, bowtie and Fedora hat. He is looking at Sylvia Beach, who is standing on the pavement – a bit less sheltered, a bit lower down – leaning against the other doorpost, looking out into the street, her left hand in the pocket of her jacket: unassuming and a bit diffident (see figure 4, p. 21).

What became one of the famous pictures of the two, however, was taken from inside the shop, apparently, as their clothes suggest, on the same day. Again they stand most symbolically on the threshold, but now Joyce is looking confidently into the camera while Beach is looking intently at Joyce. In both pictures, their eyes do not meet. The two early photos stress the distance between them, a distance that may have to do with Sylvia Beach being so much in awe of Joyce.

The earliest of the Beach letters in the Jahnke Bequest is an oddity. It dates from 11 October 1920 and Beach writes in the first person, but the letter is not from her, nor is Joyce the recipient. Starting her letter with "Je suis le peintre américain …", it becomes clear that she lends her voice, her pen and paper and most notably her French to an American artist who wishes to recommend Joyce as a tenant to a landlord whose apartment he had visited and found too dark for his work as a painter. Joyce did not move to this apartment, but Sylvia Beach invested time – if not money – on his behalf. She had, for a brief moment, given up her own identity and, probably out of necessity, even signed for the American painter, putting a tiny "par S.B." below the "signature." The fact that it is part of the Jahnke Bequest suggests that it may never have been sent off. Though not included in this edition, the letter can serve as an epitome of one of Beach's most characteristic traits, that of the helper, facilitator, adviser, intermediary.

1   A Panoramic View

The first letter of the Beach-Joyce correspondence proper, which started in early January 1921, continues in this vein: Beach suggests one of her customers as a possible typist for parts of his *Ulysses* manuscript and passes her address on to Joyce. Only one and a half months later, in late February 1921, she forwarded him a momentous letter by Valery Larbaud, the well-known poet, translator, man of letters and lover of American literature who acted as godfather to Beach's bookshop and to whom she and Adrienne had introduced Joyce the previous Christmas. On 22 February, Larbaud wrote that he was "raving mad over *Ulysses*" and had not been so enthusiastic about any book since reading Whitman at the age of eighteen (Larbaud, *Lettres* 40). Ending her cover letter to accompany Larbaud's with "Hurrah for 'Ulyssees'! [sic]" (Beach to Joyce, 22 February 1921), Beach must have known that Larbaud could be instrumental in promoting *Ulysses*. She would become the publisher of *Ulysses* only a few weeks later, when at the end of March 1921 Joyce "immediately and joyfully" accepted her offer to publish his novel, as she records in her memoirs that came out in 1959, *Shakespeare & Company* (p. 47).

It is noteworthy that the first draft of the account of how she came to publish *Ulysses* made it clear that Joyce suggested that she should publish the book, and it also showed her hesitancy. This was in 1937. Some twenty years and many revisions later, it was Beach offering Joyce to publish the book, and this final version was to persist, not least through Ellmann's rendering of this important moment (*JJII*, p. 504). Even Beach's biographer, Noël Fitch, by quoting from Beach's memoirs *Shakespeare and Company* (1959), gives the latter version more weight, even though she does mention that in an early draft Joyce had thought of asking her to publish (see Bishop, pp. 7-12, and Fitch, p. 77f.).

The letters start in January 1921, with Sylvia Beach at the beginning of an adventure undreamt of a year before: publishing *Ulysses* – in English – in France. Initially the correspondence shows her as an inexperienced but enthusiastic publisher; we see her grow into her role as an agent and arts manager, but frequently also catch a glimpse of the secretary, bookkeeper, moneylender and errand girl. Many of the letters are short notes about daily business, which formed quite a substantial part of their relationship. From April 1921 to February 1922, a great deal of daily business must have consisted of her correspondence with the printer of *Ulysses*, and to judge by the surviving letters from Darantiere[1] to Beach at Buffalo, one would have expected a greater pres-

---

1   The printer in Dijon. See undated letter [between 10 June and 27 July 1921], note 3. There are 67 letters from that period at Buffalo.

ence of that protagonist in her letters to Joyce. There are only four extant Beach letters to Joyce in this period; but why write letters, when he would come to her shop almost every day? It is also notable that from the most active years of correspondence in the 1920s, i.e. from 1924 to 1928, more than 160 letters, cards and telegrams have survived from Joyce to Beach whereas we have only 51 letters and statements from Beach to Joyce (see Appendix B: Survey of Correspondence).

As to his letters: they include thanks for (no longer extant) holiday greeting cards from her, or requests for a reply, which most probably were not ignored by the conscientious Sylvia Beach. He asked her to send books to various people, or when he was on holiday, money or medicines to him; he wanted her to order books for him or to copy letters he received which he was going to pass on to somebody else; or he asked her to write letters on his behalf to printers, publishers, friends and foes.

Her letters convey a portrait of the artist as a manager: an author managing, with the indispensable assistance of Sylvia Beach, his own work, and his self-promotion of his life. In addition to Joyce's never-ending money troubles, she was looking for a flat for his family and trying to find a suitable typist for the *Ulysses* manuscript; she first organized the subscription of *Ulysses* and then took care of the subsequent sale of the book. There was a translation of *Dubliners* on its way, and she was also concerned with the translation of *Ulysses* into French and with a new edition of *A Portrait of the Artist* by Jonathan Cape, who had taken over after the closure of Harriet Weaver's Egoist Press.[2] All of this must have made Joyce realize just how generous an arrangement he enjoyed with Sylvia Beach as the publisher of *Ulysses*. And then there was *Exiles* that Joyce so much wanted to see performed on a Parisian stage, and time and again there were Joyce's eye troubles.

The 1920s letters also mention a gramophone record with Joyce reading from the "Aeolus" episode of *Ulysses*, the publication of the first passages from *Work in Progress* in the avant-garde journal *transition*, and, to top it all, the pirating of *Ulysses* by Samuel Roth,[3] which came to a head in a quite unprecedented way, culminating in the famous letter of protest signed by 167 prominent writers, artists and thinkers from all over the world, released on Joyce's birthday on 2 February 1927. As in the Samuel Roth case, most of the 1920s letters are only the tip of the iceberg, and as editors we can at least reveal some of the stories below the surface. The added context to the letters may broaden the view of present-day readers, offer them access to another perspective and thus make

---

2   See statement of accounts, 27 July 1922, note 2.
3   See letter of 9 September 1926, note 2.

the letters come alive. There may be a great deal of subtext to the often hastily written letters, and the annotations often create a shift in perception for the present-day reader, by adding a second eye to a previously monocular vision. It is, however, not only the contemporary context, but also the appraisal of the past events from today's perspective that enhances our perception. This is particularly obvious not only for the complex case of Samuel Roth, but also for *Exiles*, which is only marginally treated in the letters. Through the added context we come to realize how much Joyce cared for his play, how he not only dealt with the literary elite when it came to *Ulysses*, but, with Sylvia Beach's connections, also managed to get the attention of the *crème de la crème* of the Parisian theatre world with his much less prominent play.

2   High Drama 1: Staging *Exiles*

To savour the full drama of the (non-) staging of *Exiles*, we must go back to Zurich. As early as 1915, Joyce had offered the play to the leading theatres in Berne and Zurich, and he even considered Geneva for a French version,[4] as well as to theatres in England, but his efforts were all in vain.[5] He also asked Pound to try and have *Exiles* staged in America, and he offered it to Yeats and the Abbey Theatre in Dublin. Yeats, having read Joyce's *Portrait*, even thought that the Abbey "should [dare to] face a riot for [a play by Joyce]",[6] but then he rejected it on the grounds that the Irish theatre was not good at the type of play since *Exiles* was "too far from the folk drama."[7] In 1918, briefly, he considered producing it with The English Players in Zurich, the company he himself had founded together with Claud Sykes after receiving a generous stipend from Edith Rockefeller McCormick (*JJII*, pp. 422-23).

Incidentally, *Exiles* was the first of Joyce's works to be published in translation. Stefan Zweig, a great admirer of *Exiles*, found the Austrian-Czech Hannah von Mettal to translate the play into German (Faerber and Luchsinger, p. 56); it was published in Zurich in 1919 by the bookseller and publisher Rascher Verlag and the same year it was performed in Munich. But the reception was poor, and so the play did not sell: there is a statement from 1926 in the Rascher Verlag papers declaring that only nine copies had been sold,[8] which gave rise

---

4   Letter to Michael Healy, 2 November 1915 (Letters I, p. 85).
5   Letter to Harriet Shaw Weaver, 1 July 1916 (*Letters I*, p. 92).
6   Letter from Yeats to Pound, 11 February 1917 (qtd. in *JJII*, p. 401n).
7   Unpublished letter (at Cornell) by Yeats to Joyce (qtd. in *JJII*, p. 401f.).
8   24 March 1926. Zentralbibliothek Zürich, MS 74.

to Joyce's statement in a letter to Beach: "[t]he deuce take that tiresome Swiss" (*JJtoSB*, 2 May 1928) No wonder: Rascher agreed to publish the play at Joyce's cost. Later in the year Joyce wrote to Harriet Weaver that there was a case pending between "Rasher" and the Rheinverlag (see Joyce to Weaver, 20 Sept 1928 (*Letters I*, pp. 268f.).

Sylvia Beach mentions that *Exiles* was one of the first problems that Joyce brought to her (*Sha&Co*, p. 163): very soon after his arrival in Paris – and not very long after the Munich performance – Joyce had agreed to a contract offered to him by Aurélien Lugné-Poë, who, at that point, thought it would bring in no money but intended to stage it nonetheless.[9] In autumn 1920, Joyce wrote to his brother Stanislaus that *Exiles* was being translated into French – by Lugné-Poë's then-secretary Jacques Natanson, who was himself to become a playwright – and would be produced by Lugné-Poë's Théâtre de l'Œuvre in December.[10]

Lugné-Poë brought cosmopolitan avant-garde drama to Paris, with new playwrights like Maeterlinck, Wilde, Ibsen, Strindberg, Hauptmann, d'Annunzio, and Jarry.[11] Beach saw him as one of Paris' "most esteemed theatrical managers" (*Sha&Co*, p. 163), and he was a brilliant promoter of budding playwrights. Unfortunately, by June 1921 Lugné-Poë had changed his mind and to Joyce's great disappointment declined to stage *Exiles*, saying that "he was not such a fool as to put on the piece and lose 15,000 francs."[12]

Beach, in her account of the story, shows some understanding for Lugné-Poë, who maintained that he had to consider the demands of present-day theatregoers who asked for something that made them laugh (*Sha&Co*, p. 164). While it is true that at that time he concentrated on comedies and farces, he also staged Strindberg's *Dance of Death* in 1921.[13] However, it was Lugné-Poë's success with his production of Fernand Crommelynck's farce *Le Cocu magnifique*, which had premiered in December 1920,[14] that forced a postponement of *Exiles* until spring, when he finally declined (*JJII*, p. 498). "*Le Cocu* took the wind out of the sails of *Exiles*," Joyce told his friend Frank Budgen, "as the jealousy motive is the same in both cases. The only difference is that in my play the people act with a certain reserve, whereas in *Le Cocu* the hero, to mention only one, acts like a madman" (Budgen, p. 350).

---

9   Joyce to Jenny Serruys, 20 October 1920 (*Letters III*, pp. 24-5).
10 Letter to Stanislaus Joyce, 28 October 1920 (*Letters III*, p. 26).
11 Styan, pp. 30-38 and 45-47 and https://www.britannica.com/topic/Theatre-de-lOeuvre, accessed 12 December 2020.
12 Joyce to Harriet Weaver, 24 June 1921 (*Letters I*, p. 166).
13 www.lesarchivesduspectacle.net; accessed 30 March 2020.
14 www.lesarchivesduspectacle.net; accessed 30 March 2020.

In 1922, Jacques Copeau came onto the scene – again, one should say. The French actor, literary critic, stage director, and dramatic coach, was at the forefront of a movement against realism in early twentieth-century theatre. In 1913, he had founded the Théâtre du Vieux Colombier. Together with Louis Jouvet,[15] he sought to break down the barrier between actor and audience by redesigning the 1920 theatre as a reconstruction of the Elizabethan apron stage without the proscenium arch and with simple screens to suggest locale. The atmosphere of each play was created almost entirely by lighting. Emphasizing the play rather than its trappings, Copeau concentrated on training the actors, and eventually his company ranked with the great Moscow Art Theatre of Konstantin Stanislavsky.[16]

Beach had every hope that Jacques Copeau would produce Joyce's play (*Sha& Co*, p. 165). Although he turned down *Exiles* in October 1920, he came back almost two years later, in July 1922, and offered to consider it for the Théâtre du Vieux-Colombier. He even added that the role of Richard attracted him personally.[17] There were great hopes that things would work out this time, and Beach felt that Copeau should be able "to get into Richard's skin and communicate the Joycean subtleties to his attentive listeners." But at the end of the 1923/1924 season, to everyone's surprise, Copeau retired from the Théâtre du Vieux Colombier to the country and to a life of contemplation without having produced the play (*Sha&Co*, p. 165).

At roughly the same time, Edouard Bernaert,[18] a Belgian poet and journalist who also worked for the Éditions de la Sirène, had prepared a translation

---

15   Louis Jouvet (1887-1951). He was to become one of the most influential figures of the French theatre in the 20th century. He joined Jacques Copeau's theatre group in 1913 to establish the Théâtre du Vieux Colombier. In 1922 he accepted the technical direction of the Comédie des Champs-Elysées that Jacques Hébertot (see note 20) had offered him and two years later took over as sole director until 1934, when he changed to the Athenée, a position he retained until his death. Cf. Whitton, p. 81; also: https://www.britannica.com/biography/Louis-Jouvet; for playbills: http://www.evene.fr/celebre/biographie/louis-jouvet-744.php, both accessed 14 December 2020.

16   Jacques Copeau (1879-1949). https://www.britannica.com/biography/Jacques-Copeau, accessed 12 December 2020.

17   Letter of 28 July 1922. (Princeton, *Jacques Copeau to James Joyce*). Copeau's appraisal was enthusiastic: "I was eagerly interested in the play ... I am slightly disconcerted by the third act which in fact I will reread. However, the first and the second seemed to me first class. I haven't read anything so valuable for quite a long time.... and I must say that the role of Richard attracts me very much personally." (Original in French)

18   Edouard Bernaert worked for the Éditions de la Sirène (see Hélène du Pasquier to Joyce, 27 Oct [1923] where she says that she met Bernaert "de la Sirène", at Princeton). They successfully published translations and the editors had a flair for good work in the fields of

of the play together with Hélène du Pasquier,[19] who had already translated stories from *Dubliners*. They proposed it to Jacques Hébertot[20] of the prestigious Théâtres des Champs Elysées. Their performances, thus Beach, were "events nobody could afford to miss; or to attend, unless you were invited, as I was" (*Sha&Co*, p. 164). In previous years such an event was the première of Stravinsky/Dhiagilev/Nijinsky's *Sacre du printemps* which created a scandal at the Grand Théâtre des Champs Elysées. Once again, a performance seemed near, with "Hébertot's little bulletin announcing [it]" (*Sha&Co*, p. 14), once again, the plans eventually came to nothing "as everybody connected with the Champs Elysées Theatre was in a great mixup" (letter of 24 July 1924; see also *Sha&Co*, p. 165) and the Bernaert /du Pasquier translation was never published. Needless to say, in this matter too, Sylvia Beach acted as Joyce's agent.

At least, things looked brighter on the other side of the Atlantic: the Neighborhood Players in New York planned to put on *Exiles* and sent a contract, which Beach mentioned in the same letter of 24 July 1924. And indeed, they performed it 41 times in February and March 1925, but without creating the sensation that Joyce had hoped for.[21]

There were other attempts by various people to translate and/or stage Joyce's play in Paris in the 1920s, but France had to wait until 1950 for the first published French translation – by Jenny Serruys Bradley, who had already been working on it in the very early 1920s (Larbaud, *Letters*, p. 111). France had to wait until 1954 to see *Exiles* on stage.[22]

---

drama, cinema or musicology. https://portail-collections.imec-archives.com/ark:/29414/a011457630726BwAldw, accessed 14 December 2020.

19   Hélène du Pasquier (née Gibert, d. 1941). By 1923, she had published translations of two *Dubliners* stories, in *Les Écrits Nouveaux*; "Éveline" in VIII:11 (Nov 1921) and "L'Arabie" in IX:2 (February 1922). (Slo + Ca, D 19 + 20, p. 112). In 1926, the full collection of stories was published by Plon-Nourrit as *Gens de Dublin*, with translations by du Pasquier, Yva Fernandez and Jacques-Paul Reynaud. Apart from the above stories du Pasquier also contributed "An Encounter" and "After the Race." (See also letter of 27 July 1923, note 1).

20   Jacques Hébertot (1886-1970). Director of the Théâtre des Champs Elysées since 1920. Besides the Grand Théâtre there was the Comédie and as from 1923 also the tiny Studio. Together with Lugné-Poë, Hébertot was the driving force in internationalizing the Parisian stage. He had to close down his theatre in 1924. https://catalogue.bnf.fr/ark:/12148/cb129185413, and Aslan, p. 13f.

21   See Joyce's letter to Harriet Weaver, 11 July 1924, *Letters III*: p. 100, note 1.

22   In 1922 there was another attempt to have the play staged, by Marcel Ray. Ray wanted to make another, more literary translation, which would not compete with the stage adaptation based on Serruys' translation by Lugné-Poe's secretary, the playwright Jacques Natanson (letter from Valery Larbaud to Marcel Ray, 13 October 1922 (Larbaud, *Correspondance*, pp. 54-55, 302 n.3, and 303 n.1).

3 High Drama II: Samuel Roth and the Pirating of *Ulysses*

From 1926 no less than 23 letters from Beach to Joyce have survived, which is the annual record of the 1920s. Fifteen of them were written after the summer break, when news had reached her that *Ulysses* had been pirated by Samuel Roth: in the same month, the prestigious American journal *The Dial* had accepted the "Shaun" section of *Work in Progress* (later *FW* III: 403-590) but would not print it in full length, which Joyce, in turn, could not accept, as he wrote to Harriet Weaver on 24 Sept 1926 (*Letters I*: 245). And further, Wyndham Lewis was eager to print another excerpt from *Work in Progress* called the "Triangle" piece[23] in his new review *The Enemy* but eventually decided otherwise.

Beach mentioned the pirating of *Ulysses* for the first time in her letters to Joyce on 1 September 1926, on her return from her holidays. Apparently, it had been a topic before, as she merely informed him that Lewis Galantière, a mutual friend, had offered to write a letter about the case to the American papers. While Joyce was still holidaying at the Belgian seaside at Ostend – but also working with Georg Goyert on the German translation of *Ulysses* – Beach informed him on 9 September that Gorman[24] had called before sailing to the States and would do anything Joyce wished him to do about Samuel Roth. Joyce's eight letters to Beach in the remaining weeks of September show that he still had other concerns: besides the German translation, he was busy with the two excerpts from *Work in Progress* for both *The Dial* and Wyndham Lewis, and finally he needed more money as the holidays turned out to be very expensive. The scant traces of the matter in the Beach-Joyce correspondence, however, belie the extent of it. But so far no sign of the storm that was to develop was visible in the letters.

However, Joyce had been warned. As early as 1920, B.W. Huebsch, the American publisher of *A Portrait of the Artist*, foresaw the activities of American pirates,[25] and urged Joyce to publish *Ulysses* first in the United States, admittedly at the cost of having to revise strong passages. Huebsch's argument was that if Joyce published *Ulysses* – unexpurgated – in France first, this would cost him the American copyright, "as this would leave the book free for a pirate after sixty days,[26] and the pirate, in order to overcome the objections that now lie

---

23 This became *FW* II, 282.05-304.04.
24 See undated letter [after 14 June, before 22 July 1924], note 4.
25 This was before the *Ulysses* instalments in Margaret Anderson and Jane Heap's *The Little Review* (which appeared between March 1918 and December 1920 in New York) were stopped by an action brought by the American Society for the Suppression of Vice.
26 A work in English first published outside the United States had to be manufactured and published in America within two months in order to enjoy a U.S. copyright. After sixty days, it was free for anyone to pirate it (Spoo 2013, p. 68f.).

against it, would eliminate the offensive passages" without Joyce in control of the alterations (Spoo 2013, pp. 66f.).

The prelude was Roth's letter to Joyce in 1922 about his plans for a new quarterly journal, *Two Worlds*:

> Among other things we shall try to publish a novel complete in every issue – I already have one very fine one in view. But if possible I would like to begin the series with a novel by you. On its appearance in my first issue I shall send you an advance royalty of one hundred dollars and later fifteen percent on the sales of the issue.
> ROTH to JOYCE, 10 May 1922, Princeton

Joyce turned this down and urged Beach to ask Harriet Weaver "to reply to *Two Worlds* one or two words to the effect that he would be unable to accept this proposition" (Beach to Weaver, 6 June 1922 [Walsh, p. 92]). Weaver even wrote to Roth again in September 1922, "definitely declining on Mr Joyce's behalf" (Weaver to John Quinn, quoted in Spoo 2012, p. 103). Roth had also invited Ezra Pound to be on the board of editors, and Pound accepted, suggesting that he could also use Joyce's new *Work in Progress* (Kugel, p. 243). It was only in September 1925 that *Two Worlds* was launched, not with a serialized *Ulysses* as anticipated three years earlier, but with instalments of *Work in Progress* that were then available in Europe, for which Joyce accepted $200 from Roth. (Gertzman 2009, p. 36).[27] The real trouble started when Roth launched the publication of *Two Worlds Monthly* in July 1926 with instalments of *Ulysses*.

Gertzman claims that we do not know whether Roth had permission to publish *Ulysses* excerpts in *Two Worlds Monthly* (2009, p. 36). Although missing, a letter of permission dating from 3 July 1922 may be inferred from a follow-up letter by Pound on 4 July (Kugel, p. 243). However, Pound, who approved of the suggestion at that time, would no longer have been authorized to give permission for printing, as in July 1922, *Ulysses* had been published by Shakespeare and Company, and therefore, the request for permission should have been addressed to Sylvia Beach or Joyce himself (Gertzman 2009, pp. 41-2). Beach could not have consented: in a letter of 5 December 1925 (Gertzman 2009, p. 43) she rebuked Roth for publishing excerpts from *Work in Progress* without permission. This was not justified: Joyce wrote to Harriet Weaver on 5 March 1926 that he "wanted to revise Shaun abc[28] for Mr Roth [but] could not do so" as

---

27 *Two Worlds* published 5 instalments, from September 1925 to September 1926 (Slo + Ca, C 65, pp. 99-100).
28 The *Finnegans Wake* section "Shaun" consisted of four parts, which Joyce labelled a, b, c, and d.

he was too tired (*Letters III*, p. 139). The same letter also contains a paragraph showing that Joyce and Roth had some kind of agreement involving money (Roth's cheque of $100 for two pieces printed in September and December 1925 respectively) as well as Roth's offer for future printings. Mysteriously, Ellmann omitted this paragraph in the third volume of the Joyce Letters Edition; the relevant passage is quoted in Kugel (p. 244).[29]

Things were made even more complicated by the fact that Joyce had not received any money from the editors of *The Little Review* for printing instalments of *Ulysses*; thus Roth could claim that it was quite customary among little magazines not to pay their contributors (Margaret Anderson qtd. in Saint-Amour, p. 463). Joyce was advised against a law suit since Roth's printing meant no violation of American law. Because it was banned in the U.S., *Ulysses* had never been printed and therefore never been copyrighted in the United States. Moreover, magazine copyright was precarious, and none of the segments published in *The Little Review* had had a separate copyright notice in Joyce's name. (Spoo 2013, pp. 155-56.) Also, the United States had not signed the Berne Convention, which would have protected the book against piracy (Fitch, p. 244). In 1926, many copies of the Shakespeare and Company edition of *Ulysses* had been confiscated, and as a result, Gertzman suggests, Joyce and Beach were worried that Roth would sell large numbers of his excerpts and would thus ruin their profits on *Ulysses*, which they hoped to make not least through limited editions. But why would buyers of beautiful editions be worried about the cheaply produced excerpts in a little magazine (Gertzman 2009, p. 47)?

The protest initiated in late 1926 was published exactly 5 years after the publication of the first edition of *Ulysses*, on 2nd February.[30] Beach had collected 167 signatures, and it was first and foremost a moral appeal to boycott Roth[31] on the grounds that he had not obtained permission nor paid any money to the author, and for mutilating the text. Both accusations are neither true nor false. As Amanda Sigler and others have stated, it is true that Roth did expurgate the text in order to appease the censors, but critics also note the extent of expurgation that was performed by Pound for the *Egoist* and by Margaret Anderson and Jane Heap for *The Little Review* and for the same reasons: if anything, their changes were more, not fewer than Roth's. Roth actually printed

---

29   It was in fact Roth's daughter Adelaide Kugel, who had started the ball rolling with a short article in the *Joyce Studies Annual* in 1992.

30   It had been drawn up by Ludwig Lewisohn and Archibald MacLeish. See letter of 26 October 1926, note 2.

31   The text of the protest ended by appealing to the American public "to oppose Mr Roth's enterprise [with] the full power of honorable and fair opinion" (Walsh, Appendix II, 315).

the "Nausicaa" episode – the one that led to the trial – unaltered in *Two Worlds Monthly*, which was not acknowledged by Joyce's supporters (Gertzman 2013, p. 72). The international protest contributed to Samuel Roth being ostracized by the literary establishment both as a publisher of pornography and a literary pirate. As a result of extended research into the transatlantic asymmetries of copyright law and the difficulties of European authors to have their works protected in America at that time, Roth's position and contribution to Modernism have been re-evaluated. While not everything he did was above suspicion, his dealings are now seen in a wider context, and above all a re-evaluation has made us realize that things were most probably not as black and white as Joyce and Beach made them appear.

So it is remarkable that there are only four Beach letters about this case, all sent in September and October 1926, and they merely mention people who offer their help. From Joyce's side, we have five letters to Beach, all written between January and May 1927.[32] Very little is revealed in their correspondence of the absorbing affair that kept both of them extremely busy, especially Beach, who received many more orders from Joyce than the ones he gave her in the five letters. She wrote to innumerable American papers, on top of all the other letters that Joyce asked her to write, and not to speak of the 167 signatures for the protest letter, which she collected mostly herself by sending a personal letter to each of the renowned artists and thinkers (*Sha&Co*, p. 181). There is a touching memento of her incredible efforts at Princeton: a small box with all the carefully wrapped and labelled little printer's plates of all the signatures.[33]

In her letter of 22 October 1926 to Joyce, which is still at the beginning of the whole drama, Beach is quite dispirited:

> Dear Mr Joyce,
> I enclose a letter from a Hungarian publisher about Ulysses.
> I didn't understand very well your remark today about Samuel Roth's edition of Ulysses preventing the money from coming into my coffers. I have thought more of your interests in the matter than of mine as usual.
> Yours faithfully
> Sylvia Beach

---

32   *JJtoSB*, letters 30 January 1927 (no. 94), p. 115; n.d., probably February (no. 95), p. 116; n.d. probably Spring (no. 101), p. 118; n.d. possibly Spring? (no. 102), p. 118; and n.d. probably May (no.108), p. 121.
33   Princeton, Pirating Protest, Plates of Signatures.

"Yours faithfully": this is the first of five letters to Joyce (the last one is from 5 November 1926) that she closes in this highly formal way. In its brevity, it reflects a deep hurt and foreshadows a crisis between the two that came to a head after the protest had been released on Joyce's birthday in 1927. As Fitch notes, this most complex story put a strain on the relations between the two. Joyce even suggested to Beach that she should transplant her shop to the United States in order to fight against the piracy "presumably by arranging an American edition" (Fitch, p. 259). From notes that Beach did not include in her memoirs, we learn that she felt that Joyce saw "Shakespeare and Company as something God had created for him, but to me it had other sides than the Joycean. Happily for Joyce himself as that was one of the reasons why my little enterprize was so useful to him" (Beach qtd. in Fitch, p. 260). On the other hand, Joyce seems to have realised that his claims on her were beyond any limit, as he wrote to her on 17 March 1927, after a [financial] "bombshell" that had fallen the very morning:

> It is a hard thing, so I am told, to be a 'genius' but I do not think I have the right to plague and pester you night, noon and morning for money, money, and money. You are altogether overworked without my rapping at the door, I am almost inclined to let the bailiffs in and watch them walk off with the furniture and animals in the ark.
> With kindest regards
> sincerely yours
> James Joyce
> *JJtoSB*, p. 116

On 12 April 1927, around the time when the protest appeared in the April issue of the *Humanist*, Beach wrote her famous letter to Joyce, which she did not send but kept in her files. It was first published in "Appendix C" in Banta and Silverman's Joyce-Beach letters edition, and it was the first and only letter from Beach to Joyce published before the present volume. The opening is quite calm in spite of the uncomfortable fact that she owes the English publishers some £200 (ca. £12,600 nowadays), and she tells him that she cannot finance his and Nora's trip to London "with money jingling in [his] pocket"; then, in the second part, she questions his never-ending demands:

> The reward for my unceasing labour on your behalf is to see you tie yourself into a bowknot and hear you complain. (I am poor and tired too) and I have noticed that every time a new terrible effort is required from me, (my life is a continual 'six hours' with sprints every ten rounds) and

I manage to accomplish the task that is set me you try to see how much more I can do while I am about it. Is it human?
With kindest regards
Yours very sincerely
Sylvia Beach

The unsent letter of 29 April 1927 is no longer just a complaint, she rebukes Joyce for not realizing what she is in fact doing for him. It is the only time when she loses her temper in her (surviving) letters to Joyce. After giving him some figures about his considerable earnings thanks to the sales of *Ulysses*, she makes it clear that she would have expected her efforts to be appreciated and that she will no longer hide her disappointment at his failure to do so. She ends her letter with a blunt accusation:

> [It] would have been more sportsmanlike of you to own up to spending this considerable amount of money than to tell a lot of cock-and-bull stories to me who is your friend if ever you had one. You are the greatest writer who ever lived but even Pound has more sense. Do go to the moneylender. [...]
> With kindest regards
> Yours very sincerely
> Sylvia Beach

"With kindest regards, Yours very sincerely": is it that speaking her mind in her two letters allowed her to keep her countenance in the closing salutation?

From early on in their relationship, Sylvia Beach must have had a close-up view of Joyce the author and Joyce the man, and she enjoyed it. From the very first she admired the author, she was fascinated by the man and his personality (*Sha&Co*, p. 37), but she always knew that pleasure comes with a price:

> I understood from the first that, working with or for James Joyce, the pleasure was mine – an infinite pleasure; the profits were for him. All that was available from his work, and I managed to keep it available, was his. But it was all I could do to prevent my bookshop from getting sucked under.
> *Sha&Co*, p. 201

Now, she allowed herself in this letter to let Joyce know that she had seen the underside of "the greatest writer who ever lived," that her reverential respect for him was, at least temporarily, suspended.

It is an open question why Joyce, who had up until then never deemed a contract for *Ulysses* necessary between him and his publisher, all of a sudden wanted a contract for *Pomes Penyeach* that was to be published by Shakespeare and Company at the beginning of July that same year.

The Letters of Sylvia Beach to James Joyce, 1921-1929

January 3rd 1921

Dear Mr Joyce,

   I think that one of my abonnées,[1] Mademoiselle Marie Latrasse,[2] 30 rue Bobillot, would type your manuscript satisfactorily. She works at the American Express but has time free for your work and she says nothing you tell in the book can terrify her. She knows English or American or something quite well and is not at all stupid. If you write to she will call on you to arrange matters [sic].

Yours very sincerely
Sylvia Beach

>   ALS, 1 leaf, 1 side, Sha&Co stationery. ZJJF Jahnke.
>   The letter was folded in half across its length before the ink was dry: the writing, which starts only in the middle of the page, is mirrored in the upper half of the sheet.
>   To JJ at 5, Boulevard Raspail, Paris VII

---

1 French for 'subscribers' – i.e. a subscriber to Beach's lending library.
2 Marie Latrasse's is not among the borrowers' cards (Princeton, *Borrowers cards*).

February 16th 1921

Dear Mr Joyce

Raymonde Linossier[1] has just been in to see me. I told her about our plan to go on with "Ulyssees" together here. She said it would be difficult on account of constant interruptions on the part of the subscriber birds[2] and clients and that you must send "Ulyssees" back to her at once; she will copy it very legibly by hand so that any typist can read it. In fact she knows someone who will "taper"[3] it for you.

Raymonde's father is better now,[4] but his daughters have to stay with him all the time and Raymonde says she can easily go on with your manuscript.
I am very sorry for myself not having the pleasure of helping a little with the great "Ulyssees" but perhaps I shall still have a chance if there are other strokes or anything coming.

Yours very sincerely
Sylvia Beach

> ALS, 1 leaf, 2 sides, Sha&Co stationery. ZJJF Jahnke.
> To JJ at 5, Boulevard Raspail, Paris VII

1 Raymonde Linossier (1897-1930). One of Beach's "most interesting French friends"; she was the "carefully brought-up daughter of a famous physician", studied law and was a "prominent member of Adrienne Monnier's literary family" but also had musical friends such as Poulenc, Satie and Milhaud and his wife Madeleine (*Sha&Co*, p. 152). Linossier was recruited early in 1921 as one of the many typists to help with the "Circe" episode of *Ulysses* (Groden, p. 185). She later took up orientalism and started to work at the Musée Guimet in Paris. Also, she was the author of a very short Dadaist novel, entitled *Bibi-la-Bibiste*, which was quite a literary event when it was published in Paris in 1918. On Ezra Pound's recommendation (*Sha&Co*, p. 153f.), it was also printed in *The Little Review*, VIII, 3 (Sept.-Dec. 1920), pp. 24-29. Cf. also Fitch, pp. 48-9, 88, and 149.

   Raymonde's name also made it into the "Circe" episode: "Even their wax model Raymonde I visited daily to admire her cobweb hose and stick of rhubarb toe, as worn in Paris." (*U* 15.2817).

2 In an undated letter (c. 1940) to Adrienne Monnier, Beach still refers to her subscribers affectionately as "Bunnies" (Walsh, p. 187), a word her sister Holly had coined for the subscribers – from the French *abonné* for [a] subscriber (*Sha&Co*, p. 22). The "birds" are simply yet another nickname for them.

3 *Fr.* to type.

4 Apparently Linossier started in early February 1921 and was forced to stop because of her father's heart attack (Letter to Claud W. Sykes, n.d. [early 1921], *Letters I*, pp. 157-8; letter to Daniel Hummel, 14 February 1921, *Letters III*, p. 38; and postcard to Harriet Weaver, 9 April 1921, *Letters III*, p. 40).

February 22nd 1921

Dear Mr Joyce

The enclosed[1] just came and perhaps you would like to reply yourself to Larbaud[2] or I will do it if you tell me what to say.

Hurrah for "Ulyssees"!

yours sincerely
Sylvia Beach

P.S. The "N.R.F." is the Nouvelle Revue Française[3] as of course you know.

> ALS, 1 leaf, 1 side, Sha&Co stationery. ZJJF Jahnke.
> Enclosure missing. At Princeton, *Larbaud, Valery*.
> To JJ at 5, Boulevard Raspail, Paris VII

1 A letter by Valery Larbaud, dated 22 February 1921, printed in: Larbaud, 1991, p. 40.
2 Valery Larbaud (1881-1957). Well-known translator and poet, and lover of American literature. He translated literary works from English, Spanish and Italian into French. Very early on, he became not only a member of Beach's lending library, but also called himself its godfather. He was to be "her steadiest customer" (Fitch, 45), and Beach introduced him to Joyce at Christmas Eve 1920 – the two immediately struck up a friendship. Larbaud gave his flat to the Joyce family for three months in the summer of 1921 (Norburn, pp. 98-100), and he became a tireless advocator of Joyce's work. Before *Ulysses* was published, he gave a legendary lecture at Adrienne Monnier's Bookshop. Later he also supervised the French translation of *Ulysses*, published in 1929. See also letter of 7 April 1921, note 2.

After reading parts of *Ulysses* in *The Little Review* that Beach had loaned him, Larbaud wrote the letter in question: "I am raving mad over 'Ulysses'. Since I read Whitman when I was 18 I have not been so enthusiastic about any book." And as a postscript: "It's wonderful! As great as Rabelais; Mr Bloom is an immortal like Falstaff. As grand" (Larbaud 1991, p. 40). Joyce answered him on 23 February 1921 (*Letters III*, p. 39).

3 *Nouvelle Revue Française*: leading French review of literature and the other arts, founded in February 1909 by a group that included André Gide, Jacques Copeau, Jean Schlumberger and Gaston Gallimard. They wished to emphasize aesthetic issues and to remain independent of any political party or moral or intellectual school. Between the two world wars, the NRF was France's leading literary journal, but after the German occupation of France in 1940, the NRF became pro-fascist; it ceased publication in 1943. The review was revived in 1953 as *La Nouvelle Nouvelle Revue Française* and resumed its original name in 1959. See also letter of 1 May 1931, note 13. http://www.gallimard.fr/Catalogue/GALLIMARD/La-Nouvelle-Revue-Francaise, https://www.britannica.com/topic/La-Nouvelle-Revue-Francaise, accessed 6 May 2019.

The NRF was to publish two translated texts by Joyce: "Protée", tr. Auguste Morel and Stuart Gilbert, and reviewed by Valery Larbaud (1928), and "Anna Livia Plurabelle", tr. Samuel Beckett et al. (1931). (Slo + Ca, D 30 + 32, p. 113f.). See also letter of 1 May 1931, note 1.

April 7th 1921

Dear Mr Joyce,

I enclose a form[1] which I hope will meet with your approval. Adrienne Monnier[2] helped me with it and as she has had some experience in that sort of thing I think you can trust her not to make any mistakes. She says the extracts from the press are very essential and that the stuff about payment is of great importance.

We have an English printer in Paris who will get out this bulletin at once, and a notice will appear in the "Bibliographie de la France" to attract the attention of the Dutchmen, Belgians and Swiss.

I've had two more subscriptions today. There will be a French translation of the bulletin. I hope you don't object to the bulletin in this form and that you will pardon me for suggesting these improvements.

My sister and I are very happy when Lucia pays us a visit.

yours very sincerely
Sylvia Beach

> ALS, 1 leaf, 2 sides, Sha&Co stationery. ZJJF Jahnke.
> Enclosure missing. Original at Buffalo, XVIII. E.1, Folder 4.
> To JJ at 5, Boulevard Raspail, Paris VII

1 The form is Adrienne Monnier's proposal for what became the four-page prospectus for *Ulysses*.
2 Adrienne Monnier (1892-1955). Owner of the bookshop and lending library "La Maison des Amis des Livres" in the rue de l'Odéon, Sylvia Beach's life-long friend and companion. She was an influential figure in the French literary scene and inspired and in 1919 helped Beach to open her own bookshop "Shakespeare and Company". She not only advised Beach in her venture of publishing *Ulysses*, but also, as early as 1921 initiated the French translation. First passages were translated for Larbaud's lecture on 7 December 1921 at Monnier's bookshop (McDougall, pp. 126-29). In 1925, she was the first to publish an extract from *Work in Progress* – the first version of "Anna Livia Plurabelle" – in a French journal, her own *Le Navire d'Argent* (Slo + Ca, C 66, p. 100). The entire French *Ulysses* by Auguste Morel (assisted by Stuart Gilbert under the supervision of Valery Larbaud and the author) came out in February 1929 under the imprint of her bookshop. This brought her Joycean enterprise to a close. (See also EDITORS' INTRODUCTION, pp. xvf).

FIGURE 4   Joyce and Beach at 8, rue Dupuytren, 1921
PHOTOGRAPHER UNKNOWN. COURTESY OF THE POETRY COLLECTION,
UNIVERSITY AT BUFFALO

No date [April 10, 1921]

Dear Mr Joyce – I was out this morning when your [...?] came so I didn't get it until nearly five o'clock. I'm sure that Sylvia sent the 18 sheets[1] to a typist yesterday afternoon but I don't know the address. I have just been to Mlle Monnier's apartment[2] but can't find Sylvia.

If you will telephone to my hotel tomorrow morning between <u>nine</u> and <u>nine thirty</u> in the morning I will speak with you and take any message to Sylvia. My number is <u>Saxe</u>[?] <u>29-04</u>. I'm sorry that you have been ?already? inconvenienced by my having been out. Please keep this card for me. Sincerely yours C. Beach[3]

> ACS; 1 card, two sides. Buffalo.
> recto: Joyce to Beach, dated 9 April 1921.
> verso: Cyprian Beach to James Joyce
> Dating: Cyprian's message is on the verso of Joyce's calling card, on which he wrote a message to Sylvia Beach, dated 9 April 1921.
> Written on left-hand margin, with small part of corner of the card missing:
> "... s address is 8 rue Dupuytren" [Sylvia Beach's address]

1 In his message of 9 April 1921 to Beach, Joyce asked her not to forget to immediately send the end of the Circe MS, which he had left with her, to Larbaud. In turn, he would send it back the following Monday. These 18 sheets might therefore be the MS referred to.
2 See letter of 7 April 1921, note 2.
3 Cyprian Beach (1893-1951). Sylvia Beach's younger sister.

June 28th, 1921

Dear Mr Joyce,

I am so sorry to hear that you are having trouble with your eyes. Those Nouvelle Revue Française birds[1] only receive on Tuesdays and Fridays so I have not been able to get A Portrait of the Artist yet but will go this afternoon and will take it to Edmond Jaloux[2] myself.

Adrienne Monnier[3] has given me the typed Sirens that she had at her shop. Since I saw you last 6 signed orders for Ulysses have arrived

> Alexander Kaun, Berkeley, California[4]
> John M. McCormack, Noroton, Connecticut[5]
> John Dos Passos, Paris[6]
> Spencer Heafield, Chicago[7]

---

1 For NRF see letter 22 February 1921, note 3. For "birds" see letter of 16 February 1921, note 2.
2 Edmond Jaloux (1878-1949). French literary critic, founder and collaborator of literary reviews as well as novelist. He was above all interested in German and Anglo-Saxon authors; he introduced Henry James in France and also wrote essays on German authors such as Rilke and Goethe. He was elected a member of the Académie Française in 1936, the same year as Louis Gillet. From 1923 onwards, Jaloux wrote numerous articles on Joyce. (*Letters III*, p. 74, note 4). Willard Potts ranks him "next in importance to Valery Larbaud and Louis Gillet as a champion of Joyce's work in France" (Potts, p. 218, note 9). http://www.universalis.fr/encyclopedie/edmond-jaloux and http://www.academie-francaise.fr/les-immortels/edmond-jaloux, both accessed 14 December 2017.
3 See letter of 7 April 1921, note 2.
4 Alexander Kaun (1889-1944). Slavic scholar of Russian origin whose merits were above all in his untiring effort to introduce American readers to Russian literature. Cf. Simmons, pp. 137-39.
5 John McCormack (1884-1945). The world-famous Irish tenor who, in 1904, entered the singing competition at the Feis Ceoil, the Irish cultural festival of music and dance, together with Joyce. John McCormack won, Joyce received the bronze medal, which made him decide against a singing career. Cf. *JJII*, p. 151f.
  McCormack owned an estate at Noroton, which he sold in 1922. Cf. *The New York Times*, 26 February 1922. https://www.nytimes.com/1922/02/26/archives/buying-in-the-suburbs-john-mccormack-the-tenor-sells-farm-at.html, accessed 26 November 2020.
6 John Dos Passos (1896-1970). American novelist and artist. In his early novel about contemporary life in New York, *Manhattan Transfer* (1925), he used stream-of-consciousness and collage techniques just as Joyce had done in his *Ulysses*.
7 Identity unknown. There is a Spencer Heafield on the passenger list of S/S Antonia from Southampton to New York, arrival date 16 April 1923. Heafield was recorded as 22 years old on arrival, a resident of Chicago and member of the ship crew. http://www.ellisisland.org/search/FormatPassRec.asp?ID=603104100041&BN=P50310-4&sship=Antonia&line shipid=52, accessed 23 March 2011.

Louis Untermeyer, New York[8]
Madame Mayrish de St Hubert, Chateau de Colpach, Grand Duché de Luxembourg[9]

and letters asking for Ulysses, from

John M. Cameron, Chicago[10] (enclosing cheque)
Nat Wollf, Lyceum theatre, Rochester, N.Y.[11]

and Theodore Stanton[12] writes from Freiburg that if we send him a copy <u>at once</u> he will write it up in the Mercure de France in which he edits the "department of American books". I'm afraid he thinks you are American.

Also Mr P. Beaumont Wadsworth, Wallington, Surrey[13] sent Fr 150 in a letter asking for Ulysses.

---

[8] Louis Untermeyer (1885-1977). American poet, essayist, and editor, best known for his numerous poetry anthologies, which were widely used in American schools and colleges as textbooks. His works helped establish the reputations of such literary figures as Amy Lowell and Robert Frost and were influential in dispelling the belief that poetry was pretentious. He also published two autobiographies, in 1939 and 1965. Adapted from: https://www.britannica.com/biography/Louis-Untermeyer, accessed 20 March 2019.

[9] Aline Mayrisch de Saint-Hubert (1874-1947). After her studies in Bonn Aline de Saint-Hubert married Emile Mayrisch, who was to become an important figure in the steel industry. Apart from her dedication to social and health issues and particularly women's education, she also had a great interest in literature and the arts and she created a salon for artists, writers, philosophers and politicians at her home, Château de Colpach, assuming the role of intermediary between German and French culture in the years between the two wars. She died in 1947. https://www.autorenlexikon.lu/page/author/282/2820/DEU/index.html, accessed 26 November 2020.

[10] The Chicago Bar Association lists a John M. Cameron as President for the year 1925. http://www.chicagobar.org/AM/Template.cfm?Section=Past_CBA_Presidents&Template=/CM/HTMLDisplay.cfm&ContentID=9159, accessed 20 November 2017.

[11] Nat Wollf: one of the many young American people who were devoted to Beach and her shop. His enthusiastic subscription letter is at Princeton. See Bishop, p. 22f.

[12] Theodore Stanton (1851-1925). Best known as the author of *The Woman Question in Europe* (1884) and *A Manual of American Literature* (1909). Grown up in the US, Stanton worked from 1880 onwards as a journalist and literary critic in Germany and later in France. He was also a representative for American publishing houses and got Emile Zola's novel *Travail* published in America (Harper & Brothers, 1901). He was the son of Elizabeth Cady Stanton, probably the most important feminist in 19th century America. See also Maman, p. 808.

[13] P[ercy] Beaumont Wadsworth (1895-1983). English free-lance journalist who first read parts of *Ulysses* in *The Little Review* given to him by Ezra Pound in 1919 in London. Wadsworth was Harriet Weaver's guest in June 1921 where he might have heard of the subscription. He visited Joyce in Paris in August 1921. See Wadsworth, pp. 15-16.

I'm so sorry about your eyes. Please take good care of them.
No more proofs have come but when they do I will send them to you at once.
Please give my love to Lucie.

Yours sincerely
Sylvia Beach

> ALS, 1 leaf, 2 sides, Sha&Co stationery. ZJJF Jahnke.
> Indentation merely to show where paragraphs are.
> To JJ at 71 rue du Cardinal Lemoine, Paris V

No date [between 10 June and 27 July 1921]

Dear Mr Joyce

Don't pay the gentleman with the voiture à bras[1] – its included in my moving arrangements.[2]

He is taking you another package from the printer.[3] It arrived just after Lucia left. Also the enclosed letter for you.

Yours sincerely
Sylvia Beach

> ALS, 1 leaf, 1 side, Sha&Co stationery. ZJJF Jahnke.
>
> Dating: between 10 June 1921, when Beach mentioned the first galley proofs arrived, and 27 July, when she opened her shop at 12, rue de l'Odéon (Norburn, pp. 98-9).
>
> Enclosure missing.
>
> To JJ at 71 rue du Cardinal Lemoine, Paris V

---

1 *Fr.* hand cart.
2 Her own moving arrangements for her shop.
3 Maurice Darantiere (1882-1962). Known as the Master Printer of Dijon. A good friend of Adrienne Monnier's, he spent much of his time in Paris and was familiar with the French avant-garde who in turn were allied to Sylvia Beach's expatriate American customers. Beach had offered Joyce to publish *Ulysses* under the imprint of "Shakespeare and Company", after W.B. Huebsch in New York, publisher of *A Portrait of the Artist* and *Dubliners*, had declined on 5 April 1921. Through Monnier's good offices, Darantiere agreed to print *Ulysses*, even though Beach had made it quite clear that her financial situation was far from comfortable and that he would not see any money before the subscriptions – if any – came in (*Sha&Co*, pp. 48-50). As Joyce added to the textual body every time he received the page proofs, mistakes were bound to happen – not least because the printers were not fluent in English, and "without Darantiere's combination of devotion and open-mindedness, *Ulysses* would have been a much different book – if it had been printed at all" (Rabaté, p. 248). And owing also to Sylvia Beach's generosity the text could be published without any compromises.

July 27, 1922[1]

[1st sheet]

Ulysses Account Rendered

	Frs.
Stamps	3,200,00
Sundries (taxis, etc.)	2,670,00
Transportation	1,800,00
String	300,00
Paper (wrapping & carton ondulé)	650,00
Envelopes	500,00
Wires (including those to Miss Weaver)[2]	645,00
Trip to Dijon of A. Monnier and S. Beach	235,00
Printing of Ulysses	42,492,00
" " Prospectus & cards to subscribers	747,00
Myrsine Moschos[3]	1,200,00
Cable to Rosengren for Arabian Nights	44,70
Arabian Nights[4]	642,00

---

1 The day when Beach officially opened her shop at the new address, 12, rue de l'Odéon.
2 Harriet Shaw Weaver (1876-1961). Joyce's most important patron and close friend. She grew up in a well-to-do staunch Church of England family in Cheshire (North of England). After private tuition by a governess, she was not allowed to go to university but started out as a daughter at home. She read extensively and, dissatisfied with her role, engaged in social work and became a feminist and political activist. Weaver's first acquaintance with Joyce's work goes back to January 1914, to the early stages as an editor of *The Egoist*, where on 2 February 1914 the first instalment of *A Portrait* appeared. She saw the whole serialisation through to the end in September 1915. She then published *A Portrait* as a book in England under the imprint of *The Egoist*. This was only possible after Benjamin Huebsch's First Edition (New York: December 1916) had appeared, as she had not been able to find a printer in England for her venture. Between September 1915 and December 1919 five instalments of *Ulysses* appeared. Aware of Joyce's financial difficulties, she started to support him anonymously on a regular basis, only revealing her identity in 1919. She also had the first English Edition of *Ulysses* published by John Rodker for The Egoist Press in Paris in October 1922. Her selfless friendship and loyalty helped Joyce to devote his life to his art, and she supported the family personally and financially. After Joyce's death she was his literary executor and she continued to support the family members (*JJAtoZ*, p. 231; Lidderdale and Nicholson, passim).
3 Myrsine Moschos, a young Frenchwoman of Greek descent, joined the lending library in May 1921, and asked whether she could assist. The minute wage was no deterrent for her (Fitch, p. 89).
4 Joyce had an Italian translation of *Arabian Nights* in Trieste, since he had also used it for his work on *Ulysses*. The reference here is to the 17-volume edition by Sir Richard Burton,

Case of portraits delivered at 12, rue de l'Odéon	30,50
Dr. Borsch[5]	500,00
Dr. Merigot de Treigny[6]	560,00
Paid to Mr. James Joyce	39,505,80
" " S. Beach	13,978,80
Total	109,700,00

[2nd sheet]

Ulysses Account Rendered

Total receipts net from Ulysses to July 27th, 1922	Frs. 142,000,00
Total deducted for expenses & James Joyce & S. Beach	109,700,00
Credit Balance	Frs. 32,300,00

TD, 2 sheets, 2 sides, Sha&Co stationery. ZJJF Jahnke.

To JJ at 9 rue de l'Université, Paris VI

The Book of The Thousand Nights and a Night with Introduction, Explanatory Notes on the Manner and Customs of Moslem Men and a Terminal Essay Upon the History of the Nights (together with) [7 vols.] *Supplemental Nights to the Book of the Thousand Nights and a Night with Notes Anthropological and Explanatory.* Printed by the Burton Club for private subscribers only. 17 vols., n.d. [Denver, Colorado, 1919]. Joyce's reading of the so-called *Terminal Essay* (240 pages in vol. 10) spanned the entire writing of *Finnegans Wake* and the Burton edition of the *Arabian Nights* were an important structural book for Joyce's work on the *Wake* (Yared, pp. 124ff.). Of the *Supplemental Nights*, esp. vol. IV, Joyce took extensive notes in 1926 (notebook VI.B.12, 145-147 in *JJA* 31, pp. 298-99). Apart from two expressions, none of his notes made it into the book. We owe this latter information to Geert Lernout and his colleagues from the Centre of Manuscript Genetics at Antwerp University.

5 Dr. Louis Borsch (1873-1929). Prominent ophthalmologist and Beach's oculist. He was called upon for the first time at the end of May 1922 at the height of a renewed attack of iritis. For his first attack that month, Joyce had consulted Dr. Victor Morax, another well-known ophthalmologist who sent his assistant Dr. Mérigot de Treigny to give him some relief from this second attack. Mérigot de Treigny warned Joyce that he would need an operation (*JJII*, p. 535f.). Then Borsch was called to give a second opinion and he confirmed the glaucoma. As Joyce had hoped, he recommended to wait until the attack had abated before operating. From that day on, Joyce had a new doctor, "and his fees amounted to so little that Joyce (...) seemed to feel quite insulted that [they were] so small" (*Sha&Co*, pp. 66-68).

6 See previous note.

" SHAKESPEARE AND COMPANY "
— SYLVIA BEACH —

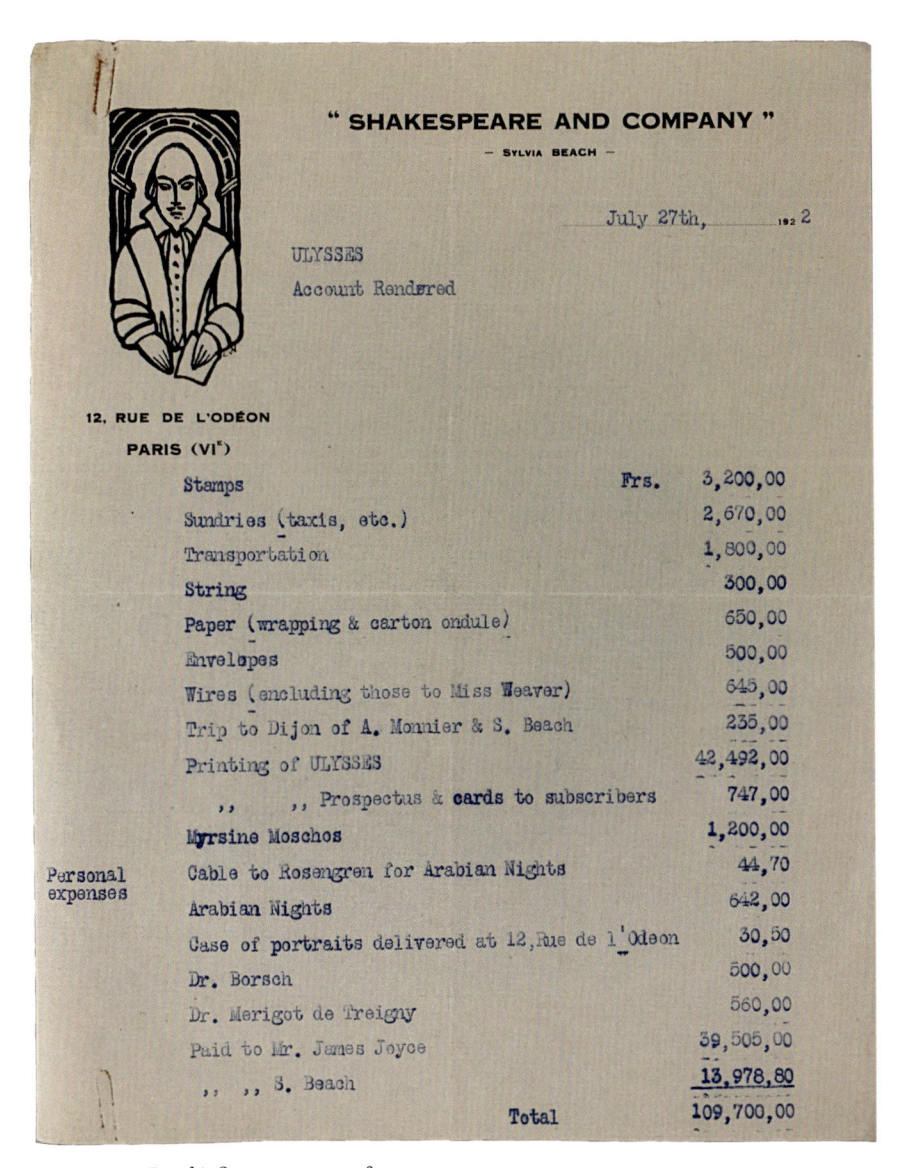

July 27th, 1922

ULYSSES
Account Rendered

12, RUE DE L'ODÉON
PARIS (VIᵉ)

Stamps	Frs.	3,200,00
Sundries (taxis, etc.)		2,670,00
Transportation		1,800,00
String		300,00
Paper (wrapping & carton ondule)		650,00
Envelopes		500,00
Wires (encluding those to Miss Weaver)		645,00
Trip to Dijon of A. Monnier & S. Beach		235,00
Printing of ULYSSES		42,492,00
,, ,, Prospectus & cards to subscribers		747,00
Myrsine Moschos		1,200,00
Cable to Rosengren for Arabian Nights		44,70
Arabian Nights		642,00
Case of portraits delivered at 12,Rue de l'Odeon		30,50
Dr. Borsch		500,00
Dr. Merigot de Treigny		560,00
Paid to Mr. James Joyce		39,505,00
,, ,, S. Beach		13,978,80
	Total	109,700,00

Personal expenses: Cable to Rosengren for Arabian Nights, Arabian Nights, Case of portraits, Dr. Borsch, Dr. Merigot de Treigny

FIGURE 5A   Beach's first statement of accounts
© SYLVIA BEACH ESTATE

Page 2.

" SHAKESPEARE AND COMPANY "

— SYLVIA BEACH —

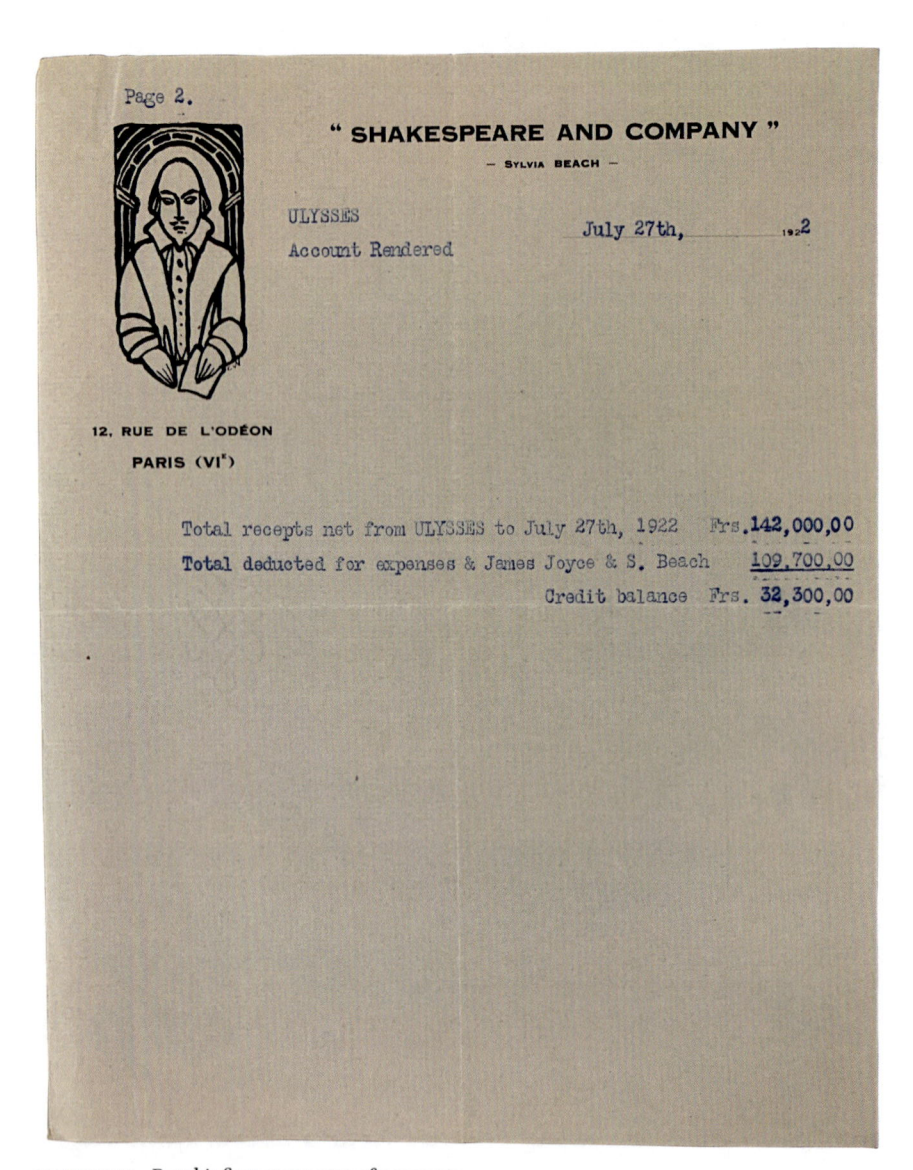

ULYSSES
Account Rendered

July 27th, 1922

12, RUE DE L'ODÉON
PARIS (VIe)

```
Total recepts net from ULYSSES to July 27th, 1922    Frs. 142,000,00
Total deducted for expenses & James Joyce & S. Beach    109,700.00
                                        Credit balance  Frs.  32,300,00
```

FIGURE 5B   Beach's first statement of accounts
© SYLVIA BEACH ESTATE

No date [on/after 12 August 1922]

ULYSSES

July 27th Mr. George Joyce,[1]	Frs.	4000,00
August 4th Mr. James Joyce,		4000,00
August 9th Mr. James Joyce,		4000,00
August 12th Mr. James Joyce,		<u>8000,00</u>
	Frs.	20,000,00

still to come in,   Frs. 4,475.00

> TD, 1 sheet, 1 side, Sha&Co stationery. ZJJF Jahnke.
> Dating: on or after 12 August, 1923.
> To JJ at 9 rue de l'Université, Paris VI

---

1 Joyce's son Giorgio (1905-1976). This is the only time in her letters to Joyce that Beach uses the English version of his name. See letter of 29 June 1923, note 1.

June 26, 1923

Dear Mr Joyce,

The postcard from you and Mrs Joyce and Lucia has just arrived. <u>Yes I have a beautiful apartment for you!</u>[1] Right in this house first floor above the entresol! A superb a princely apartment five thousand & five hundred frs a year. Large Salon – dining room – small salon – kitchen on the front – large bedroom and 2 other bedrooms almost as large at the back – and a bathroom with a 'chauffe-bain'[2] and a shower, – electric light & gas throughout – the whole apartment very light. Large fireplaces very long windows. You could use the big room at the back as a cabinet de travail.[3] It is quite cut off from noises and has a separate entrance from the stairway. There is also a servant's entrance – (3 doors to the apartment). Then there is a servant's room upstairs and you have 2 cellars. There is no central heating. You will not need a lease as Mme Tisserand[4] says the proprietor will let you stay as long as you like. The price per year is Frs 5,200 which with about Frs 220 of "charges" makes a little less than five thousand five hundred a year. I think you should give three thousand francs to Mme Tisserand for getting a fine flat for you in her house, do you not think so? It will suit you exactly I feel sure. It is free now and if you take it it will be from July 15th. Will you please send me a wire to say you will take the apartment so that I can fix it up at once with Mme Tisserand. Perhaps you or Mrs Joyce come over to see whether you like it before anything is decided.

With kind regards

yours sincerely
Sylvia Beach

unfurnished flat, Frs. 5,500
12, rue de l'Odéon, 1st floor
Big salon – small salon – dining room –
kitchen – bathroom – 3 bedrooms
2 rooms in the cellar – 1 servant's
room upstairs
gas – Electric light

---

1 Beach's answer to Joyce's inquiry of 25 June 1923 (from London) whether there is any news of a flat.
2 *Fr.* water heater.
3 *Fr.* study.
4 Madame Tisserand: the concièrge at 12, rue de l'Odéon.

ALS, 1 leaf, 2 sides, Sha&Co stationery. ZJJF Jahnke.

A part of the last sentence of the letter, "come over to see whether you like it", is written diagonally in the lower left corner

Postscript written in left margin on first page.

To JJ at Belgrave Hotel, London

June 29, 1923

Dear Mr Joyce,

Georgio[1] came at noon to-day to see the apartment.[2] He did not seem to think much of it and said he was afraid you and Mrs Joyce would not like it because it isn't modern. The bedrooms have no cabinets de toilette[3] with running water, the bathroom is not very elegant, there is no central heating, the walls need repapering.

When I saw that Georgio felt that way I advised him not to take it, particularly as I could see that he thought he could find something much nicer. He said he was going to look about now that he has all his time free.

I have been thinking this over this afternoon and I am sure that you will make a great mistake if you turn down this flat. If Georgio can find one with all the rooms and comforts that you naturally want it will be five times as expensive as this one and probably not as pleasant. Besides that, are there any unfurnished flats to let in Paris? You know the situation. Georgio is feeling rather disgusted with this town just now after his disagreeable experiences at the bank and he says you might all just as well move out to Africa if he doesn't find a perfect flat here.[4] But Baernaerts has come to tell me that he and Mme du Pasquier have proposed <u>Exiles</u> to Hébertot and that they have every hope that it will be given at the Théâtre des Champs Elysées next season.[5] If you come back to Paris where will you live? In another expensive unfurnished flat or perhaps at a hotel? It makes me sick to think of it. This flat is so large and spacious and on the first floor and has so many advantages that I can't imagine how you can let it go in the vague hope that you will find something absolutely perfect. Adrienne says to tell you that she feels sure that it would be a wise thing for you to take it. We both urge you to do so. I see nothing but wanderings for <u>Ulysses</u>

---

1 As a rule, Beach used an English-Italian form of writing Joyce's son's name.
2 Giorgio was the only one to remain in Paris while Joyce, Nora and Lucia had left for England.
3 *cabinet de toilette* toilet or bathroom.
4 Giorgio had worked at "the Banque Nationale du Crédit ... but disliked the long tedious hours, and eventually, like his father before him, gave up banking as a career." His father always sought Giorgio's financial advice, however brief his experience at the bank had been (cf. *JJII*, p. 556).
5 On Edouard Bernaert, Hélène du Pasquier and Jacques Hébertot, see INTRODUCTION to the 1920s, pp. 8.

in the future if we let this opportunity pass. It would bring bad luck. Madame Tisserand is holding on to the flat till we hear from you.[6]

Yours very sincerely
Sylvia Beach

>ALS; 2 leaves, 3 sides, Sha&Co stationery. ZJJF Jahnke.
>To JJ at Belgrave Hotel, London

---

6 Joyce told Beach that Giorgio's information had been what made him decide against the flat, and that he [Joyce] suggested to "take it and barter it if it proved unsuitable – that is, dispose of the bail without profit in exchange for a more suitable flat of similar size but of a much dearer rent" and he asked Beach to pay Mme Tisserand (see previous letter, note 4) 100 francs out of his account for her trouble (*JJtoSB*, 12 July 1923). As Fitch states, the transaction "had been awkward and embarrassing for Beach. She had done her best, but it had not been good enough" (p. 145).

July 27, 1923

Dear Mr Joyce,

Mr du Bos has just called to see me about the clause you wish to have added to the contract with Plon for Dubliners.[1] He said to tell you that "payable à la mise en vente du volume"[2] see article 11 is according to the custom of La Maison Plon and that they will on no account pledge themselves to pay by a certain date if the book has not appeared. He himself however promises you in very dignified language that you will receive twelve hundred francs by December 31 at very latest and he has every hope that the book will be out by the end of November although there is a chance that it might not really appear until the end of January. He says that it is an old custom in France not to bring out so very many books in December, owing to Christmas coming in that month as a rule. As to Mademoiselle Fernandez,[3] she is not to receive any part of the sum mentioned in your contract – all that vast fortune is for only you. The translators are to divide the same amount among themselves according to a separate contract which Plon has drawn up with them. So you are not to worry about Yva. Mr du Bos called my attention once more to the fact that it was through his efforts that Plon was prevailed on to agree to such an exceptionally large sum. du Bos' address is 1, rue Budé, Paris, IVe.

More about Mr du Bos

Mr du Bos has been ordered to bed by his doctor for a week beginning next Monday. He will rise after that time and revise very carefully the translations of Dubliners as he is not perfectly satisfied with them. He said something about something – I think proofs – that will be ready by the middle of August at

---

1 Charles DuBos (1882-1939). A French critic of French and English Literature whose support Joyce was seeking. (*JJtoSB*, Letter 15, note 5, p. 23) In 1926 a translation of *Dubliners* appeared in the "Collection d'auteurs étrangers" under the direction of Charles DuBos; the contract with Plon-Nourrit had been signed on 12 July 1923. (Banta and Silverman, INTRODUCTION 1921-1923, p. 7. It was to be the only Joyce publication by Plon (Slo + Ca, D 13, p. 111). See also INTRODUCTION to the 1920s, note 19.

With his letter of 20 July 1923 to Beach, Joyce had returned the contract unsigned, because he felt that a clause should be added guaranteeing that a small sum – more for the benefit of the translator than himself – would be paid over by a certain date.

2 *Fr.* payable when the volume is being put on the market.

3 Yva Fernandez was the sister of Emile Fernandez, a friend of Giorgio Joyce's. She translated ten of the fifteen stories into French for the 1926 *Gens de Dublin* edition by Plon-Nourrit. Her translation of "A Painful Case" had already appeared in the *Revue de Genève* in March 1922 (Hayman and Nadel, p. 53) The other translators were Jacques-Paul Reynaud ("The Sisters") and Hélène du Pasquier ("An Encounter", "Araby", "Eveline", "After the Race"). See also Banta and Silverman, note 1 above.

latest, although he is really ill. Do send him saluti on a post card to keep up his spirits. He looks more than ever as if he were going to fall apart.

Please send me soon the contracts signed[4] as I am leaving with Adrienne for Savoie on the 3rd of August.[5]

Copeau[6] sent a lady to see me this morning. She asked me if I could call on Copeau at once as he wanted absolutely to see me before he left Paris. I said I would go on Sunday afternoon at 3 o'clock. <u>Exiles</u> again?

Larbaud[7] has returned to Paris and is complaining of his liver.

Fargue is cruising but not in the nice costume you suggested.[8] He had already left when I got your letter. He collected several trunks from his friends and as none of them he bought one [sic]. Some princesses gave him donations of money.

With kind regards

yours very sincerely
Sylvia Beach

    ALS, 2 leaves, 4 sides, Sha&Co stationery. ZJJF Jahnke.
    To JJ at Alexandra House, Clarence Road, Bognor, England

---

4 Joyce sent them on 29 July 1923.
5 Beach and Adrienne Monnier usually spent their summer holidays at Les Déserts in the Savoie mountains. See letter of 7 April 1921, note 2.
6 Jacques Copeau. See INTRODUCTION to the 1920s, p. 8.
7 See letter of 22 February 1921, note 2.
8 Léon-Paul Fargue (1878–1947). French poet and one of Beach's very close friends. Fitch notes that "[h]e was a poet of the streets, invoking the sounds of light, the smell of alleys, the shadows of buildings" (p. 46). A frequent visitor at Shakespeare and Company, he helped prepare the first extracts of *Ulysses* in French for the first issue of *Commerce* in 1924 (cf. *JJtoSB*, Letter 15, note 6, p. 23). Fargue did not speak a word of English and was, in Beach's eyes, "a bohemian, [with] no sense of time, unaware of the existence of anyone but himself, but a genius in poetry" (Beach quoted in Fitch, p. 46). Of his verbal inventions Beach notes that they were "unimaginatively obscene ... and nothing in *Ulysses* ... could shock me after Fargue" (Beach quoted in Fitch, p. 47).

"The nice costume you suggested" may be a reference to a funny advertisement Joyce had sent to Fargue for which he instructed Beach to translate it to him while Fargue fanned himself with his hat. In his next letter Joyce suggested that Fargue should dress in the "best *angliche* fashion", i.e., "tarpaulins, a sou'wester, tarry pigtail, a hamfrill beard, Wellington boots, cutlass, tomahawk and a 40 foot telescope" when crossing the stormy sea (*JJtoSB*, 12 July and 20 July 1923, p. 18).

June 12, 1924

Dear Mr Joyce,

Lucia has given me news of your operation.[1] I am glad everything is satisfactory and hope you will be out of the hospital soon. I thought of you all day yesterday and suffered almost as much as you did and dreamed last night that the operation had been successful.

Yours very sincerely
Sylvia Beach

> ALS, 1 leaf, 1 side, Sha&Co stationery. ZJJF Jahnke.
> To JJ at Dr. Borsch's Clinique des Yeux, 39 rue du Cherche-Midi, Paris VI

1 This was the second iridectomy on his left eye, on 11 June, the first one having been performed in Zurich on 23 August 1917 by Prof. Sidler. (*JJII*, p. 536; Norburn, p. 78) In early summer 1922 he had also had a severe attack of iritis, but could avoid an operation. His Paris ophthalmologist Dr Borsch "intended [the operation] as a precaution against glaucoma, which seemed imminent." (*JJII*, p. 566). See also statement of accounts of 27 July 1922, note 5.

No date [after 14 June, before 22 July 1924]

all fear of the ocean once you wuz on one of those floating palaces. As for being interviewed – Conrad too was the modest violet till he saw the New York sky line –then he dropped that and told the noospaper men to come on. Gee they're human after all those big fellas.

Yesterday a seeing-Paris car drove up to Shakespeare and Company and a perspiring guide ushered in his flock to buy a gross of Ulysses and Frank Harris[1] and Boccaccio. Then he asked me for 10% but didn't get it.

McAlmon[2] has got tossed by a bull but only the bull was injured.

Did you send Dujardin's letter[3] to Larbaud?

---

1   Frank Harris (1856-1931). Irish-born American who made his career as a journalist and editor of various journals, notably the *Saturday Review* (1894-98), where he published a series of articles on Shakespeare. His *The Man Shakespeare and His Tragic Life-Story* (London, 1898) was one of Joyce's sources for Stephen's ex tempore Shakespeare biography in the library episode of *Ulysses*, "Scylla and Charybdis". See Gifford, pp. 204-53 (9.165-1134) passim.

    However, Harris is best known for his unreliable autobiography *My Life and Loves* (3 vols. between 1923-1927). The sexual frankness of it was new for its day and created trouble with censors in England and the United States. https://www.britannica.com/biography/Frank-Harris, accessed 26 November 2020.

    Being banned, *Ulysses* sold quite well; yet Beach was saddened to see that it was also listed in catalogues of erotica & pornography. Moreover, after the success of *Ulysses*, many writers thought that Beach was going to specialize in erotica. One of them was Frank Harris who claimed that he was "really the only English writer who had got under a woman's skin." Beach turned him down as she did other writers, most notably D.H. Lawrence: she wanted to be a one-book publisher. See *Sha&Co*, pp. 91-95.

2   Robert McAlmon (1896-1956). American poet and author and a close friend of Joyce's from the beginning of his Paris years. Married at the time to Bryher (Winifred Ellerman, 1894-1983), whose father was one of the richest men in England, he helped Joyce financially (*JJII*, p. 514). Early recollections of Joyce and Beach are recounted in McAlmon's *Being Geniuses Together* (1938) and Bryher's *Heart to Artemis* (1962). See *JJtoSB*, Letter 11, note 1, p. 22. He wrote one of the essays in *Our Exagmination*, for which see letter of 8 July 1931, note 8.

3   Édouard Dujardin (1861-1949). One of the early pioneers of the stream of consciousness technique, exemplified in his 1887 novel *Les lauriers sont coupés*. Banta and Silverman state that "Joyce received a letter from Édouard Dujardin dated 14 June 1924 inviting him to spend a day at his house in Avon, Seine-et-Marne, where George Moore was visiting. In the same letter Dujardin praised *A Portrait* in the French translation" (*JJtoSB*, 4 July 1924 [no. 32], note 2, p. 78). And he continued: "Thanks to you, dear Sir, I will publish a new edition of those 'Lauriers son coupés' to which you have given [new] life. (...) Because I can't even begin to tell you what stimulant and what joy you have brought to my old age". (Original in French, at Buffalo).

I enclose one of Herbert S. Gorman[4] and a press cutting about his book.
I hope your eye is improving.
With kindest regards

Yours very sincerely
Sylvia Beach

Arthur Symons[5] is here again until Friday.

> ALS, 1 leaf, 2 sides, Sha&Co stationery. ZJJF Jahnke.
> Fragment (first part missing).
> Dating: after 14 June (the date of Dujardin's letter that she mentions), but before 22 July 1924, when she mentions that she asked Larbaud to return Dujardin's letter. Her hope for an improvement of his eye suggests that she wrote the letter in June rather than in July.
> Enclosures missing.
> To JJ in Paris or, from 7 July, at Saint-Malo.

---

4 Herbert S. Gorman (1893-1954). American newspaper reporter, critic and writer – mostly of historical novels – and the author of *James Joyce: His First Forty Years* (New York: B.W. Huebsch, 1924), which he had "written with a good deal of help (and a measure of censorship) from Joyce himself." Gorman later published an expanded version in 1939 (rev. 1948). From a present-day perspective, Gorman's biographies give "a greater sense of how Joyce wished himself to be seen than of how his contemporaries actually saw him" (*JJAtoZ*, p. 95). See also letter of 1 May 1931, notes 6 and 11.

5 Arthur Symons (1865-1945). English poet and critic born in Wales of Cornish parents. He was well-versed in European literature and the first English champion to the French Symbolist poets. He was the author of *The Symbolist Movement in Literature* (London: William Heinemann, 1899), which influenced both Yeats and Eliot. In it he characterized Symbolist literature as suggesting or evoking the "unseen reality apprehended by the consciousness." https://www.britannica.com/biography/Arthur-Symons, accessed 25 March 2019.

June 23 [?1924]

Dear Mr Joyce

Adrienne has no copies now of Gide's book[1] but she will have some tomorrow and will send you one. This book of Ramón's is just to put the thousand francs in. I will send you more tomorrow and Fitzgerald.

Yours very sincerely
Sylvia Beach

> ALS, 1 leaf, 1 side, Sha&Co stationery. ZJJF Jahnke.
> Dating: To judge from the stationery, the letter must have been written either in 1923 or more likely in 1924. See also note 1 below.
> To JJ at Victoria Palace Hotel, Paris (1924)

---

1 André Gide (1869-1951). French writer and co-founder of the *Nouvelle Revue Française* in 1909. Winner of the Nobel-Price in 1947. He was one of the very early callers to Shakespeare and Company in 1919. Beach's initial timidity was to disappear and Gide became one of her most loyal supporters, leading the group that saved the shop in the mid-1930s (Fitch, pp. 49, 97, and 358f.); see also letter of 22 February 1921, note 3.
  The book could have been Gide's *Corydon* (publ. 1924), which Beach mentioned only three weeks later in her letter of 16 July 1924.

July 1, [1924]

Dear Mr Joyce

Isn't this printer an impertinent fool! Is there anything you would like to have me say to Jonathan Cape?[1]

Yours very sincerely
Sylvia Beach

> ALS, 1 leaf, 1 side, Sha&Co stationery. ZJJF Jahnke.
> Dating: The year must be 1924. See note 1 below
> To JJ at Victoria Palace Hotel, Paris

---

1 Jonathan Cape (1879-1960) founded his own publishing house in 1921 and soon became a notable British publisher also of American authors like Sinclair Lewis, Ernest Hemingway, Eugene O'Neill, Robert Frost, Ian Fleming or Wyndham Lewis. https://www.britannica.com/biography/Jonathan-Cape, accessed 27 November 2020.

In his letter of 11 July 1924 to Harriet Weaver, Joyce complained about "Mr Cape and his printers", who had set the book with "perverted commas" – whereas he preferred dashes to quotation marks – and "underlined passages which they thought undesirable" (*Letters III*, p. 99f.).

In 1924 Harriet Weaver closed down her Egoist Press. It had published the first English edition of *A Portrait of the Artist as a Young Man* in 1917 and Weaver arranged the transfer of the publishing rights to Jonathan Cape. The new agreement with Cape was in stark contrast with those Joyce had had with Shakespeare and Company and The Egoist Press. Both Beach and Weaver had been extremely generous; Beach gave him 66% of her net profit, and Weaver, too, accorded him 25% royalties, not to mention that very often he received more. Cape offered 15%, in addition "he and Miss Beach were to occupy themselves with preparations for the publication and with the reading of proofs for the Cape edition of *A Portrait*" (*JJtoSB*, INTRODUCTION 1924-26, p. 30).

July 11, 1924

Dear Mr Joyce

I have copied Yeats' letter[1] for myself, Miss Weaver[2] and your brother and return it herewith. Yes Yeats knows.[3] And Jane Heap[4] tells me he was singing your praises long ago in New York. She came to see me this afternoon at your suggestion.

---

1 W.B. Yeats (1865-1939). Poet, dramatist, essayist, and a driving force of the Irish literary revival He had been awarded the Nobel Prize the previous year. As a very young man Joyce admired Yeats's poetry; he got to know him personally in 1902 and Yeats was, in spite of Joyce's youthful arrogance, impressed by the young artist (*JJII*, pp. 100-104). Through Yeats and Ezra Pound Joyce received first grants from British public funds in 1915 and 1916 when he was in Zurich. Yeats also became one of the first subscribers to *Ulysses*. Though their literary work and their political views differed greatly, Yeats influenced Joyce's work to some extent, and their mutual artistic respect never diminished (*JJAtoZ*, pp. 235-36).

  Joyce asked Beach in his letter of 10 July 1924 to have these three copies made of Yeats's letter, dated 1 July 1924, because it contained "news of an unusual kind" (Joyce to Weaver, 11 July 1924, *Letters III*, p. 100). Only the second sheet of this letter by W.B. Yeats with a postscript dated 5 July is at zJJF Jahnke. By oversight, Beach might not have returned the first – and now missing – sheet to Joyce after copying. However, one of the three copies of this first sheet is now at Buffalo.

  The letter was a very kind, second invitation from Yeats, who had already invited Joyce the previous year (*Letters III*, 26 June [1923], p. 77). The "news of an unusual kind" was Yeats's account of his intervention with the Tailteann Committee to have Joyce invited "as the guest of the nation" to the Tailteann Games (see below), even though, as Yeats stated, he had been very doubtful whether he would succeed, not least because he anticipated "the horror with which the suggestion will be received by, for instance, the Marquis McSwiney, Chamberlain to the Pope." Also the committee's invitation policies were a bit less than straight-forward. The postscript of 5 July then confirms Yeats's scepticism: "Yes the committee did all but unanimously decide not to send you an official invitation. "

  As to the Tailteann Games: Nationalist legend has it that they were first held beside the hill of Tara in 632 BC, and the last time in 1168. In 1924 the first revived Tailteann Games – said to be the biggest sporting event organised across the world in that year and bigger even than that year's Paris Olympic Games – were celebrated in Dublin's Croke Park. http://www.irishexaminer.com/sport/columnists/paul-rouse/when-irelands-tailteann-games-eclipsed-the-olympics-431134.html, accessed 5 December 2017.

2 See statement of accounts of 27 July 1922, note 2.

3 "Yes Yeats knows": not clear what he should know.

4 Jane Heap (1887-1964). Together with Margaret Anderson, she edited *The Little Review* in which "13 and part of the 14th of the 18 episodes of Ulysses" had appeared (Slo + Ca, C 53, p. 97).

The weather in Paris is stuffy. I am glad you are in St Malo. Ulysses is going well[5] and Darantiere[6] is sending some more cases.

With kindest regards

Yours very sincerely
Sylvia Beach

> ALS, 1 leaf, 1 side, Sha&Co stationery. ZJJF Jahnke.
> Enclosure: First sheet of letter missing.
> To JJ at Hôtel de France et Chateaubriand, Saint-Malo

---

5 The 4th printing had appeared in January 1924, and the 5th was on its way to be published in September 1924.
6 See undated letter [between 10 June 1921 and 27 July 1921], note 3.

July 16, 1924

Dear Mr Joyce,
Adrienne and I thought that "gâteau aux amants"[1] might do but Fargue[2] turned it down. He says it's rather feeble. There is a cake called "puyt d'amour"[3] – round with custard in the middle – but Adrienne thinks it too messy for the purpose. She thinks 'brioche' will have to do if you are willing. Fargue paid a nice visit to his friend the pastrycook's wife but he found nothing in her repertory corresponding to a seed cake.

Larbaud[4] has written to Adrienne that Penelope (Gide[5] calls her "hideuse femelle sans accents")[6] (see Corydon)[7] is to appear without accents and no

---

[1] For Valery Larbaud's talk on *Ulysses* in December 1921, first excerpts from *Ulysses* were translated into French by the very young Jacques Benoist-Méchin in collaboration with Léon-Paul Fargue. Along with further passages they were published in *Commerce* 1 (summer 1924), among them also passages from the last episode, "Penelope" (see McDougall, pp. 126-31). Joyce suggested "gâteau aux amants" – i.e. gateau of lovers – as a translation for the English "seedcake", which occurs twice in the novel); it seems that "madeleine" was an option at one point, which Joyce wanted to avoid (cf. *JJtoSB*, 13 July 1924). Eventually, "gâteau aux amants" was chosen for the excerpt from "Penelope" published in *Commerce;* for Adrienne Monnier's first edition of *Ulysse* (1929) however, Auguste Morel opted for the less specific "gâteau chaud mâché" for the seedcake in "Lestrygonians" and for "gâteau au cumin" ('caraway') in "Penelope" (*U* Morel, p. 173 and p. 709). Aubert et al. (2004) chose "gâteau à l'anis" for both (*U* Aubert et al., p. 222 and 967).
[2] See letter of 27 July 1923, note 8.
[3] *Fr.* literally meaning 'a well in a mound of flour'.
[4] See letter of 22 February 1921, note 2. Larbaud had supervised the translation of the "Penelope" fragment which was to be published in *Commerce* (see note 1). Monnier, in her article about the translation of *Ulysses*, mentions that Joyce had suggested "that it would be good, for the translation of the fragment of "Penelope", to suppress not only the punctuation, as had been done, but also the accents over the letters and the apostrophes". Monnier was "frankly against it" but to her surprise Larbaud's telegram answer from Italy was: "Joyce is right Joyce ha ragione".
[5] See letter of 23 June [?1924], note 1.
[6] *Fr.* hideous accentless female.
[7] Gide's *Corydon* (1924) consists of four dialogues on the subject of homosexuality and its place in society. Corydon, named after the shepherd whose love for a boy is described in Virgil's *Eclogues*, "marshals an erudite range of evidence from naturalists, historians, poets, and philosophers to support his contention that homosexuality has pervaded the most culturally and artistically advanced civilizations (...). The evidence, *Corydon* suggests, points to heterosexuality as a socially constructed union, while the more fundamental, natural relation is the homosexual one." (Gide, Engl. transl. Cover text). In *The Hours of James Joyce*, Jacques Mercanton recalls that Joyce "admired Gide, *The Pastoral Symphony* or *Lafcadio's Adventures*, but not what he had written about Russia ... As for *Corydon* – he looked toward the sky, with the look he would assume when he meant to mock the universe: 'Will you explain to me how an intelligent man could have written that!'" (Mercanton in Potts, p. 222).

remarks or explanations or apologies of any sort and he will take the entire responsibility for the translation.

I got a letter from Miss Weaver yesterday. She was very much pleased with Yeats' letter.[8] I showed it to some of our friends here and they were impressed. May I send a copy to Larbaud?

The enterprising Jew[9] who wrote to ask you to lecture for the League of Public Discussion in America[10] has now come to Paris to fetch you. He wants to take you back alive or dead with Shaw[11] and George Moore[12] for a whirlwind tour of the States. You would lose [continuation missing]

    In the second dialogue, part III, which is about the relationships between male and female in the animal world, there is the passage referred to: "Look," he said, opening an enormous book of zoology, "this shows you the hideous female *Chondracantus gibbosus* with her dwarf male attached to her...." (Gide, English transl. p. 40). This is the translation of: "Voyez, me dit-il en ouvrant une énorme zoologie: ceci vous représente la hideuse femelle du *chondracanthus gibbosus*, avec son mâle nain fixé sur elle ..." (Gide, p. 65).

8   This is the one mentioned in Beach's letter to Joyce of 11 July 1924, which she had copied for herself, Miss Weaver and Stanislaus Joyce. There is no reaction to this letter from Stanislaus in his letter of 7 August 1924.

9   Unidentified; Symore Gould?

10   The League for Public Discussion was quite a prestigious society. In 1924, its director Symore Gould invited Eugene V. Debs, an eminent American Social and Labour Leader and candidate for the U.S. presidency for a lecture or debate, offering him $300 plus expenses. Among the past speakers he mentioned the philosopher Bertrand Russell and a notable Unitarian minister and pacifist, John Haynes Holmes. Gould's postscript matches Beach's letter: "I saw Mr Shaw (Bernard) in London and he was very pleased to see your letter asking him to come. But it seems that Mrs Shaw is unalterably opposed, feeling that an American trip might prove his undoing" (Letter Symore Gould to Eugene V. Debs, 22 December 1924. Cunningham Memorial Library at Indiana State University). http://timon.indstate.edu/iii/encore/search/C__Rx1002880__SLeague%20for%20Public%20Discussion__Po%2C1__Orightresult__U__X3?lang=eng&suite=gold#resultRecord-x1002880, accessed 30 November 2020.

11   George Bernard Shaw (1856-1950). Dublin-born like Joyce, the pre-eminent playwright was to be the winner of the Nobel Prize for Literature in 1925. Joyce and Shaw never met, as Shaw told Beach in a note on 22 January 1950. Joyce believed that it had been Shaw who had prevented *Exiles* to be put on by the Stage Society in London in 1917 (cf. *JJII*, p. 443); later, in 1921 Shaw wrote a witty letter to Beach explaining why he would not subscribe to *Ulysses* (Sha&Co, p. 52).

12   George Moore (1852-1933). Novelist and man of letters who had lived in Paris for many years before taking up residence in London and Dublin. Because he knew Moore to be a friend of Édouard Dujardin's, Joyce picked up his *Les lauriers sont coupées* during his first stay in Paris in 1902-03, the book he would always claim as the inspiration for his use of the interior monologue. See *JJII*, p. 126, footnote, and also undated letter [after 14 June, but before 22 July 1924], note 3. But Joyce also came to consider Moore as a rival, e.g. mocking his short novel *The Lake* (1905), not least because he was also experimenting with the stream of consciousness.

ALS, 1 leaf, 2 sides, Sha&Co stationery; fragment. Buffalo.
"(Gide calls her "hideuse femelle sans accents") (see Corydon)" is added diagonally towards upper right corner of the page.
To JJ at Hôtel de France et Chateaubriand, Saint-Malo

July 22, 1924

Dear Mr Joyce,

It was a great pleasure to receive such a nice long letter from you.[1]

I caught Gilbert Seldes[2] with his bride to-day at the Medicis Grillroom and this is his address: chez Murphy, 1 rue Git-le-Coeur, Paris, until August 1 – then Guaranty Trust Co, rue des Italiens.

I have ordered Jim the Penman.[3]

I got some copies of the Chicago Tribune[4] and put one in your seaman's chest[5] and will send one to Gorman.[6] Will you please send me his letter whenever convenient for you, or his address which I forgot to keep. He does not seem to be coming over this summer.

Adrienne says it will be gâteau aux amants if you want it to be.

A Jewess named Mrs Gabel,[7] Hotel Majestic,[8] came and confided to me blushingly that she would like to make you a little present of a little money – she

---

1 His letter was indeed quite long, but her remark may also be ironic: Apart from asking many questions, he makes no less than ten requests which she is answering or commenting on in this letter (*JJtoSB*, 17 July 1924).

2 Gilbert Seldes (1893-1970). American writer and cultural critic. Managing editor of the *The Dial* in 1922-1923. For *The Dial* see letter of c. 28 August 1926, note 3. With his 1924 book *The Seven Lively Arts*, he was among the first to insist that popular culture deserved serious attention from cultural critics https://www.ibdb.com/broadway-cast-staff/gilbert-seldes-5909, accessed 26 November 2020.

3 A play by Sir Charles L. Young (1839-1887). Joyce asked Beach in his letter of 17 July 1924 to order it for him. The play is based on the Victorian English barrister and forger James Townsend Saward, also known by the nickname of Jim the Penman. In addition to his legal career he forged money orders for almost 30 years. http://www.sensationpress.com/jim_the_penman.htm, accessed 30 November 2020. The play can be found in *English and American Drama of the Nineteenth Century, English 1801-1900*, ed. Allardyce Nicoll and George Freedley (New York: Readex Microprint Corporation, 1965), and the title page reads "Printed as Manuscript, not published." The play was first produced at the Haymarket Theatre, 25 March 1886. (*JJtoSB*, letter 40, note 4, p. 81).

   At the time he ordered *Jim the Penman*, Joyce had started on "Shem the Penman", a section of *Finnegans Wake*, with Shem as the archetypal artist figure and a self-parody. The relevant passage opens with "Shem was a sham and a low sham ..." (*FW* 170.25). A first version of "Shem the Penman" was published in *This Quarter* 1.2 (Autumn-Winter 1925-26). See also Atherton, p. 70, and p. 247, entry "Dilnot", and Landuyt in Crispi and Slote, pp. 142-62.

4 Founded in 1847, it still exists today.

5 Joyce had one in Beach's shop as a repository for books, journals etc. that he wanted her to collect for him.

6 See undated letter [after 14 June, but before 22 July 1924], note 4.

7 Not identified; she is also referred to as Mrs Gobel by Joyce in a letter to Beach (*JJtoSB*, 25 July 1924, p. 43).

8 Probably the luxury hotel at 30 rue La Pérouse, Paris XVI.

had come from Brentanos[9] with Ulysses under her arm – and did I think 100 francs was all right. I said it was rather trifling for a James Joyce but you could get yourself a few flowers with it. Then she decided to make it 200 francs although I suggested 500 francs would buy a regular bouquet. But she decided that 200 was more within her means and she said to tell you that she felt that in getting Ulysses for 60 francs she owed you 200 francs as it was worth at least that much more to her. I could make a joke about Mrs Gabel forking out 200.[10] Before she left New York her brother had told her to be sure to give a present to James Joyce as soon as she came to Paris so that the booksellers wouldn't get all the profits from the sales of Ulysses. I promised to send it to you and said you would drink the health of the Gabels in a little bottle of wine.

I am selling lots of Ulysses,[11] and am very busy as Myrsine[12] is off on her vacation which she is spending as the guest of the Maharanee of some Indian name at Plombières.[13] Her little sister Ellen[14] helps me as much as she can.

Mr David O'Neil[15] says your genius cannot be measured. Mademoiselle Théry[16] had such a lump in her throat that she could not swallow a bite of her

---

9   American Bookstore in Paris. Frequented by American expatriates, Brentano's also distributed American newspapers and books by American authors that were not well-known outside of the United States. https://en.wikipedia.org/wiki/Brentano%27s#cite_note-nyt-18870ct17-36.
10   "Gabel" is the German word for fork. For the position of this remark in Beach's letter, see also material description.
11   This would be from the 4th edition, which had appeared in January 1924. According to Beach's *Ulysses* accounts, she sold 174 copies to other bookshops and 32 directly in the shop. In July she recorded 83 copies to bookshops in the period of July 1-9, and 13 to the public (Princeton, *Ulysses – Accounts and Royalties*).
12   See statement of accounts of 27 July 1922, note 3.
13   Maharanee: 1. The wife of a maharajah. 2. A princess in India ranking above a rani, especially the sovereign ruler of one of the former native states. Myrsine's father, a physician, had travelled widely, thus it was only natural that she had a good many friends from oriental countries (*Sha&Co, p.* 50).
14   One of the many Moschos sisters who could be asked for help if needed (*Sha&Co*, p. 49).
15   Not identified.
16   Simone Téry. In his letter to Beach, Joyce mentions that he met her twice at the Trianon before he left Paris (*JJtoSB*, 17 July 1924). "Her book, *L'Ile des Bardes* (Paris: E. Flammarion, 1925), which gives her views on contemporary Irish literature, includes an essay about Joyce (pp. 202–243) and recounts a meeting with him at a restaurant 'en face de la gare Montparnasse'" (*JJtoSB*, letter 36, note 6, p. 80).

dinner because she was going to talk with such a great man that evening at the Trianon.[17] McAlmon has come back.[18]

I hope you are finding St Malo restful after the Paris discomforts. Larbaud[19] is in the Republic of San Marino at the Albergo del Titano. I sent him the letter by registered post and asked him to return Dujardin's[20] by registered post.[21]

Arthur Symons[22] is an old friend of Dujardin's and was much interested in the letter. Was it all right to show it to him? It is too late to ask you now.

With best wishes

Yours very sincerely
Sylvia Beach

Mr John Quinn[23] is dying. No hope, the doctors say.

    ALS; 2 leaves, 4 sides, Sha&Co stationery. ZJJF Jahnke.
    Postscript in left margin on first page, written from bottom to top
    "I could make a joke about Mrs Gabel forking out 200" is written horizontally in the left margin on page 4 (instead of page 2) and is thus out of context in the autograph.
    "Arthur Symons" to "Yours very sincerely Sylvia Beach" is written diagonally in the left-hand margin of page 4.
    To JJ at Hôtel de France et Chateaubriand, Saint-Malo

17 Restaurant des Trianons (5, Place de Rennes, Paris VIe, Gare Montparnasse) was one of Joyce's favourite restaurants. One of his letters to Beach bears the restaurant's address (*JJtoSB*, 1 May 1924).
18 See undated letter [after 14 June, but before 22 July 1924], note 2.
19 See letter of 22 February 1921, note 2.
20 See undated letter [after 14 June, but before 22 July 1924], note 3.
21 In her previous letter of 16 July 1924, Beach asked whether she may send a copy of Yeats's letter to Larbaud, and in his reply of 17 July Joyce instructed her to send it along with Dujardin's letter (both of which Larbaud was to return).
22 See undated letter [after 14 June, but before 22 July 1924], note 5.
23 John Quinn (1870-1924). Second-generation Irish-American lawyer, art and book collector in New York. In 1921 Quinn defended – without success – Margaret Anderson and Jane Heap, the editors of *The Little Review*, from the charge of publishing indecent matter, as they had published instalments of *Ulysses* in their magazine. Quinn died 28 July 1924 (*JJtoSB*, Letter 40, note 1, p. 81). In his letter to Beach of 5 August 1924 Joyce wrote that Quinn's death "greatly shocked" him, even though Joyce had been very disappointed and distressed at Quinn selling his *Ulysses* manuscript at a price which was even $25 below its reserve price of $2000. See *JJtoSB*, INTRODUCTION 1924-26, pp. 29-30, and Joyce's letter to Weaver, 16 August 1924 (*Letters I*, pp. 219-21).

THE LETTERS OF SYLVIA BEACH TO JAMES JOYCE, 1921-1929　　　　　　51

July 24, 1924

Dear Mr Joyce,

The contract for <u>Exiles</u> came this morning and I have stored it away with Jonathan Cape's.[1] The Neighbourhood Players[2] are surely going to put on <u>Exiles</u>. As for Hébertot[3] he is in a mess just now; Jouvet[4] wants to leave him and take over the Vieux Colombier for himself and he and Romains[5] and the

---

1 In his letter of 23 July 1924 (*JJtoSB*, p. 42), Joyce mentioned that he enclosed a contract he signed for the production of *Exiles* in America, and asked Beach to keep it with Jonathan Cape's contract for reference. See also Beach's letter to Joyce, 1 July 1924, note 1.
　　A second English edition of *Exiles* was published by The Egoist Press in 1921 from new type, in an edition of 1,000 copies. There were 168 bound copies and 500 sets of sheets on hand unsold when The Egoist Press disposed of the book to Jonathan Cape in 1924. Cape continued to issue these sheets in a new binding, with the Egoist dust wrapper. In 1936 Cape issued *Exiles* as No. 6 of the New Plays Series. (Slo + Ca, A 14, p. 22).
2 In a letter to Harriet Weaver (11 July 1924) Joyce mentioned that the Neighborhood Playhouse in New York sent him a contract "agreeing to all terms of last year: advance of £250, limit of one year or retainer of $500 for another, accounts weekly and stipulation as to production. I have signed and am returning it." (*Letters III*, p. 100). This had been arranged by the American sculptor Jo Davidson (*JJII*, p. 569n) who in 1930 made a bust portrait of Joyce in Paris and after Joyce's death contributed a pencil drawing for the memorial publication *Pastimes of James Joyce*. The first performance of *Exiles* at the Neighborhood Playhouse (1915-1927) was on 19 February 1925. The play, directed by Agnes Morgan, continued for forty-one performances, though it did not create the sensation for which Joyce had hoped. (*JJII*, p. 569; *Letters III*, p. 100, note 1; https://www.ibdb.com/broadway-show/exiles-3409, accessed 27 September 2020.
　　Founded by Alice and Irene Lewisohn in 1915, the Neighborhood Playhouse was "one of the first 'Off-Broadway' theatres", and was "committed to the community and devoted to renewing the roots of drama in ritual, pageant, song and dance." It was a critical favourite for much of the early 1920s, staging art plays by Lord Dunsany and continental dramatists. http://neighborhoodplayhouse.org/about/our-history, and https://www.broadway.cas.sc.edu/content/alice-lewisohn, accessed 27 November 2020.
　　Joyce and Beach consistently used British spelling for the theatre's name. See also letter of 14 August 1924, note 10.
3 Jacques Hébertot, see INTRODUCTION to the 1920s, p. 9.
4 Louis Jouvet, see INTRODUCTION to the 1920s, note 15.
5 Jules Romains (1885-1972). French poet, novelist and dramatist, elected a member of the Académie Française in 1946. His play *Knock ou le Triomphe de la médecine*, was staged at the Comédie des Champs-Elysées in 1923. Louis Jouvet directed the play, made the stage-set and was also an actor. Playbills viewable at https://www.google.com/culturalinstitute/beta/exhibit/TwLyuSoDjNxoJg, accessed 27 November 2020. It was performed 1.500 times.
　　Romains was an early patron of Adrienne Monnier's bookshop and lending library. Beach had read his work in the New York Public Library in 1914 and she met him personally in 1917. She soon became part of Romains' "group of copains, [which] exemplified his doctrine of *unanimisme*, a sort of urban pantheism which held that the individual becomes a part of the

Pitoeffs[6] and Hébertot and everybody connected with the Champs Elysées Theatre are in a great mix up. If Hébertot lives through it he will probably put on <u>Exiles</u> next winter we think.

It's too bad the British authorities are spoiling your holiday with their tiresome red tape.[7] I have never declared the lodgers in my rooms to the commissaire as it is forbidden to sublet so I couldn't give you a paper stating that you rent rooms here. But we can draw up a statement to the effect that the permanent domicile of James Joyce is an apartment at 12 rue de l'Odéon which his publisher S.B. has placed at his disposal. The apartment is the 3 rooms on the entresol of course. We might add that the bulk of your baggage is on the premises. Please let me know just how you want to word it and I will type it and sign it. Also Madame Tisserand[8] will sign a declaration as 'gérante' that you reside in this house as my guest. With kindest regards

yours sincerely
Sylvia Beach

---

spirit of the group or country, a doctrine similar to Whitman's theory of universal brotherhood" (Fitch, pp. 50-51).
6 Georges Pitoëff (1884-1939) and Ludmilla Pitoëff-de Smanov (1895-1951). Both were from Tbilissi, Georgia, and they met in Paris in 1914, where Ludmilla had been attending drama courses since 1910. They spent most of the First World War years in Geneva as actors, with Georges Pitoëff also increasingly as a stage director in various theatres. In January 1922 the couple moved back to Paris and greatly influenced French theatre through their subtle and inventive productions of more than 200 plays, from Shakespeare to works by French innovators such as Cocteau and Anouilh.
    (adapted from Aguet, pp. 1413-15, and "George Pitoëff." *Encyclopædia Britannica*. 13 September 2018. https://www.britannica.com/biography/Georges-Pitoeff, accessed 25 March 2019).
7 In his letter to Beach, Joyce wrote that the British authorities, before exempting him from income tax on the ground of residence abroad, wanted him to state his exact domicile. So he sent them a list of his "several thousand addresses ... since 1904". He thought that the authorities wanted him to state a domicile in Paris and that there would be no option but to rent a room from Beach at 12 rue de l'Odéon. To make it more plausible, he also mentioned that they should make out (fictional) receipts, typed and dating from January or so (*JJtoSB*, 23 July 1924).
8 See letter of 26 June 1923, note 4.

As soon as I got your letter[9] I instructed Lloyds Bank by 'pneu'[10] to send you a draft for four thousand francs. It would reach you by tomorrow morning at latest.

Will you please answer Larbaud's inquiry[11] very soon. It seems to be urgent.
S.B.

> ALS, 1 leaf, 2 sides, Sha&Co stationery. ZJJF Jahnke.
> Postscript written in left margin.
> To JJ at Hôtel de France et Chateaubriand, Saint-Malo

9   Joyce's letter of 23 July 1924 (see above, note 7). At the end he added that this boring formality was holding up two remittances of interest on his capital and that he should therefore appreciate a cheque if there was any balance for him.
10 *Fr.* short for "pneumatique". A message sent via pneumatic tube. In the 1860s a network of tube lines was installed between telegraph offices and large firms to ensure fast communication in Paris. In 1879 it was opened to the public and the "pneu" became immensely popular as the messages reached recipients in less than two hours. https://www.paris zigzag.fr/secret/histoire-insolite-paris/la-poste-pneumatique-et-souterraine-de-paris.
11 To judge from Joyce's letter of 28 July 1924 to Larbaud (*Letters I*, pp. 217-8), Adrienne Monnier had sent Joyce a copy of a passage from Larbaud's letter of 16 July 1924 to her (Larbaud, 1991, p. 177). In it he had asked some questions about Irish and Breton, as he wanted to answer Ernest Boyd's attacks on his views in Boyd's chapter on Joyce in the revised edition of his *Ireland's Literary Renaissance* (Boyd, 402-12). See also letter of 1 August 1924, note 3. For Larbaud see letter of 22 February 1921, note 2.

July 29, 1924

Dear Mr Joyce,

This telegram for you came last night. Was it all right to open it? I thought it might be something very urgent. I had already written to this Potsdam publisher[1] asking him what terms he was prepared to offer you for the German rights. Jonathan Cape[2] had a letter from him and he sent it on to me. Germany is getting more and more excited about <u>Ulysses</u>; a number of booksellers have been ordering it and another publisher the Deutsche Verlags-Anstalt in Stuttgart[3] wrote again and I finally replied, asking him his intentions.

I had a letter from Miss Weaver.[4] She is spending the summer in London and Eliot[5] is taking over the office of the Egoist[6] for the Criterion Publications.[7]

---

1 The publishing house of Gustav Kiepenheuer, who in 1919 moved his firm from Weimar to Potsdam before moving to Berlin in 1928. Among their published authors were Bertolt Brecht, Ernst Robert Curtius, Gustave Flaubert, André Gide, Nikolai Gogol, Ivan Goll, Hermann Hesse, Anna Seghers, George Bernard Shaw, Carl Sternheim, and Ernst Toller (Tripmacker, p. 248).
2 Jonathan Cape had taken over the publication of *A Portrait* from The Egoist Press in 1924. Cape had nothing to do with *Ulysses*, however. See letter of 1 July 1924, note 1.
3 German publishing house founded in 1881. Among the authors published were Theodor Fontane, Albert Einstein, José Ortega y Gasset, Erich Fromm and Tania Blixen. https://www.randomhouse.de/DVA-Verlag-Geschichte-Neuerscheinungen-und-Autoren/Gruendung-und-Geschichte/aid55925_11786.rhd#, accessed 26 November 2020.

  Beach sent an item by registered post to the Deutsche Verlags-Anstalt on 8 Nov 1924 (Princeton, *Record Books 1924-25*). Probably this was the *Portrait* as Joyce suggested to Beach in his letter of 8 November 1924 (*JJtoSB*, p. 51).
4 See statement of accounts of 27 July 1922, note 2. Beach actually referred to two letters, the first being that of 14 July, where Weaver said that she "expect[ed] to remain [in London] till the autumn except for a few weekends in the country"; the second is dated 26 July 1924: "I ought to have written (...) before this but have been very much rushed this week clearing up at my office in order that Mr Eliot may get into it soon." (Princeton).
5 T.S. Eliot (1888-1965). American-born poet, essayist, dramatist, and critic. Nobel Prize winner 1948. He was assistant editor of Weaver's *The Egoist* (1917-19), and later editor of the journal *The Criterion*. Eliot first met Joyce in Paris in 1920. In 1923 his influential essay "*Ulysses*, Order, and Myth" – one of the first published critiques – appeared in *The Dial*. He was also an early supporter of *Finnegans Wake*, and published a "Fragment of an Unpublished Work" in *The Criterion* in 1925 (FW 104.1-125.23). As an editor at Faber & Faber of London, he was very much involved in a possible publication of *Ulysses* after the US ban was lifted. This came to nothing, but he finally brought out *Finnegans Wake* at Faber & Faber (*JJAtoZ*, p. 64, and see *Fahy*, pp. 178f.).
6 Beach here referred to the offices of the Egoist Press which Weaver had established in 1920 shortly after *The Egoist* magazine ceased publication in 1919, and it closed down again in 1924. The Egoist Press was the publisher of the first British edition of *Ulysses*, in Paris on 12 October 1922. See also statement of accounts of 27 July 1922, note 2.
7 London-based literary review founded in 1922 by Lady Rothermere, wife of the newspaper magnate Viscount Rothermere; its editor was T.S. Eliot. In July 1925 the contributions

I shall be in Paris until September. If you come up to see Dr Borsch[8] I should like to have the phonograph record made of your reading of the four old gentlemen.[9] I am going to see about the arrangements immediately.

What have you managed to do about the English authorities and your income? You may forge my signature if you like or I will forge it myself whenever you have drawn up a paper.[10] I'm afraid you are feeling rather upset with the worry and the bad weather.

With kindest regards

yours very sincerely
Sylvia Beach

ALS, 1 leaf, 2 sides, Sha&Co stationery. *ZJJF Jahnke.*
Enclosure missing.
To JJ at Hôtel de France et Chateaubriand, Saint-Malo

included a fragment of *Work in Progress* (FW 104.1-125.23) – the second one to be published (Slo + Ca, C 64, p. 99). Joyce's poem "Ecce Puer", celebrating the birth of his grandson Stephen and mourning the death of his father, also first appeared in *The Criterion* in 1933 (*JJAtoZ*, p. 45).

8   See statement of accounts of 27 July 1922, note 4.

9   The first published fragment from *Work in Progress*, which Joyce referred to as "the four old men, *Mamalujo*" [an abbreviation of the four evangelists' named Matthew, Mark, Luke, John] in a letter to Harriet Weaver on 24 March 1924 (*Letters I*, p. 213). The passage (FW 383-399) was published in its first form in Ford Madox Ford's new journal *transatlantic review* 1.4 (April 1924), pp. 215-23. Supposedly, it was he who gave Joyce's unfinished work the title *Work in Progress* (Slo + Ca, C 62, p. 99).

Beach referred to a recording again in her letter of 14 August 1924, but there is no extant recording of such a reading; however, there are two other recordings of Joyce reading from his own work. The first was "Mr Taylor's Speech" from the "Aeolus" episode of *Ulysses* (U 7.828-870). Slocum and Cahoon give 1926 as the year, they quote Sylvia Beach's catalogue of 1935, No. 4, where, according to them, it is described as follows: "Phonograph record of a reading by James Joyce from 'Ulysses' pages 136 – 137, recorded by His Master's Voice (...) Signed: James Joyce, Paris, 17 november 1926 (sic; date of recording). Only remaining copy of the 30 that were made. Paris 1926." (Slo + Ca, p. 173) In a handwritten note, however, Beach stated that "on the 25th of November 1924 ... a reading by James Joyce of a passage from "Aeolus" was recorded at the Paris factory of His Master's Voice". She also gave 1924 as the year in an answer to a query about this recording; moreover, there are hand-written labels by Joyce for the record which clearly give the date as 27 November 1924 (Princeton, *Letters and related material concerning James Joyce recordings*).

The second recording was made in 1929 of Joyce reading the last pages from "Anna Livia Plurabelle" (FW 213.11-216.5).

10   See letter of 24 July 1924. The paper referred to is the statement she mentioned in her previous letter, regarding Joyce's permanent domicile at 12, rue de l'Odéon, so as to provide Joyce with an address abroad during his stay in England.

August 1, 1924

Dear Mr Joyce,

Your books have just arrived from Burns, Oates & Washbourne (but not the catalogue yet)[1] and I have sent them on to you.

Jim the Penman[2] is only a manuscript. Shall we buy it?

Larbaud asked me to show you his letter for Boyd.[3] I enclose a copy. He wanted me to return the original immediately so that he could send it right over to New York.

This afternoon I went to the phonograph place[4] to find out how to go about having a record made. They gave me the address of their establishment where the arrangements must be made but it will be closed until August 11.

I will go there after that date and let you know what happens.

---

1   In his letter to Beach of 25 July 1924 Joyce thanked her for the 200 francs from Mrs Gabel (see Beach's letter of 22 July 1924) and for the catalogue from Burnes, Oates and Washbourne, asking her to send a more recent one and enclosing a slip of paper with a list of the books he wanted Beach to order for him (*JJtoSB*, p. 43). For bibliographic details see APPENDIX D, Book Orders, pp. 309-10.
2   See letter of 22 July 1924, note 3.
3   Ernest Boyd (1887-1946). Irish critic and author living in New York. His study *Ireland's Literary Renaissance* (1916) was a milestone in Irish literary criticism. A revised edition with an additional chapter was published only seven years later (Boyd 1923, pp. 402-412). In this chapter, Boyd also mentioned Valery Larbaud and his views on Irish literature, and he stated condescendingly that "[it was] natural, perhaps, that [Larbaud] should know nothing whatever about Irish Literature, and prove it by comparing the living Irish Language to Old French" (Boyd, p. 404). Boyd was also among the early voices on *Ulysses* in the *New York Tribune* (28 May 1922). A polemic was eventually sparked off by Boyd's review of Herbert Gorman's *James Joyce: The First Forty Years* (New York: W.B. Huebsch, 1924) in *The New York Times Book Review* of 2 March 1924, where Boyd attacked some of Larbaud's views on Joyce. Beach sent Larbaud a copy of the review, and Joyce wrote to Larbaud that he thought it 'ought to be answered' (Joyce to Larbaud, 24 March 1924 in *Letters III*, p. 91). Larbaud's answer was published in the *Nouvelle Revue Française* of January 1925. See also Beach's letter of 24 July 1924, note 11.

The (typed) copy of Larbaud's letter to Boyd is undated, but judging by its contents it must be the one in question. Larbaud maintained that Boyd had quoted him out of context and he gave a brief outline of his planned 10-page answer "to his criticisms" to be published in the *Nouvelle Revue Française* (January 1925). Above all he hoped to convince Boyd and his readers that Boyd's attacks were "not based on very firm ground" and that what Boyd called his "sweeping judgements" were not the result of "ignorance or conceit". Boyd justified his stance in a two-page hand-written letter to Larbaud in French on 20 January 1925 in the form of a personal reply to the publication of Larbaud's article in the January issue of the *NRF*, and with an article in the *NRF* in March 1925, pp. 309-313 (cf. *Letters III*, p. 115, note 8). The Larbaud and Boyd letters mentioned here are at Princeton.
4   See letter of 29 July 1924, note 9.

I suppose you know of Quinn's death.[5] Ezra Pound[6] was here this afternoon and said it was cancer.
Bill Bird[7] has brought out an interesting book on wines by himself.
With kindest regards

yours sincerely
Sylvia Beach

>ALS, 1 leaf, 2 sides, Sha&Co stationery. ZJJF Jahnke.
>Enclosure missing.
>To JJ at Hôtel de France et Chateaubriand, Saint-Malo

---

5   See letter of 22 July 1924, note 23.
6   Ezra Pound (1885-1972). American poet, critic and mentor to a number of modernist writers. Pound's first encounter with Joyce's writing was through W.B. Yeats in 1913. In the following year he arranged for the serialization of *A Portrait of the Artist as a Young Man;* later also for parts of *Ulysses* in the English journal *The Egoist* as well as the American magazine *The Little Review*. However, he was less than enthusiastic about *Work in Progress*: in November 1926 Pound wrote to Joyce that he could make nothing of the typescript and wished him "every possible success" (*JJII*, p. 584).
7   William Augustus Bird (1888-1963). American journalist, now remembered for his hobby, the Three Mountains Press, a small press he ran while in Paris in the 1920s, whose carefully made books (handprinted on a seventeenth-century press) were also sold at Beach's bookshop. Ezra Pound had a position as editor for Three Mountains from 1923. An early work was his own *A Practical Guide to French Wines* (1922). Bird was very friendly with Joyce and his family from the early 1920s. See Fitch, pp. 155-6, and *JJII*, passim.

August 7, 1924

Dear Mr Joyce,

The paper[1] went off to London this morning. I was not able to get Dr Borsch[2] to sign it until 7 last evening. Myrsine's little sister[3] took it over at 2 and again at 5 and waited till 7. I hope the delay won't inconvenience you too much.

Thank you for your letter

yours very sincerely
Sylvia Beach

> APCS, Sha&Co stationery, pm Paris 7-8-24, and St Malo 8-8-24. ZJJF Jahnke.
> To JJ at Hôtel de France et Chateaubriand, Saint-Malo

1 In his letter of 5 August 1924, Joyce asked Beach to have Dr Borsch or his assistant Dr Collinson sign yet another document for the British authorities (the fifth, he thought), as they required it before exempting Joyce from income tax, presumably for the gift of 47,000 francs received from Harriet Weaver. See Joyce's letter of 12 August 1924 [in *JJtoSB* wrongly dated 12 July 1924], where he told Beach of Weaver's gift "about 10 days ago" i.e. at the end of July or beginning of August. See also letter of 24 July 1924, note 7.
2 See statement of accounts of 27 July 1922, note 4.
3 Probably Ellen Moschos. See statement of accounts of 27 July 1922, note 3, and letter of 22 July 1924, note 14.

FIGURE 6   Postcard of 7 August 1924
© SYLVIA BEACH ESTATE

[August 8, 1924] Friday evening

Dear Mr Joyce,

Your wire[1] came too late to telegraph the money. I sent it by mandat-carte[2] – they said it would arrive just as quickly and I do hope it will. I have come to the Bourse P.O.[3] to try to wire you a thousand in case the other money is too late but they tell me it wouldn't even leave Paris till tomorrow morning. Stupid system! I'm so sorry. Please let me know when you need more.

With kindest regards

yours very sincerely
Sylvia Beach

> ALS (carte lettre), 1 leaf, 1 side. ZJJF Jahnke.
> To JJ at Hôtel de France et Chateaubriand, Saint-Malo
> Dating: pm Paris 8-VIII-24, and St Malo 10-8-24

1 Joyce sent Beach a telegram from Saint-Malo on 8 August 1924 (a Friday) asking her to send 2000 francs, which he would return the following Monday.
2 *Fr.* money-order.
3 Beach must have gone from Shakespeare and Company in the 6th arrondissement to the Bourse Post Office (bourse = stock exchange) in the 2nd arrondissement, which involved quite a journey across the Seine.

August 14, 1924

Dear Mr Joyce,
    Thank you for your letter and the photo of you and Lucia which I like very much.[1] Adrienne is looking up the French book you ordered and I am ordering the others from London.[2] I am glad you have been comfortable in the Hotel Chateaubriand and hope all the trouble you had getting your affairs straightened out did not prevent you from enjoying the holiday that you needed so much. Please do not worry about the 2000 [francs] but let me know if you need some more.[3] So Miss Weaver[4] has come across again – forty-seven thousand francs! What a remarkable woman!
    <u>Commerce</u> will appear at the end of this month. Everything except Fargue has been ready since the 1st of July.[5] What a madman. Poor Adrienne. We shall not be able to go away before September on account of it.

---

1   There is a photo at Buffalo which is identified as "Joyce and Lucia at Brittany 1924" (Basinski, p. 86). Joyce sent it with his letter of 12 July 1924 – whose date should read 12 August (see note 2 below) – noting that he no longer wore a patch, though he might as well do so "for all the seeing I can see" (*JJtoSB*, p. 40).

2   In his letter to Beach – wrongly – dated 12 *July* 1924, Joyce asked her to get some books for him. There is an enclosure consisting of a list of four books written in Joyce's hand and dated 1924, which is kept together with this letter (Buffalo). The first on the list is French: Camille Jullian, *De la Gaule à la France. Nos origines historiques* (Paris: Hachette, 1922), and Joyce suggested that she could perhaps get this book at the Odéon gallery. It is odd that Beach should react to this request and so many other queries, or indeed the news of Miss Weaver's generous gift only a full month later. A juxtaposition of the letters of Joyce to Beach of 12 July and of Beach to Joyce of 14 August reveals that the date of Joyce's letter should read 12 *August* 1924, as in his letter of 17 August 1924 he told Beach that Jullian's book had not come yet. Moreover, the Buffalo catalogue lists an orphan envelope stamped 12 August 1924 St. Malo at the end of the Joyce to Beach correspondence. ("General Note" following *X.C. 279). See APPENDIX D, Book Orders (p. 310) for full list of books.

3   On 12 August (Tuesday) Joyce promised to repay her on the following Monday. On Sunday 17 August, however, he asked her to send another 1000 francs.

4   See statement of accounts of 27 July 1922, note 2. Joyce also mentioned this in his letter to Beach on 12 July [= August]. The sum, according to Weaver, was a "windfall", £550 (≈ 47,000 francs) that came from her aunt Emily's estate (Lidderdale and Nicholson, p. 243).

5   *Commerce* (1924-1932). This literary magazine soon became "a great European light" (McDougall, p. 51). The first parts of the French translation of *Ulysses* were published in the first issue of *Commerce*, which was established and funded by the American Marguerite Gibert Chapin who married an Italian prince. Adrienne Monnier was initially its administrator and publisher, and it was edited by Paul Valéry, who was assisted by Valery Larbaud and Léon-Paul Fargue (*Sha&Co* pp. 142-3; for Fargue see letter of 27 July 1923, note 8).

I have just been interrupted by the visit of Mrs Theodore Bernstein[6] from the Neighbourhood Playhouse.[7] She says she is the Producer and she seems very intelligent and would like to see you about some things. But she is on her way to London and will be here again later. I asked her politely what had happened to your cheque.[8] She replied that she knew nothing of the financial side of the theatre, but that she would ask Miss Lewisohn[9] about the cheque.

The Irish Book Shop[10] has sent a cheque all in Irish for 10 Ulysses.

I went to the place where discs are made but the manager was away on his vacation. He will be there after the 20th so I shall see him next Wednesday or Thursday probably. Could you let me know when you expect to be in Paris? We might arrange to have the record done soon after September 15 when any holiday of mine will be over, and perhaps yours.[11] I am so impatient to get this record.

---

6 Mrs Theodore Bernstein, née Aline Frankau (1880-1955). She became "the first woman designer to achieve professional recognition in the American theatre. She was an artist of many talents who didn't start her stage and costume designing career until she was in her early forties." She was above all doing costume and scenic design at the Neighborhood Playhouse. (Florida Atlantic University Library, "Jewish Heroes and Heroines in America". Exhibition text). http://seymourbrody.com/heroes_1900/bro59.htm, accessed 5 January 2018). On the Internet Broadway Database she is listed as "designer, performer, production crew" (https://www.ibdb.com/broadway-cast-staff/aline-bernstein-24670, accessed 1 December 2020).

7 See letter of 24 July 1924, note 2, and note 9 below.

8 In his letter of 12 July [actually August] 1924 Joyce told Beach that he had wanted to refund her the 2000 francs she had sent, as he knew this to be an excess beyond the royalties. Yet he thought that the American cheque for *Exiles* might have reached Paris, since he had signed the contract on the 15 or 16 of July and, being an advance receipt, the amount (about 5000 francs) should have arrived by the time of writing (*JJtoSB*, p. 40).

9 Alice Lewisohn (1883-1972) or her younger sister Irene Lewisohn (1892-1944). See letter of 24 July 1924, note 2. On 15 August 1923 a telegram arrived for Joyce at Gloucester Place from Miss Lewisohn (most probably Alice) who offered to produce *Exiles* (Lidderdale and Nicholson, p. 228). On 28 June 1924, Helen Arthur, Manager of the Neighborhood Playhouse, sent a letter to Joyce to say that "Before Miss Alice Lewisohn sailed, ... she asked me, as the Manager of the Neighborhood Playhouse, to conclude with you a contract for your play *Exiles* ..." (Princeton, *Exiles*). The contract stipulated that Joyce would receive $250.

10 The Irish Book Shop in Dublin. On the sale of *Ulysses* in Dublin in the early days, see Bishop, p. 14f.

11 Beach had plans – which did not materialize – to have a recording done of Joyce reading "the four old men", a passage from *Finnegans Wake*. See letter of 29 July 1924, note 9.

Your conundrum.[12] Answer: nothing makes me happy except to do anything at all for you.

With kind regards

yours very sincerely
Sylvia Beach

> ALS, 2 leaves, 3 sides, Sha&Co stationery. ZJJF Jahnke.
> To JJ at Hôtel de France et Chateaubriand, Saint-Malo

---

[12] As a P.S. to his last letter, Joyce put a riddle to Beach, asking her the following question: "When is he more troublesome, when he is in Paris or when he is out of Paris?" (*JJtoSB*, Letter 34, 12 July [actually 12 August], 1924, p. 41).

No date [20(?) November 1924]   12, rue de l'Odéon, Paris (VIe)

Dear Mr Joyce,

Mr Coppola[1] has just telephoned to say they will do the record at 11 instead of 10 Thursday morning.[2] I hope that is convenient for you. I asked him whether the Company often made such records privately. He said: very seldom. Never in Paris. They made an exception in this case as Mr Coppola thought it would be an interesting record. He said the Company's trade mark on it would mean that they would control the selling price whereas we could sell the records for "a thousand pounds apiece" this way. Also we avoid drawing up a complicated contract and having a lot of delay. He said the reason they won't let the newspaper correspondents be present is, they want the name of the Company that made the record to be kept a secret, otherwise they would be immediately besieged by everybody wanting records made and this is the only one they want to make (at their Paris House). The process is so expensive that there is no profit, etc.

I am so sorry I couldn't hear what you were saying about the book on glaucoma yesterday – something about cataract and a Dublin review.

It was so exasperating! I suppose I must wait to find out until the next time you come over.

With kindest regards

yours very sincerely
Sylvia Beach

Thursday

---

1 Mr Coppola: of the record company "His Master's Voice".
2 This seems to be the recording project Beach mentioned in her letters to Joyce on 29 July and 14 August 1924. In Sylvia Beach's catalogue from 1935 the dates given for the recording are the 17th November (Monday) and a note of hers gives the 25th (Tuesday), but the two dates do not tally with the Thursday given as a recording day in the present letter. However, it might be Thursday 27th November, which would be in line with the labels Joyce dated "27th November 1924" (see letter of 29 July 1924, note 9). Also, they must have changed their mind about the passage Joyce was going to read: no longer was it to be from the "four old gentlemen" from *Work in Progress*, but Mr Taylor's speech from *Ulysses*.

ALS, 1 leaf folded in half and turned 90°, 3 sides, neutral paper. ZJJF Jahnke.
Dating: 20(?) November, 1924. Joyce was only in Paris from 5-16 September, when it seems that Beach was not (see letter of 14 August 1924), and again from 12 October onwards. Also the letter was written on a Thursday, probably one week before the recording day. See note 2 to this letter.
"(at their Paris House)" is inserted above the line.
To JJ at 8 avenue Charles Floquet, Paris VII

January 29, 1925

Dear Mr Joyce,

I have been trying to telephone to you for the last thirty-five minutes but have had to give it up. Do you not need some more of your royalties by this time?[1] I can spare Frs 3000 and enclose cheque.

With kindest regards

yours very sincerely
Sylvia Beach

> ALS, 1 leaf, 1 side, Sha&Co stationery. zJJF Jahnke.
> To JJ at 8 avenue Charles Floquet, Paris VII

1 From the 5th edition of September 1924.

March 14, 1925

Dear Mr Joyce,

many thanks for remembering my birthday![1] The rhododendron is magnificent and is making a great stir in my shop! Thank you!

With kindest regards

yours very sincerely
Sylvia Beach

> ALS, 1 leaf, 1 side, Sha&Co stationery. ZJJF Jahnke.
> To JJ at 8 avenue Charles Floquet, Paris VII

1   Beach turned 38 on 14 March.

March 30, 1925

Dear Mr Joyce,

The nearest thing I can find to the life story of John Sims Reeves is: Charles E. Pearce. <u>Sims Reeves. Fifty Years of Music in England</u>.[1] This is in the 1924 catalogue. Is it the book you want?

I am sending you the Theatre Arts Magazine[2] for April with your portrait as frontispiece.

With kindest regards,

yours very sincerely
Sylvia Beach

>APCS, 1 side, neutral brown postcard. Verso: with diagonal stamp "Shakespeare & Company | Bookshop | 12, rue de l'Odéon, Paris VIe" in the upper left corner. ZJJF Jahnke.
>
>To James Joyce, 8 Avenue Charles Floquet, E.V. [?en ville] 7e; post mark Paris, 30.3.1925.

---

1 John Sims Reeves (1818-1900), an English vocalist, opera and music hall singer; according to the National Portrait Gallery website "the premier English tenor." The book about Sims Reeves was published in London by S. Paul in 1924. In his letter to Harriet Weaver of 5 March 1926, Joyce mentioned having read "the Life of Sims Reeves"(*Letters III*, p. 139). His notebook (VI.B.13) also gives evidence of his reading (see Lernout 1988). Sims Reeves's name appears also in *Finnegans Wake*: "and what Sim sobs todie I'll reeve tomorry" (*FW* 408.21f.).

2 The magazine began publication in 1916 under the editorship of Sheldon Cheney. It became the significant voice of the new movement in the theatre (Vols. 1-48, November, 1916 – January, 1964). "Broad in scope, handsomely designed, and containing in-depth coverage of every aspect of the theatre-world, the magazine provided a permanent record of American dramatic art in its formative period, and directed readers to dramatic trends and events, and to the emergence of new and important dramatists, directors, playwrights and stage designers." http://snbehrman.com/reference/1916cheney.htm, accessed 27 November 2020.

On account of *Exiles* being performed at the Neighborhood Playhouse (New York) in February and March 1925, he made it to the frontispiece of the magazine. See also letter of 24 July 1924, note 2.

Mardi Gras [February 16]

Dear Mr Joyce,
 Darantiere has signed a contract[1] to have the new edition of <u>Ulysses</u> ready on the 1st May or to pay me for the damages caused by his failure to have the edition ready by that date. This arrangement only holds good if the proofs are returned immediately. The prospects do not seem to be very good. We are waiting until we can call in the opinion of an expert drinker[2] or two. If I am to be confronted with the problem of how to provide you with royalties without being able to obtain your book from the printer, I prefer to resign in favour of anybody you choose.
 With kindest regards

Yours very sincerely
Sylvia Beach

1926

> ALS, 1 leaf, 1 side, on neutral paper. ZJJF Jahnke.
> To JJ at 2 Square Robiac, Paris VII

1 Dated 4 February 1926, for the second edition, also known as the 8th printing of *Ulysses* (Buffalo).
   The type was entirely reset and corrections were incorporated in the text, resulting also in different pagination; so the printing costs were considerable. The damages Darantiere promised to pay were 500 francs per week from 1st May for the first 1000 copies promised for that date.
2 Beach probably refers to the carnival festivities which culminate on Mardi Gras, or Fat Tuesday, the day before Ash Wednesday, the beginning of ritual fasting (Lent).

May 22, 1926

Dear Mr Joyce

The young Italian editor[1] of this review came at André Salmon's[2] suggestion to ask if you could give him something for the next number. It is to appear on the 15th of June. I thought perhaps you would give him some poems from Chamber Music. He would be very glad to have them he said. Georges Duplaix[3] can translate them. Mr San Lazzaro said his paper used to be in Italian and was called Cronache d'Attualità 1914-1920[4] and is widely spread in Italy and he is a Roman. After the June No there will be none till November.

With kindest regards

Yours very sincerely
Sylvia Beach

>   ALS, 1 leaf, 1 side, Sha&Co stationery. ZJJF Jahnke.
>   To JJ at 2 Square Robiac, Paris VII

1   Gualtieri di San Lazzaro (1904-1974). He was the editor of the review *Les Chroniques du Jour*. See letter of 28 September 1926, note 12.
2   André Salmon (1881-1969). Journalist, poet and art critic working with many magazines and journals in the 1920s. http://www.andresalmon.org/index.html, accessed 2 December 2020.
3   Georges Duplaix translated two poems from *Chamber Music*, v and xxxvi: they were published by *La Revue Nouvelle* III.27 (February 15, 1927); (Slo + Ca, D 28, p. 113).
    Duplaix was to acquire a reputation in publishing. He instigated the Little Golden Books series for children, which proved to be an immense success. He also brought the famous Tintin to the US. http://www.tintinologist.org/articles/goldenpress.html, accessed 6 February 2018.
4   *Cronache d'Attualità* was a magazine devoted to contemporary art and was published by A. G. Bragaglia of the Casa d'Arte Bragaglia in Rome, whose importance as a European centre for the arts was comparable to that of the Bauhaus in Dessau. http://www.scuolaromana.it/luoghi/casabrag.htm, accessed 2 December 2020. No publication details for a contribution by Joyce could be found. It seems that the *Cronache d'Attualità* found a continuation in Paris as *Les Chroniques du Jour*, see note 1 above.

July 13, 1926

Dear Mr Joyce,

The enclosed letter is from a Japanese schoolteacher[1] who admires you and would like to translate some of your works into Japanese. Mr Tuohy[2] saw him in Dublin and told him to call on you but he is diffident and I told him it was difficult to see you. He leaves on Sunday morning. Could you let him call on you Thursday afternoon or Friday or something? He is coming for his reply Thursday morning the day after tomorrow.

With kindest regards

yours faithfully
Sylvia Beach

>   ALS, 1 leaf, 1 side, Sha&Co stationery. ZJJF Jahnke.
>   Enclosure missing.
>   To JJ at 2 Square Robiac, Paris VII

---

1 Unidentified. The first of Joyce's works to be published in Japanese was "A Painful Case", translated by Tomoji Abe. It was included in an anthology of English and American short stories in 1926 (Slo + Ca, D 85, p. 122).
2 Patrick Joseph Tuohy (1894-1930). Irish painter. Without having met him, Joyce had commissioned Tuohy to paint his father in 1923. In May 1924 Tuohy finally persuaded Joyce to sit for his own portrait, which took innumerable sittings and was finished only in January 1927 (*JJII*, pp. 565-66). Both portraits are at Buffalo.

No date [c. 10 August 1926] Les Déserts[1]

Dear Mr Joyce,

Thank you for your postcard which arrived this afternoon. I am sorry you are leaving A L P[2] if you are comfortable there. As soon as there is any news up here I will telegraph you.

This is such a fine place. The Désertiens have not even heard of the fall of the franc.[3] They are hoping for rain as the springs are drying up, but dreading a storm. The house across the road is in ruins. It was struck by lightening (sic) in March. Adrienne said you would be interested. She is reading Vico.[4] I brought Chamber Music with me. It's a nice quiet place for reading poetry, and I only wish I had Shaun.[5]

With kindest regards

yours very sincerely
Sylvia Beach

---

1 Les Déserts, [Haute-]Savoie, or more precisely, the high plateau above it called La Féclaz, was the isolated and peaceful place "without postal facility, transportation or modern conveniences" where Sylvia and Adrienne usually spent their summer holidays (Fitch, p. 202). For Adrienne Monnier, see letter of 7 April 1921, note 2.
2 See "Dating" for the letter.
3 There was a serious 'exchange crisis' in France in July 1926. See Asselain and Plessis, pp. 187-213.
4 Giambattista Vico (1668-1744). Neapolitan philosopher. Joyce was particularly drawn to Vico's use of etymology and mythology as well as his "division of human history into recurring cycles, each set off by a thunderclap, of theocratic, aristocratic and democratic ages, followed by a *ricorso* or return" (*JJII*, p. 554). In 1924 he urged Miss Weaver to read Vico's *Scienza Nuova*, as with *Ulysses* he had urged her to read the *Odyssey* (*JJII*, p. 564). Joyce once said that his imagination grew when he read Vico as it did not when he read Freud or Jung (*JJII*, p. 693).
5 Shaun was Joyce's working title for Book III of *Finnegans Wake* (pp. 403-590), which he had started in March 1924 and consisted of four parts or "watches". It encompasses "a dream whose central character is Shaun, who emerges in various forms as the embodiment of [his father's] aspirations and his hopes for overcoming the failures that have dogged his own life. The dream records Shaun's flaws as well as his virtues, and it chronicles his defeats as well as his triumphs. While his dream reveals a desire for the future, an intrusive pragmatism insistently displaces the optimism that initiates them" (*JJAtoZ*, p. 201f.). To Harriet Weaver Joyce wrote on 17 April 1926 that he had finished revising the four parts (*Letters III*, p. 140), and he sent her the typescript in early June (*Letters I*, p. 241). It is possible that Beach had received a copy of this typescript and left it in Paris.

ALS, 1 leaf, 1 side, on neutral paper. ZJJF Jahnke.

To JJ at Ostende [poste restante].

Dating: between 7 and 11 August 1926, as Joyce sent an undated postcard stamped 6 August 1926 to say that they stopped "by chance" at the Auberge Littoral Palace A.L.P. but moved to a cheaper place. He also instructed Beach to add "poste restante" in the address. (*JJtoSB*, p. 67)

August 12, [1926]   Les Déserts Savoie

Dear Mr Joyce,
  What would you like me to do about the enclosed letter?[1]
  I hope you have found a good hotel and that you are enjoying your holiday.
  We had a storm yesterday. All the people ran out of their houses lamenting when they saw a blaze. Four men jumped on the roof and pulled it all down and the rest of the house was saved.[2] It was Gay's brother's.[3]
  There is no news.
  Kindest regards

yours very sincerely
Sylvia Beach

> ALS, 1 leaf, 1 side, on neutral paper. ZJJF Jahnke.
> Dating: it was in August 1926 that the fire occurred (Fitch, p. 241).
> Enclosure missing.
> To JJ at Ostend, poste restante.[4]

1 With his letter of 24 August 1926 Joyce returned Beach's "enclosures" and instructed her "not [to] do anything till [her] return to Paris and till the Dial replies". Thus "the enclosed letter" could have been about his four watches of Shaun, which he had sent to *The Dial*. See her previous letter of c. 10 August 1926, note 5, and undated letter of c. 28 August 1926, note 3.
2 Elsewhere, the story of the storm is told differently: "The thatched roof blazed, lighting the faces of Adrienne, Sylvia and their neighbours as they helplessly watched it burn" (Fitch, p. 241).
3 Gay was the husband of a cousin (Josephine) of Adrienne's at Les Déserts. See *Sha&Co*, p. 192f, and Fitch, p. 203, where Fine [Josephine] and Gay are referred to.
4 See previous letter, material description, dating.

FIGURE 7   Adrienne Monnier's cottage at Les Déserts, Haute Savoie
PHOTOGRAPHER UNKNOWN. COURTESY OF SPECIAL COLLECTIONS,
PRINCETON UNIVERSITY

August 19, 1926

Dear Mr Joyce

Please excuse this card in haste. The Navire d'Argent[1] was sent to Mr Patrick Hoey[2] the day I received your card asking for it. It was sent not registered as it generally goes quicker so but fearing it is lost. I sent another one to day – registered this time. I took also the enveloppe to the concierge 2 Square Robiac[3] and gave the perfume (+ address & hundred frs) to Mr Mc Almon[4] who is going to England today.

With kindest regards

Yours sincerely
Myrsine Moschos[5]

---

1   A monthly literary magazine published by Adrienne Monnier 1925-1926. Contributions were in French, among them many translations mostly from English (William Carlos Williams, Hemingway, T.S. Eliot et al.) In October 1925 she published "Anna Livia Plurabelle" from *Work in Progress*, in English, preceded by an explanatory note about the London "Calendar" having asked for changes in the text and, when Joyce refused, declining to print the fragment. "We hope to be obliging those of our readers who are lovers of literature in English by offering the incriminated text in this issue" (originally in French, *Navire d'Argent*, Oct 1925, p. 59).

2   Hoey from Dublin, worked as a chemist's assistant at a pharmacy in Ostend where Joyce went to buy cotton wool. In his postcard to Beach of 10 August 1926 (*JJtoSB*, p. 68) Joyce mentions that Hoey recognized him after 25 years, having been present at a farewell dinner given for Joyce in 1902. In his letter to Weaver (*Letters I*, p. 244) he said it was 24 years.

   Joyce asked Beach to send a copy of *Le Navire d'Argent*, and mentioned in a letter to Weaver that Hoey was "a great admirer of [his] works and pomps" and had all the first editions ... "He is in fact a very good [Shaun] all the more as his name is the same as my own. Joyeux, Joyes, Joyce (Irish Sheehy or Hoey, the Irish change J into Sh e.g. James Sheumas, John Shaun, etc). He very often uses the identical words I put into [Shaun]'s mouth at the Euclid lesson before coming down here" (18 August 1926, *Letters I*, pp. 243-44). Hoey then wrote to Beach to have his *Ulysses* autographed. He had been told by Joyce that he would need her consent for this (Buffalo).

   Hoey also made it four times into Joyce's notebooks VI.B.12, p. 163 "Hoey dillidantus" (1), VI.B.12, p. 178: "Hoey – sure you'd write as good as that yrself. Pat" (2) and "Hoey – Mind yr boot going out" (3), as well as "Hoey – I haven't much of a brogue" (4): No 1 and 4 made it, in slightly changed form, into *FW* (cf. Lernout, "The Beginning: Chapter I.1", in Crispi and Slote, p. 52).

3   Joyce's Paris address from June 1925 to April 1931 and thus the most permanent of Joyce's addresses.

4   See undated letter [after 14 June, but before 22 July 1924], note 2.

5   See statement of accounts of 27 July 1922, note 3.

Mr Lyons[6] did not call.

>APCS, Sha&Co stationery. ZJJF Jahnke.
>Dating: *pm* Paris 20-8-26
>Salutation and postscript witten vertically, at the top left.
>To JJ at Hôtel de l'Océan, Ostende, Belgium

---

6   James Lyons, a relative of Joyce on his mother's side who visited Joyce at Ostend after he had revised a section of the German translation together with Georg Goyert. Lyons flew in by plane, stayed for a few hours and flew out again, and Joyce was appalled by his daring, saying that he would have to be chloroformed before he would venture into a plane (*JJII*, p. 580).

No date [28 August 1926]
Les Déserts
Savoie

Dear Mr Joyce,
Thank you very much for your letter. It was curious about the little girl and the shells.[1] I also received Lucia's letter enclosing the photos[2] which amused me very much, and the list of corrections to be copied and sent to the Dial[3] as soon as they let me know that they have taken in ʌ.[4] We are going back to Paris tomorrow night. Adrienne will send Mr Carducci's[5] article to La Revue Nouvelle.[6]

---

1 In his preceding letter to Beach of 24 August 1926 Joyce describes a "curious thing" that happened to him on the beach, when a child of about four approached him and insisted on filling his pockets with tiny shells and was not deterred from doing so even though Joyce told her in Flemish – by then he had taken 43 lessons in it – that he did not want them.
2 A letter from Lucia dated 25 August 1926 is at Buffalo, but no photos are mentioned.
3 *The Dial* was an American magazine published intermittently from 1840-1929, in its final phase (1920-29) with patronage from Scofield Thayer, the editor at the time. It could also afford to pay fees to its contributors and was, with Ezra Pound as a foreign editor, an international forum for the dissemination and discussion of modernism. Among the illustrious list of contributors were W.B. Yeats, T.S. Eliot, and Marcel Proust. *The Dial* also reported on the cultural life of European capitals, with Eliot from London, John Eglinton from Dublin, Ezra Pound from Paris, and with occasional letters from Vienna and Berlin and Prague, expanding the geographical range to Central Europe (Britzolakis, pp. 85-90 passim).
    The story with *The Dial* and Joyce's piece "four watches of Shaun", which were to become Book III of *Finnegans Wake*, was not a happy one. On 25 July 1926 Joyce informed Weaver that he had sent the typescript of Shaun to *The Dial*, feeling "about as diffident as a young lady of 19 at her first coming-out" (*Letters I*, p. 243). On 24 September 1926 he wrote her that *The Dial* had accepted the piece for $600, only to decline to print the text "as it stood" a week later, whereupon Joyce withdrew the manuscript (*Letters I*, p. 245). See Beach's telegram to Joyce of 10 September 1926, and Joyce's letter to Beach of 19 September 1926 where he commented wryly that *The Dial's* decision not to print his piece "close[d] temporarily [his] financial stabilisation scheme" and asked for the return of the manuscript (*JJtoSB*, p. 72).
    The piece was published eventually in four instalments in *transition* (March 1928 to November 1929, vols 12, 13, 15 and 18).
4 ʌ: Joyce's siglum for "Shaun". See letter of c. 10 August 1926, note 5.
5 Edgardo Carducci (1898-1967). Composer and librettist and Paris friend of Joyce. In 1930, in an article on the tenor voice in Europe, he favourably mentioned the tenor John Sullivan – whom Joyce greatly admired – crediting Joyce for having made him [Carducci] understand Sullivan's voice (*Letters III*, p. 205, note 6). He also set Joyce's poem "Alone" to music (see letter of 25 April 1931, note 8). In 1935 he suggested writing the music for the film project of *Ulysses* (Joyce to his son Giorgio, 3 June 1935; *Letters III*, p. 358).
6 In his letter of 24 Aug 1926, Joyce asked that Monnier should withdraw Carducci's article from *Mesures* and give it to *La Revue Nouvelle*, which had published "Cendres" ("Clay") in its

I am glad you are having a satisfactory holiday this time, and that you are learning Flemish.

But I have lost count of the languages that you know. It is worse than Gulliver.[7]

We have had a good holiday and no rain since the storm.

The pig had an accident that gives him a tendency to turn inside out he has had to be stitched up twice.

And the black cow has had an albino calf which is very vexatious, and Gay Marie[8] and his wife say that's what comes of the bull being black too, but otherwise everything has gone well.

Adrienne was interested in the picture of you waiting for the Queen of Belgium. The day before she had been telling me of a dream that the queen went to a place where she was.

I will let you know immediately if there is any news.

With kindest regards from Adrienne and myself to you, Mrs Joyce and Lucia

yours very sincerely
Sylvia Beach

> ALS, 1 leaf, 1 side, on neutral paper. ZJJF Jahnke.
>
> Dating: Beach's reference to the little girl in the first paragraph means that the letter was written after having received Joyce's letter of 24 August 1926 (see below, note 1).
>
> Enclosures missing.
>
> To JJ at Hôtel de l'Océan, Ostende, Belgium

February 15, 1926 issue, 1-[7], translated from *Dubliners* by Yva Fernandez (*JJtoSB*, letter 81, note 5).

7 Gulliver and the Lilliputians could not understand each other, even though Gulliver tried very hard: "I spoke to them in as many languages as I had the least smattering of, which were High and Low Dutch, Latin, French, Spanish, Italian, and Lingua Franca, but all to no purpose" (Swift, p. 65f.).

8 See also letter of 12 August [1926], note 3.

September 1, 1926

Dear Mr Joyce,

We arrived yesterday morning but were so tired after sitting up all night on the train that we didn't come to work until today. I found your postcard and was glad to hear from you. It is a pity that you have to attend to the German translation of Ulysses when you are supposed to be taking a holiday.[1] We had such a good rest at Les Déserts.[2] I'm afraid you were afraid of disturbing me and ran short of money. I hope everything is arranged satisfactorily now, and that you will let me know otherwise.

Galantiere[3] is sailing the day after tomorrow. He is going to be only a few days in New York and come right back. He offered to write a letter to the papers about the pirating of Ulysses[4] but I said you would have to be consulted first. Gorman[5] and his wife are coming here on the fifth to stay with Mrs Galantiere.

I enclose some press extracts.

With kindest regards

---

1   The postcard (dated 29 August 1926) tells of Georg Goyert, the German translator, arriving [at Ostend] with the complete *Ulysses*. Joyce complained that the publishers only wanted to give them a fortnight for the revisions when at least 6 weeks were needed.
2   See letter c. 10 August 1926, note 1.
3   Lewis Galantière (1895-1977). Translator of French literature, playwright, journalist. He owned a copy of *Ulysses* with Joyce's dedication dating from 11 February 1922 (https://www.raptis rarebooks.com/product/ulysses-james-joyce-first-edition-signed/, accessed 22 November April 2020). Between 1920 and 1927 he worked for the International Chamber of Commerce in Paris where he came to know many French writers and American expatriates. He also worked with the Federal Reserve Bank of New York, the Office of War Information, and Radio Free Europe. He was president of the American branch of P.E.N., 1965-1967. Cf. Lewis Galantière Colletion (1920-1977) at Columbia University Library http://www.columbia.edu/cu/lweb/eresources/archives/collections/html/4078798.html, accessed 15 February 2018.

In 1927 he went back to the States to work for *Vanity Fair*. Apart from his engagement with the Roth case, Galantière also tried, at the end of 1926 and in early 1927, to place fragments from *Work in Progress* (one of them the "triangle piece" (*FW* 282.05-304.04) in the U.S., but without success. See Fitch, p. 247; Galantière to Beach 31 October 1926 (Princeton), and 26 January 1927, incl. a typed note, undated, after 26 January 1927 (Buffalo).
4   While on holiday Joyce received the disturbing news that *Ulysses* was being pirated by Samuel Roth. Roth had first written him in 1922 to regret that *Ulysses* was not available in America, and that he had now set himself to repair the lack without authorization. See INTRODUCTION to the 1920s, pp. 10-13, on the pirating case, and letter of 9 September 1926, note 2.
5   See undated letter [after 14 June, but before 22 July 1924], note 4.

yours very sincerely
Sylvia Beach

>ALS, 1 leaf, 2 sides, Sha&Co stationery. ZJJF Jahnke.
>Enclosures missing.
>To JJ at Hôtel de l'Océan, Ostende, Belgium

September 9, 1926

Dear Mr Joyce,

    Gorman[1] has just been here. He asked me to send you the enclosed press cutting. He is to sail on the 15th and I gave him your address in case he wants to communicate with you. He says he will do anything you wish about Samuel Roth.[2] A number of people from America this summer have mentioned the edition of <u>Ulysses</u> that is coming out there.[3]

    There is no news from the Dial[4] but I am expecting it on one of the next few boats.

    I hope you are not working too hard.

    With kindest regards to all

yours very sincerely
Sylvia Beach

Did you get my letter from the Deserts?[5]
    Thank you for the Punch[6] which is very funny and The Daily Mail.
    S.B.

A Cambridge student told me that they had no other god before you in Cambridge. He said that no man would dare to say anything against a line you had written. He would be 'beyond the pale'. The professors lecture principally

---

1 See undated letter [after 14 June, but before 22 July 1924], note 4.

2 Samuel Roth (1893-1974). Austrian-born American poet, editor and avant-garde publisher. He attended Columbia University on a faculty scholarship and published a poetry magazine, *The Lyric*, that included works by, among others, D.H. Lawrence and Archibald MacLeish (who would help draw up the International Letter of Protest against Roth that was published in 1927). After World War I, he opened the Poetry Bookshop in Greenwich Village, and in 1921, while in England as a correspondent for the *New York Herald*, Roth wrote to Joyce expressing his admiration for his work and attempting unsuccessfully to arrange a meeting. In 1925 he launched his quarterly *Two Worlds*, and in 1926 *Two Worlds Monthly*, in which he printed 12 instalments of *Ulysses*. Legal action by Joyce's American lawyers was necessary to stop further publication. As a result of the protest letter, Roth became a literary pariah (*JJAtoZ*, pp. 192-93). See also INTRODUCTION to the 1920s, pp. 10-13.

3 See letter of 1 September 1926, note 4.

4 See letter of c. 28 August 1926, note 3.

5 Beach refers to her letter of c. 28 August 1926, sent from her holiday in the Haute Savoie. Joyce acknowledged receipt in his letter of 11 September, stating that it had been delayed.

6 The most famous magazine of satire and wit, it ran from 1841-2002; a very British institution that published the work of some of the greatest comic writers and shaped the cartoon as we know it today. See also https://www.punch.co.uk/about/index, accessed 19 December 2020.

on the works of James Joyce and the students of English have <u>Ulysses</u> given to them and are obliged to read it twice.

> ALS, 1 leaf, 2 sides, Sha&Co stationery. ZJJF Jahnke.
> Postscript 1: written diagonally in lower left edge
> Postscript 2: written on verso in lower part of sheet after letter was folded in two and turned by 90°.
> To JJ at Hôtel de l'Océan, Ostende, Belgium

September 10, 1926   Telegram

DIAL[1] ACCEPTS I WILL SEND YOU LETTER AND LIST OF CORRECTIONS TO DIAL IMMEDIATELY.
SYLVIA BEACH

> TG, 1 leaf, one side, grey-coloured form, stamped "Oostende 10 IX. 1926". ZJJF Jahnke.
> To JJ at Hôtel de l'Océan, Ostende, Belgium.

1   See letter of c. 28 August 1926, note 3.

September 10, 1926

Dear Mr Joyce,
The enclosed letter from the Dial has just arrived and there will be another very soon I suppose. I am sending the list of corrections.[1]

With kindest regards

yours sincerely
Sylvia Beach

> ALS, 1 leaf, 2 sides, Sha&Co stationery. ZJJF Jahnke.
> Enclosure missing.
> To JJ at Hôtel de l'Océan, Ostende, Belgium

---

1 Beach sent three lists of corrections to *The Dial* between July and mid-September 1926. See her letters of 21 July and 16 September 1926 in Walsh, p. 112. There are various extant manuscripts of emendations concerning Joyce's piece for *The Dial* (Buffalo, VI.I.29, 31-41, VI.I. 42a and possibly VI.I.43); at least one of them (Buffalo, VI.I.42.a) is a list on two sheets of Hôtel de l'Océan stationery that was most probably enclosed in Joyce's letter to Beach the next day (11 September), in which he thanked her for the telegram and stated that he had been going over [Shaun] abcd all day and sent her the final corrections, asking her to copy and send them on to *The Dial* (*JJtoSB*, p. 70f.).

No date [before 16 September 1926]

Dear Mr Joyce
there was no information at the American Library[1] so I will write to the Public Library of Dublin, Georgia and Texas Dublin
SB

> APCI, 1 side, Sha&Co stationery. Without addressee's address. ZJJF Jahnke.
> Dating: Some days/weeks before 16 September 1926.
> To Joyce [most probably] at Ostend

---

1 Joyce asked an American visitor, Julien Levy, to look up Dublin, Georgia, for him. Joyce was also anxious to know if there was a river (*JJII*, p. 583). Apparently, he received no or insufficient information and asked Beach to make inquiries. See also letter of 16 September 1926, note 8. Some of the information made it into the first draft of the first chapter of *Finnegans Wake* in October 1926 (cf. Lernout, "The Beginning: Chapter I.1" in Crispi and Slote, p. 53).

He sent a first draft to Harriet Weaver on 15 November 1926 (*JJII*, pp. 582-3; *Letters I*, pp. 247-8).

September 16, 1926

Dear Mr. Joyce,
There has been no further news from the Dial.[1] I suppose the cheque will come soon.[2] The Olympic, the Leviathan, and the Paris are due tomorrow.[3] I sent off the third list of corrections on the Berengaria last Saturday[4] and wrote to Miss Moore[5] today about everything mentioned in your letter.[6] Do you object to her chopping up ʌ abcd so small?[7] I don't know when he will appear.

The librarian in Dublin, Ga,[8] has sent the enclosed literature about it. Her handwriting seems difficult so I had the historical sketch typed. The prospectus[9] is done by the Lyons Club, I see.

Gorman[10] and Lloyd Morris[11] sailed yesterday. They were very much disappointed at not seeing you. Lloyd Morris sent his "love". Gorman said he had written to you, I believe.

---

1   See letter of c. 28 August 1926, note 3.
2   An advance on the $600 that *The Dial* was willing to pay for the whole piece. See undated letter of c. 28 August 1926, note 3.
3   Olympic, Leviathan, Paris (and Berengaria): names of Atlantic Ocean liners. "Tomorrow", 17 September, was a Friday.
4   11 September 1926. See also letter of 10 September, 1926, note 2.
5   See Beach's letter of 16 September 1926 to Marianne Moore in Walsh, p. 112. Moore (1887-1972), one of America's foremost poets and winner of the Pulitzer Prize in 1951, was the editor of *The Dial* from 1925-29 when *The Dial* closed down. https://www.poetryfoundation.org/poets/marianne-moore, accessed 25 May 2020. See also letter c. 28 August 1926, note 3.
6   In his letter of 11 September 1926 Joyce instructed Beach to send the final corrections to Marianne Moore and give her instructions as to his biographical note (take it from Who's Who or Gorman's biographical notes) as well as the title of the piece, for which she may choose something in the line of what the European reviews *The Criterion* (London), *This Quarter* (Paris) or the *transatlantic review* (Paris) used. He also offered to read the proofs (*JJtoSB*, p. 70f.).
7   This may have been suggested in the letter from *The Dial* that Beach referred to in her letter of 10 September 1926.
8   See previous document, undated [before 16 September] from Beach to Joyce.
    In his letter of 19 September 1926 to Beach (*JJtoSB*, p. 72) Joyce suggested that "the communal library of Dublin GA ought to have an autographed copy of *Dubliners*", which he enclosed to his letter of 2[3] September 1926 (*JJtoSB*, p. 73).
9   Not clear, it could be a leaflet about Dublin from the local Lyons Club.
10 See undated letter [after 14 June, but before 22 July 1924], note 4.
11 Lloyd Morris (1893-1954). American author and critic. He wrote critical studies, fiction, plays, and a series of books on American culture.
    In his letter to Beach of 5 August 1924 (*JJtoSB*, p. 45) Joyce mentions an outing with Morris and his mother. They went to see the megalithic stones at Carnac in Brittany

A Berlin bookseller[12] who is connected with the Rhein Verlag[13] came to see me about supplying him with prospectuses of your works in English. He said he would send out hundreds of them in Germany and wanted them at once. If you will give me an idea of the way you would like to have them done I will go ahead with them at once. But you mustn't bother about it as you are trying to take a holiday. I can arrange something.

There was a 'bumper' sale of Ulysses this summer. I am afraid I have mislaid the photos that Lucia sent me.[14]

With kindest regards

yours very sincerely
Sylvia Beach

>   ALS, 1 leaf, 2 sides, Sha&Co stationery. ZJJF Jahnke.
>   Salutation written in lower left margin verso, diagonally from top to bottom.
>   Enclosure missing.
>   To JJ at Hôtel Poste, Ghent, Belgium

described in Morris's *A Threshold in the Sun* (New York: Harper & Brothers, 1943), pp. 242-243. See also *JJII*, p. 567.

12 Unidentified.
13 Joyce's German publisher, founded in 1920 in Basel and later based in Zurich, with its operating office in Munich. They published *Jugendbildnis* [1926] (*A Portait of the Artist as a Young Man*), *Ulysses* (1927, 2nd rev. ed. 1930) and *Dublin. Novellen* [1928].
14 See undated letter of c. 28 August 1926, note 2.

September 28, 1926

Dear Mr. Joyce,

The copies of the new extract[1] and your letter and all came.[2] Wyndham Lewis[3] rushed in yesterday to tell me to tell you that he would not be able to go to Brussells after all and he said he was going to London and to send the manuscript there as soon as I got it. I think it will be all right not to send him a post card first.[4]

The Ms will be registered and he will get my letter besides. I made the corrections,[5] all but 'aquilittoral' which I couldn't find on page 3 nor on any other. I am asking W.L. to send a proof[6] and it can be corrected on that, or if you prefer I will send him a wire.

---

1 Banta and Silverman argue that although not clearly identified in the letters, this new extract is in all probability from "The Triangle" (FW Book II.2, pp. 282-304), also known as "The Euclid" or "Geometry Lesson", all the more so as he signs off an undated letter in this late September exchange with "Goodbye now, geometry" (*JJtoSB*, letter 89, p. 74). Moreover, there is a typescript of a fragment of *Finnegans Wake* in the Lewis papers at Cornell University, which corresponds to this section of FW and is undoubtedly the manuscript Lewis never returned (*JJtoSB*, letter 87, note 2, pp. 88-89).

2 This is to sum up a bit of excitement about four letters to Beach from 22-26 September 1926. Joyce first announced that he was sending a piece for Wyndham Lewis and asked her to have it typed and to send the original and 3 copies back to him to check. Next he told her that he had lost the postal receipt for the manuscript he sent and he worried that he would not be able to repeat it if it were lost; in the third letter he assured Beach that everything had arrived safely, and in the last letter he returned the letter from *The Dial* in which the editors reversed their decision to print the four watches of Shaun and asked Beach to retrieve the manuscript from them (*JJtoSB*, pp. 72-75; see also letter of c. 28 August 1926, note 3).

3 Wyndham Lewis (1882-1957). British artist, critic, satirist and novelist. Co-founder of vorticism, an artistic movement that was partly inspired by cubism and futurism, which rejected romanticism and sentimentality in art.

   Joyce was in Brussels and could have met him there. In his letter of 22 September Joyce had announced Lewis's call at Shakespeare and Company, assuming that Lewis wanted "his piece", which was to appear in his new review *The Enemy* to be published in January 1927. But Lewis changed his mind and instead published an attack on Joyce who was, according to him, suffering from a fixation on time. In his fable 'The Ondt and the Gracehoper' (FW 414-419) Joyce defends his work by satirizing Lewis as the humourless Ondt (ant) in contrast to himself, the prodigal Gracehoper. (*JJAtoZ*, p. 135); see also Joyce to Beach, 22 September 1926, notes 1 and 2 (*JJtoSB*, pp. 88-89), and Luca Crispi's essay "Storiella as She Was Wryt, Chapter II.2" in Crispi and Slote, pp. 214-49.

4 On 26 September 1926 Joyce asked Beach to write two postcards to Lewis – to his Brussels and London addresses – to find out where to send the typescript (*JJtoSB*, p. 74).

5 This, and the reference to 'aquilittoral' is in response to Joyce's request in his letter of 26 September 1926 (*JJtoSB*, p. 74).

6 Beach was carrying out Joyce's instructions of 26 September, i.e. to ask for a proof if Lewis accepted the piece (*JJtoSB*, p. 74).

I am very happy to have a copy for myself. You forgot to sign his so I forged as you requested, and centuries from now the professors will be wrangling about your different signatures.

Thank you for the Brussells Post Office pictures.[7]

Larbaud[8] is due in Paris on October 1st.

Adrienne tells me that Dédalus[9] and Gens de Dublin[10] are very much in demand and are having a great success.

I hope you didn't strain your eyes correcting the typescript.[11] It was very kind of you to correct my copy and I feel much honoured.

With kindest regards

yours very sincerely
Sylvia Beach

---

7   Banta and Silverman annotate the Brussels post office pictures as follows:
"The correspondence side of these postcards is blank. On the picture side Joyce wrote Λ a, Λ b, Λ c, and Λ d, respectively, his signs for the Shaun sections. Each of the postcards is meant to tell of events in the French [and Belgian; eds.] mails. In Joyce's letter to Miss Weaver of 24 September 1926 in reference to the return of Λ abcd, he comments: '(I enclose [Λ abcd] in four pictures from the G.P.O. vestibule here.)' *Letters*, I, 245" (*JJtoSB*, letter 91, note 2, p. 89). The connections of the pictures and Joyce's piece are very loose indeed.

Below the captions (orig. French and Flemish) Photographs by J. Emmanuel Van Den Bussche.

Λ a Charlemagne institutes the post offices of his Empire. The Ambassadors of Calif Haroun-al-Raschit hand him the keys of the Holy Sepulchre

Λ b Charles v receives the oath of J.B. Tour & Taxis, the Grand Master of the Postal Service of the Empire (1520)

Λ c Brussels Central Post Office, Universal Postal Union: procession of the people, members of the postal services, inventors, officers

Λ d Brussels Central Post Office, Arrival in Antwerp of a mail boat from the Congo. Disembarkation of Baron Dhanis (1885). Governor General Wahis introduces him to the authorities and the public.

The postcards are at Buffalo.

8   See letter of 22 February 1921, note 2.

9   *Dédalus – Portrait de l'artiste jeune par lui-même*. First French translation of Joyce's *A Portrait of the Artist as a Young Man* by Ludmila Savitzky (Paris: Editions de la Sirène, 1924).

10 First complete French translation of *Dubliners*. See letter of 27 July 1923, note 3.

11 Joyce wrote that he corrected it in bad light (26 September 1926, *JJtoSB*, p. 74). In the preceding undated letter (*JJtoSB*, letter no. 89, pp. 73-74) he had told Beach that he could not do it and that, perhaps, if she had time to read it, she should do it as it strained his eyes.

P.S. We have never received Les Chroniques du Jour[12] | S.B.

ALS, 1 leaf, 2 sides, Sha&Co stationery. ZJJF Jahnke.
P.S. written diagonally in left-hand corner verso.
To JJ at Hotel Astoria & Claridge, Brussels, Belgium

12 *Les Chroniques du Jour*. An art journal as well as a publishing house [1919]-1931. See letter of 22 May 1926.
   Poèmes, a small collection of poems by various writers, was published on 10 July 1926 (Paris: Les Chroniques du Jour: chez Oreste Zeluk) in an edition of 175 copies, 25 of which were *hors commerce*. The poems were accompanied by hand-coloured drawings by A. Fornari. It included Joyce's *Chamber Music* poems II, XI, XXIV, XV, translated by Auguste Morel. Incidentally, the collection also contains poems by André Salmon. He had suggested that Mr San Lazzaro should ask Beach for a contribution by Joyce.
   Two Joyce poems were reprinted in the periodical *Les Chroniques du Jour*, Paris, VII.6 (Nov. 5, 1926). See Slo + Ca D 12 and D 26, pp. 110f, and 113. https://catalogue.bnf.fr/ark:/12148/cb32742010g and https://renouvaud.hosted.exlibrisgroup.com/permalink/f/gt86ri/41BCU_ALMA7149054540002851.

September 29, 1926

Dear Mr Joyce,

I am returning herewith your copy of the new extract[1] and hope I didn't make too much of a mess with the corrections. And I could scarcely hold a pen for laughing. What a funny piece you have written! I found 'aquilittoral' on page 2 as soon as I took the typescript home last night.[2] Excuse me for overlooking it. There was too much confusion in my shop yesterday while I was trying to do everything.

page 3 l 9   instead of 'volvamns' is it not 'volvamus'?
           13   'rivalibns'   'rivalibus'?
page 6 l 5   from end I couldn't read your correction for 'lilying'
page 7 l 1-2   is it 'diarmuee'?
                  (I left these two uncorrected)
last page   is there a fullstop after 'Romeopullupalleaps'?

I am enjoying it so much! What "fun for all"! Why does it talk about <u>taxis</u> in the Post pictures?[3] Yours very sincerely

Sylvia Beach

---

1 See Joyce to Beach, 26 September 1926 (*JJtoSB*, p. 74). A facsimile of the typescript that was sent to Wyndham Lewis (at Cornell, Wyndham Lewis Collection) and can be consulted in the *James Joyce Archive*, Vol 53, pp. 45-55.
2 See previous letter, 2nd paragraph.
3 Beach here referred to the second of the four postcards "from the G.P.O vestibule" as he called them in his letter to Weaver (cf letter of 28 September 1926, note 7, ʌ b). The reference is to the (German) House of Thurn & Taxis, who were instrumental in founding the European postal service. From c. 1500-1700 the family had organized the postal services for the whole of Europe from Bruxelles. In Belgium, the family is known by the frenchified name of "Tour & Taxis". "Taxis" derives from the name of the Italian branch of the family, "Tasso", who had a badger in their coat of arms. Another source derives it from Mount Tasso, the family seat, where "tassi", (from Latin 'taxus') "yew tree" grew. The Tour & Taxis also played an important role in bringing all the goods from the colonies to Belgium. In *Finnegans Wake* we find "turn-intaxis" among a number of allusions to early means of transport and horses in particular (*FW* 554.1). https://de.wikipedia.org/wiki/Thurn_und_Taxis#Taxis, and https://fr.wikipedia.org/wiki/Maison_de_Thurn_und_Taxis, both accessed 2 December 2020.

I wrote to M.M. confirming cable of 19th[4]

    ALS, 1 leaf, 1 side, Sha&Co stationery. ZJJF Jahnke.
    Postscript written diagonally, in the margin.
    To JJ at 2, Square Robiac, Paris

---

4 M.M.: Marianne Moore (1887-1972). Poet and editor of *The Dial* 1925-29. See letters of c. 28 August 1926, note 3, and 16 September 1926, notes 5 and 6. On 19 September 1926 Joyce instructed Beach to cable the *Dial* to return the typescript (*JJtoSB*, p. 72).

October 22, 1926

Dear Mr Joyce,
    I enclose a letter from a Hungarian publisher about Ulysses.[1]
    I didn't understand very well your remark today about Samuel Roth's edition of Ulysses[2] preventing the money from coming into <u>my</u> coffers. I have thought more of your interests in the matter than of mine as usual.

Yours faithfully
Sylvia Beach

> ALS, 1 leaf, 1 side, Sha&Co stationery. ZJJF Jahnke.
> Enclosure missing.
> To JJ at 2, Square Robiac, Paris

---

1 Slocum & Cahoon only list a Hungarian translation published in 1947. In his letter of 15 July 1926 to Weaver Joyce mentions that "requests for translation rights [had] come from Hungary, Poland, Czecho-Slovakia and Japan" (*Letters I*, p. 242).
2 See letter of 9 September 1926, note 2, and INTRODUCTION to the 1920s, pp. 10-13.

October 25, 1926

Dear Mr Joyce,

Do you remember a synopsis of a novel by a Japanese named Ken Sato?[1] He is leaving for Japan on Friday and wants to translate Ulysses into Japanese. Perhaps it would be a good idea for you to let him call on you if you are not too busy. He would be glad if you could see him. He can go Wednesday afternoon or Thursday. I can't find the address of that other Jap who is going to translate A Portrait of the Artist[2] but they ought to get in touch with each other.

Yours faithfully
Sylvia Beach

>   ALS, 1 leaf, 1 side, Sha&Co stationery. ZJJF Jahnke.
>   Date: written in pencil
>   To JJ at 2, Square Robiac, Paris

1 Ken Sato translated a collection of tales by Saikaku Ibara "from the old original" – a Japanese classic – which was printed for private distribution in 1928 by Maurice Darantiere (the printer of *Ulysses* up to 1930) and was available in 2018 for $1000). The stories were then published by Robert McAlmon, a good friend of Joyce's, at his Contact Publishing Company in 1929 in Paris (see also *JJtoSB*, Letter 115, note 2, p. 148). http://www.biblio.com/books/161751007.html, accessed 25 May 2020.

   Further mention of Japanese translators inquiring for copyright is made in letters from 22 August 1931 onwards, but Ken Sato was not among the translators involved then, nor did he take part in later published translations of *Ulysses* (Cf. Slo + Ca, D 91-93, p. 123). Joyce already mentioned in his letter of 15 July 1926 to Weaver that, among other countries, a request for translation rights had come from Japan (*Letters I*, p. 242).

2 *A Portrait of the Artist as a Young Man* first appeared in 1932 in a Japanese translation by Matsuji Ono and Tomio Yokobori. Another one followed in 1937 by Kozaburo Nabara (Slo + Ca, D 87 and 88, pp. 122-23).

October 26, 1926

Dear Mr Joyce,

Hemingway[1] brought Archibald MacLeish[2] who is a lawyer as well as a writer and he wrote this cable. He said Mr Kieffer[3] would be able to consult all the papers in the Ulysses dossier if he is in the law office of John Quinn and we only need to authorize him to enjoin the Roth publication[4] and to refer him to my letter in which I exposed the whole matter to him.

Yours faithfully
Sylvia Beach

>   ALS, 1 leaf, 1 side, Sha&Co stationery. ZJJF Jahnke.
>   Enclosure missing.
>   To JJ at 2, Square Robiac, Paris

1   Ernest Hemingway (1899-1961). American author and journalist, a central figure in modernism. In 1954 he won the Nobel prize. Hemingway first walked into Beach's bookshop late in 1921 and he became her "best customer" as he was not only a regular visitor but actually spent money on books (*Sha&Co*, p. 77). They soon became good friends, a friendship that extended to Joyce as well. His first collection of short stories was published by William Bird at his Three Mountains Press in Paris in 1924. See also letter of 1 August 1924, note 7.
2   Archibald MacLeish (1892-1982). American poet. He arrived in Paris in 1923 and soon became a regular visitor and friend of rue de l'Odéon. He was the only lawyer in Joyce's circle of friends at the time and it was he who, together with Ludwig Lewisohn, drew up the text of the protest against Samuel Roth (*JJII*, p. 585; see also *Letters III*, pp. 151-153). Joyce was particularly taken with Ada MacLeish, who had a lovely soprano voice (Fitch, pp. 174-75).
3   Mr Kieffer was John Quinn's law partner. The Joyces seem to have been friendly with the family. Ellmann notes that their daughter Helen was dining with the Joyces on the day *Ulysses* was published on 2nd February 1922 (*JJII*, p. 524). On Quinn, see letter 22 July 1924, note 23.
4   Samuel Roth published an unauthorized version of *Ulysses* in his *Two Worlds Monthly* from July 1926-October 1927. The pirating of *Ulysses* is first mentioned in Beach's letter on 1 September 1926. See letter of 9 September 1926, note 2, and INTRODUCTION to the 1920s, pp. 10-13.

November 2, 1926

Dear Mr Joyce,

Paul-Emile Bécat[1] thanks you for consenting to sit for a portrait. He asks if it would be convenient for you to give him a sitting tomorrow afternoon at your house at 2 o'clock, and on Thursday at the same hour. It gets too dark later in the afternoon. He says there's no light after 3. If you prefer a later hour he could work by electric light but it would have to be a strong one.

Excuse me for not remembering the 'Mercure' before.[2] I don't know whether it's the Oct 1st or Oct 16th so am sending both.

I enclose a letter from Ezra Pound to George Antheil.[3]

Herr Curtius[4] is thinking of lecturing on you to his students this year.

---

1   Paul-Emile Bécat (1885-1960). Painter and printmaker. He is now known as an illustrator of erotic literary texts, and for his portraits of artists. Authors for which he illustrated works include Voltaire, Diderot, Pierre Louÿs, Baudelaire, Verlaine. http://en.wikipedia.org/wiki/Paul-Émile_Bécat, accessed 19 February 2018.

    Bécat was married to Adrienne Monnier's sister Marie (Fitch, p. 98) who was to make "a wonderful carpet (...) representing the Liffey flowing through Dublin into the Irish Sea" as Joyce wrote to Harriet Weaver on 20 September 1928 (*Letters I*, p. 268).

    There is a photo of a drawing of the double portrait of Joyce and Robert McAlmon, dated 1921 (Princeton, *James Joyce and Robert McAlmon*). He then painted a double portrait in 1923, but apparently did not do a portrait in 1926-7. There is also a drawing of Sylvia Beach (Princeton, *Sylvia Beach*). Joyce and Bécat shared the 2nd February as their birthday.

2   *Mercure de France*, a bimonthly literary journal whose origins go back to the end of the 17th century. The October 1926 issues are available online at the bibliothèque nationale de France, http://gallica.bnf.fr/ark:/12148/cb34427363f/date1926, accessed 19 February 2018.

    In the section "Lettres anglaises" in the issue of 15 October, Henry D. Davray reviewed May Sinclair's new novel *Far End* whose techniques he hailed as new and original (*Mercure de France*, 15 October 1926, pp. 469-72). This may have been what Joyce was interested in. May Sinclair, a friend of Ezra Pound, is reputed to have been the first critic to use the term "stream of consciousness" for a literary technique when reviewing Dorothy Richardson's novels in *The Egoist* in April 1918. Cf. Rebecca Bowler, "'Stream of Consciousness', Drama and Reality" available at https://maysinclairsociety.com/may-sinclair-and-stream-of-consciousness/, accessed 19 February 2018.

3   George Antheil (1900-1959). American pianist and composer. He came to Paris in 1923. Beach introduced him to her circle of friends and he even lived in a flat above her shop. Antheil's best known work is the "Ballet Mécanique", first performed in Paris in 1926. Joyce and Antheil collaborated on Circe but the project never came off the ground (Fitch, p. 271). Ezra Pound was an enthusiastic promoter of George Antheil and when composing his operatic work "Le Testament de Villon", Pound relied on advice from Antheil. "Villon" premiered in Paris in 1926 with violin virtuoso Olga Rudge, who was Antheil's touring partner and Ezra Pound's mistress. For Pound see letter of 1 August 1924, note 6.

4   Ernst Robert Curtius (1886-1986). German literary scholar and Romance language literary critic with strong Anglophone affinities, best known for his study *European Literature and the Latin Middle Ages* (German 1948, English 1953). Curtius was an important mediator

The banks are closed today, so I have not been able to attend to that matter yet.[5]

Yours faithfully
Sylvia Beach

>   ALS, 1 leaf, 2 sides, Sha&Co stationery. ZJJF Jahnke.
>   Enclosure missing.
>   To JJ at 2, Square Robiac, Paris

---

between French and German culture at a time when it was most needed, and he had many friends among those who were connected with Shakespeare and Company, such as Charles Du Bos, T.S. Eliot, André Gide, Valery Larbaud. In 1926 Curtius was a professor at Heidelberg university (Lausberg, "Curtius, Ernst Robert", pp. 447-48).

5 Beach may be referring to the draft to be sent to Joyce's brother Stanislaus (see letter of 5 November 1926).

November 5, 1926

Dear Mr Joyce,

I enclose the draft for Mr Stanislaus Joyce[1] and hope his name is spelt right. If not will you please ask him to endorse the draft with the wrong spelling anyhow. He will have no difficulty in cashing it. As it is uncrossed,[2] the letter in which it is sent must be registered.

Ivan Goll[3] came to see me. He is going to take up the matter with the Rheinverlag.[4] He is very unpleasant and bad for the health.

Yours faithfully
Sylvia Beach

ALS, 1 leaf, 1 side, Sha&Co stationery. ZJJF Jahnke.
To JJ at 2, Square Robiac, Paris

1 Stanislaus Joyce (1884-1955). Joyce's younger brother who in 1905 came to live with him in Trieste. He was the first confidant of the writer and a great help to Joyce's young family, also financially. During the First World War he was interned for his pro-Italian views while Joyce chose to move to Zurich. After a short post-war return, Joyce moved to Paris with his family; Stanislaus stayed in Trieste. Their relationship cooled considerably and they hardly met afterwards (*JJAtoZ*, pp. 125-26).
2 An uncrossed draft (or cheque) is one which does not have two lines across it: the holder can cash it anywhere. It is therefore not very safe. In contrast, a crossed draft or cheque can only be paid into an account.
   In his letter to Stanislaus of 5 November 1926, Joyce enclosed a bank draft of Lire 6000 (about £65) on the occasion of Stanislaus having announced his wedding to Nelly Lichtensteiger. They eventually got married on 13 August 1928. (*JJII*, p. 585, *Letters III*, p. 145) http://en.wikipedia.org/wiki/Italian_lira, accessed 12 March 2018.
3 Ivan Goll (1891-1950). French-German poet with Jewish origins. Born in Alsace, he studied in Freiburg Strasbourg and Munich. He lived in Switzerland from 1914-19 and knew Joyce superficially (*JJII*, p. 491). His move to Paris brought him nearer to surrealism, and he started to write in French and to translate literary works into German and French. https://hls-dhs-dss.ch/de/articles/028050/2005-11-25/, accessed 3 December 2020. In 1920 Goll approached Joyce on behalf of the Rhein-Verlag about publishing *A Portrait of the Artist* in German. (*JJII*, p. 491) He was one of the seven who worked on the first French translation of "Anna Livia Plurabelle" which appeared in the *Nouvelle Revue Française* on 1st May 1931.
4 This probably refers to the German translation of *Ulysses* for which, Joyce wrote to Beach, the "Rheinverlag want[ed] to rush the publication for November at latest" (letter 2 September 1926, *JJtoSB*, p. 70). See also Beach's letter to Joyce of 1 September 1926.
   The Rhein-Verlag had already published the German translation of *A Portrait of the Artist as a Young Man* early in 1926. In 1927 the first German edition of *Ulysses* came out – the first ever translation of the entire book, and in 1928 *Dubliners* appeared.

November 24, 1926

Dear Mr Joyce,

Here is a statement and I hope I haven't made too many mistakes in doing the sums. Myrsine[1] wasn't here.

That's a very funny poem for Pound[2] by "Giacomo Giocondo",[3] and what can he say after that?

I like ⊣'s alphabet[4] and thank you for giving me a copy.

---

1 Myrsine Moschos. See statement of accounts of 27 July 1922, note 3.
2 See letter of 1 August 1924, note 6.
3 Troppa grazia, Sant'Antonio!
   E.P. is fond of an extra inch
   Whenever the 'ell it's found.
   But wasn't J.J. the son of a binch
   To send him an extra pound?
   "Giacomo Giocondo"
   Parigi, 19-11-1926
   (*James Joyce Archive*, Vol. 1, p. 336)
   Joyce may have written this poem after receiving Ezra Pound's letter dated 15 November 1926, in which Pound acknowledged receipt of the Λ a,b,c,d MS (see letter c. 10 August 1926, note 5) that Joyce had sent him after *The Dial* had first accepted and then refused it, and telling him that he could not make head or tail of it (*Letters III*, pp. 145-46).
   He added the poem as a P.S. to his letter to Pound of ?8 Nov 1927, having mentioned "a few halfpennies of encouragement" that he had received from various sources:
   "I forgot to send a little epigram I made after our last conversation, I think, about my new book. So here it is. I am writing it legibly.
   E.P. exults in the extra inch
   Wherever the ell it's found
   But wasn't J.J. a son of a bitch
   To send him an extra pound?
   The title I gave it (the epigram) was:
   Troppa Grossa, San Giacomone!" (*Letters III*, p. 166)
   Ellmann's footnote to "Troppa Grossa, San Giacomone":
   'Too heavy, great Saint James'. A parody of the Italian expression 'troppa grazia, San Antonio' ('too much grace, St Anthony'), denoting too much of a good thing. St Anthony of Padua is known as a worker of miracles. (*Letters III*, note 2, p. 166):
   "Troppa Grazia Sant Antonio", Joyce's original title, could also be understood ironically, according to an Italian native speaker, i.e. in the sense that the person asked to give something could have given more than just the little bit she or he gave, reflecting Joyce's disappointment at the meagre support he received from Pound.
4 The ⊣ is Joyce's shorthand (or "siglum") for Issy, the daughter character in *Finnegans Wake*, and the alphabet leads to a passage in *Finnegans Wake*:
   There is an undated manuscript at Buffalo, VI.J.4, headed "⊣'s alphabet of 29 letters (Izzy is born|on last day of February of a leap year)":

Yours sincerely
Sylvia Beach

    ALS, 1 leaf, 1 side, Sha&Co stationery. ZJJF Jahnke.
    To JJ at 2, Square Robiac, Paris. With attachment. See below.

    It must have been an early version of the alphabet he later inserted on the first set of galley proofs for the publication as "A Work in Progress" in *transition* 6 (September 1927). The catalogue states that this note was an "extradraft fair copy".... and was not sent to the printer but may have been a gift for Beach."
    In the final printing of *Finnegans Wake* Issy's alphabet occurs in Book I, 6 (*FW* 147.9-15).
    They're all of them out to please. Wait! In the name of. And all the holly. And some the mistle and it Saint Yves. Hoost! Ahem! There's Ada, Bett, Celia, Delia, Ena, Fretta, Gilda, Hilda, Ita, Jess, Katty, Lou, (they make me cough as sure as I read them) Mina, Nippa, Opsy, Poll, Queeniee, Ruth, Saucy, Trix, Una, Vela, Wanda, Xenia, Yva, Zulma, Phoebe, Thelma. And Mee!

[Statement of accounts: enclosure to letter of 24 November 1926]

ULYSSES
Total no of copies sold from June 8 to Nov 24, 1926[1]

2400

From June 8 to July 20   158 copies at Frs 100

(Royalties 25%)
           Frs. 3.950
Since July 20 2242 copies at Frs 125 70.062.50

          Frs. 74.012.50
Total of royalties paid to James Joyce, 61.627.50
 Balance to credit of Frs. 12.385.00

Shakespeare and Company [stamp]

 Typed note, 1 leaf, 1 side, graph paper torn from pad. ZJJF Jahnke.
 Attached to letter of 24 November 1926.

---

1 Between February 1922 and May 1930 Shakespeare and Company had published 11 editions of *Ulysses*. The edition sold here was the 8th (see letter of Mardi Gras [February 16], note 1), which had come out in May 1926. The amounts are in old French francs. By 24 November 1926 Joyce's royalties for the 8th edition would have amounted to c. € 49,000 in 2019. See APPENDIX E, Currencies, p. 311.

November 29, 1926

Dear Mr Joyce,

I have to go to Georgette Leblanc's concert[1] this evening with Adrienne.

There is a young man, American living in Switzerland, whose dream is to see you before he goes back there. He expects not to be even able to stand up in your Presence. Dante would not have been so aweinspiring, he says, he was not so great. You are "the Deity". He is hoping to have the privilege of going to see you and you need not speak to him. He will just see you and be able to remember it all his life.

I hope this has not given an impression of a precious person or a cheeky one. He is a nice fellow, sensitive and seems to look like a poet. He trembles at the very mention of your books. It would be very kind of you to let him call on you although he hardly dares to hope you will. He is leaving in a few days. Mr Emo Bardeleben is his name.[2] He has made several visits to Paris and my shop in the last few years with the hope of seeing you. I loaned him the reviews containing fragments of your new book.

Yours sincerely
Sylvia Beach

> ALS, 1 leaf, 2 sides, Sha&Co stationery. ZJJF Jahnke.
> To JJ at 2, Square Robiac, Paris

1 Georgette Leblanc (1869-1941). Well-known French soprano and author. In 1895 she met the Belgian playwright Maurice Maeterlink and in the years to come would perform several roles in his plays. In the early twenties, after her marriage broke up, she met Margaret Anderson (editor of *The Little Review* in which instalments of *Ulysses* had been published). She turned to writing, publishing also two autobiographies. https://www.fembio.org/biographie.php/frau/biographie/margaret-anderson/, accessed 10 December 2020, and Brognier, p. 130.

2 According to the Ellis Island Immigration Website there was one Emo Bardeleben (1901-1966) who arrived in 1919 at Ellis Island and whose place of residence had been New York. He would have been 25 at the time of Beach's letter. http://www.ellisisland.org/search/matchMore.asp?LNM=BARDELEBEN&PLNM=BARDELEBEN&first_kind=1&kind=exact&offset=0&dwpdone=1, accessed 12 March 2018.

He seems to have been a friend of artists. Balthus gave him a picture ("Joueuse de Diabolo"), and he sat for René Auberjonois for a "Portrait of a Man") https://www.swissinfo.ch/eng/lost-balthus-painting-found-in-switzerland/2787964, accessed 26 May 2020. http://www.artnet.de/künstler/rené-victor-auberjonois/portrait-of-a-man-emo-bardeleben-Lwogak8WgqRqB_6KZIR8gg2, accessed 26 May 2020.

No date, Monday [early December 1926]   18 rue de l'Odéon[1]

Dear Mr Joyce,

Adrienne thinks the best way of getting the signatures[2] is to get Larbaud[3] to organize the affair at Nouvelles Littéraires,[4] all the signatures to be sent in there, and we will send a lot of them from our shops. She says it's the only way to do it properly. Larbaud would be very much interested in the plan, and it would be much more impressive for the papers in America.

The letter must be translated into French.

Yours sincerely
Sylvia Beach

    ALS, 1 leaf, 1 side, bluish-grey sheet torn in half and used upright. ZJJF Jahnke.
    Dating: Beach refers to the signatures for the international letter of protest against the pirating of *Ulysses* by Samuel Roth (see INTRODUCTION to the 1920s, pp. 5, 12-13). By mid-December 1926 the collection of signatures was well under way as letters from Beach to Bryher and Gertrude Stein suggest (Walsh, pp. 114-5), so the letter probably dates from *early* December 1926.
    To JJ at 2, Square Robiac, Paris.

1 Monnier and Beach lived at 18, rue de l'Odéon from 1921-1936 (Fitch, p. 367).
2 See "Dating" of this letter.
3 See letter 22 February 1921, note 2.
4 *Les Nouvelles Littéraires* was a weekly journal published by the Librairie Larousse from October 1922 to 1985. In the years between the wars and beyond it was a most important forum for contemporary literature. http://www.fabula.org/colloques/sommaire1451.php, accessed 12 March 2018.

    Articles on Joyce include "Rencontre avec James Joyce, Irlandais" by Simone Téry, (issue of March 14, 1925), and "Une Soirée James Joyce [at Adrienne Monnier's bookshop]" by Edouard Marye (April 4, 1931), as well as articles by Marcel Brion, Edmond Jaloux, Alfred Kerr, and others. The international letter of protest was not an issue. https://gallica.bnf.fr/ark:/12148/cb328268096/date, accessed 4 May 2020.

December 17, 1926

Dear Mr Joyce,

It seems to me that when writing to your agents[1] you should say that, although you have an offer from your publishers in Paris you would prefer to have your new book[2] brought out in America, if satisfactory arrangements could be made. I have been thinking about it since I saw you today and I believe it would be a good thing to have such an important book "handled" by a big New York publishing firm with their enormous mailing lists and facilities for distribution, and all the friends you have over there to push it. The publishers would probably pay a large sum in advance and their edition might bring in far more than one in Paris. You have put time, labour and genius so unsparingly into your book that you must get every penny you can out of it. There's no need for Christ to be born in a stable this time with a comfortable lodging at hand.

Yours sincerely
Sylvia Beach

> ALS, 1 leaf, 2 sides, Sha&Co stationery. ZJJF Jahnke.
> To JJ at 2, Square Robiac, Paris

1   The agents may have been the Bradleys (see letter of 29 April 1927, note 3), but there is no such letter at the William A. Bradley Agency Archive at the Harry Ransom Center in Texas (personal communication, 5 December 2012).
2   The "new book" is most probably one of the earliest references to publication plans of what was known as *Work in Progress* and later became *Finnegans Wake*. The Samuel Roth case (see INTRODUCTION to the 1920s, pp. 10-13) had alerted him to the copyright problem. In January 1928, and only in order to secure copyright, Part 1 of *Work in Progress* was published as a not-for-sale item by Donald Friede in New York. Slocum and Cahoon list four more such publications in 1928-1930 (Slo + Ca, A 30 + 31, 34 + 35, 38).
    In June 1928, Joyce wrote to Harriet Weaver that he had received two more offers from US publishers "for a book which a year ago they had called gibberish" (*Letters III*, p. 178).

January 3, 1927

Dear Mr Joyce,
I hope you are better.[1] I am forwarding your letter to Miss Weaver.[2] It is very good. I join in the kick to A D 1927.

With kindest regards

yours very sincerely
Sylvia Beach

> ALS, 1 leaf, 1 side, Sha&Co stationery. ZJJF Jahnke.
> To JJ at 2 Square Robiac, Paris VII

---

1 In a letter to his friend Frank Budgen on 13 January 1927, Joyce wrote that he had had the worst Christmas and New Year ever, suffering from an inflammation of intestines. He blamed overwork and worry (*Letters III*, p. 168).

2 See statement of accounts of 27 July 1922, note 2. It is not clear what letter Beach is forwarding to Weaver. In his letter of 24 September 1926 (*Letters I*, p. 245), Joyce had prompted Weaver to order a piece from him; she obliged and received a sample by mid-November including a key to it (*Letters I*, p. 247). She tentatively voiced her reservations about the opaque language in his work in progress (Weaver to Joyce, 20 November 1926, in *JJII*, p. 584). On 21 December he sent her the finished piece, mentioning the successful reading he had given a few days before, and with the hope that she would like it. No letter of his to Beach or any other addressee that could be relevant for Weaver to receive could be located in the period of 21 December to 3 January.

April 12, 1927

Dear Mr. Joyce,

I see that I owe the English publishers[1] over two hundred pounds. The 15th is the date on which they must be paid. I have not a sufficient provision in the bank to meet all the bills and shall try to get some of the more lenient publishers to wait a fortnight, but it makes business relations very unpleasant. There are a lot of American bills too. I never try to borrow from my family. They are too poor. From what you tell me, you have only a few thousand francs left, and the balance of your royalties for *Ulysses* will barely cover your rent on the 15th. You will get a big price for the manuscript of *Dubliners*, but I imagine that Rosenbach[2] will pay only a small part of the sum down. The rest he will settle up later. Meanwhile I am afraid I and my little shop will not be able to stand the struggle to keep you and your family going from now till June, and to finance the trip of Mrs Joyce and yourself to London "with money jingling in your pocket."[3] It is a very terrifying prospect for me. I have already many expenses for you that you do not dream of, and everything I have I give you freely. Sometimes I think you don't realize it, as when you said to Miss Weaver[4] that my work was "easing off." The truth is that as my affection and admiration for you are unlimited, so is the work you pile on my shoulders. When you are absent, every word I receive from you is an order. The reward for my unceasing labour on your behalf is to see you tie yourself into a bowknot and hear you complain. (I am poor and tired too) and I have noticed that every time a new terrible effort is required from me, (my life is a continual 'six hours' with sprints every ten rounds[5]) and I manage to accomplish the task that is set me you try to see how much more I can do while I am about it. Is it human?

With kindest regards

---

1 Jonathan Cape, who took over *Dubliners* from The Egoist Press in 1924 and reset the text for its publication in Cape's Travellers' Library in 1926. See letter of 1 July 1924, note 1.
2 A.S.W. Rosenbach (1876-1952). American collector and dealer. He bought the manuscript fair copy of *Ulysses* in 1924 from John Quinn at a price of $1975. See letter of 22 July 1924, note 23. In 1927 Joyce tried to sell a proof copy of *Dubliners* to Rosenbach, but he was not interested.
3 The Joyces were in London from early April and left Paris again on 21 May to stay a full month at The Hague (mainly) and in Amsterdam.
4 See statement of accounts of 27 July 1922, note 2.
5 This is a reference to "six day" bicycle races where "three times in each twenty-four hours ... the waiting fans are treated to an hour of sprints, ten two-mile speed dashes" (*Popular Mechanics Magazine*, 45.2 (February 1926), p. 251. I owe this information to Geert Lernout. https://books.google.be/books?id=n9cDAAAAMBAJ&pg=PA251&dq=five+series+of+ten+sprints+every+twenty-four+hours&hl=nl&sa=X&ved=0ahUKEwiIkc-k2fnWAhVI6RQKHR54C1MQ6AEINDAC#v=onepage&q&f=false.

Yours very sincerely
Sylvia Beach

    ALS, 2 leaves, 2 sides, Sha&Co stationery. Buffalo.
    Permission to print Miss Beach's letter to Joyce was granted to Professor Silverman by Miss Beach in 1959. (*JJtoSB*, Appendix C, p. 209).
    To JJ at 2 Square Robiac, Paris VII. This letter was never sent off.

April 29, 1927

Dear Mr Joyce,

I have thought over the question of your finances. I am quite unable to think of them clearly in your presence on account of the spell cast by your genius and the slowness of my arithmetic.

You said you had only 9000 francs a month to live on and then I reminded you that Ulysses had brought you in 125 000 since last August.[1] It makes about 12 000 francs a month doesn't it, which added to 9000 makes about 21 000 francs a month. You didn't consider the Ulysses royalties important enough to mention. But it would have been more sportsmanlike of you to own up to spending this considerable amount of money than to tell a lot of cock-and-bull stories to me who is your friend if ever you had one. You are the greatest writer who ever lived but even Pound[2] has more sense. Do go to the moneylender. The Bradleys[3] cannot get a more false notion of your circumstances than you yourself have. And what does anything matter?

With kindest regards

yours very sincerely
Sylvia Beach

> ALS, 1 leaf, 2 sides, Sha&Co stationery. ZJJF Jahnke.
> To JJ at 2 Square Robiac, Paris VII

1 Beach refers to the sales of the 8th edition of *Ulysses*, which came out on 26 May 1926 and for which she had sent Joyce a statement for copies sold up to 24 November 1926. In her *Ulysses* accounts book Beach notes under her entry "Royalties": "8th ed. 126,272 Frs by April 15 (overdrawn 1,272)", which tallies with the 125,000 Frs she mentions. See also note 1 to attachment to letter of 24 November 1926.
2 See letter of 1 August 1924, note 6.
3 Through Ezra Pound Joyce got to know Jenny Serruys, then fiancée of (and later married to) William A. Bradley. Serruys became a friend and quasi-patron of Joyce, loaning him furniture when he first arrived in Paris with his family. It is said that she loaned him the table upon which he completed *Ulysses*. Her friendship with James Joyce led to her translation of Joyce's *Exiles* into French which was eventually published in 1950.
   Around 1923 the Bradleys founded a literary agency. At its height, it was the pre-eminent literary agency in Paris, representing major authors on both sides of the Atlantic, cultivating new talent, and bringing European literature to a larger American audience. According to Gertrude Stein, William Bradley was "the friend and comforter of Paris authors" and he handled the majority of the "Paris exiles" in the 1920s and 1930s. The Bradleys influenced the shape of modern literature by taking risks on experimental writings at a time when both American and European publishers were hesitant to pursue new and different works. See Texas, Harry Ransom Humanities Research Center http://norman.hrc.utexas.edu/fasearch/findingAid.cfm?eadid=00300, accessed 6 December 2020, and *JJII*, p. 487f.

August 11, 1927   Le Désert Savoie[1]

Dear Mr Joyce,

I am hoping every day to get the 'questionnaire'.[2] You must be very busy getting it into shape for the 15th so perhaps I shall not see it before it appears in <u>Transition</u>.[3]

I hope you are not working too hard and that all the family is well.

Yours very sincerely
Sylvia Beach

Adrienne received the review and will write to you about the article and a dream she had about your new book.

> APCS, picture overleaf is a dancing bear: Text: En Savoie – Montreurs d'Ours [In Savoy – Bear tamers]. ZJJF Jahnke.
> Postscript written at the top, between date and postal stamp, from bottom to top.
> To JJ at 2 Square Robiac, Paris VII

---

1 See letter of ca. 10 August 1926, note 1.
2 This refers to *Finnegans Wake*, Book I, chapter 6, which contains 12 questions, and was to be published in *transition* 6 (September 1927). On 14 August 1927 Joyce replied that he had sent the first draft of the questionnaire with a letter a week before, but feared that he sent it to Savoie not H[aute] S[avoie]. He went on to say that in question 11 he had allowed Shaun, one of the protagonists, to speak with the voice of *The Enemy* (*JJtoSB*, p. 129), by which he meant Wyndham Lewis's new review in which Lewis had attacked Joyce for his experimental work (see letter of 28 September 1926, note 3, and "The Mookse and the Gripes", *transition* 6, 101-106 and 106a-f).
3 Edited by the polyglot Eugene Jolas, the first issue of *transition* (April 1927) made a programmatic statement with its first contribution "Opening pages of a Work in Progress" by James Joyce, and it soon became the most important avant-garde literary magazine of the 1920s and 30s. It ran 17 instalments of *Work in Progress*, the last one in No 27 (May 1938), which was also *transition*'s closing number. The deadlines turned out to be the right measure of gentle pressure for Joyce, and with hindsight, *transition* became the transitory port of call for Joyce's new work as in each case where *transition* duplicated a previous publication there was extensive revision of the text, which was usually revised again before the final publication in *Finnegans Wake* in 1939 (see Slo + Ca, C 70, p. 101).

December 5, 1927

Statement
James Joyce, Esq.,
Paris.

From November 1 to November 30[1]

Copies of ULYSSES sold: 176 at Frs 125
                          25%   Frs. 5.500

(booksellers: 161 other customers 15)

    TD, unsigned. 1 leaf, 1 side, Sha&Co stationery. ZJJF Jahnke.
    To JJ at 2 Square Robiac, Paris VII

---

1 9th edition, May 1927 (Slo + Ca A 17, p. 25).

July 30, 1928 [postmark]   Les Déserts Savoie[1]

Dear Mr Joyce

thank you for your card from Innsbruck.[2] I hope Salzburg is cooler. Miss Weaver says she enjoyed 'Shaun' so much.

With best wishes to you all

yours very sincerely
Sylvia Beach

The Isère and her reflection at this point have a bottle shape, the people say.

> APCS, 2 sides. Picture overleaf Montmélian – Vue prise de la Rive gauche de l'Isère [Montmélian – view from the left bank of the river Isère]. ZJJF Jahnke. Postscript/comment on verso, on right margin of the picture, written from bottom to top.
> To JJ at Hotel Mirabell, Salzburg, Austria

---

1 See letter of ca. 10 August 1926, note 1.
2 The Joyces stayed in Innsbruck from c.17-23 July 1928 (Norburn, p. 134).

FIGURE 8   Sylvia Beach at Les Déserts, undated
PHOTOGRAPHER UNKNOWN. COURTESY OF SPECIAL
COLLECTIONS, PRINCETON UNIVERSITY

August 10, [1928]¹   St Claude [Dept. Jura, France]

S B
A.M.

> APCI, picture overleaf "Le Jura, Saint-Claude – Pont d'Avignon et Faubourg des Moulins | Le pain de sucre (altitude: 888 m.)" [the name of the mountain could be translated as 'Sugarloaf'] ZJJF Jahnke.
> To JJ at Hotel Mirabell, Salzburg, Austria

---

1 This and the following postcard must have been written on their way home from Les Déserts, their summer holiday place in Haute Savoie.

No date [after 10 August 1928]   Besançon[1]

This is the clock in the Cathedral of St Jean

S B
A.M.

APCI, picture overleaf of cathedral clock, with lateral view from left, front view and lateral view from right; with oval stamp "Souvenir | de l'horloge astronomique | Besançon". ZJJF Jahnke.
Dating: see note 1 of 10 August [1928].
verso, beneath picture:
Besançon. – Astronomical Clock.
Commissioned by Cardinal Mathieu, archbishop of Besançon, conceived and executed by Mr. Vérite de Beauvais. Started in March 1858, finished in August. The clock contains 30.000 mechanical devices, is 5.80 m high and has 72 dials. Refurbished in 1900 by Mr Florian Goudey, clock maker in Besançon. Edition Brandibas-Goudey. (Original in French).
To JJ at Hotel Mirabell, Salzburg, Austria

---

1   See postcard of 10 August [1928], note 1.

August 18, 1928

Dear Mr Joyce,

I am very sorry to hear that your eyes are troubling you. We got home on the 14th and went out to Rocfoin[1] over the 15th which was a holiday. Myrsine[2] then started her vacation. She gave me Lucia's letter asking for the gouttes jaunes, the lotion etc[3] and for the money from Crosby Gaige to be sent to you.[4] On the morning of the 16th I went to the bank where they had the sum of money for you and when I showed them my chargé d'affaires paper,[5] they consented to send you the money. Otherwise a signed authorisation from you would have had to be obtained from you (not Lucia). I hope they sent it promptly – by telegraph as I instructed them. Ellen[6] got the gouttes jaunes without any trouble and you must have received them long ago. But the lotion. Ever since I came back I have been struggling with your pharmacien to get four bottles and with

---

1 Rocfoin is some 80 kms southwest of Paris on the road to Chartres, where Adrienne Monnier's family lived and where Sylvia Beach and Adrienne Monnier went most Sundays (Fitch, p. 267 and *Sha&Co*, p. 191).
2 See statement of accounts, 27 July 1922, note 3.
3 There are requests for 'gouttes jaunes' (*Fr.* yellow drops) in various letters by Joyce; the first time Joyce mentioned "drops" is on 5 September 1922: "Will you thank Miss Moschos for sending me the cocaine. Fortunately I have not been obliged to use any drops, as the pain has subsided" (*JJtoSB*, p. 13). In 1925 he requested them from his son Giorgio (Joyce to Giorgio, 1.9.1926, at ZJJF Jahnke), a day or two later he asked Beach to get some and send them registered to his hotel in Bruxelles. On 22 August 1928, in a typed letter written on Joyce's behalf by Stuart Gilbert in Salzburg, Joyce had him acknowledge receipt of the medicine ordered in the present letter, and he asked him to say that "his eye [was] better today." (Princeton, *Joyce to Beach, Stuart Gilbert Correspondence*). On 3 September 1928 Joyce asked for "two large bottles of the lotion and a fresh supply of yellow drops" (*JJtoSB*, p. 142-3).
4 Crosby Gaige (1882-1949). According to Colin Smythe a very colourful figure. His first career had been in the theatre, and in the 1910s and 20s he was making a fortune by producing Broadway hits. He had also "one of the best private libraries of his time and handset and printed fine editions on a press he kept in a huge barn at his home." Among his friends was also Bennett Cerf, the founder of Random House, who suggested that he should start his own publishing house, which he did in 1927, specializing in limited signed editions of original works of well-known writers, "whom he paid handsomely". (Colin Smythe, "Crosby Gaige and W.B. Yeats's *The Winding Stair* (1929)". http://colinsmythe.co.uk/crosby-gaige-and-w-b-yeatss-the-winding-stair-1929/, accessed 12 March 2018.

In October 1928 Crosby Gaige published a deluxe edition of *Anna Livia Plurabelle*, „a third and final version of [it], unpublished and known only to a few of Mr Joyce's friends who heard him read it at his house a fortnight ago. He made at least three hundred alterations and additions to the text that appeared in *transition* 8" (unpublished draft of a letter by Beach and Joyce to James R. Wells [of Crosby Gaige], 5 December 1927 (Buffalo).
5 *Fr.* power of attorney.
6 See letter of 22 July 1924, note 14.

the P.O. to send them. The pharmacien has to be prodded and shaken up all the time and makes one blunder after another (my coiffeur M. Auguste who had his shop next door told me the pharmacien took dope) and the P.O. wants the bottles to be half the size and packed in wooden boxes which have to be made to order by a carpenter-packer and take forever. So that is why you have been waiting all this time for your lotion. Last evening I sent you two bottles in cardboard boxes by post-express in hopes that they would reach you safely. The post office people said they would surely be broken before they got out of France. The others I am sending today in wooden boxes made to fit the bottles. The contents of the large bottles has been put into small bottles, making eight instead of four. There was no way of sending the large ones. Now the wooden boxes are too heavy to send as échantillons[7] so they will have to go as 1st class mail at the rate of about 35 frs per box. They could be all packed in a case and go by freight but I am afraid you would never get them. I sent Georgio only 1400 frs by mistake, yesterday. I am telegraphing him another thousand this morning. Ellen will get the draft for Mrs Schaureck on Monday.[8] She has not had time to go to the bank yet.

Gorman[9] writes that he fears you have not received his letter that he wrote soon after reaching Cannes. He wonders if you are back in Paris.

Protée[10] has bowled over the gentleman who is at the head of the librairie "Au Commerce des Idées". He says he is "bouleversé"[11] that it is a formidable chef d'oeuvre etc.

McGreevy[12] came in yesterday. He conducts tourists to Versailles and other monuments. He says he can arrange to work for you the first week in September

---

7   *Fr.* commercial sample.
8   Mrs Eileen Schaurek (1889-1963). One of Joyce's sisters whom Joyce brought to Trieste to live with them. In 1915 she got married to Frantisek Schaurek, who was employed at a bank in Trieste, and they went to Prague after their wedding. After the war they returned to Trieste where Joyce and his family joined them in 1919 before leaving for Paris in 1920. In November 1926, when Eileen was in Dublin, her husband committed suicide. In Beach's 2nd Accounts Book there are entries for fairly regular monthly payments to Eileen of £5 between April 1928 and May 1930 (Princeton, *Accounts and Royalties*).
9   See undated letter [after 14 June, but before 22 July 1924], note 4.
10 The third episode of *Ulysses*, "Protée", translated by Auguste Morel and Stuart Gilbert and reviewed by Valery Larbaud in *La Nouvelle Revue Française*, Paris, xv.179 (1 août 1928), [204]-226. (Slo + Ca, D 30, p. 113). For the choice of the title see letter to Valery Larbaud of 10 February 1927, where Joyce asks if there ought not "to appear a footnote to say that this title is not in the original text?" (*Letters III*, p. 154).
11 *Fr.* bowled over.
12 Thomas MacGreevy (1893-1967). Irish poet, literary and art critic. He has been called the first Irish modernist; he wrote hundreds of articles on art, literature, dance and religion. Educated at Trinity College Dublin, he moved via London to Paris in 1927 where he was a

as you wanted.[13] I hope you have been resting this summer but fear you have gone on working and not taking care of yourself as you should have done.

Adrienne and I are about to translate two missing pages of <u>Ulysses</u>.[14] Morel[15] asked us to. They had got lost somehow.

I have sent Miss Duncan's[16] copy of <u>Ulysses</u> and <u>Transition</u> No 13.[17]

With best wishes to all the family

yours sincerely
Sylvia Beach

---

lecturer at the Ecole Normale Supérieure and soon got to know Joyce and later Beckett, his successor at the Ecole in 1928. It was MacGreevy who introduced Beckett to Joyce. MacGreevy wrote several articles to explicate Joyce's latest work to the readers of *transition*. He must have been working on the first of them around the time of this letter: it appeared as "A Note on *Work in Progress*" in *transition* no. 14 (Autumn 1928). It was included as "The Catholic Element in *Work in Progress*" in *Our Exagmination* (1929), see letter of 8 July 1931, note 8, and Deming 1977, item 5459. MacGreevy had assisted Joyce in his *Work in Progress* before (see letter of 10 May 1928, *JJtoSB*, p. 139). In his later years MacGreevy worked above all as a critic and arts editor in London until he finally moved back to Dublin, as director of the National Gallery of Ireland between 1950-63. (*Encyclopaedia of Ireland*, "Thomas MacGreevy") See also Susan Schreibman at the Thomas MacGreevy Archive at http://www.macgreevy.org/about.jsp, accessed 12 March 2018.

13 Unverifiable.
14 They must be pages for the French translation published by Adrienne Monnier's printing press 'La Maison des Amis des Livres' in February 1929 (Slo + Ca, D 17, pp. 111-2).
15 Auguste Morel, a young university graduate and translator who was teaching in the provinces and whom Ellmann describes as a young Breton "who had translated with great dexterity Thompson's 'The Hound of Heaven' and other English poems ... and was imaginative and gifted, but did not know English as well as Larbaud" (*JJII*, p. 562). He had been called in by Adrienne Monnier after Larbaud had not made much headway and thought it too demanding. In 1924 Morel agreed to translate *Ulysses*, on condition that Larbaud should revise his work, which he in turn accepted because he had Joyce's assurance that he himself would help. Finally, around 1927-8 Stuart Gilbert also offered to help. (Auguste Anglès and Philippe Soupault in Aubert, pp. 41-42).
16 Most probably Elizabeth Duncan. Lucia received lessons at her Dancing School at Schloss Kleßheim near Salzburg (Shloss, p. 160f.). Isadora, her more famous sister, had died the previous year.
17 *transition* 13 (Summer 1928) contained instalment no 11 of *Work in Progress* which became *Finnegans Wake* Book III, chapter 2 (*FW* 429-73).

Most probably the recipient of *transition* issue was not Miss Duncan, as in his letter of 3 September 1928 he hoped that she had sent *transition* 13 to Prof. Fischer in Salzburg – where the Joyces had stayed the whole month of August – as Prof. Fischer had published five articles in the Austrian press about Joyce. (By 3 September Joyce had probably forgotten that she had already told him she had sent the item.)

I will send you any presscuttings that come in.

>ALS, 3 leaves, 6 sides, half-size Sha&Co stationery. ZJJF Jahnke.
>Postscript added to recto 1, in top left margin.
>To JJ at Hotel Mirabell, Salzburg, Austria

May 15, 1929

Dear Mr Joyce

am I to send Miss Weaver the Preface?[1] I forget. And The Revue Hebdomadaire[2] and Européenne?[3] SB

> [added in Joyce's hand, in ink:]
> Oui, ja, jo[?], si, yes
> J.J.

This is the proof of the ad in <u>Transition</u>.[4] What do you think of one in the New Statesman[5] as well as Times Lit Supplement?[6]

(over

The printer told me it was too late to add an m to incammination in the title on cover. The plate has been engraved.

It will be added to the title page inside.[7] SB

> [rather illegible, in Joyce's hand in ink, to the right of Beach's initials:]
> Lea[?ve] it ?with 1 'm' Tl. [?Title] ?Tan ?bi[s] !⁸
> Yes, ?do put? the ad in T.L.S + N.S.

---

1 It is not clear what preface Beach refers to. There was no preface in the first edition of the publication that is the subject of the second part of this letter.
2 *La Revue hebdomadaire* was a weekly journal devoted to literature, history and travelling, published from 1892-1939. https://gallica.bnf.fr/ark:/12148/cb34350607j/date, accessed 2 December 2020.
3 *La Revue Européenne* was directed by Valery Larbaud and he used it to promote non-French literature (cf. Soupault in Aubert, p. 42, and see also Laurent in Dezalay and Lioure, pp. 163-170).
4 The ad in question was for the forthcoming publication of *Our Exagmination*. See letter of 8 July 1931, note 8. It appeared in *transition* 16/17 (Spring-Summer) 1929, which came out in June without an instalment of *Work in Progress*.
5 Founded in 1913, a leftist weekly journal with a strong focus on politics still published today.
6 The *Times Literary Supplement* first appeared in 1902 as a supplement to *The Times* and became an independent publication in 1914. It has long been considered one of the pre-eminent critical publications; astonishingly though, there was only a lukewarm review of *Dubliners*, fairly favourable ones of *A Portrait of the Artist* and *Exiles*, but no review of *Ulysses*, which Virginia Woolf called "a memorable catastrophe – immense in daring, terrific in desaster" in her "How It Strikes a Contemporary", a tour d'horizon to the *Lit. Supp.* of masterpieces of the past years (cf. May, passim and in particular p. 158f.).
7 There was no second "m" in any of the later editions and there was none either on the title page inside. Joyce's wish for a second "m" may have derived from the fact that "incammination" was probably derived from the Italian "incamminarsi", 'to set out'/'to set forth'.
8 A playful "Tant pis"? The "p" of pis could also be read as a "b".

ALS, 1 leaf, 2 sides, Sha&Co stationery. Unusually large handwriting, probably black crayon. Buffalo.

"Lit Supplement?" is written from bottom to top along the lower right hand edge of the paper.

To JJ at 2 Square Robiac, Paris VII

6.8. 1929 Monastère de la grande Chartreuse

Sylvia Beach
Adrienne Monnier

APCS, picture overleaf of St Bruno: Text: – Dauphiné. – La CHARTREUSE – La Statue de Saint Bruno. ZJJF Jahnke.
To JJ Esq, at Imperial Hotel, Torquay, Angleterre

No date [1928/29]

SELECTIONS FOR THE ANTHOLOGY[1]

No 4 p. 47 "This wastohavebeen underground heaven" [FW 76.33]

St. Patrick in Ireland.
No 2 p. 10 "and in point of fact" [FW ?30-47]

A mysterious character appears in the book.
No 1 p. 20 "in the name of Anem" [FW 15.29]

The elder brother paints himself black in contrast to the spotless Shaun.
No 7 p. 55 "He points the deathbone" [FW 193.29-195.06]
    to the end of the section

Shaun defends himself.
No 12 p. 14 "O murdewr mere," [FW 411.25 (O murder mere)]
    to "Phwum" [FW 412.06]

A description of one of the brothers of the book. He is a postman.
No 12 p. 8 "Ay he [who] so swayed a will of a wisp" [FW 404.15-405.02]
to "Shaun himself"

History.
No 1 p. 23 "Mutt. – Quite agreem. [FW 17.17-30]
to "O pride thy prize."

>   TD, 1 leaf, 1 side, Sha&Co stationery. ZJJF Jahnke.
>   "A Mole" is written in pencil in the right margin next to "No. 4, p. 47 ..." (unknown hand).
>   References to the passages in *Finnegans Wake* by the editors

---

1   This must have been a first list, presumably by Beach, for "A Muster from *Work in Progress*", for inclusion in *transition stories*, an anthology edited by Eugene Jolas and Robert Sage. (Jolas, pp. 177-191). The numbers indicated for each item refer to the *transition* volume number. The first suggestion on the list, "This wastohavebeen ..." is the only passage that made it into the selection under the title "A Mole". There is another handwritten list by Joyce with seven items; six of them appeared in the final publication (Buffalo, MS VI.B.50.f; see *JJA* 40, p. 349).
   The anthology that Mary Colum wanted to publish (see Joyce's letter of 22 December 1930) was not exclusively devoted to the not yet named *Finnegans Wake*.

Introduction to the 1930s

Ursula Zeller

The new decade brought a decisive change in the relationship between Beach and Joyce. Their friendship, having cooled off over the last few years, became even more strained due to professional conflicts of interest, which eventually led to a breakup. In autumn 1932, their business relations came to an end.

Beach's health problems, her chronic migraine and a general exhaustion with depressive periods, Joyce's constant demands and repeated overdrawing of royalties, as well as her own financial straits: all this added to the difficult atmosphere in which their communication was taking place – as did Joyce's situation. He, on his part, was likewise afflicted with various health issues and nervous bouts, and he had to undergo a critical eye operation in May 1930, which, though successful, did not put an end to these problems. After his father's death in December 1931 he fell into a depression, such that he considered abandoning *Work in Progress* altogether, with which he had been struggling for quite some time. More importantly, his daughter's mental illness came to overshadow the last decade of his life and he was increasingly faced with worries and expenses for Lucia's treatments. This made him all the keener to republish portions of *Work in Progress* in deluxe editions and, most of all, to enter the American market with *Ulysses*. Three fourths of Joyce's income, as Paul Léon noted, would go into Lucia's therapies (*JJII*, p. 687). At the same time, Joyce did not think of changing his extravagant lifestyle, but continued to dine at the best restaurants and stay at expensive hotels, and to ask Beach for money when sales were low, while she and Adrienne Monnier were "travelling ... third class", as Monnier wrote in her famous letter to Joyce (May 1931, qt. in *JJII*, p. 651f.)

The early 1930s still yield an intense exchange of letters between author and publisher, with a special concentration in 1931, while Joyce was living in London and crucial, sensitive issues were being negotiated. A few of these continued over the following year, when written communication often went through Beach's successor as Joyce's secretary, Paul Léon, his devoted friend and consultant since 1928. At the peak of Joyce's and Beach's estrangement, Léon formally took over, Joyce typically having a third party steering him through the final crisis with his publisher.

INTRODUCTION TO THE 1930S

1   "Don Leone"

Joyce had met Paul Léon, a Russian Jew from St. Petersburg, in 1928 through Léon's brother-in-law Alex Ponisovsky, with whom Joyce had been taking Russian lessons. According to his wife, Léon, a professor of philosophy and sociology, was less interested in Joyce's works than in the man and the artist; apparently he had not even read *Ulysses*. He was fascinated by Joyce's creative process, into which their nearly daily meetings allowed him frequent insights. Fluent in seven languages, Léon would not only help with proofreading, but also conduct lexical research for Joyce and collaborate in the collective translation of "Anna Livia Plurabelle" into French (Noël, pp. 7f. and 16). At the same time, he acted as Joyce's manager and "lawyer", introducing himself to Beach in that role in his very first letter to her (3 February 1932, Buffalo). While admiring Joyce deeply, Léon could also be quite frank, teasing and even critical at times, and it was this "irreverent reverence", as Ellmann called it, that Joyce found particularly engaging. (*JJII*, p. 630) Since Léon wished to remain independent from Joyce, he chose not to accept a salary for his services (Noël, p. 9). Vis-à-vis others, Léon was utterly loyal to him, defending his interests, not least against Beach's. Speaking for Joyce in a voice of his own, he assumed a rather cool tone from early on, referring to Joyce as "my client" in a draft letter to Beach. Apparently Joyce found this too offensive, so that in the final letter his name was reintroduced (?8 February and 8 February 1932, NLI Léon)

Some months into World War II, the Joyces joined Maria Jolas in St-Gérand-le-Puy. After the German invasion of Paris the Léons followed, and the two men resumed their collaboration, correcting misprints in the recently published *Finnegans Wake*. The Léons were the only ones to return to Paris, and over several days, Paul Léon would go and rescue Joyce's documents from the abandoned flat, storing them in a large brown suitcase, the contents of which may to some extent overlap with the papers from Maria Jolas' famous trunk (see Noël, p. 40, and for the trunk, EDITORS' INTRODUCTION, p. XVII). He also bought back items from the Joyce household at an illegal auction, such as most of the first editions and some personal belongings. (Noël, p. 36ff.) All this was done at great personal risk.

Léon put his own correspondence with Joyce in a large separate envelope, which he entrusted to the head of the Irish legation in Paris and which, as he stated on a note, he would "in the event of death" bequeath to the National Library of Ireland. This tragically occurred far too soon: in August 1941, Paul Léon was arrested by the Gestapo and in April 1942 he was killed in the concentration camp at Auschwitz.

Among the dominant issues in the letters of those years is, to begin with, the topic that would lead to ultimate falling-out between Beach and Joyce: the American edition of *Ulysses* and what subsequently came to be called the continental edition. Beach's arranging for the various publications of *Work in Progress*, profitable editions by fine arts presses among them, as well as her support in negotiating for the publication of *Finnegans Wake*, are another instance of her selfless engagement for Joyce's interests reflected in this correspondence. And finally, there is the curious *Frankfurter Zeitung* episode, which takes up just a few months in Joyce's life and a paragraph or two in Ellmann's biography. With Beach's letters to Joyce in the ZJJF Jahnke Bequest, however, there emerged a significant number of items that deal with this curious issue: a baffling third of her 41 letters from 1931. In view of Joyce's heavy investment, the rather trivial, if amusing anecdote calls for a closer examination, which first and foremost gives a vivid picture of the paranoid and litigious side of Joyce's personality.

2   Crossing the Atlantic: An American Edition of *Ulysses*

While only a very few short letters survive from 1930, there is an important document among them: on 9 December Joyce and Beach signed a contract, or "Memorandum of Agreement", as they called it, concerning the rights on *Ulysses*. After Joyce had declined Beach's earlier suggestions for a contract for *Ulysses*, he suddenly insisted on having one. With the fees for the suit against Samuel Roth, as well as a general wish to settle family inheritance and to provide for Giorgio's "dowry", as Stuart Gilbert facetiously called it (p. 43), he was in particular need of money. At a time when his relationship with Beach was strained, he no longer seemed to trust his publisher to provide a reliable source of income. Ironically, as Fitch points out, Joyce would be the one to breach the contract he had initiated. (p. 309) With exclusive world rights for Beach and a uniquely generous 25% of royalties for Joyce, it was for both sides a comfortable agreement. If "deemed advisable by author and publisher", Beach's rights on Joyce's novel would be sold to another publisher "at a price set by herself". (see "Memorandum", p. 147f.)

Soon after this settlement, in spring 1931, Joyce was aiming for the American market with its enormous economic potential and he contacted his agent Pinker to sound out the possibilities. As a result, two offers came, the first from Benjamin Huebsch of Viking Press and another from Curtis Brown, a literary agency in London, which acted on behalf of Claude Kendall, a small New York publisher mostly of erotica. As Kendall wrote, he wanted to publish *Ulysses* as a "test case" in America, where *Ulysses* was still banned, and he was prepared to do so at his own expense regarding legal costs. (Pollinger of Curtis Brown to Joyce, 26 May 1931, and to Beach, 25 June 1931; Princeton)

In June, rumours of another pirated edition of *Ulysses* of 10.000 copies – more than a third of the number of copies Beach had sold in a decade – added considerably to the dynamics, even though such a new pirated edition "almost certainly never existed". (Slo + Ca, p. 28f.) More likely, Roth started circulating his 1929 copies again some time after his release from jail in July 1930:[1] the New York authorities had confiscated the plates for Roth's *Ulysses* edition, but not the copies in his brother's warehouse.[2] Pinker decided the only way to stop Roth's piracy and to obtain copyright was to have an official American edition as soon as possible. (Joyce to Harriet Weaver, 1 October 1931, *Letters III*, p. 230).

While Joyce and Beach were both sceptical about the offer from the unknown Kendall, Beach's objections to him as well as to Huebsch were of a more fundamental nature. Neither offer contained a word about her rights on *Ulysses*. As a result, Beach developed a parallel strategy: one the one hand, she did as Joyce instructed her and asked for offers without giving any terms herself. On the other, she communicated with both agencies, Curtis Brown and Pinker, on her own (see her letters to Joyce of 5 June, 1 and 12 July 1931) – though, loyal as always, not without first sending Joyce a draft. He decided to leave that letter uncommented, just asking her to "keep it by [her] for the moment". (*JJtoSB*, 8 June 1931, p. 171) Which, however, she did not.

In both letters to the agencies she stated her conditions for securing the American rights on *Ulysses* and at the same time asked for conditions for Joyce that approached the outstanding shares he received from her own publication: a 20% royalty should be paid to him. As his publisher she was to receive the sum of $25,000,[3] since in her view yielding the American rights was tantamount to giving up her rights on *Ulysses* altogether. With an official American publication there would no longer be a market for the Paris edition, all the more so as the former was planned as an inexpensive trade edition. To Pinker

---

1 Roth had reset the text, it was not the "photographic forgery" Joyce believed it was (Joyce to Bennett Cerf, 2 April 1932. *Letters III*, p. 243). (Gertzman 2013, p. 104).
2 Joyce's description of the pirated copy Beach had "just received from America" confirms this, as it matches the bogus edition Roth had published in 1929: "It is the exact reproduction of the ninth Paris edition, the title page and even the printer's 'justification' (Darantiere, Dijon) are reproduced." (Joyce to Pinker, 19 October 1931, Princeton).
3 Today $25,000 in 1931 would be worth something between $420,000 and $1,580,000, depending on the calculating parameters (relative price based on the Consumer Price Index, or relative wage/income). www.measuringworth.com/calculators/uscompare, accessed 24 August 2020. The same calculation applies in subsequent instances. See also APPENDIX E.

she justified her large sum not only as a compensation for future financial losses, but also retrospectively as recognition of her investment that had made *Ulysses* the success it had become: "Considering that much time, expense and influence have been used in developing the sales during all these years, this is a modest estimate of the value that 'Ulysses' represents for me."[4] (4 July 1931, Princeton)

As Joyce's agent, Pinker continued to disregard her role, just informing her of the offers. In any event, he seems to have simply ignored her letter. Joyce himself, throughout their (surviving) correspondence, remained silent on Beach's claims, even when she expressly asked for his opinion. Instead, he repeatedly used an intermediary. Only Curtis Brown would, in reply to Beach's letter, acknowledge her "English language rights in this book"– without, however, addressing the terms she had stated (Pollinger of Curtis Brown to Beach, 25 June 1931, Princeton). It was only upon Beach's persistence that Pollinger eventually responded to her claims. Rejecting them as an impossible "economic proposition for any American publisher to pay you £5000 ..." (8 July 1931, ZJJF Jahnke), he had a colleague at Curtis Brown ask Beach the following day to state her "minimum terms which would be acceptable" (Michael Joseph to Beach, 9 July 1931, Princeton).

When Beach sent Joyce a copy of her reply to Pinker, his answer again contained no explicit comment on the matter and yet it bespeaks their antagonism. Most of his letter is concerned with various offers for *Work in Progress*, English and American, that were pouring in during those months. At the same time as asking her for her views, he made Beach an offer to publish the book herself. By giving her precedence over large, prestigious publishing houses, Joyce acknowledged Beach's crucial role as his publisher and her engagement in the prepublications of *Work in Progress*, which had been a frequent subject in their letters. On the other hand, he made it clear that a deal had to be closed very soon, as he was sorely in need of money. All he gave her was two days to consider his last-minute offer, and he was certainly aware that Beach could not financially compete with these firms. Joyce's statement, "I have had an enormous lot of worry lately which I could have coped with better if I had not been left in the lurch for money" reads like an implicit criticism of Beach' insistence on the *Ulysses* contract – all the more so, as these remarks conclude

---

4   To stay within Beach's time: Joyce would get $25,000 in royalties from Random House, who eventually secured the contract, if 56,250 copies were sold – precisely twice as many as Beach had sold in the first decade of *Ulysses*. Calculation based on facts and figures from Crispi, p. 36-38. Starting sales in late January 1934, Random House had already sold more than 35,000 copies by mid-April – more than all of Beach's editions. (Fitch, p. 342).

with the brief information that another U.S. offer for *Ulysses* has arrived from the Grabhorn Press: "but as I possess no rights in this book I sent it on to you via Pinker." (*JJtoSB*, 13 July 1931, p. 173)

This is little more than a tactical, symbolical gesture and cannot be considered a serious offer. The previous year, writing to Weaver about the tensions with Beach, Joyce had clearly stated his priorities. Affirming Beach's great help with his new book, which Beach felt was "not being energetically enough given to her by [him]", he riposted: "This is not a case for energy, but for prudence and some form of compromise, American wealth, law and power being what they are." (18 March 1930, *SL*, p. 352) Shortly after this letter, Joyce signed a contract with both Viking and Faber for what came to be *Finnegans Wake*.

At that stage Beach seemed to accept with relative ease the priority of Joyce's monetary interests concerning *Work in Progress*.[5] But *Ulysses* remained an altogether different matter. While it was clear that her insistence on the price for the American rights would block all negotiations, it was not due to her claims that neither Viking nor Kendall succeeded in securing a contract: Joyce himself thought their nearly identical offers far too small.[6] Moreover, Viking – if not both publishers[7] – at some stage suggested that Beach get some share of the royalties, but Joyce would not consent to a reduction of his royalties. "He felt no financial obligation" to Beach, as she wrote in a suppressed portion of her memoirs. (Fitch, p. 321)

Given Joyce's attitude, it is unlikely that in later negotiations his associates seriously tried to find a compromise to accommodate Beach's rights in some way or other. Rather, she was "advised to accept the inevitable and consider the cession of the American rights", in view of Roth's recent activities, as Joyce wrote to Pinker in autumn. (19 October 1931, Princeton)

After August 1931, Beach's letters do not bring up the subject again until half a year later, this time to her successor and new vis-à-vis in her correspondence with Joyce. In reply to Paul Léon's request to set up a new contract to replace

---

5   As early as 1926 (and years before here rights on *Ulysses* were contested), Beach had in fact suggested to Joyce that rather than entrusting the book to her, he should benefit from a big American publisher (letter of 17 December 1926, see also *Sha&Co*, p. 179).

6   "an advance of 1000$ on account of 10% the first 3000 copies and 15% thereafter" (Pinker to Beach, 25 June 1931, Princeton) – indeed a rather meagre figure compared to the 25% Joyce was used to getting from Beach.

7   In a letter to Pollinger, Kendall writes that Beach never considered how much money she and Joyce were losing through the sales of a pirated edition. "Our contract could have provided that she share in the royalties of the American edition." (29 July 1931, Princeton) Apparently, however, as Beach recalled in a letter to Léon, he never made her such an offer (see her letter of 3 March, 1933).

"the Memorandum of Agreement" on *Ulysses* – and in reply to similar moves from others – she formally relinquished all rights in the book.

The development and final escalation in this matter, bracketed by these two letters, took place in personal encounters after Joyce's return from London in late September. While briefly united in debating a common strategy for the new chapter in the Roth case, Joyce and Beach soon came to disagree over who would have to pay the lawyer's fees from previous episodes – depending on who owned the rights on *Ulysses* at the time of Roth's major piracies between 1926 and 1929 (see letter of 4 February 1932, note 8, and INTRODUCTION to the 1920s, pp. 10ff.). Regarding the present situation, that central issue was hardly addressed in their conversations, despite Joyce's continued negotiations with U.S. publishers in the background – or rather: behind Beach's back. Towards the end of 1931, Padraic Colum, whom Joyce would also call upon for difficult missions, visited Beach regularly, insinuating she had no rights in the novel, until one day he shouted at her that she was standing in Joyce's way. (Fitch, p. 322f.) She called Joyce immediately. "Miss Beach screamed at me as I told you and said she would give the rights to me as a Xmas present (she did not)", as Joyce reported to Weaver (17 January 1932, *SL*, p. 361) In his *Paris Diary*, remembering with ironic amusement the "Joyce – Beach battle" Gilbert notes that over the telephone Beach apparently called Joyce "a liar" (p. 43f.) – she who in her correspondence would hardly ever lose her patience.

In his reply to Beach's letter that unconditionally cancelled her contract for *Ulysses*, Léon, relentlessly loyal to Joyce, coolly acknowledged her "recognition ... of his ownership of the rights for *Ulysses*." (8 February 1932, Princeton) No longer a *cession* of her rights, as had been Joyce's words to Pinker; no longer, in Beach's own words, a *present* to Joyce.

This new situation accelerated the negotiations with various U.S. publishers and in March 1932, with the intercession of Robert Kastor, the brother of Joyce's daughter-in-law, a contract was signed with Bennett Cerf of Random House. Nevertheless, it would take almost another two years for the book's legal status to change and the American *Ulysses* to appear.

3   From Shakespeare to Homer:
    The Odyssey Press Continental Edition

In several letters to Beach expressing his (premature) satisfaction with the development on the American front, Léon addressed the issue of the rights for a continental edition. He suggested setting up a new contract with her for the purpose, particularly as her 11th edition, the largest so far, would soon run out of print. Joyce and Léon argued that the American and the continental editions were complementary rather than competing enterprises,[8] whereas Beach continued to be convinced of the opposite and consequently lost "all interest in *Ulysses* since [Joyce] decided on an American edition", as he wrote to Weaver (7 May 1932, qt. in Crispi, p. 39).

For Joyce, the prospect of *Ulysses* out of print and the resulting loss of the cash flow was a disaster. With the Random House edition still in abeyance, he needed Beach to bring out a 12th edition (a cheap one, so as to reach new readership segments) – all the more so as Pinker's negotiations for a British edition had remained fruitless. But after brief consideration, Beach decided against another Shakespeare & Co. edition. Her scepticism about its financial success was anything but diminished by Joyce's refusal to prepay the printing costs and moreover, she felt that she neither had the physical nor the emotional strength for another Joyce venture. (Fitch, pp. 326 and 334)

Apparently it was Beach who suggested to Albatross Press that they take over *Ulysses*, as she writes in her memoirs (p. 205) and as correspondence from that Hamburg publisher indicates – but then, Joyce and Léon were at the same time negotiating a *Dubliners* paperback edition with Albatross, who had also expressed a keen interest in *Ulysses*. It seems that by the end of July they were coming close to an agreement about the novel (the contract was signed in October). For this purpose, they decided to create a new imprint, the Odyssey Press, so as to protect Albatross from potential lawsuits.[9] This subsection was to publish only two books, the other being *Lady Chatterley's Lover*, with a similarly turbulent legal history. During that summer Beach conducted her separate talks with the publisher, and she did so without Joyce's knowledge (Fitch, pp. 331 and 335). Joyce, likewise, had hardly informed Beach of their negotiations, still hoping and urging her to continue bringing out the book herself. When after the summer Joyce returned to Paris, Beach had already closed a deal with Albatross on her continental rights.

These uncertainties in their scant and mostly indirect communication reflect, and added to, the strains in their relationship. Nevertheless, Joyce did eventually try to achieve an agreement that should satisfy all parties. As

---

8 E.g. Léon to Beach, 14 July and 30 August 1932 (Buffalo). Cf. also Lawrence Pollinger to Beach, 8 July 1932 (ZJJF Jahnke). However, in a draft letter to Beach (?8 February 1932, NLI Léon) Léon had specified Joyce's request or need for a new, 'continental' contract: "as long as *Ulysses* has to be published for continental circulation" – a qualifying modification that, interestingly, was suppressed in his final letter to her of the same date.

9 There were further reasons for this: Albatross was a paperback reprint house, a brand distinctiveness they wishes to retain, and their books as such were for circulation only outside Britain. (McCleery, p. 95).

he wrote to Léon: "The fact that she did not inform me of her arrangement with the Albatross Press is of no importance. My aim is simply to act fairly." (20 September, 1932, NLI Léon, qt. in Cripsi, p. 46) When Beach refused to meet Joyce, he initiated talks with the publisher about her interests without involving her. In the end, he succeeded in securing a better arrangement from Albatross than she herself had negotiated.[10] At the same time, Joyce took great care to make Beach believe the surplus came from his share – something he had opposed in the American negotiations – rather than from the publisher, and she promptly rejected the offer.

It was only Léon's report that her refusal of the offer "hurt" Joyce that made her change her mind to accept an offer, which Joyce deemed "a fair and equitable arrangement considering the energy which she had applied during so many years in bringing out *Ulysses*". (31 October 1932, Buffalo) It seems that in the case of the continental edition, Joyce made a particular point of acknowledging Beach's engagement – and of cutting a better, less "merciless"[11] figure than he had in the issue of the American edition. In December 1932, the Albatross/Odyssey Press published their first edition in a text version proofread by Stuart Gilbert, that on the verso of its title page boasted to be "the definitive standard edition, as it has been specially revised, at the author's request". This does not stand up to closer examination; Gilbert neither had the time nor the skill for a thorough revision and the claim was withdrawn in later Odyssey Press editions. However, the statement served both the author's and the publisher's interests, as McCleery points out. Its main purpose was to distinguish the Odyssey Press book from a potential U.K. pirated edition that Joyce feared was being produced – as well as from Beach's earlier editions and "to advantage and position [it] in the marketplace". (pp. 101 and 103)

It was the very first time that *Ulysses* was printed outside France. And it was also the only time that Beach received proportional royalties from subsequent *Ulysses* editions. She would get nothing whatsoever from the far more lucrative sales both in America and later in Britain. Nevertheless, in one of her last letters to Joyce, coincidentally written three years to the day after the *Ulysses* memorandum (on 9 December 1933), Beach congratulated him on the lifting of the ban on *Ulysses*, emphasizing twice within a paragraph how "very glad of it" and "very happy over it" she was, as if she had to convince herself of her undivided joy in Joyce's American triumph.

---

10   2,5% instead of the initial 1% from her own deal. For further details see Beach to Joyce, 24 October, 1932, notes 4-6, Fitch, p. 335, and Crispi, pp. 45ff.
11   Beach's word in a suppressed portion of her memoirs. (Fitch, p. 326)

Even while heading for the high-point of their crisis at the end of 1931, Beach would remain at Joyce's service. She did her usual, still almost daily secretarial work for him, and persistently negotiated on his behalf also where she was not involved in the role of his publisher. "Nobody had the slightest illusion on the subject," she commented in that context, "Shakespeare&Co was given the power of attorney by Joyce to deal with his affairs, but no profit was derived from it – services were free". (*Sha&Co*, p. 137) Through 1932 and into 1933, even after their business relations had come to a close and Léon had taken over, Beach took care of the Japanese piracies of *Ulysses*. She consulted a Sorbonne professor specializing in copyright law, corresponded with the Japanese translators, and with a Tokyo professor of law about possible measures against their (partly) illegal acts.[12] While apparently Joyce was ready to pay Léon a certain salary for his assistance, he took Beach's services for granted even beyond her activities as his publisher, considering her profits from her *Ulysses* edition reward enough. On the other hand, Beach's claim that she did not earn anything from *Ulysses* can hardly be seen as correct, as Crispi demonstrates in detail (p. 50f.)

In any event, there is one most curious issue, which left Beach with nothing but costs – an issue, moreover, that can hardly be counted as a professional activity on behalf of Joyce. She invested an enormous amount of time, energy and even empathy, sacrificing a good part of her summer recreation in 1931.

4   "The Frankofurto Siding, a Fastland Payrodicule":[13]
     The *Frankfurter Zeitung* Affair

Some time in 1937, during one of their conversations in Paris, Beckett mentioned to Joyce that many intellectuals were turning to Kafka. Joyce was perplexed and bothered by this new figure of literary pre-eminence, as Beckett remembered, since "[t]he name was known to Joyce only as that of the sinister translator of the *Frankfurter Zeitung*, Irene Kafka" (*JJII*, p. 702). Oddly enough, the primary source of Joyce's irritation was not artistic rivalry per se, but the coincidence of names by which he associated his new rival (who had died in 1924) with quite another person and another conjunction of names, a vexing

---

12   Equally problematic, and illegal, was the preventive censorship they applied to their translation: in order to avoid the fate of *Ulysses* in America and Britain, the Japanese translators omitted certain phrases and even entire paragraphs. An intervention, unbeknownst to Joyce, that would have been absolutely unacceptable to him. (Ito, p. 197)
13   FW 70.05f.

incident six years earlier, which also implicated questions of artistic recognition and reputation.

The story involving one Kafka and two Joyces, the so-called *Frankfurter Zeitung* affair, began on 19 July 1931, when the prestigious German newspaper mistakenly published a short story – a genre mix of crime and fantasy entitled "Vielleicht ein Traum" – under Joyce's name: "We hereby publish a fragment by James Joyce, the author of the great English novel *Ulysses*," while a certain Irene Kafka is credited as its translator "from the English manuscript."

In the Weimar Republic, the *Frankfurter Zeitung* (FZ) was one of the leading liberal German daily newspapers of international reputation, particularly famed for its sophisticated *feuilleton* for a progressive cultural elite. Since the 1920s, the German *feuilleton* had been aspiring to overcome the traditional opposition between "high" literature and *feuilleton* journalism. Part of their strategy was to employ established as well as avant-garde writers such as Thomas Mann, Stefan Zweig, Max Weber, Theodor W. Adorno, and Walter Benjamin (Todorow, "Eintagsfliegen", pp. 729ff.). The pre-publication in installments of Alfred Döblin's *Berlin, Alexanderplatz* in 1929 – a novel that is often compared with *Ulysses* – was a prime instance of the FZ's role as a forum to explore new literary aesthetics and changing social realities, as was the ensuing dialogue with scandalized readers that the paper carried out publicly in their pages. In this respect, it had more in common with the debates in little magazines such as *The Little Review* than with the English newspaper arts pages of the time.

Joyce of course did not know this, but he was not unaware of the FZ's outstanding reputation (letter to Stanislaus, 22 August 1931,[14] *Letters III*, p. 227): in his Zurich years, he had been an occasional reader of the *Frankfurter Zeitung*, which is evidenced by two entries in the Subject Notebook for *Ulysses* that can be traced to this newspaper (van Mierlo, n.p.). No other German daily newspaper featured more articles on Joyce than the *Frankfurter Zeitung*: they even published a report on the reading of the French version of "Anna Livia Plurabelle" at Adrienne Monnier's bookshop, some three months before the FZ incident, and the newspaper continued to publish articles on Joyce's work after the conflict over "Vielleicht ein Traum". The reviews were in the main favourable, especially when compared to most early German criticism. (Mitchell, p. 19) The FZ incident, then, has to be read against the backdrop of hitherto excellent relations between writer and newspaper.

---

[14] Since virtually all correspondence concerning the FZ affair dates from 1931, subsequent letter dates will indicate the year only if it is other than 1931.

It was Joyce's German publisher Daniel Brody, who by chance discovered the story in the FZ and immediately inquired at the newspaper, where he was told that the translator Irene Kafka had received a written authorization from Joyce to translate it. It later turned out that the story was by a certain Michael Joyce and that Irene Kafka or, as Kafka claimed, her secretary, had confused the two names. Joyce was more than upset. "Vielleicht ein Traum, aber gewiss eine Schweinerei," as he put it bluntly in a letter to Ivan Goll, the Rhein-Verlag representative in France (30 July, *Letters III*, p. 224): perhaps a dream, but most certainly a filthy disgrace. What followed was a big whirl of excitement that lasted for nearly three months and turned an embarrassing, but minor mistake into an international affair, involving people in Ireland, England, Germany, Austria, France and Switzerland.

Joyce forwarded the matter for further investigation to Monro, Saw and Co., his legal representatives in London and he cabled Brody to "intervene at once" (Brody to Broch, 28 July, Hack and Kleiss, column 225). At the same time, he sent out a first round of letters in various directions for help to identify the obscure Michael Joyce and Irene Kafka: from Ivan Goll and Pinker to his German translator Georg Goyert.[15] Joyce had Harriet Weaver search the British Museum catalogue and he rang up several literary agencies in London (Joyce to Beach, 14 August),[16] all to no avail. He suspected his namesake to be the newspaper's invention and hence a cheap excuse for their error, until it transpired that the other Joyce was an occasional contributor to journals and literary monthlies such as the *New Statesman* or *London Mercury*, where the story had first appeared.

Michael Joyce's literary career was less impressive than his main career in the Bank of England. After an early novel, the subtitle of which sounds like a reference to the FZ incident, *Peregrine Pieram: The Strange Power of His Pen and the Story He Never Wrote* (1936), he wrote mostly literary and historical monographs and continued to publish the occasional short story.[17] "Perchance to Dream," the original title of "Vielleicht ein Traum" (a quote from Shakespeare's *Hamlet*), made its way into various anthologies, one of them published by Joyce's publisher Faber & Faber, where it enjoyed the company of work by Poe, Baudelaire and Verlaine.

Irene Kafka, in turn, was associated with more distinguished writers than Michael Joyce. Primarily a translator from the French, she translated Molière, Alfred de Musset, Pierre Ronsard and Julien Green, as well as poems by Proust

---

15 For all correspondents see APPENDIX C, Overview of Correspondence re F.Z. Affair.
16 All referenced letters from Joyce to Beach are in *JJtoSB*.
17 "Michael Joyce" (retirement notice) p. 174.

and Jules Romain. Little else is known about her, except the tragic end of her life: Kafka was killed in May 1942 in the concentration camp Ravensbrück. (Dokumentationsarchiv)

Meanwhile, Kafka was merely the victim of what Mary Colum called Joyce's "persecution complex". (p. 194) Joyce's obsessive preoccupation distracted him from the urgent and vital professional concerns, the ongoing negotiations for an American edition and with Faber and Viking for *Work in Progress*, as well as the promotion of the latter, which had not yet received much attention, let alone praise. Thus, when six weeks into the affair, Beach told Joyce about the great effect Louis Gillet's article had on the French reception (and sales figures) of *Work in Progress*, she concluded: "But it doesn't interest you particularly, I imagine, with this Frankfurter Zeitung business engrossing you at present." (1 September)

Whereas usually Joyce was eagerly looking out for reviews and was "anxious for a good press in French journals" (Banta and Silverman, p. 7) he now was too preoccupied with the seeming damage to his reputation to savour its actual, and profitable, increase on another front. Instead, Joyce was busy launching his campaign against the F.Z. On 13 August, he wrote to Beach, "Have now sent off 36 letters and 11 wires on the F.Z. affair" and signed the brief note with "salutations cordiales," a remarkable departure from his standard "kindest regards" and "sincerely yours," which expresses more affection than he could muster in all his letters to Beach over a 17-year period.[18] It was as if the conflict and the prospects of litigation had an energizing effect on him that warmed him up to his fellow campaigner, even at a time when his relation with Sylvia Beach had become tense.

The extant correspondence in the matter, both published and unpublished, yields an approximate total of 120 letters and telegrams regarding the affair.[19] In addition, there were handwritten and typed copies of many of these letters that at Joyce's request Beach forwarded to friends or was to show to her customers at Shakespeare and Co. to publicize the affair; these have not been included in the count (see APPENDIX C). All in all, Joyce called upon at least 25 people to join him in his campaign, among them T.S. Eliot, Sean O'Casey, Harriet Weaver, Adrienne Monnier, Philippe Soupault, Ernst Robert Curtius, Padraic Colum – but first and foremost: Sylvia Beach.

In his campaign, Joyce followed two main lines of attack. The first was a series of protest letters which he had his legal representatives, his agent Pinker,

---

18 There is one other exception to be found in a telegram announcing that the German translation of *Ulysses* was completed.

19 This figure includes those not extant, but referred to in other correspondence.

as well as some author colleagues send to both Kafka and the *Frankfurter Zeitung*, demanding immediate financial redress and public rectification, some combined with the threat of a lawsuit (Joyce to Beach, 7 August, and Joyce to T.S. Eliot, 27 August, *Letters III*, p. 228). One of Beach's letters to Joyce reveals that in his view, the magnitude of the damage he suffered through the *FZ*'s erroneous attribution was no less than that of a state affair. (11 August) Joyce further suggested that, apart from her role in the orchestration of the affair, Beach herself, in her capacity as his publisher and as holder of all his unpublished manuscripts, write a letter of protest to the *FZ* and to Irene Kafka and to "denounce this affair as a fraud" (Joyce to Beach, 9 August). And this at the same time that he was challenging her rights as his publisher.

Beach, as always, was willing to do his bidding. She promptly replied with a rather grandiose suggestion (13 August), which mainly seems to reflect Joyce's own exaggerated claims. At the same time, however, she thought it worth mentioning that Ivan Goll, the Paris representative of Rhein-Verlag, had asked "what good was it to put yourself on bad terms with them" (ibid.).

Even though Goll was not the only one who tried to dissuade Joyce from pursuing his *idée fixe*, Joyce, with his penchant for litigation, remained intent on suing the newspaper. It was not enough – as nothing in this matter could ever be enough – that Irene Kafka had already written three personal apologies: to the newspaper, to the Rhein-Verlag and to Joyce's Zurich friend Georges Borach to convey to Joyce her "deepest regrets" in this "painful affair," as she would sum up in a fourth apology to Joyce's London lawyers, expressing her astonishment at his persistent complaints (Kafka to Monro Saw & Co., 17 August, Princeton).

Meanwhile, Joyce's obsession had grown to such an extent that he began to distrust Brody, one of his strongest supporters. While at first Brody, in his capacity as Joyce's German publisher and copyright holder, was supposed to sue the newspaper, Joyce now wanted to keep him out of it. Giorgio, who seemed to have inherited his father's all-round suspicion of nearly everyone outside the family, was instrumental in this dynamic, and he managed to convince Beach, too (see her letter to Joyce, 6 August).

Naturally there is no indication that Brody ever meant to keep potential damages for the Rhein-Verlag. At any rate, for him as a publisher, it would have made sense to let the matter drop, since he could have no interest whatsoever in spoiling his good relations with such a prominent newspaper, a prime forum for advertising the Rhein-Verlag's modernist literature. Brody repeatedly brought this argument up, in particular the *FZ*'s good coverage of Joyce's work, and Joyce might soon benefit again "in the matter of Anna Livia Plurabelle or of the Gilbert-book." (30 July, Princeton) But Joyce was not willing to capitulate, not even for the sake of promoting his work. Nor did he mind that a breach between newspaper and publisher would also affect the publicity of other Rhein-Verlag authors, among them Hermann Broch, Italo Svevo, Ivan Goll, and Ilja Ehrenburg.

Joyce's second line of attack was a publicity campaign involving the international press, which again was supposed to be managed by Beach. The writer and former diplomat Harold Nicolson, who had changed to a post on the London newspaper *Evening Standard*, should be asked to take care of the English scene (Joyce to Beach, 13 August). In this context, Joyce also mentions the BBC to Beach (ibid.), which suggests that he also wished the FZ scandal to be broadcast on radio (though there is no further evidence of this).

Despite Joyce's overblown battle plan and despite Beach's countless endeavours, the publicity campaign never really got off the ground. If in 1927, Ezra Pound had been nearly the only international writer who refused to sign the international protest against Roth's piracy of *Ulysses*, arguing that Joyce was using "a mountain battery to shoot a gnat" (*JJII*, p. 586), this time he was obviously in good and numerous company. Two short newspaper articles were the meager outcome of it all.

Nevertheless, in this case, the repeated threat of a campaign was apparently enough for the FZ to eventually yield to one of Joyce's unrelenting claims: to get a public rectification. Naturally, the FZ literary editors were most reluctant to publicize their embarrassment in their own pages, "the biggest disgrace they had ever met with" (Brody to Joyce, 30 July, Princeton), their good name being at stake just as much as Joyce's. On 9 August, after repeated appeals to Joyce's understanding, the newspaper published an apology entitled "Michael und James." It started off by asserting that of course they had asked Frau Kafka concerning authorization[20] and it then continues:

> What editor would not have jumped at a story by James Joyce even if it did not reveal the powerful archery of "Ulysses"? Perhaps it was an early work, perhaps it was a by-product, or perhaps a work written for self-relief in an hour of relaxation as Goethe turning from his "Elective Affinities" wrought a story of a man of fifty or as Thomas Mann turning from his longer novels gives us an occasional tale. [...]

---

20   According to Michael Joyce, however, he had not been contacted either, as he writes in a letter to Joyce, expressing his regrets that his work had been attributed to him (3 September, Princeton). According to his daughter, Michael Joyce was "utterly horrified and wrote in strong terms to the paper about the liberty they had taken in publishing his story without his permission" and he was also convinced "that they had deliberately taken the name of a more renowned writer" (personal communication from Louise McConnell, 20 September 2013).

We ourselves remembered his book of stories "Dubliners," which show the great poet not as advancing the claims of "Ulysses" but in mood of leisure. After all, no master is obliged to produce only master-pieces and every lion in his tenderer moments draws in his claws and becomes playful.

"Michael and James", translation made for Beach, ZJJF Jahnke

On the whole, "Michael und James" is an awkward self-justification that tries to play down Kafka's mistake by presenting it as a "happy coincidence of sur-names," which brought Michael "before the notice of the German-speaking public". (ibid.) It is ironical that a *feuilleton* like that of the *Frankfurter Zeitung* should defend a publication which more than ever ran counter to its self-image as a critical and avant-garde cultural forum. In the editors' need to save their face, their so-called apology was obviously directed at their readership rather than Joyce, with whom they essentially must have agreed. But in no way could they afford to publicly expose their lack of critical judgment or lack of diligence (whichever it was).

5   "My Maturer Work Disfigured by the Hallmark of the Beast"[21]

Naturally, Joyce was not willing to accept this apology, more intent than ever on suing the newspaper. He was *fuchsteufelswild*, ('mad as hell'), as Brody with some amusement described Joyce's reaction in a letter to Hermann Broch (Hack and Kleiss, column 235) and he wanted to send his namesake to hell, too. "Nothing emerges as to a Michael Joyce. There is a Michael Scott (not to be confused with Walter Scott) mentioned in Dante's Inferno," Joyce wrote to Brody (qt. ibid.). Another conflation of names, willful and arbitrary this time, in an affair that was characterized particularly by Joyce's paranoia of the name. As he wrote to his brother Stanislaus, he was most of all displeased with the title of the piece, "Michael und James." The conjunction of the two names apparently irritated him just as much as the initial misappropriation of his name (22 August, *Letters III*, p. 227) So Joyce sent a second letter of protest to his lawyers to send on to the FZ, signed not only in his own name but also in that of Sean O'Casey and T.S. Eliot. "I have used your name and O'Casey's," he wrote to Eliot, "coupling them with my own" (27 August, *Letters III*, p. 228), thereby uncoupling it, as it were, from his unfortunate namesake.

When referring to the FZ incident, Joyce would often use a pun: "another piece of Frankfurt's furto franco" he wrote to Giorgio and Helen (21 August, ZJJF

---

21   U 15.844f.

Jahnke) and to Stanislaus he sent "Three hoots for Furtofranco" (22 August, *Letters III*, p. 227). With *Furto franco*, open or obvious theft, Joyce described the erroneous ascription of a text to (or use of) his author's name, as an act of piracy damaging his work.[22] In his letter to Stanislaus, he explicitly drew a parallel between the FZ affair and Samuel Roth's unauthorized publication of *Ulysses* four years earlier, which had come to preoccupy him again in the spring of 1931. Conversely, Joyce understood Roth's offence as both "misuse of my name and mutilation of my work," as he put it, in that order, to Benjamin Conner, his American lawyer in the suit against Roth (1 September 1928, *Letters III*, p. 181). To Joyce, they were identical offences, both damaging to his reputation – no matter that in the Roth case a lot of money was at stake, the illegal edition robbing him of substantial profits from the American market. However, Joyce's inflated concern about his name, his marked sense of self-worth also translated into economic terms.

When in late August, Joyce proceeded to sue the German newspaper for damages, he instructed his lawyers to aim for the generous figure of $5,000, as a notice in the *Chicago Tribune* announced (issue of 28 August, Princeton). The equivalent today of $5,000, would be something between $83,900 and $315,000. To put it in relative terms, the sum Joyce demanded from the FZ was 130% of the advance on royalties he could expect for *Work in Progress*, which was being negotiated at the time: Viking offered him an advance of $3,850, or £850 (Joyce to Beach, 19 July).

In October Joyce's lawyers advised him to let the matter drop. In fact, they refused to pursue it any further, as chances of winning the case were minimal. Appealing in turn to Joyce's good name, the German lawyer Willi Rothschild, who had looked into the matter for Joyce's London lawyers, wrote that "in Frankfurt, the slip would be regarded as trifling, and a lawsuit on account of it would seem vindictive and exacting, unworthy of a writer of repute," thus Ellmann's summary of Rothschild's letter (*Letters III*, p. 230). The most Joyce could expect in case he should win, would be £25. In the end, instead of getting him any redress, Joyce's campaign cost him £48 in lawyers fees, or some £3,300 to £17,100 in today's money.

Joyce's appreciation of coincidences and mistaken identities, that elsewhere inspired him as a writer, could not arouse his sense of humor in the FZ case. In *Ulysses*, he self-ironically comments on his vain youthful efforts to place a short story, "Matcham's Masterstroke," for easy money ("one guinea a column", *U* 4.503f.) in the penny magazine *Titbits* by having Bloom wipe

---

22 Ironically, some had actually understood that the FZ had announced the story as a portion from his *Work in Progress* (*L'Intransigeant*, issue of 1 September, Princeton).

himself with it in the jakes; a story which Joyce may well have plagiarized from a prize-winning piece by the ever-successful Philip Beaufoy (Kenner, p. 11). This fraud is mockingly mirrored in "Circe" when a furious Beaufoy reviles Bloom as "a soapy sneak masquerading as *littérateur*" (*U* 15.822f.). But in the FZ affair Joyce insisted on accurately behaving as he had depicted the hilariously raging author.

The Letters of Sylvia Beach to James Joyce, 1930-1939

June 24, 1930

Statement ULYSSES

10th edition:	copies sold May 7 to June 7: – 243 (balance of edition) at Frs 125 Royalties 25%	Frs 7.593,75
11th edition:	copies sold June 7 to 24th: – 85 at Frs 125 Royalties 25%	2.656,25
		Frs 10.250,00
	Paid to James Joyce May 7-June 24	2.506,80
		Frs 7.743,20
	Credit of James Joyce	Frs 7.743,20
	+ Balance in Trust A/C	269,25
	+ Rhein Verlag remittance[1] RM[2] 1200 (about: (buying rate for Mark in Paris probably 6.6.)	Frs 7.272,00)
		Total, Frs 15.284,45

AD without signature, 1 leaf, 1 side, Sha&Co stationery. ZJJF Jahnke.
To JJ at 2 Square Robiac, Paris VI

---

1 The three-volume German translation of *Ulysses* appeared as a 'private print' in 1927. A revised edition came out in 1930. It was listed in *Die Literarische Welt*, III.44 (October 28, 1927) at the price of [R]M 100. (Slo + Ca, D 45.6, p. 117), which was also the price of the subscription ending on 30 September 1927. See publisher's subscription brochure "The Homer of our Time – Germany Awaiting Joyce's *Ulysses*" (Original in German), p. 15; at ZJJF.

2 RM = Reichsmark, the German currency at the time.

August 12, 1930 | Joyeuse

Best greetings
S B

This is now the Hotel des 3 Pigeons[1]

> APCS, picture overleaf of La Recluse [The Hermit]. Text: Joyeuse (Ard[èche]) – The Hermit, tower of the dukes of Joyeuse. (Original in French). ZJJF Jahnke. Postscript added on picture in Beach's hand
> To Mr & Mrs JJ c/o Miss Harriet Weaver, 74 Gloucester Place, London W 1, Angleterre

FIGURE 9A   Postcard of 12 August 1930
© SYLVIA BEACH ESTATE

---

1 "The pigeons" is quite probably a hint to "Crouch low, o pigeons three" (*FW* 480.03) and this passage was printed in *transition* 15 (Feb 1929, p. 201, ll. 33-34). The "Three Jolly Pigeons" is an inn in Oliver Goldsmith's poem *The Deserted Village* whose first line "Sweet Auburn! loveliest village of the plain" Joyce parodies several times in *Finnegans Wake*.

JOYEUSE (Ard.) — La Recluse, tour des ducs de Joyeuse

This is now the Hotel des 3 Pigeons

FIGURE 9B Postcard of 12 August 1930
© SYLVIA BEACH ESTATE

August 25, 1930

Dear Mr Léon,[1]

I have received a cable from Mr Colum[2] asking for the rights for a publisher in New York[3] to bring out a limited edition of Mr Joyce's essay on Mangan.[4] Could you come to see me? Perhaps this afternoon between six and seven or tomorrow morning if convenient for you. Meanwhile if Mr Joyce telephones to you, will you please tell him about it. The affair is complicated on account of Jacob Swartz's[5] edition which constitutes the first edition. We would have to inform the New York publishers.

---

1 Paul L. Léon (1893-1942). Philosopher and sociologist of Jewish descent who emigrated from Russia in 1918. In 1928 Joyce got to know him and his wife Lucie Noël, and they became close friends. Léon had enormous linguistic gifts and also a good understanding of legal affairs and was to work with Joyce from 1930 onward for the rest of his life, not charging Joyce anything for his services, as he wanted to be independent. He could only do so because his wife was the breadwinner, working as a fashion editor for the New York Herald Tribune. By 1932, Léon had replaced Beach as his personal secretary and consultant. In 1941, it was Léon who rescued Joyce's papers and belongings in besieged Paris. He was arrested in August of that year and was killed in Auschwitz in April 1942. In her account of their friendship, Lucie Noël writes poignantly about these years. (*JJAtoZ*, p. 131f., and Alexis Léon (Léon's son) in https://www.irishtimes.com/culture/in-memory-of-true-friendship-1.208492, accessed 7 December 2020; see also INTRODUCTION to the 1930s, p. 125).
  Joyce was away in England from 2 July 1930, first in Wales, then in Oxford and around 25 August moved on to Dover, so Beach wrote to Léon. This is the first extant letter of Sylvia Beach to Paul Léon.
2 Padraic Colum (1881-1972). Irish playwright, novelist and poet. He got to know Joyce in the literary Dublin circles around 1902. (Colum, p. 10). From 1914 he lived mainly in the US, together with his wife Mary (née Gunning Maguire), a literary critic and author. In the 1920s and 30s they frequently met Joyce in Paris. Colum wrote the preface to the deluxe edition of *Anna Livia Plurabelle*, published by Crosby Gaige in 1928 (see letter of 18 August 1928, note 4). Joyce relied on their advice in many of his plans. (*JJAtoZ*, p. 42).
3 Most probably James R. Wells of The Fountain Press. See Beach's letter to Jacob Schwartz, 13 December 1930 (Princeton, *Ulysses Bookshop to Sylvia Beach Regarding the Unauthorized Publication of Two Joyce Essays*). See also letter of 1 May, 1931, note 5.
4 Joyce's essay on the Irish poet James Clarence Mangan, first delivered as an address to the Literary and Historical Society of University College Dublin on 15 February 1902, and published in the unofficial college magazine *St. Stephen's* in May 1902 (Mason and Ellmann, p. 73).
5 Jacob Schwartz, collector and proprietor of the Ulysses Bookshop in London. On 7 March 1930, Schwartz' bookshop published the essay – along with Joyce's essay "Ibsen's New Drama" – in a small edition of 40, which, according to Schwartz, was not for sale, but solely for libraries and friends. (Schwartz to Beach, 16 December 1930 [Princeton, *Ulysses Bookshop to Sylvia Beach Regarding the Unauthorized Publication of Two Joyce Essays*). However, the copies are missing from many libraries to which they had supposedly been supplied, and soon a trade

Yours sincerely
Sylvia Beach

    ALS, 1 leaf, 2 sides, Sha&Co stationery. ZJJF Jahnke.
    To Paul Léon at 27, Rue Casimir Périer, Paris VII

---

developed among collectors and dealers (Brockman, "Jacob Schwartz", p. 177). See also letter of 1 May 1931, note 5.

December 9, 1930 [no address]

MEMORANDUM OF AGREEMENT[1] made this nineth day of December, 1930 BETWEEN James Joyce, Esquire, c/o Shakespeare & Co., Rue de l'Odeon Paris (Hereafter called the Author) of the one part and Miss Sylvia Beach, Shakespeare & Co., Rue de l'Odeon, Paris (Hereafter called the Publisher) of the other part, whereby it is agreed by and between the parties as follows:
THE AUTHOR HEREBY AGREES:

1. To assign to the Publisher the exclusive right of printing and selling throughout the world, the work entitled ULYSSES.

THE PUBLISHER HEREBY AGREES:

1. To print and publish at her own risk and expense the said Work
2. To pay the Author on all copies sold a royalty on the published price of twenty-five per cent.
w. To abandon the right to said Work if, after due consideration such a step should be deemed advisable by the Author and the Publisher, in the interests of the Author, in which case, the right to publish said Work shall be purchased from the Publisher at the price set by herself, to be paid by the publishers acquiring the right to publish said work.

lu et apprové

---

1 For a facsimile of the officially signed and stamped contract see *Sha&Co*, p. 203. "lu et approuvé" in Joyce's hand, followed by his signature and hers. With hindsight, Beach states that
> [c]ontracts didn't seem important to either Joyce or myself. At the time I published *Ulysses*, I did mention the subject, but Joyce wouldn't hear of a contract and I didn't care, so I never brought up the question again. But in 1927, when I brought out *Pomes Penyeach*, Joyce himself asked me to have a contract drawn up; and in 1930 he suddenly wanted a contract for *Ulysses* too. The wording of these contracts was as Joyce wanted it. He read and approved them, and he signed them. The paper of the contract for *Ulysses* was stamped, official stationery. To be sure, it wasn't witnessed by an "avoué" [witness], but nobody seemed to think that necessary.
> I think Joyce's purpose in having this contract must have been to prove [...] that *Ulysses* was not his property but mine. In a letter to the lawyer who was prosecuting the pirate of *Ulysses*, Joyce stated plainly that *Ulysses* was not his property but belonged to Sylvia Beach (*Sha&Co*, p. 204).

As early as 1922 John Quinn (1870-1924), art and book collector who had acquired and later sold Joyce's manuscript of *Ulysses*, had serious doubts about this unresolved contractual situation. See Banta and Silverman, p. 5.

James Joyce
Sylvia Beach

COPY.

 TDTS, 1 leaf, l side. Carbon copy [?] ZJJF Jahnke.
 With two some small emendations by hand.

No date [?late 1930]

A List of English articles on Joyce

ENGLISH ARTICLES

Ford Madox Ford: The English Review, December 1922. "Ulysses" and the Handling of Indecencies"[1]
Edwin Muir: The Calendar, July 1925. James Joyce: the Making of "Ulysses"[2]
Herbert Read: The Listener August 20, 1930. The High Priest of Modern Literature
Rebecca West: The Bookman, September 1928. The Strange Case of James Joyce
"   " N.Y. Herald Tribune January 12, 1930. James Joyce and his Followers[3]
Stephen Gwynn: The Manchester Guardian, March 15, 1923. Modern Irish Literature[4]
E.M. Forster: The New Leader, March 12, 1926. The Book of the Age? James Joyce's "Ulysses"
J. Middleton Murray, The Athenaeum, April 23, 1922. Mr Joyce's "Ulysses"[5]
John Eglinton: The Dial, August 1923. Irish Letter[6]

ENGLISH ARTICLES continued

Cecil Maitland: The New Witness, August 4, 1922: Mr Joyce & the Catholic Tradition[7]
Gerald Griffin: Everyman, August 14, 1930 James Joyce and his Method
Shane Leslie: The Quarterly Review, October-Sept 1922
Domine Canis: Dublin Review July-Aug-Sept 1922.[8]
Oliver Scribe: T.P.'s Weekly February 13, 1926 The Modern Rabelais James

---

1   FORD MADOX FORD. Extract in Deming 1970, Vol. 1, pp. 276-278.
2   EDWIN MUIR. Deming 1970, Vol. 1, pp. 327-34. Listed as "James Joyce: The Meaning of Ulysses", *Calendar of Modern Letters*, i, No. 5 (July 1925), pp. 347-55.
3   REBECCA WEST. Extract in Deming 1970, Vol. 2, pp. 534-37.
4   STEPHEN GWYNN. Extract in Deming 1970, Vol. 1, pp. 299-301. Full article in Stephen Gwynn, *Irish Literature and Drama in the English Language: A Short History*. London: 1936. Repr. Folcroft, Pa.: The Folcroft Press, 1969, pp. 192-202.
5   J. MIDDLETON MURRAY. Deming 1970, Vol 1, pp. 195-198.
6   JOHN EGLINGTON. There is a "Dublin letter" by John Eglington in *The Dial* lxxv, No. 2 (August 1923), pp. 179-83. An extract of another "*Dublin Letter*" of 1922 in Deming 1970, Vol 1, pp. 271-2.
7   CECIL MAITLAND. Deming 1970, Vol 1, pp. 272-73.
8   'Domini Canis', SHANE LESLIE. Deming 1970, Vol 1, pp. 200-3.

Joyce's Novel[9]
D.M. Curtnesse: The New Age November 29, 1923 <u>The English Novel since 1914</u>

Leading Article in the Times Literary Supplement March 4, 1926
Giving a passage from "Ulysses" and comparing it with Strachey[10]

I haven't got Gilbert's article in the Fortnightly Review and Sisley Huddleston's in the Manchester Guardian hasn't turned up yet.[11]
S B

>TDI, 2 leaves, 2 sides (top copy). Sha&Co stationery. NLI Léon.
>Underlined article titles (as well as her initials at the end of the list) in Beach's hand, with some of the article titles added in ink in Beach's hand on second leaf.
>The list begins with a list of German and Swiss Articles, not transcribed.

9   OLIVER SCRIBE. "The Modern Rabelais | James Joyce's Novel that startled Europe". *T.P.'s and Cassell's Weekly*, February 13, 1926. p. 580.
10 TLS, March 4, 1926, No. 1,259. anon. Leading Article "English Prose", pp. 149-50. The article is a review of the *Oxford Book of English Prose*, ed. Sir Arthur Quiller-Couch, 1925. The passage mentioned by Beach is on p. 149. The Strachey quote is from the very end of his *Queen Victoria*, the Joyce quote is from "Proteus" (*U* 3.147-56).
11 Review of *"Ulysses"* by Sisley Huddleston in the *Observer* (No 6823, 5 March 1922), p. 4.

April 25, 1931 (one of Shakespeare's birthdays)

Dear Mr Joyce,

Thank you for your letter from Calais. I hope you had a good crossing and are comfortably settled in London. Neither "Don Leone"[1] nor Soupault[2] have come to see us yet. Soupault fixed a rendez-vous but called it off afterwards. Léon sent me the photo.[3]

I am sending you a letter which I received from Knopf.[4] The Colums[5] think something should be arranged with him. Will you let us go ahead and see what

---

1 See letter of 25 August 1930, note 1.
2 Philippe Soupault (1897-1990). French writer, poet, novelist, journalist, (film) critic, radio pioneer, and long-time friend of Joyce. He took an active role in the Paris Dadaist movement, and founded the surrealist movement with André Breton. https://www.met museum.org/art/libraries-and-research-centers/leonard-lauder-research-center/research/index-of-cubist-art-collectors/soupault, accessed 22 May 2020.
3 Most probably a photo of James Joyce examining the French translation of "Anna Livia Plurabelle" with Philippe Soupault, who was one of the collaborators on it. The photo appeared in Soupault's *Souvenirs de James Joyce*, published in 1943. See also letter of 1 May 1931, and *JJII*, plate XLIII.
4 On 4 March 1931 Beach wrote to Alfred A. Knopf that she had heard from Mary Colum (see note 5) that he was interested in bringing out an anthology of Joyce's work and invited him to make her an offer. In a letter to Harriet Weaver of 11 March 1931 Joyce mentioned that "[t]he only good news is that Mrs Colum ... is confident that she can arrange for an American publisher named Knopf to bring out ... an anthology of mine for which she expects they will pay me an advance" (*Letters I*, p. 303).

Despite Knopf's considerable interest, nothing came of it. On 21 March 1931 Knopf expressed the hope that the terms (an advance of $250 plus 10% royalties) would satisfy Joyce and asked Beach to send "an outline" for him to bid in case Joyce did not agree. He even renewed his request for the outline immediately after receiving the telegram of Joyce's refusal on 3 April 1931. There is a note in Joyce's hand on that letter from Knopf, asking Beach to "tell him to go and better[?] himself" (Buffalo). In his letter to Beach of 5 May 1931 Joyce wrote: "People here [in London] who ought to know tell me he [Knopf] is not to be trusted" (*JJtoSB*, p. 168).

Alfred A. Knopf (1892-1984) and Blanche Knopf founded the Publishing House Alfred A. Knopf, Inc. in 1915. They paid special attention to the quality of printing, binding, and design, and earned a reputation as purists in both content and presentation. https://norman.hrc.utexas.edu/fasearch/findingAid.cfm?eadid=00301, accessed 23 November 2020.
5 Padraic and Mary Colum. For Padraic see letter of 25 August 1930, note 5. Mary Colum (1884-1957). Literary critic and author. From the 1910s to the 1950s she wrote more than 160 articles, among them, an early review of *Ulysses* for the weekly literary magazine *The Freeman* (ed. Albert Jay Nock). She also published a critical enquiry on the foundations of modernist literature (1937) and a semi-fictional autobiography in 1947. Though Joyce relied on her in many ways, her outspokenness once led him to pronounce that he hated intellectual women (Budgen, p. 354). Colum was also of great help with Lucia's illness (*JJII*, pp. 649-51). See also www.marycolum.com, accessed 10 December 2020.

we can do? Also I enclose a letter from a person named Buchman[6] whom I have never [heard] of, announcing that he is pirating your "Pomes Penyeach", and asking for your autograph on one of the copies for "a very dear friend". I have written to my father to have them printed at once by the Princeton Press and to send copies to Washington and take out a copyright, but I suppose this fellow's edition will be out before anything can be done.[7] I wonder when the Oxford edition[8] will be ready. Will you please return the two letters to me. I have no copies of them. Messrs. Augener[9] have sent me a guinea for "A Flower given to my daughter" set to music by Moeran,[10] and I have placed it to your credit.

With best greetings to all,

Yours very sincerely
Sylvia Beach

TLS, 1 leaf, 1 side, Sha&Co stationery. ZJJF Jahnke.
Enclosures: letters from Alfred A. Knopf and Alexander Buchman, at Buffalo, XIII.
To JJ at Hotel Belgravia, London

6 Alexander Buchman from East Cleveland, Ohio, wrote to Beach on 15 April 1931 (Buffalo) that he had found that *Pomes Penyeach* was not copyrighted in the US, that he was printing 100 copies, and whether Joyce would sign one.
7 Thanks to Beach's father's connections with Princeton University Press, 50 copies were published "for Sylvia Beach of Paris solely to copyright the work in the United States" on 2 May 1931 (Fitch, 315; Slo + Ca, A 25, p. 37). On the same day Beach wrote to Buchman that *Pomes Penyeach* was copyrighted, whereupon Buchman repeated his request. In her "Pomes Penyeach diary of publication" (Princeton) she wrote that Buchman's letter never received a reply. Buchman did publish 103 copies, probably in September. See Slo + Ca, A 25 and A 26, pp. 36-7; all letters mentioned between Buchman and Beach are at Buffalo.
8 The 'Oxford edition', published as *The Joyce Book* (The Sylvan Press and Humphrey Milford, Oxford University Press [1933]), was compiled by Herbert Hughes (1882-1937), a composer, musicologist and critic for *The Daily Telegraph*. It included musical settings of all of the poems of *Pomes Penyeach*, set by thirteen different composers: E.J. Moeran, Arnold Bax, Albert Roussel, Herbert Hughes, John Ireland, Roger Sessions, Arthur Bliss, Herbert Howells, George Antheil, Edgardo Carducci, Eugene Goossens, C.W. Orr, and Bernard Van Dieren. See also Slo + Ca A 29, p. 40, and F 15, p. 165f.
9 Music publisher in London. Augener's Edition of Classical and Modern Music was world-famous. They published a setting of "A Flower Given To My Daughter" in E.J. Moeran's setting as "Rosefrail" in 1931. See Slo + Ca, F 14, p. 165.
10 Ernest John Moeran (1894-1950). A website devoted to his work calls him "perhaps the greatest unsung genius of English composition" (www.moeran.com). He set "Tilly" from *Pomes Penyeach* to music for *The Joyce Book* (see above, note 8). He had already set poems from *Chamber Music* to music, published as *Seven Poems by James Joyce* (Oxford University Press, [1930]). See Slo + Ca, F 13, p. 165.

April 27, 1931

Dear Mr Joyce,

I am sending you herewith a cheque on Lloyds Bank, City Office, Threadneedle Street, for twelve pounds. After the radio séance in Berlin[1] I sold some copies of ULYSSES to Germany, but this is the last of the money from those sales, and the last penny of your royalties.[2]

With best greetings,

Yours very sincerely
Sylvia Beach

> TLS, 1 leaf, 1 side, Sha&Co stationery. ZJJF Jahnke.
> To JJ at Hotel Belgravia, London

1 See letter of 22 August 1931, note 9.
2 In his letter to Beach of 25 April 1931, Joyce instructs her to send "any royalties you may have" (*JJtoSB*, letter p. 167).

May 1, 1931

Dear Mr Joyce

I hope you got the N R F.[1] I sent a copy to Miss Weaver too. And did you get the Intran?[2] I suppose that was another of Soupault's[3] activities.

Padraic Colum[4] asked me if he fixed it up with Wells[5] for three hundred and fifty dollars would you accept. He wants to write to him and say that's the last price. He is willing to take twenty-five dollars less for himself.

---

1   *La Nouvelle Revue Française*. NRF XIX.212 (1 mai 1931): contains "Anna Livia Plurabelle" (*FW* 196-201, 215-216), tr. Samuel Beckett, Alfred Péron, Ivan Goll, Eugène Jolas, Paul L. Léon, Adrienne Monnier, and Philippe Soupault, with the author ([633]-646; Slo + Ca, D 32, p. 114) For *NRF* see also letter of 22 February 1921, note 3.

2   *L'Intransigeant*, a French newspaper, founded in 1880 by Henri Rochefort. Though initially politically oriented to the left, it moved to the right when in 1898 it joined the anti-semitic campaign against Dreyfus. It ceased publication in 1940. https://gallica.bnf.fr/html/und/presse-et-revues/les-principaux-quotidiens?

3   See letter of 25 April 1931, note 2. By the late 1920s Soupault had become a well-known journalist – beside his career as a writer – and contributor to *L'Intransigeant*. It is more than likely that Soupault arranged for something to appear in the *Intran*.

4   See letter of 25 August 1930, note 2.

5   James R. Wells was the partner of Crosby Gaige, at the time of the publication of the deluxe edition of *Anna Livia Plurabelle* in October 1928. He had been largely responsible for the production of Gaige books. Wells later became the publisher, together with Elbridge I. Adams, of the Fountain Press, successors to Crosby Gaige (*JJtoSB*, letter 133, note 3, p. 152).

Beach already mentioned Joyce's essay on Mangan in her letter to Paul Léon, 25 August 1930. By the end of 1930 there must have been negotiations still, thus a telegram to Wells in New York, dated 11 December 1930 and signed by Colum and Beach: "MUST HAVE CABLE REPLY ABOUT JOYCE ESSAY COLUM SYLVIA BEACH" (Buffalo), and Joyce mentioned the project in a letter to Weaver of 22 December 1930. This edition could not be traced (Ellmann, *Letters III*, p. 209, note 2). The whole story was rather complicated as Schwartz himself had published the Mangan essay (see letter of 25 August 1930, note 5). This meant that *de facto* the publication of the Mangan essay by the Fountain Press would no longer have been a first edition and Wells may have lost interest in the venture, reducing the offer from the original $375 to $120 (see remonstrative letter from Beach to Schwartz, 31 January 1931; Buffalo). Colum's last offer to Wells in question here would tie in with the original sum. There is no written evidence anywhere that a de luxe edition did materialize. In his letter of 3 February 1931 to Beach, Schwartz suggested how to compensate Joyce for this loss by publishing a limited edition of "all the collected early essays" and the three stories that had appeared in the *Irish Homestead* (all three letters at Princeton, *Ulysses Bookshop to Sylvia Beach Regarding the Unauthorized Publication of Two Joyce Essays*). There was no traceable reaction from the Joyce/Beach side (cf. also Slo + Ca, A 39, pp. 51-2).

That "cahier d'étudiant"[6] that you had in 1903 is beautiful. Adrienne likes it very much too. I will pass it on to Georgio soon. I hope he will be very careful of it – keep it under lock and key.

I sent you H C E No 3 signed copy as soon as I got your letter.[7] It's a pity you had to have it in such a hurry – cost you 28 frs 90 plus Taxi Myrsine[8] to Poste Central 6,20 total Frs 35,10 – simply by registered post you would have Frs 6,90 'comme frais'.

Gorman[9] and McAlmon[10] seem to be great chums now. They drop in together every day. Gorman says he thinks Pound[11] will give him the "stuff" he wants for his book on you, and that Mr Stanislaus Joyce too is getting the "stuff" together for him.[12] He is coming to see me for my "stuff" next Tuesday.

Pound had a narrow escape from the Italian who tried to stab him during the dinner given by Putnam[13] in his honour at the Brasserie de l' Odéon. But

---

6   *Fr.* student's notebook. Probably the 'commonplace book' Joyce used in 1903 and 1904 and later around 1912 (often referred to as 'The Paris Notebook' and 'The Pola Notebook'); considered to be "one of the most revealing memoirs of any period in his life." (Crispi 2009, p. 1).

7   The de luxe first edition of *Haveth Childers Everywhere* published by Henry Babou & Jack Kahane in Paris and by The Fountain Press in New York on 30 June 1930 (Slo + Ca, A 41, p. 53). Joyce had asked Beach in his letter of 29 April 1931 to send him a signed copy "by air mail or radio at once" (*JJtoSB*, letter 161, p. 168), as he wanted it for Herbert Hughes for his work on the 'Oxford edition' (see letter of 25 April 1931, note 8).

8   Myrsine Moschos, Beach's long-time employee at Shakespeare and Company (see letter of 22 July 1924, notes 12+13).

9   See undated letter [after 14 June, but before 22 July 1924], note 4.

10 See undated letter [after 14 June, but before 22 July 1924], note 2.

11 See letter of 1 August 1924, note 6.

12 Gorman's *James Joyce, His First Forty Years* had appeared in 1924 and he agreed to write a biography of Joyce and started work at the end of December 1930. Joyce turned out to be a difficult subject, at times generous with information, at others withdrawn. Gorman "had difficulty also with some of Joyce's friends such as Ezra Pound, who refused to be bothered with the past, or with others who planned their own volumes of reminiscence". Also, Joyce did want an authorized biography and asked his brother Stanislaus to send Gorman copies of his letters, yet at times he lost interest (*JJII*, p. 631-2). However, Gorman was allowed to copy material from Joyce's commonplace book (see note 6 above) and to use it for his 'definitive biography', published in 1939. It became the source text for almost all the information scholars had about this manuscript, presumed lost until 2002 (Crispi 2009, p. 2).

    Joyce's brother Stanislaus transcribed the majority of the 150 letters from Joyce, and included letters from Joyce to his mother, his wife, and himself (Harley K. Croessmann Collection Carbondale; https://archives.lib.siu.edu/?p=collections/finding aid&id=475&q=&rootcontentid=6609#id6609, accessed 20 December 2020).

13 Samuel Putnam (1892-1950). American editor, publisher, and author, best known for his translations of works by authors in Romance languages. A literary and art critic for various

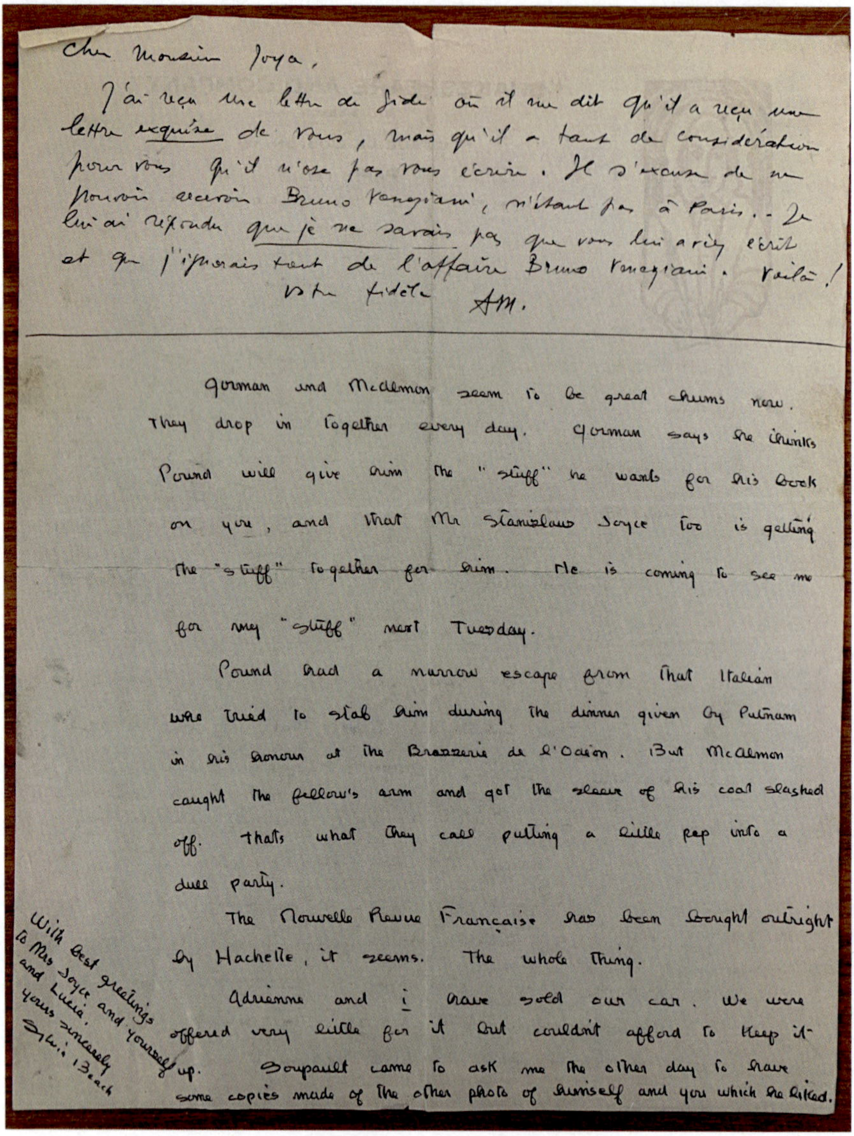

> Cher Monsieur Joyce,
>
> J'ai reçu une lettre de Gide où il me dit qu'il a reçu une lettre exquise de vous, mais qu'il a tant de considération pour vous qu'il n'ose pas vous écrire. Il s'excuse de ne pouvoir recevoir Bruno Venaziani, n'étant pas à Paris. Je lui ai répondu que je ne savais pas que vous lui aviez écrit et que j'ignorais tout de l'affaire Bruno Venaziani. Voilà!
>
> Votre fidèle AM.

Gorman and McAlmon seem to be great chums now. They drop in together every day. Gorman says he thinks Pound will give him the "stuff" he wants for his book on you, and that Mr Stanislaus Joyce too is getting the "stuff" together for him. He is coming to see me for my "stuff" next Tuesday.

Pound had a narrow escape from that Italian who tried to stab him during the dinner given by Putnam in his honour at the Brasserie de l'Odéon. But McAlmon caught the fellow's arm and got the sleeve of his coat slashed off. That's what they call putting a little pep into a dull party.

The Nouvelle Revue Française has been bought outright by Hachette, it seems. The whole thing.

Adrienne and I have sold our car. We were offered very little for it but couldn't afford to keep it up. Soupault came to ask me the other day to have some copies made of the other photo of himself and you which he liked.

With best greetings to Mrs Joyce and yourself and Lucia,
Yours sincerely
Sylvia Beach

FIGURE 10   Letter of 1 May 1931, with Adrienne Monnier's postscript
© SYLVIA BEACH ESTATE

McAlmon caught the fellow's arm and got the sleeve of his coat slashed off. That's what they call putting a little pep into a dull party.

The Nouvelle Revue Française has been bought outright by Hachette,[14] it seems. The whole thing.

Adrienne and I have sold our car. We were offered very little for it but couldn't afford to keep it up. Soupault came to ask me the other day to have some copies made of the other photo of himself and you which he liked.[15]
[diagonally in the left-hand margin]
With best greetings to Mrs Joyce and yourself

yours sincerely
Sylvia Beach

Chicago newspapers, he moved to Europe in 1927. He founded and edited a critical magazine, the *New Review* (1931-32), where Ezra Pound was an "associate editor". According to Carpenter's Pound biography, the dinner was given "to celebrate the opening number of the *New Review*, where [Pound] was attacked by a drug-taking Surrealist, who had turned up hoping to stab Jean Cocteau but in his absence settled for Ezra instead. The man, said Putnam, was about to plunge 'a long, wicked-looking knife' into Ezra's back but 'luckily Bob McAlmon ... [seized] the assailant's arm'. Putnam adds that Ezra was 'not in the least ruffled'" (Carpenter, p. 484; single quotation marks and ellipsis are Carpenter's).

14 One of the foremost French publishers. The editors of the *Nouvelle Revue Française* had very high ideals about independence (see letter of 22 February 1921, note 3), so the sale of the NRF to Hachette would have been newsworthy. But neither Hachette nor the NRF or Gallimard mention this momentous step in their companies' histories.

15 See letter of 25 April 1931, notes 2 and 3.

Dear Mr Joyce

I have received a letter from Gide[16] in which he tells me that he has received an exquisite letter from you, but has such high regard for you that he dare not write to you. He apologizes for not being able to receive Bruno Veneziani[17] as he is not in Paris. I answered him that I did not know that you had written to him and that I didn't know anything about the Bruno Veneziani affair. Voilà.

Your faithful
AM.

    TLS, 1 leaf, 2 sides, Sha&Co stationery. ZJJF Jahnke.

    Postscript message from "Dear Mr Joyce" to "Your faithful AM": written at the top of verso, in Adrienne Monnier's hand; original in French.

    To JJ at Hotel Belgravia, London

---

16   See letter of 23 June [1924], note 1.

17   Bruno Veneziani (1890-1953). Ettore Schmitz's (Italo Svevo's) brother-in-law. Chemist, and musician. Experimenting with drugs and homosexual, he was the black sheep in the Veneziani family. For some time in the 1910s, he had been treated by Sigmund Freud in Vienna (Ghidetti, pp. 181 and 328f.).

    On 15 April 1931 Joyce had written to his brother Stanislaus that Veneziani had turned up in Paris, asking him for "letters of presentation to Gide, Milhaud, etc.". He added that he was inclined to give them, as Veneziani seemed "normal enough, socially at least", and asked for his brother's opinion (*Letters III*, p. 216).

    On 30 April 1931 Gide wrote to Joyce that he had written to Veneziani that he was not in Paris and unfortunately could not receive him (*Letters III*, p. 218).

May 2, 1931

Dear Mr Joyce,
    MacLeish's[1] address is Farmington, Connecticut.
    I enclose a cable from my father.[2] I wrote to Buchman that <u>Pomes</u> was now copyrighted.

Yours very sincerely
Sylvia Beach

> APCS, Sha&Co stationery. Address side empty. ZJJF Jahnke.
> Enclosure: at Buffalo, XIII. *Sylvester Beach*
> To JJ at Hotel Belgravia, London

---
1 See letter of 26 October 1926, note 2.
2 See letter of 25 April 1931, notes 6 and 7. Beach received the cable on 2 May 1931.

May 2, 1931

Dear Mr Joyce

Kahane[1] called up this morning to say that he gives his consent to go ahead with the shilling H C E,[2] that he gave it some time ago in fact. He asked whether the 1st fragment of Work in Progress[3] is still available. I told him you were not interested in talking about it any more.

I hope your weather is better than ours.

Yours sincerely
Sylvia Beach

>APCS, Sha&Co stationery. Address side empty. ZJJF Jahnke.
>To JJ at Hotel Belgravia, London

---

1 Jack Kahane (1887-1939). A francophile Manchester-born writer in Paris who sought his luck in publishing when he entered into partnership with Henri Babou in 1929, considering this also an opportunity for his own work after his publisher Grant Richards went bankrupt in 1925. Babou and Kahane published Joyce's *Haveth Childers Everywhere* in 1930 (see below), but soon after the partnership came to an end. In 1931, Kahane published his first book under the Obelisk imprint. He financed the publication of slow-selling works of genuine merit by running a sideline in so-called 'dirty books' and contributed many a title under various pseudonyms. (Pearson, pp. 63-70 passim).
  Kahane published three books by/for Joyce:
  (1) *Haveth Childers Everywhere*. De luxe first edition published on 30 June 1930. 600 copies + 85 writer's copies. Selling price: $20. See also letter of 1 May 1931, note 7.
  (2) *Pomes Penyeach*. De luxe limited edition (25 copies) with initial letters for each poem designed and illuminated by Lucia Joyce, and the text in facsimile of the Joyce's handwriting. Paris: The Obelisk Press and London: Desmond Harmsworth, October 1932. Selling price: 1'000 frs. (Slo + Ca A 27, pp. 38-9).
  (3) *A Chaucer A.B.C.* With Initial letters designed and illuminated by Lucia Joyce, with a preface by Louis Gillet. 300 copies. Paris: The Obelisk Press, 1936 (Pearson, p. 217).
2 In his letter of 25 April 1931 Joyce told Beach that he had repeatedly asked Paul Léon to get written permission for the trade edition by Faber & Faber from Babou & Kahane. It was published on 8 May 1931 in Faber & Faber's *Criterion Miscellany*, No. 26 (Slo + Ca, A 41, p. 54).
3 *Anna Livia Plurabelle*, published in 1928 by Crosby Gaige in New York. The second fragment was *Tales told of Shem and Shaun*, published in 1929 by The Black Sun Press in Paris and the third the above HCE of 1930 (cf. *JJtoSB*, p. 159f.).

May 9, 1931

Dear Mr Joyce,

It was a great pleasure for me to get your letter. You didn't say how you were but I hope the rest is doing you good. Gide's letter which I am returning to you herewith, is a marvel.[1] Adrienne says it is rare to have such a letter from Gide.

I sent off (or had Adrienne's girls send off) all the copies of the N R F[2] to the people you mentioned, and I think Adrienne sent you yesterday the seven copies for you to sign.[3] She was amused by the things "Le Monde"[4] and Lefèvre[5] said about A L P and hopes there will be some more attacks to make it lively.

I gave your messages to the Colums.[6] Padraic laughed and said you were like the old woman who had the Sibylline Books for sale in old Rome.[7] Kahane is buzzing around but doesn't come out with anything definite. He promised me that he would send Léon[8] a paper signed by himself and Babou[9] with the

---

1 See letter of 23 June [?1924], note 1. This is André Gide's letter of 30 April 1931, expressing his great admiration for Joyce (*Letters III*, p. 218).
2 *Nouvelle Revue Française*. See letter of 22 February 1921, note 3.
3 In his letter to Beach of 5 May 1931, Joyce named T.S. Eliot, C.K. Ogden, Daniel Brody, Georges Borach, Georg Goyert. (*JJtoSB*, p. 168) He also requested that copies be sent to him to sign them for "The Septuagint", i.e. the seven people involved in the French translation of "Anna Livia Plurabelle" published in NRF. See letter of 1 May 1931, note 1.
4 A communist weekly newspaper with "literary, artistic, scientific, economic and social information" as the subtitle ran. Founded by Henri Barbusse, it existed between 1928 and 1935, on its board were, among others, Albert Einstein, Maxim Gorki, and Upton Sinclair. https://fr.wikipedia.org/wiki/Monde_(revue), accessed 25 April 2020.
5 Frédéric Lefèvre (1889-1949). French novelist, essayist and literary critic, co-founder and editor-in-chief of the weekly *Nouvelles Littéraires*, for which see letter of 17 July 1931, note 12.
6 See letter of 25 August 1930, note 2, and letter of 25 April 1931, note 5.
  Joyce was planning two projects, one with each of the Colums. Together with Padraic he was negotiating with James R. Wells of Fountain Press for a publication of Joyce's essay on James Clarence Mangan, for which Colum was to write an introduction, while Mary Colum was arranging for Alfred A. Knopf to bring out a Joyce anthology. For details on the Mangan publication see letter of 1 May 1931, note 5; for the planned anthology see letter of 25 April 1931, note 4. In his letter of 5 May 1931 to Beach, Joyce comments on the two publishers and the projects, which both came to nothing.
7 A famous collection of prophecies sold by the sibyl of Cumae (the old woman) to Tarquinius Superbus, the last king of Rome. Kept in the temple of Jupiter and consulted in emergencies, the books were destroyed in the fire of 83 BC. (https://www.britannica.com/topic/Sibyl-Greek-legendary-figure#ref202173, accessed 25 November 2020)
8 See letter of 25 August 1930, note 1, and INTRODUCTION to the 1930s, p. 125.
9 Henry Babou, French publisher of deluxe editions and *livres d'artistes*, who met Jack Kahane in 1928. For their collaboration and for Kahane see second letter of 2 May 1931, notes 1 and 2.

permission for Faber[10] to publish 'Haveth Childers Everywhere'. My copies came yesterday. It is a goodlooking little book. I read it again last night and enjoyed it more than ever. There are some of the funniest and some of the finest things in 'Work in Progress' in it, I think. The English papers seem to be taking it in quite a sporting manner, judging by the ones you have sent me, which just arrived.

You ought to let Augustus John[11] do an oil painting of you while you are there. I wonder why he didn't send the 'sanguine' one just the same. It would have been the very time along with Yeats and Gogarty.[12] I saw an awful poem by Gogarty in an old London Mercury[13] the other day. I hope he does better as a nose-and-throat specialist.

In his letter of 5 May 1931, Joyce wrote to Beach: "In view of my unfortunately worded agreement with them I would like something in writing 'consenting' to the publication of H.C.E. here in a trade edition. T.S.E. refuses to delay issue any longer so it comes out on 7." T.S. Eliot brought out the first English edition in the Faber & Faber series *Criterion Miscellany*, No. 26 (8 May 1931). Miss Beach's presentation copy dated 5 October 1931 is at Buffalo (Banta and Silverman, note 2 to letter 160, p. 188). https://seriesofseries.owu.edu/criterion-miscellany, accessed 12 April 2019.

10   Faber & Faber, founded in London in 1929, grew out of an originally scientific publishing house, Faber and Gwyer, established in 1925. T.S. Eliot joined the firm as both literary advisor and author, whose poems (including *The Waste Land*) were published in the first season of their new focus. Soon Eliot would introduce other leading authors such as Ezra Pound, Marianne Moore, or Wyndham Lewis to their programme and they also took over Eliot's influential literary review, *The Criterion*. In 1929 the two publishers went separate ways and Geoffrey Faber duplicated his own name to replace Gwyer's. Eliot would remain director at Faber & Faber for almost 40 years. https://www.faber.co.uk/blog/about/faber-1920s/, accessed 12 January 2020.

11   Augustus John (1878-1961). Welsh painter, best known for his portraits of European personalities, writers and artists. Joyce sat for him in October and November 1930 (*Letters III*, p. 206, PC to Gorman. According to Ellmann, Joyce did not like John's drawings, which he thought failed to represent accurately the lower part of his face (*JJII*, p. 627).

12   "The Royal Academy is open", Joyce wrote to Beach on 5 May 1931. "John exhibits his portraits of Yeats, Gogarty etc. but not mine. Or perhaps it is face to the wall like its original." (*JJtoSB*, p. 168f.)

For Yeats see letter of 11 July 1924, note 1. Oliver St. John Gogarty (1878-1957). Irish surgeon, man of letters and politician, known for his caustic wit and ribald humour. A close friend – and rival – of Joyce's in their youth until their falling-out in 1904, Gogarty served as an inspiration for Buck Mulligan in *Ulysses*. In his memoirs, *As I was Going Down Sackville Street* (1939) and *It Isn't This Time of Year At All!* (1954) he wrote about his friendship with Joyce and other Irish writers. (*JJAtoZ*, p. 94)

13   A major monthly literary magazine (1919-1939), with a wide editorial scope and great critical influence. With its Neo-Georgian values and conservative position on art, it became an antipode to avant-garde modernism and the canon of little magazines. After its founding editor J.C. Squire retired in 1934, *The London Mercury*'s success was gradually dwindling. (Huculak, p. 240f.) Gogarty had published the poem "Portrait. Jane W ..." in the *London Mercury* of June 1925 (p. 93).

Gorman[14] spent an afternoon with me last Tuesday and I showed him lots of stuff. Among others the letter from Lady Gregory[15] and your reply and Yeats' letter.[16] He is going to ask you about them. The article about your acting in that play in Dublin[17] I have not yet come across, but I have it somewhere.
Yours sincerely
Sylvia Beach

>ALS, 2 leaves, 3 sides, Sha&Co stationery. ZJJF Jahnke.
>Enclosure: letter from André Gide, in *Letters III*, p. 218.
>To JJ at 28b Campden Grove, London

14 See undated letter [after 14 June, before 22 July 1924], note 4.
15 Lady Augusta Gregory (1852-1932). Irish playwright, essayist, translator, folklorist, and a leading figure of the Irish Literary Revival. Born in Co. Galway into a protestant upper-class family, she early developed an interest in Irish language and culture, which in her forties was increased by a mutually creative friendship with W.B. Yeats. With him, Douglas Hyde and others she founded the Irish Literary Theatre and the Abbey Theatre in Dublin. (Welch, p. 226)
16 Probably Lady Gregory's letter of 27 July 1922, in which she asks Joyce about his relationship to the Irish Renaissance. In his reply of 8 August (Buffalo) he "vehemently declined to be considered a part of the Irish literary movement". (*Letters III*, p. 77, note 2) Yeats' letter to Joyce could either be the one of 26 June 1923, in which he invites Joyce to his home in Dublin, where he could meet some of his admirers – a new literary generation. Joyce seemed pleased at the invitation, but again declined. (*Letters III*, ibid.) Or else, and more likely, Beach is referring to Yeats' letter of 1 July 1924, with another invitation to Dublin, on occasion of the revival of the Tailteann games. See letter of 11 July 1924, note 1. (Buffalo)
17 In 1898, his last year at Belvedere College, Joyce played the role of a schoolteacher in the annual school performance. The play was F. Anstey's *Vice Versa: A Lesson to Fathers* (*JJII*, p. 56). The occasion, however, is a rather unlikely subject for a newspaper article.

May 12, 1931

Dear Mr Joyce,

I am sending you the copy of <u>Pomes Penyeach</u> that the Princeton U.P. has just sent me,[1] and the letter from the manager.[2] Will you please return them if it is not too much trouble.

The N R Fs[3] and H C Es[4] that you signed arrived and I have been busy distributing them. I called up Babou[5] and told his secretary who said as usual that he was out, that I would send him H C E and would he please give my errand girl at the same time the letter authorising the Faber & Faber H C E.[6] She promised but Léon[7] who I then called up warned me not to give Babou or Kahane the copies until after they gave their paper – good advice I think.

Léon says he has been after Babou every day for some time and finally was just about to get hold of the famous paper when Babou told him he had heard from Kahane that it was to be sent to Miss Beach not to Léon so that threw out his entire plans again. I think if Léon is attending to the matter for you it will only give them a few more excuses for delay if they hear all the time from me at the same time. Léon says he will go to Babou's tomorrow morning and try to get the document from him finally. He will let me know what happens. It seems to me suspicious, their behavior, Babou & Kahane's.

Léon was very much pleased with the signed H C E and N R F and is writing to you. He came to the shop to get them as soon as I told him they had arrived. Colum[8] hasn't come yet. I will send it to him. I gave him a review copy meanwhile several days ago. He is sending a notice to the Dublin Review.[9] Stuart

---

1 In the U.S. *Pomes Penyeach* was not under copyright and in spring 1931 it was threatened to be pirated. In order to ensure copyright Beach arranged for a small number of copies immediately to be printed by Princeton University Press. See letter of 25 April 1931, notes 6 and 7.
2 Paul G. Tomilson of Princeton University Press, letter to Beach, 9 May 1931. (Buffalo)
3 *Nouvelle Revue Française*, with the French translation of *Anna Livia Plurabelle*. See letter of 22 February 1921, note 3.
4 The trade edition of *Haveth Childers Everywhere*.
5 See preceding letter note 9.
6 See preceding letter, notes 9 and 10.
7 See letter of 25 August 1930, note 1, and INTRODUCTION to the 1930s, p. 125.
8 See letter of 25 August 1930, note 2.
9 An influential Catholic periodical, with a broad range of topics as well as prominent contributors. Founded in 1836 and (despite its name) published in London, it ceased publication in 1969. http://en.wikipedia.org/wiki/Dublin_Review_(Catholic_periodical), accessed 12 April 2019.

Gilbert[10] was just here. He read all the press cuttings and showed me Moore's letter.[11] Old imbecile!

Yours sincerely
Sylvia Beach

>   ALS, 1 leaf, 2 sides, Sha&Co stationery. ZJJF Jahnke.
>   Last paragraph, from "Léon was very much pleased" onwards, is written in the broad top margin, at a 90°degree angle from the main body.
>   Enclosure: letter from Paul Tomilson, at Buffalo.
>   To JJ at 28b Campden Grove, London

10   Stuart Gilbert (1883-1969). British critic, translator and friend of Joyce. He first read *Ulysses* in Burma, where he had served as a judge for nearly two decades. Returning in 1927 with his French wife to Paris, he soon became acquainted with Beach, who described him as "delightfully humorous, witty, paradoxical, rather cynical, extremely kind". (*Sha&Co*, p. 144) When she showed him a literary magazine with some pre-published pages of novel's French translation, he pointed out some significant errors. Beach passed these on to Joyce, who subsequently got in touch with him. Gilbert not only became one of the supervisors of Auguste Morel's translation of *Ulysses*, with Joyce's assistance, he wrote *James Joyce's Ulysses* (1930), the first book-length study of the novel. He also contributed an essay to *Our Exagmination* (see letter of 8 July 1931, note 8) and other early works of Joyce criticism. His *Paris Journal* gives an account of their close and productive friendship. (*JJII*, p. 600f.)

11   See letter of 16 July 1924, note 12. In a letter to Joyce, George Moore had expressed his annoyance that Joyce had sent him a copy of Gilbert's study of *Ulysses*. He felt that his reading of *Ulysses* was superior to, and not in need of, Gilbert's study, and then went on to point out a section of Gilbert's explication that he thought was particularly "silly". (letter of 29 April 1931; Buffalo) In his letter of 10 May 1931 to Beach, Joyce mentioned that "most furious letter" he had received from George Moore, to which he "replied sweetly and sincerely. Old men have a right to their anger." (*JJtoSB*, p. 169).

May 15, 1931

Dear Mr Joyce

I am sending you herewith a cheque on London for seven pounds which is all you have left of your royalties after paying the gas bill of 528 and Frs 100 to Daniel.[1] Georgio brought me the gas bill. I will send him the receipt. I am trying to get the paper you want from Babou.[2] Every day they promise to send it and after Babou's secretary's assuring me the other day that he was sending it right off by post I could hardly believe it still hadn't arrived this morning. Of course yesterday was Ascension – maybe he will tell me that was the reason. But I will send him the copy of H C E that you signed for him and that may bring some result.

Thank you so much for the one for me. I will distribute the others. If you sign any more don't sign on the inside cover that's supposed to be kept folded in. It's awkward but there's only the title page.

Please thank Miss Weaver[3] for her letter and the cuttings. I will write to her.
With best greetings to all

yours hastily
Sylvia Beach

    ALS, 1 leaf, 2 sides, Sha&Co stationery. ZJJF Jahnke.
    To JJ at 28b Campden Grove, London

1 Daniel was Joyce's florist at rue S. Placide. In his letter to Beach of 10 May 1931, Joyce writes that the gas bill was 465 Francs. (*JJtoSB*, p. 169)
2 See letter of 9 May 1931, note 9.
3 See statement of accounts, 27 July 1922, note 2.

May 27, 1931

Dear Mr Joyce,

I hope you finally got the ten pounds I sent you by Padraic Colum. He was late getting there, Mary Colum tells me.[1] Perhaps you would have preferred not to have it go that way but I was afraid you needed it before the banks opened. I enclose a letter from the Viking Press.[2] They are in a great hurry for a reply – as usual when they have propositions like that to make. Also here is the letter from Pinker[3] about "A Portrait of the Artist". If they are now offering you three hundred pounds they have gone up.[4]

---

1 See letters of 25 August 1930, note 2, and of 25 April 1931, note 5.
2 Viking Press, founded in New York in 1925 by Harold K. Guinzburg and George S. Oppenheim, former employees at Simon and Schuster and Alfred A. Knopf respectively. For many years it was the exclusive American publisher of *Chamber Music, Dubliners, A Portrait of the Artist as a Young Man, Exiles* and later also *Finnegans Wake*. Joyce's links to Viking stem from his long-time close association with B.W. Huebsch, who, except for *Finnegans Wake*, had published all these works under his own imprint. His 23-year-old firm was purchased by Viking Press before they had published any titles of their own. They greatly profited from Huebsch's attractive backlist, which apart from Joyce included D.H. Lawrence and Sherwood Anderson. Viking Press were the first to send Joyce and Beach an offer for the publication of *Ulysses* in America. (McCullough, p. 184, and https://web.archive.org/web/20061028174548/http://us.penguingroup.com/static/html/aboutus/adult/viking.html, accessed 12 January 2020).
3 Joyce's literary agent since 1915. By 1931, it was Ralph Pinker (1900-1959), one of James B. Pinker's sons, who was in charge of the leading literary agency in London, founded in 1896: *James B. Pinker & Son | J. Ralph Pinker | Literary Dramatic & Film Agents, Talbot House, Arundel Street, Strand, London W.C. 2.* https://eehe.org.uk/?p=25663, accessed 29 March 2021. Since 1930, his brother Eric took care of the agency's affairs in America. On Joyce's business relation with Pinker, see Gillies, p. 103ff. J.B. Pinker is mentioned in the "Circe" chapter of *Ulysses:* "[Philip Beaufoy:] My literary agent J.B. Pinker is in attendance." (15.835)
4 Joyce wrote to Beach earlier that month: "Pinker wrote me offering me £300 if I would sign an edition of the Portrait for Ginsbourg (i.e. Viking Press). He refers to some previous similar offer. Have you the letter?" (*JJtoSB*, no date; letter 164, p. 169f.) On the basis of an accompanying letter Banta and Silverman date the letter to 11 May, which would make this an unusually late reply from Beach.

A week later, Joyce mentioned the issue again. "Ginsbourg again offered me £300 if I would sign 2500 copies of *The Portrait*. I replied I would sign 100 copies for that sum." (*JJtoSB*, letter of 4 June 1931, p. 171).

Mr "Bunny" Wilson of the 'New Republic'[5] has turned down Adrienne's conference.[6] Meanwhile Eliot[7] is chewing it over.

I haven't seen Gorman[8] lately. I'll call up Georgio about the record. He should have one of course but could get it directly from Ogden[9] I think. Georgio and Helen have come three times and every time I was absent with a headache. But we met at a talkies called 'Cocoanuts'.[10]

I will send you a few more pounds soon. Only four or five. There is nothing coming in.

Have you been having a thunder storm too? I will return the letter from Holland[11] asking for your signature in a day or two.

With best greetings to you all

yours sincerely
Sylvia Beach

---

5   Edmund Wilson (1895-1972), American critic, writer and essayist recognized as one of the leading literary journalists of his time. From 1926-1931 he was an associate editor of *The New Republic*, a liberal American weekly (today monthly) magazine, founded in 1914. A good part of his first major critical work, *Axel's Castle* (1931), had appeared in that magazine. A study of Symbolism, it also discusses its further developments in the works of Yeats, Valéry, Proust, Eliot, Joyce and Stein. https://www.britannica.com/biography/Edmund-Wilson, accessed 22 November 2020.

6   This probably refers to Monnier's talk on *Ulysses* and the French public, the first part of the Joyce soirée at her bookshop on 26 March 1931 (see Fitch p. 313f. for details). The lecture was not published by Faber & Faber either, as the following sentence might suggest, but appeared only in May 1940, in Monnier's *La Gazette des Amis des Livres*.

7   See letter of 29 July 1924, note 5.

8   See undated letter [after 14 June, before 22 July 1924], note 4.

9   Charles Kay Ogden (1889-1957). English writer, mathematician, philosopher, psychologist, and linguist. Most notably, he developed Basic English and founded the Orthological Institute for its promotion as an international second language. http://www.basic-english.org, accessed 21 October 2019. In August 1929, the last four pages of "Anna Livia Plurabelle" (FW 213-216) had been recorded by Joyce for Ogden at the Orthological Institute; three further pressings were to follow (Slo + Ca, p. 173). In 1931, Ogden translated the recorded section from ALP into Basic English, which was published by his institute's journal and reprinted in *transition* in 1932. In her memoirs, Beach writes: "I thought Ogden's 'translation' [of ALP] into Basic English deprived the work of all its beauty, but Mr. Ogden and Mr. Richards were the only persons I knew about whose interest in the English language equaled that of Joyce." (*Sha&Co*, p. 172). Ogden also wrote an introduction to *Tales Told of Shem and Shaun*, published in 1929 (Slo + Ca, A 36, p. 48).

10   The "Cocoanuts", a musical comedy, was the first feature-length film by the Marx Brothers (1929).

11   See following letter.

I sent off <u>Ulysses</u> by air mail to Mr O'Connor.[12]

> ALS, 1 leaf, 2 sides, Sha&Co stationery. ZJJF Jahnke.
> Enclosure missing.
> To JJ at 28b Campden Grove, London

---

12   Martin O'Connor (d. 1937). Barrister of Irish descent living in Wimbledon near London, and, according to an auctioneer's details on the item sold, he entertained "politicians, lawyers and literary figures, such as Joyce and Beckett." Apparently, Joyce had luncheon at the O'Connors' house on 23 May 1931. (Norburn, p. 148) At his request, Beach sent them a copy of the 11th printing of *Ulysses*, which he had signed for "Martin and Lili O'Connor|James Joyce|Wimbledon|Whitsun 5.vi.1931". https://www.bonhams.com/auctions/22714/lot/206, accessed 25 April 2020. The presentation copy had a narrow escape as Lili, who had been told that *Ulysses* was full of obscene language, attempted to destroy the book, tearing off the front cover.

May 29, 1931

Dear Mr Joyce,

Colum[1] tells me you prefer a thousand franc note in a registered letter to a cheque so I am sending you one herewith but it is risky. Did you have so much trouble cashing the cheques? The letter you received from Curtis Brown has come.[2] I showed it to Colum who says he doesn't know who Mrs or Messrs Claude Kendall[3] is and thinks you'd better ignore it. He is writing to you about it. They are in a hurry to get hold of your Ulysses. Although I would agree to anything you wished – provided they paid the price I should demand for handing over Ulysses to them – I am not very sure of those persons. If a reliable publishing house were to make you an advantageous offer, of course you would have to consider it seriously. The Viking Press is so pokey.[4]

I am not returning Curtis Brown's letter till I hear from you whether you want me to reply or prefer to do so yourself, or ignore it as Colum suggests.

Yes I know that young John Melville, Holland count, a harmless collector. He buys your work in limited editions. I like his letter, don't you?[5] Perhaps you will autograph his copy of Ulysses.

---

1   See letter of 25 August 1930, note 2.
2   A leading literary agency in London founded by the American-born Albert Curtis Brown in 1905. In 1914, he established the American branch of his firm in New York, mostly to market the U.S. rights of his British clients. He was one of the first to gain notable success as a literary agent in America. Apart from Joyce, their clients included D.H. Lawrence and Ezra Pound. http://www.curtisbrown.com/about.php, accessed 23 September 2020, and Madison, p. 256.
    The letter from Laurence Pollinger of Curtis Brown to Joyce consists basically of a transcribed telegram from the New York publisher Kendall, in which he asks the agency to negotiate the American rights to publish *Ulysses* as a "test case here". (letter of 26 May 1931, Princeton) See also INTRODUCTION to the 1930s, p. 126f.
3   The New York publisher [Mr.] Claude Kendall, who was mainly active in the 1930s. In a letter to Beach, Laurence Pollinger, Kendall's representative at Curtis Brown, recommends Kendall as a comparatively new publisher that appears to be making "distinct progress" (letter from Pollinger to Beach, 3 June 1931, Princeton). With a publisher's list of mainly murder mysteries and risqué romances, Kendall's interest in *Ulysses*, apart from its commercial potential, seems to have been due more to the novel's aura of the forbidden and obscene than to its avant-garde qualities.
4   See preceding letter, note 2.
5   John Melville's letter is at Princeton and indeed quite a charming mixture of admiration and jovial familiarity ("Should you ever come to Holland I would be delighted if you would look us up.").

The year of the Clos St Patrice in Establet's[6] bill is 1920 – the price per bottle 20 frs. With best greetings

yours sincerely
Sylvia Beach

>ALS, 1 leaf, 2 sides, Sha&Co stationery. ZJJF Jahnke.
>To JJ at 28b Campden Grove, London

---
6 Antonin Establet was the proprietor of *Les Trianons*, one of Joyce's favourite Paris restaurants (*JJtoSB*, letter of 11 May 1931, note 4, p. 189).

June 2, [1931]

Dear Mr Joyce,

Rhein Verlag[1] announces that they are sending you RM 437.[2] I will let you know when it arrives at the bank here.

yours sincerely
Sylvia Beach

> APCS, 1 side. ZJJF Jahnke.
> To JJ at 28b Campden Grove, London

---

1 See letters of 16 September 1926, note 13, and of 6 August 1931, note 10.
2 An advance royalty payment for *Ulysses*. As Beach noted in her accounts, "437 RM = 2643.85 Frs." (Princeton) While registered in Zurich, their operating office was in Munich, which is why the Swiss publisher paid in Reichsmark rather than Swiss Francs.

June 5, 1931

Dear Mr Joyce,

I am sending you herewith the notice from Lloyds that the money from Rhein Verlag[1] has arrived, and the statement[2] sent me by Rhein Verlag. Also a copy of a letter that I have written to Mr Porringer or whatever his name is,[3] at Curtis Brown but am not sending to him until it has your approval.[4] I have left the space for the sum you wish to demand in advance royalties blank as I don't know what sum you think of naming. Colum[5] to whom I showed the letter from Pollinger said he thought about ten thousand dollars but that seems to me quite inadequate. Adrienne thinks you might say twenty-five thousand dollars. Colum thinks Curtis Brown is in a great hurry to put through this affair and he is going to try to find out something about Claude Kendall from his friends in New York.

I hope you are all well and enjoying the visit of Georgio and Helen.

Last evening we dined at Jean Schlumberger.[6] He asked Adrienne to read aloud A L P out of the N R F[7] after dinner and all who were there were very

---

1 See letters of 16 September 1926, note 13, and of 6 August 1931, note 10.
2 "This payment is in advance for "Ulysses" (i.e. RM 500) which is reduced for the account of Mr Joyce with RM 63. –" (Princeton).
3 Laurence Edward Pollinger (1898-1976). English literary agent for the British-American agency Curtis Brown Ltd. (for which see letter of 29 May 1931, note 2). In 1935, after disagreements with their employer, Pollinger and two colleagues established their own literary agency, Pearn, Pollinger and Higham. Among their clients were writers such as Scott Fitzgerald, D.H. Lawrence, Dorothy Parker and Graham Greene. In 1958, Pollinger would open a successor firm with his two sons, Laurence Pollinger Ltd. (https://norman.hrc.utexas.edu/Watch/fob_search_results_next.cfm?FOBFirmName=P&FOBNote=&locSTARTROW=231, accessed 26 November 2020, and Spanier and Mandel, p. 659).
4 Draft letter not enclosed. This is an answer to Pollinger's letter of 3 June 1931 recommending Claude Kendall, who had made the second offer for an American edition of *Ulysses* (see letter of 29 May 1931, notes 3 and 4). In her letter, eventually dated 11 June, Beach named the price of 25'000$ for her rights on *Ulysses*, as well as 20% royalties, with a certain advance, to Joyce. In his reply, Joyce remained silent on this and instead asked her to write to Pollinger to say that "as you have had several U.S.A. offers you want to hear terms not to give them" (*JJtoSB*, 8 June 1931) – which Beach did, using Joyce's phrase verbatim (second letter of 11 June 1931 to Pollinger, ZJJF Jahnke). Both these letters to Pollinger were sent off the same day. See also INTRODUCTION to the 1930s, p. 127f.
5 See letter of 25 August 1930, note 2.
6 Jean Schlumberger (1877-1968). French writer, poet and journalist, co-founder of the *Nouvelle Revue Française*, in which he played a key role (for NRF see letter of 22 February 1921, note 3). His *Heureux qui comme Ulysse* ... (Happy He Who Like Ulysses ... 1906) marked his beginning as novelist. (Cap, p. 294)
7 For the French translation of "Anna Livia Plurabelle" see letter of 1 May, note 1.

much impressed and André Chamson[8] said after all it was the "jet lyrique" that "vous prenait" and Schlumberger kept saying: "c'est très beau, très très beau!"[9] A lively discussion about your method and your vocabulary took place.

yours very sincerely
Sylvia Beach

> ALS, 1 leaf, 2 sides, Sha&Co stationery. ZJJF Jahnke.
> Greetings and signature written diagonally in the left margin.
> Enclosures: Notice from Lloyds missing, statement by Rhein-Verlag and copy of Beach's draft letter at Princeton.
> To JJ at 28b Campden Grove, London

---

8 André Chamson (1900-1983). French novelist, art historian and critic, a friend and patron of Shakespeare and Company and La Maison des Amis du Livre. He also contributed to Adrienne Monnier's *Navire d'Argent*. (Fitch, p. 188).

9 *Fr.* the lyrical drive that captivates you; it is very beautiful, very very beautiful!.

June 6, 1931

Dear Mr Joyce

You mention in your letter just received, one from Huebsch which I have not seen but would like to see.[1] It must be the one sent care of Gorman[2] and that he asked me to forward.

I don't remember your speaking of a Pathé disk[3] and Adrienne.

You will have got my letters sent you yesterday by this time. I wrote that way to Curtis Brown[4] to make the situation clear but perhaps we could just let the matter drop. I sent Transition No 16-17[5] to Pollinger[6] and will send the injunction to Pinker.[7]

---

1   Benjamin W. Huebsch (1876-1964). One of the first American publishers to publish modernist literature, he launched Joyce's American career, as well as that of D.H. Lawrence and a number of Continental authors in translation. Starting out as a lithographer's apprentice and later studying violin, he got into publishing by chance. He took over his uncle's small printer's shop in New York and in 1902 gradually began to publish literature. From the outset he was interested in bringing out works regardless of their marketability and in that sense, he was not the typical modernist publisher. Each of his titles was in some way to reflect his interests in both political and aesthetic reform. With the exception of *Ulysses*, which he declined in 1920 for fear of censorship, Huebsch published all of Joyce's major work under his own imprint (*Dubliners* and *A Portrait* in 1916, *Chamber Music* and *Exiles* in 1918). He also published Gorman's Joyce biography. His firm merged in 1925 with the newly founded Viking Press, which greatly profited from his cultural capital. As Viking's editor-in-chief, Huebsch was the first to make an offer for *Ulysses* in America. (McCullough p. 184f., and Turner, pp. 40 and 47f.).
   To Beach's request Joyce replied, "There was no second letter from Huebsch." (*JJtoSB*, 8 June 1931, p. 171) See note 10 below.
2   See undated letter [after 14 June, before 22 July 1924], note 4.
3   At a soirée at *La Maison des Amis des Livres* on 26 March 1931, Adrienne Monnier had recited the French translation of "Anna Livia Plurabelle". Such séances were regularly held at her bookshop; Joyce hoped thereby to "break the back of the resistance" to his *Work in Progress*. It was an evening with an elaborate programme in four parts, with Monnier first talking about Joyce's reception in France, followed by Soupault addressing the company. Then Monnier played the record with Joyce reading ALP in English and finally, she read the French translation, upon which Joyce, who must have liked the recital, suggested, "I think Miss Monnier should record it and sell the discs" (Fitch, p. 314). He repeated this suggestion in two letters to Beach (10 May and 4 June 1931). In the latter, Joyce asked her: "Did Soupault tell her [A. Monnier] of my proposal about a Pathé record and does she agree?"
4   See letter of 29 May 1931, notes 2 and 3.
5   For *transition*, see letter of 11 August 1927, note 3. Issue no 16-17 (June 1929) contains the 1928 injunction against Samuel Roth forbidding "his publishing, printing, stating or advertising, or otherwise disseminating the name of the plaintiff in connection with ... the book *Ulysses*" (p. 205f.).
6   See preceding letter, note 3.
7   See letter of 27 May 1931, note 3. Joyce had asked Beach to "send [Curtis Brown / Laurence Pollinger] the injunction he wants and also one to Pinker ..." (*JJtoSB*, letter of 4 June 1931, p. 171). See also note 10 below.

[Sideways text at top of letter:]

Gorman says he hasn't heard from you since you left. He hasn't written to you as he has nothing to tell you. Ma Stanislaus Joyce wrote to him some time ago that in June he was going to begin drawing the Collins etc copied. He says Gorman, that he wrote to Miss Schaurek and your sister Eva and received no reply. Meanwhile as his Joyce book is not to appear till next spring he is working on his "Many". He has been invited to stay with friend at Toulon but says it would be cheaper at a hotel. He is going down there about the 10th I think. Mr Allanon has gone to the Midi.

[Main letter:]

Mrs James Stephens came and asked for your address. I was out and Myrsine didn't give it. She was going right back to London. Perhaps you will let her know. Of course you have the address: Eversleigh, Queen's Walk, Kingsway, isn't it?

Blackmail! I am curious to see his letter. What a bunch of crooks!

Yours very sincerely
Sylvia Beach

Miss Allanah Harper brought over 6 records from Ogden. I asked Georgio to tell you, and will bring me a lot himself in July. He's a great flirt according to her, very gallant with young girls

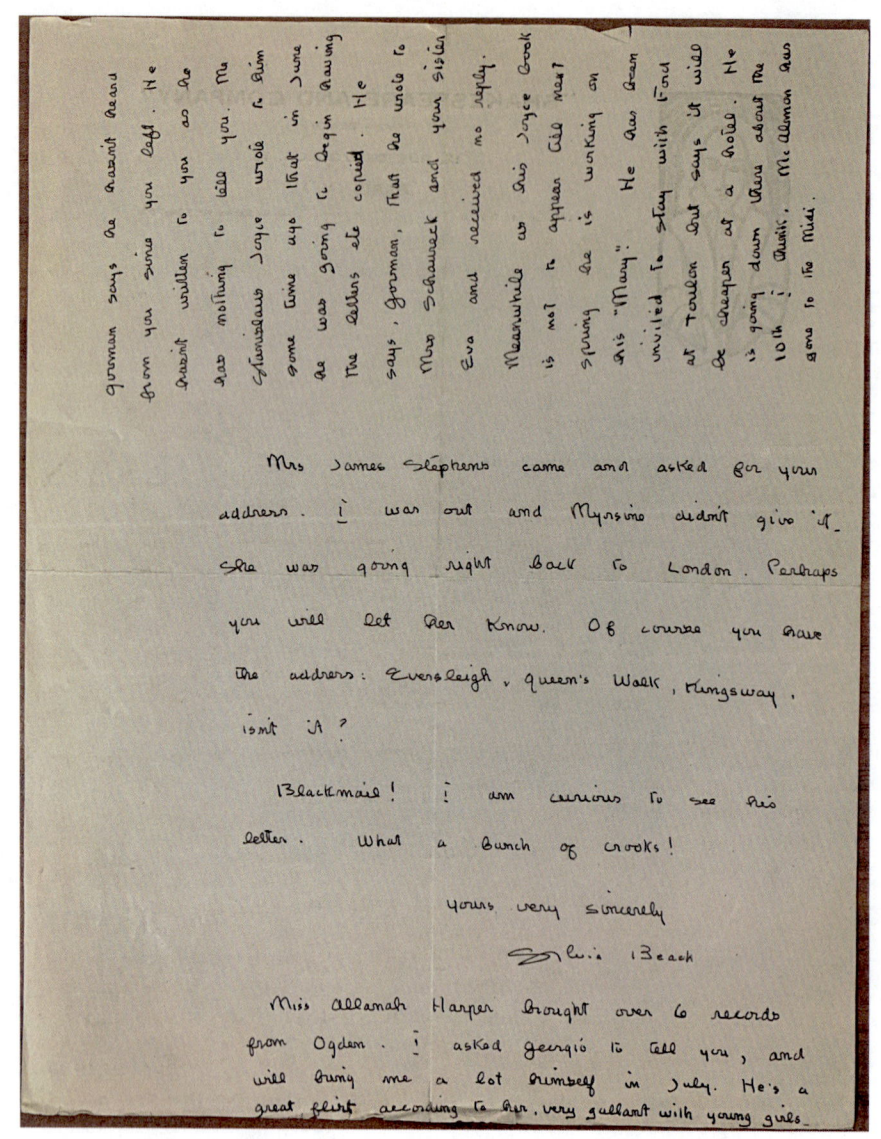

FIGURE 11   Letter of 6 June 1931
© SYLVIA BEACH ESTATE

Mrs James Stephens[8] came and asked for your address. I was out and Myrsine[9] didn't give it. She was going right back to London. Perhaps you will let her know. Of course you have the address: Evensleigh, Queen's Walk, Kingsway, isn't it?

Blackmail![10] I am curious to see his letter. What a bunch of crooks!

Yours very sincerely
Sylvia Beach

Miss Allanah Harper[11] brought over 6 records from Odgen.[12] I asked Georgio to tell you, and will bring me a lot himself in July. He's a great flirt according to her, very gallant with young girls.

Gorman says he hasn't heard from you since you left. He hasn't written to you as he has nothing to tell you. Mr Stanislaus Joyce wrote to him some time ago that in June he was going to begin having the letters etc copied. He says, Gorman, that he wrote to Mrs Schaureck and your sister Eva[13] and received

---

8 Cynthia Stephens, wife of James Stephens (1882-1950). Irish poet, short story writer, and novelist, who in the 1930s lived in Paris and London. In his younger years, Joyce had viewed him as a rival, but as Joyce became more successful his attitude to Stephens relaxed. In 1927, worried by criticism of his *Work in Progress*, Joyce was toying with the idea of asking Stephens to finish the work for him. Nothing came of it, but the two men became good friends (*JJAtoZ*, p. 209, see also *JJII*, pp. 333 and 591f.).

9 See statements of accounts, 27 July 1922, note 3.

10 "In my opinion," Joyce wrote to Beach on 4 June 1931, "one should walk warily with Mlle Kendall and Huebsch. The latter's letter is faintly suggestive of blackmail. Pollinger misreports my talk with him. All I want done at this stage is to get into the heads of Mlle K & H that *Ulysses* has been and is protected by an order of a U.S.A. court even in its unexpurgated form." (*JJtoSB*, p. 171) Thus, "blackmail" may refer to another attempt by Huebsch to suggest Joyce make some textual changes, as he had done in 1920. Alternatively, "blackmail" may suggest that in his capacity as Joyce's American publisher, Huebsch claimed a right of first refusal for an American edition (even though in the 1920s he had rejected the option to publish the novel).

11 Allanah Harper (1904-1992), an Englishwoman from a well-to-do family. Moving to Paris in her early twenties, she founded a bilingual little magazine, *Echanges: revue trimestrielle de littérature anglaise et française* (1929-1931), which was partly funded by Aga Khan. Its aim was to promote English writers among the French and vice versa. Harper thus introduced the French to W.H. Auden, T.S. Eliot, Gertrude Stein and Virginia Woolf, and introduced the English to Léon-Paul Fargue, André Gide and Henri Michaud, to name a few.
  https://norman.hrc.utexas.edu/fasearch/findingAid.cfm?eadid=00053, accessed 27 November 2020.

12 See letter of 27 May 1931, note 9.

13 Eileen Schaurek (1889-1963), the second, and Eva Mary Joyce (1891-1957), the fourth of Joyce's six sisters.

no reply. Meanwhile as his Joyce book is not to appear till next spring he is working on his "Mary".[14] He has been invited to stay with Ford[15] at Toulon but says it will be cheaper at a hotel. He is going down there about the 10th I think. McAlmon[16] has gone to the Midi.

ALS, 1 leaf, 2 sides, Sha&Co stationery. ZJJF Jahnke.
Last paragraph, from "Gorman says" onwards, is written in the broad top margin, at a 90° angle from the main body.
To JJ at 28b Campden Grove, London

14   Gorman's novel, *The Scottish Queen*, was published in 1932. He was at that time also working on the expanded version of his Joyce biography.
15   Ford Madox Ford, formerly Ford Madox Hueffer (1873-1939). English novelist, critic and editor, who in *Transatlantic Review* had published the first extract from *Work in Progress* ("Mamalujo").
16   See undated letter [after 14 June, before 22 July 1924], note 2.

June 10, 1931

Dear Mr Joyce,

I am sending you herewith a cheque on Lloyds Bank for £21-5-1 (they wouldn't let me send mark), the equivalent of RM 437[1] from the Rhein Verlag. Your letters which came this morning were the first intimation I have had from you that you wanted money sent to you at once. If you had returned the letter to me from Lloyds Bank that I sent to let you know it had come[2] I would not have had to spend the whole morning at the bank while they looked it up. But I should have asked you to.

Hemingway[3] has given me good advice about the American publishers.

yours sincerely
Sylvia Beach

you have received another bill from Establet[4] – or reminder (Frs 259,25)

> ALS, 1 leaf, 1 side, Sha&Co stationery. ZJJF Jahnke.
> The additional note is written at the bottom of the left margin.
> To JJ at 28b Campden Grove, London

---

1 This is an advance royalty payment from Joyce's German (Swiss) publisher. The Great Depression hit Germany particularly hard. In 1931 it suffered a serious banking crisis, and most of all a currency crisis that led to the imposition of money exchange controls. *Reichsmark* were hence taboo in international transactions. Beach noted in her file the equivalent in French money: "437 RM = 2643.85 Frs." (Princeton)
2 See letter of 5 June 1931.
3 See letter of 26 October 1926, note 1.
4 See letter of 29 May 1931, note 6.

June 13, 1931

Dear Mr Joyce,

You have about one thousand francs to your credit. When I have paid Establet's[1] bill Frs 259,25 you will have Frs 741,25 – about six pounds. This month up to date I have sold 34 copies of Ulysses. If as many again are sold between now and the 23rd there will be another thousand francs – about eight pounds. Business is worse and worse.[2]

Soupault[3] has written to you I suppose by this time about the record.[4] It seems the people want to ask a terrible price for making it. Adrienne is going to write to you about the A L P separate printing at the N R F.[5] Gallimard[6] won't give his copy back and Adrienne has sent word to him that there will be the hell to pay if he doesn't return it.[7]

---

1   See letter of 29 May 1931, note 6.
2   To compare: In 1929, before the Great Depression was showing its effects, the average monthly sale had been 213 copies. (Princeton).
3   See letter of 25 April 1931, note 2.
4   See letter of 6 June 1931, note 3.
5   According to La Hune Catalogue of Joyce's Paris Library, there were two offprints of that publication of the French "Anna Livia Plurabelle" (Slo + Ca, D 32, p. 114). On NRF, see letter of 22 February 1921, note 3.
6   Gaston Gallimard (1881-1975), publisher and co-founder of NRF. Gallimard had urged Joyce to agree to a French translation of Ulysses. He had wanted the whole of Ulysses for translation and publication in the NRF, but his plans came to nothing. The French Ulysses was published by Adrienne Monnier under the imprint of her bookstore, while Gallimard did not publish the novel until 1942. (JJtoSB, 25 June 1923 (no. 16), note 2, p. 23f.).
7   Joyce wanted to have the offprints of ALP destroyed, because they had been made without his consent. In a letter to Gallimard, Monnier not only asked him to return his two copies, on Joyce's behalf she also requested a written and signed statement confirming that no offprint copies were extant beyond the total of ten that were then being recalled from the various owners. (18 June 1931, http://obvil.sorbonne-universite.site/corpus/paulhan/monnier #PLH_171_095692_1931_07, accessed 12 July 2020).

Joyce apparently considered the cheap offprint format inappropriate and unprofitable, and seemed to aspire to a small bibliophile edition, as Monnier's comment in a letter to Jean Paulhan suggests: "The bibliophiles are not that silly. They want full-cream rather than low-fat milk." (23 June 1931, original in French. http://obvil.sorbonne-universite.site/corpus/ paulhan/monnier#PLH_171_095692_1931_08, accessed 12 July 2020).

By the end of the month Monnier could report to Joyce the destruction of all copies, jokingly drawing a sketch of how exactly the journals were torn into pieces, before being sent to Paulhan. (25 June 1931; Buffalo).

She discussed the matter with the Paulhans[8] at the pen club dinner last night. I sat next to André Spire.[9] He said he regretted he had not been able to come to the Joyce Séance.[10] He has been having family troubles, he told me. Dujardin was opposite. Fortunately McAlmon was not there.[11] He is in Cagnes sur Mer. Valéry[12] presided. He didn't get the Nobel Prize (think of Wyndham Lewis![13]) but Oxford is conferring some degree on him on June 24 – Honoris Causa, is that what they call it?[14] Galsworthy too.[15]

Haveth Childers Everywhere and A L P in the shilling edition sell very well.[16] No one buys anything else.

If you get a letter from Mlle Elvira de Alvear[17] asking for the honour of publishing something of yours in her review Imán she hopes you will answer it.

---

8   Jean Paulhan (1884-1968). French essayist, literary critic, publisher and teacher of oriental languages. Editor-in chief of the *Nouvelle Revue Française from 1925-1940*, and again until his death, after the *Nouvelle NRF* would reappear in 1953. He was also literary director at Gallimard for decades and was elected a member of the Académie française in 1963. http://www.academie-francaise.fr/les-immortels/jean-paulhan?fauteuil=6&election=24-01-1963, accessed 22 November 2020.
9   André Spire (1868-1966). French Jewish poet, literary critic and essayist, who published on a wide variety of topics, from a theory of free verse (*Plaisir poétique et plaisir musculaire*, 1949) to Zionism. He was an influential figure in the Parisian literary circles of that period. It was at a party at Spire's in July 1920 that Beach had first met Joyce. In "La rencontre avec Joyce" (Mathews and Saillet, pp. 41-45) he recalls his acquaintance with Joyce.
10 See letter of 6 June 1931, note 3.
11 See undated letter [after 14 June, before 22 July 1924], notes 2 and 3. For the clash between Dujardin and McAlmon, which occurred at the French "Anna Livia Plurabelle" séance and was caused by a minor misunderstanding involving Dujardin's wife, see Fitch, p. 314, and *JJII*, p. 636.
12 Paul Valéry (1871-1945), French poet, essayist and critic, belonged to the circle of French, Irish, American and English writers who frequently met at Shakespeare and Company and became a good friend of Beach's.
13 It was *Sinclair* Lewis, not Wyndham Lewis, who won the Nobel Prize for Literature in 1930.
14 Valéry was awarded an honorary doctorate from Oxford University in 1931. Cf. Gifford and Stimpson, p. 3.
15 John Galsworthy (1867-1933). English novelist and dramatist, had also received an honorary doctorate from Oxford, and was to win the Nobel Prize 1932, shortly before his death.
16 The Faber & Faber trade edition of HCE had just appeared in May 1931, their 2-shilling-edition of ALP in June of the previous year.
17 Elvira de Alvear (1907-1959). Argentinian poet, who in 1931 founded a Spanish literary journal in Paris, *Imán*, with Alejo Carpentier as its editor. It only appeared for one year; among its contributors were Eugene Jolas, Hans Arp, Léon-Paul Fargue, Philippe Soupault, Franz Kafka and John Dos Passos. Jorge Luis Borges, who was said to have been in love with de Alvear, wrote a poem about her, "Elvira de Alvear". (Monegal, p. 308f). https://www.researchgate.net/publication/330124686_El_acierto_en_el_fracaso_La_revista_Iman_1931_un_episodio_de_la_historia_literaria_latinoamericana, accessed 28 April 2019.

I told her you would be sure to. She knows a Spaniard in England who would translate a part of Ulysses for Imán if you consented she pays a high price.

AL, 1 leaf, 2 sides, Sha&Co stationery. ZJJF Jahnke.
The last few lines, from "you would be sure to.", are written diagonally in the left margin. As there is no signature, there could have been a second leaf now missing.
To JJ at 28b Campden Grove, London

FIGURE 12   Sylvia Beach and Adrienne Monnier at the desk in "Shakespeare & Co", undated
PHOTOGRAPHER UNKNOWN. COURTESY OF SPECIAL COLLECTIONS,
PRINCETON UNIVERSITY

June 19, 1931

Dear Mr Joyce,

I am sending you herewith an open cheque on London for seventeen pounds. If anything more comes in in the next few days I will send it along to you. This cheque is on the Haymarket branch which I hope will be more convenient for you than Threadneedle Street.

Thank you for your wire on Bloomsday. Georgio and Helen came to see me in the morning but I was feeling very ill from some Guinness's stout that a member of my library named Miss Killen[1] had recommended to me for headache and at noon I had to take to my bed where I have been ever since till today.

Georgio and Helen gave me good news of you.[2]

With best greetings

yours very sincerely
Sylvia Beach

    ALS, 1 leaf, 1 side, Sha&Co stationery. ZJJF Jahnke.
    To JJ at 28b Campden Grove, London

---

1 Identity unknown.
2 This probably refers to the good result of the eye operation by Professor Vogt on 15 May in Zurich. On 15 June, Vogt examined Joyce again and was pleased with the progress. (Norburn, p. 143)

July 1, 1931

La Ferme des genets
Auberville s/Mer
Calvados

Dear Mr Joyce, your letter of June 25th was sent to me here. I am so sorry to hear of your brother's illness.[1] It is not very gay for any of you there I am afraid. Also Pinker's and Curtis B's[2] propositions were forwarded to me. Pinker advises waiting till Huebsch proposes,[3] C.B. wants the matter clinched at once for his eager yet obscure client. I enclose their letters.[4] Please return them to me and tell me what to reply. I shall be in Paris Friday night but only till Saturday noon. (The 4th of July only). I am staying here for a week with friends who have taken a house. It is near Trouville. I had a letter from Gillet[5] (which I will send you soon) asking all about you, when you were to be in Paris etc and saying his article on you was finished and printed. It is not in the 1st of July No. of the Rev. des

---

1 In that letter, Joyce wrote that his brother Charles "had a bad lung hemorr[h]age two months ago. He has tuberculosis of both lungs but it seems is to be let out in a few weeks." (*JJtoSB*, 25 June 1931, p. 172)
2 See letters of 27 May 1931, note 3, and of 29 May 1931, note 2.
3 See letter of 6 June 1931, note 1. Fitch notes that Huebsch had already sent a proposal to both Joyce and Beach on 16 May 1931 (pp. 316 and 430). Pinker may be referring to a possible second offer from Huebsch, in response to competing offers.
4 In his letter of June 25, 1931, Pinker's agency informed Beach of an offer for the book rights of *Ulysses* in America: "This offer is $1000.00 advance on account of 10% on the first 3000 copies and 15% thereafter and $500 royalty for 100 signed copies. Mr. Joyce says that he would not wish to sign the copies nor would he write a preface, but he would be willing to make a prefatory note to say that the text was authentic." Pinker revealed that the offer came from Claude Kendall, a New York publisher. (Princeton) On the same day, Laurence Pollinger of Curtis Brown also sent a letter to Beach, informing her of Claude Kendall's "best offer for the U.S.A. and Canada volume rights" for *Ulysses*. (Princeton) On Kendall see letter of 29 May 1931, note 3.
5 Louis Gillet (1876-1943). A leading French literary and art critic whose work on Joyce was crucial for Joyce's early reception in France. He published on a wide range of subjects, from the medieval arts to French Impressionism, and with one of his focuses on anglophone literature from Shakespeare to Virginia Woolf. In 1935 he was elected to the *Académie Française*. While his first response to Joyce had been quite negative, Gillet with a recent convert's fervour turned into an advocate of his works. He came to regret his article on *Ulysses* (published as "Du côté de chez Joyce" in the *Revue des Deux Mondes* on 1 August 1925). Though clever and witty, it could hardly do the novel any justice, as he later admitted in a letter to Joyce. (cf. Markow-Totevy, p. 14.) Gillet gradually changed his opinion after the publication of the French translation in 1929, but this was due mainly to his personal contact with Joyce. For the story of their intellectual friendship see Markow-Totevy, "Introduction". https://data.bnf.fr/fr/documents-by-rdt/11904932/te/page1, accessed 9 May 2020.

D.M.[6] Adrienne says. We will watch for it. I enclose Gillet's letter and will reply to him that I have sent it on to you.[7]

With affectionate greetings to you all
Sylvia Beach

> APS, 1 side, picture with caption '61. CAEN – Eglise Saint-Etienne vue de la maison des étudiants'. ZJJF Jahnke.
> Enclosures: letters from R. Pinker, L. Pollinger of Curtis Brown and L. Gillet, at Princeton.
> To JJ at 28b Campden Grove, London

---

6 *Revue des Deux Mondes*. Gillet's article on *Work in Progress*, "M. James Joyce et son Nouveau Roman", the first of his two essays on Joyce's last book to appear in the *Revue des Deux Mondes*, was published on 15 August 1931, in vol. 85 (pp. 928-39). (Deming 1977, p. 205, item 5058). This essay, which compared him to Dante and Shakespeare, pleased Joyce very much, and it was translated and published in *transition* 21 (March 1932), in a special section called "Homage to James Joyce". ("L'Extraordinaire Aventure de M. James Joyce", Gillet's second article on *Finnegans Wake*, was published in the *Revue's* issue of 15 December 1940.)

The *Revue*, founded in 1829, was – and still is – a prestigious publication, by now most probably the oldest European monthly review. The *Revue's* position as a central literary journal in 19th century France was challenged when in the early 20th century the *Nouvelle Revue Française* was founded, so that it widened its focus to include history and politics. The two worlds refer to Europe and America. http://www.revuedesdeuxmondes.fr/qui-sommes-nous/, accessed 9 May 2020.

7 In his letter of 25 June 1931 to Beach, Gillet wrote that this article "has cost me immense trouble, it is all printed: I corrected the proofs, but it has been left abandoned these past two months, because of the troublesome, tactless, unbearable current affairs ... Ah! Who will save us from the nightmare of history, as Dedalus says? When shall we, as Rabelais says, be 'pickled in the scorn of fortuitous things'?" (Princeton; original in French)

July 8, 1931

Dear Mr Joyce,

Last evening I received your express letter and the other one came to day an hour before you phoned.[1] Being quite alone in the shop I had to wait till lunch time to close and wire the £10.

I am very sorry you have not had an answer to the letters addressed to me last week[2] – Miss Beach came back on Friday and went to Rocfoin[3] on Saturday with Mlle Monnier – She took both your letters and said that she had to answer them herself. She told me also that she only could give you the Ulysses accounts or send you the money[4] – and give you Dr Fontaine's reply[5] – So I thought all that was done. I tried to ask Dr Fontaine but she was always away – As soon as possible I will send you her answer (as I remember your question)

---

1   There is no extant "express letter" dating from 7 July, nor is there a document that could be identified as "the other one". (For previous letters see the following note.) The next letter from Joyce – to Beach's assistant Myrsine Moschos – dates from 8 July, in which he thanks her for the £10 she wired him that same day. (Buffalo).
2   The week before 8 July, Joyce wrote two letters to Moschos, one on 30 June, and the other on 1 July 1931. (Buffalo) Basically consisting of a litany of enquiries and requests, the first letter asked about payments of royalties; whether Beach had answered Pollinger's letter informing her of Claude Kendall's offer for *Ulysses*; and whether Huebsch had also made a proposal. In the second letter, Joyce reiterated the request about recent royalties and wrote that Pinker did not confirm rumours of any further pirating acts by Samuel Roth, of which George Antheil's wife had informed Beach in a letter: "Samuel Roth came out of jail some time ago, and started right away to set up an exact duplica of 'Ulysses' and is selling it all over New York. It is his own printing, but is an exact copy of your edition, even saying edited by Shakespeare and Co, 12 rue de l'Odéon." (Böske Antheil to Beach, 9 June 1931; Princeton)
3   See letter of 18 August 1928, note 1.
4   In the first of his two letters to Moschos, Joyce asked whether Beach had given her instructions about forwarding him royalty money during Beach's absence.
5   Dr Thérèse Bertrand-Fontaine (1895-1987). A distinguished doctor and scientist. She was the first woman to become head of the hospital system in Paris and was also elected a *grand officer of the French Legion of Honour*. She was the Joyce family doctor during those years. A member of the Shakespeare and Company library, she had been introduced to Joyce by Beach. Among her patients were other expatriates, such as Samuel Beckett, Stuart Gilbert, Ernest Hemingway, and Mary Colum (cf. Lyons, pp. 215-217).
    In his letter to Myrsine Moschos, 1 July 1931, Joyce had requested some medical information about his brother's tuberculosis as well as about his daughter, whose mental and physical health had become a constant worry: "I should also like to know from Dr Fontaine whether contact with phthysical subject who recently had a bad haemorrhage and has both lungs affected is dangerous for young persons, Lucia, for instance." (Buffalo).

I copied T.S. Eliot's letter[6] and sent the original to Miss Weaver[7] – also Our Exag[8] to Mr R. Pinker –

I sent someone to get the "gouttes jaunes"[9] which – Mr Leon[10] said – were to be called for by Mrs Stephens.[11]

Please do not trouble to send back the £10 before it is quite convenient to you – they are mine and have nothing to do with the bookshop's accounts.

I have seen the photos in the N.Y. Herald and also Chicago Tribune after you told me.[12]

---

6   See letter of 29 July 1924, note 5. Eliot's letter to Joyce dates from 6 July 1931. Writing in his capacity as editor at Faber & Faber, he puts forward the publisher's terms for negotiation of the British rights for *Work in Progress:* They could offer an advance of £300, if the book were to be sold at a guinea, with a "royalty of 15% up to 500 copies and 20% after that. Furthermore, if you agreed to the publication of a limited signed edition, we should suggest a further 100 signed copies to be sold at £5:5 each." Such a deluxe edition would be on a straight 20% royalty, i.e. would earn Joyce a further £100 besides the £300 on the ordinary edition. (Copy in Myrsine Moschos' hand; Princeton) Beach also mentions Eliot's letter in her letter of 21 July 1931.

7   See statement of accounts, 27 July 1922, note 2.

8   *Our Exagmination Round His Factification for Incamination of Work in Progress*, a collection of twelve essays instigated by Joyce in order to promote his *Work in Progress*. Published by Shakespeare and Company in May 1929, it was Beach's third and last title for Joyce. Contributors were Samuel Beckett, Marcel Brion, Frank Budgen, Stuart Gilbert, Eugene Jolas, Victor Llona, Robert McAlmon, Thomas McGreevy, Elliot Paul, John Rodker, Robert Sage, William Carlos Williams, with letters of protest by G.V.L. Slingsby and Vladimir Dixon. It was later published by Faber & Faber, London, and New Directions, Norfolk, CT.

    In his letter of 30 June 1931, Joyce asked Moschos whether "three copies of the Exag [had] been sent to my sister in Dublin, my nephew George Joyce.... Mrs. Richard Guinness 19 Great Cumberland Place, London W." (Buffalo) For his agent Pinker, however, Joyce had arranged for "two copies of Ulysses" (ibid.).

9   See letter of 18 August 1928, note 3.

10 See letter of 25 August 1930, note 1, and INTRODUCTION to the 1930s, p. 125.

11 See letter of 6 June 1931, note 8.

12 Founded in 1841 as a Whig party, penny paper, *The New York Herald* became one of the most significant American daily newspapers. In 1924, it merged with its rival, the *New York Tribune*, to form the *New York Herald Tribune*, which ceased publication in 1966. https://chroniclingamerica.loc.gov/lccn/sn83030214/, accessed 9 May 2020. *The Chicago Tribune*, then a major daily newspaper founded in 1847, still exists today.

    These two newspapers apparently published an article with pictures of Joyce and Nora on account of their wedding in London on 4 July 1931. See also letters of 17 and 21 July 1931, especially note 6 to the latter.

Veuillez recevoir je vous prie ainsi que Madame Joyce mes sentiments bien respectueux.[13]

Myrsine Moschos.

> ALS, 1 leaf, 2 sides, Sha&Co stationery. ZJJF Jahnke.
> To JJ at 28b Campden Grove, London

FIGURE 13   Summer at Rocfoin: Adrienne Monnier, Madame Monnier, Sylvia Beach, James Joyce and Monsieur Monnier, ca. 1928
PHOTOGRAPHER UNKNOWN. COURTESY OF THE POETRY COLLECTION, UNIVERSITY AT BUFFALO

---

13   *Fr.* Yours most sincerely and respectfully, and please convey my best regards to Mrs. Joyce.

July 12, 1931

Dear Mr Joyce,

I am sending you herewith the proofs of Gillet's article[1] that he has just sent me, and his letter.[2] We think it very fine.

I have replied to Pinker[3] and am sending you a copy on the back of his letter of my letter.[4] This has to get right off. Curtis Brown[5] is impatient too.

When I go to Paris next week I will ask Thérèse to write to you about the danger of infection from your brother's tuberculosis.[6] I do hope he will recover.

With best greetings to you all

yours very sincerely
Sylvia Beach

Will you please return Pinker's letter

> ALS, 1 leaf, 1 side, Sha&Co stationery. ZJJF Jahnke.
> Enclosures: letter from L. Gillet at ZJJF Jahnke, proofs of Gillet's article missing.
> To JJ at 28b Campden Grove, London

1 See letter of 1 July 1931, notes 5-7.
2 Louis Gillet's letter to Beach dates from 8 July 1931. He complained that he already had to shorten his article on *Work in Progress* by one third, and that now another two pages would have to go. He should like Joyce to approve of what the merciless editors-in-chief at the *Revue* [*des Deux Mondes*] would let them keep of his figure ... Gillet further wrote that over the past few days he had frequently met with Victor Bérard [whose book on the Semitic origins of the *Odyssey* had greatly intrigued Joyce] and that they had decided to organize a *dîner* in honour of *Ulysses* in the autumn. "You'll be there, Nausicaa", he added. (ZJJF Jahnke; original in French).
3 See letter of 27 May 1931, note 3.
4 Beach was apparently resending Pinker's letter of 25 June to Joyce that she had already mentioned and forwarded to Joyce in her letter of 1 July 1931, requesting that Joyce return the letter to her (see letter of 1 July 1931, note 4). Beach's answer to Pinker's letter dates from 4 July 1931: she deemed their offer "too small" to be of any interest to Joyce. Referring to her contract with Joyce for *Ulysses*, she continued: "If an American edition appeared I should probably have to cease publication here. Any offers must therefore include the sum of twenty five thousand dollars to be paid to me on signing the contract." (Princeton).
5 See letter of 29 May 1931, note 2.
6 See letter of 8 July 1931, note 5.

July 15, 1931

Chez Monsieur Clovis Monnier
Rocfoin
par Maintenon, Eure et Loir

Dear Mr Joyce,

I have just received your letter of the 13th (it was brought at 8.30 this morning) and as we are going back to Paris at noon to stay two days I will send you a wire as soon as we get there. It is very kind of you to give me an option on "Work in Progress".[1] I would dearly love to publish it, more than anything in the world but I am too much hampered by lack of capital to manage it satisfactorily for you. You need an advance immediately which I couldn't give you and a publisher in England or America would handle it much better in every way than I could. You must not hesitate to close with whichever of the publishers' offers you think best. You have several very good ones to choose from.[2] Can't you make a separate contract with Faber and an American house at the same time and get a double advance in that way? Or do they want the exclusive rights?[3]

I hope you have received the proofs of Gillet's article[4] by this time. They left Maintenon on Sunday. Your express letter took two days to reach there, on account of the 14th probably.[5]

Adrienne joins me in best wishes

yours very sincerely
Sylvia Beach

> ALS, 1 leaf, 2 sides, Sha&Co stationery. Stationery address crossed out. ZJJF Jahnke.
> To JJ at 28b Campden Grove, London

1 Joyce wrote to Beach on 13 July 1931: "Are you interested in publishing this book yourself? If so, wire me the word 'suspend' and I will hold up things for a week till I can hear and answer." (*JJtoSB*, p. 173) See also INTRODUCTION to the 1930s, p. 128f.
2 In the same letter, Joyce wrote: "In addition to Faber's offer for *W i P* (£400 advance of 15% royalties rising to 20%) and Viking Press (£600 of 15% royalties) Harcourt Brace cabled yesterday they would pay £600. (...) pending two other American offers and two English ones." (ibid.)
3 *Finnegans Wake* was eventually published by Faber & Faber in London as well as Viking Press for the USA; both editions appeared on 4 May 1939.
4 See letter of 1 July 1931, notes 5-7.
5 The 14th of July, *quatorze juillet*, or *jour de la Bastille*, is the French national holiday.

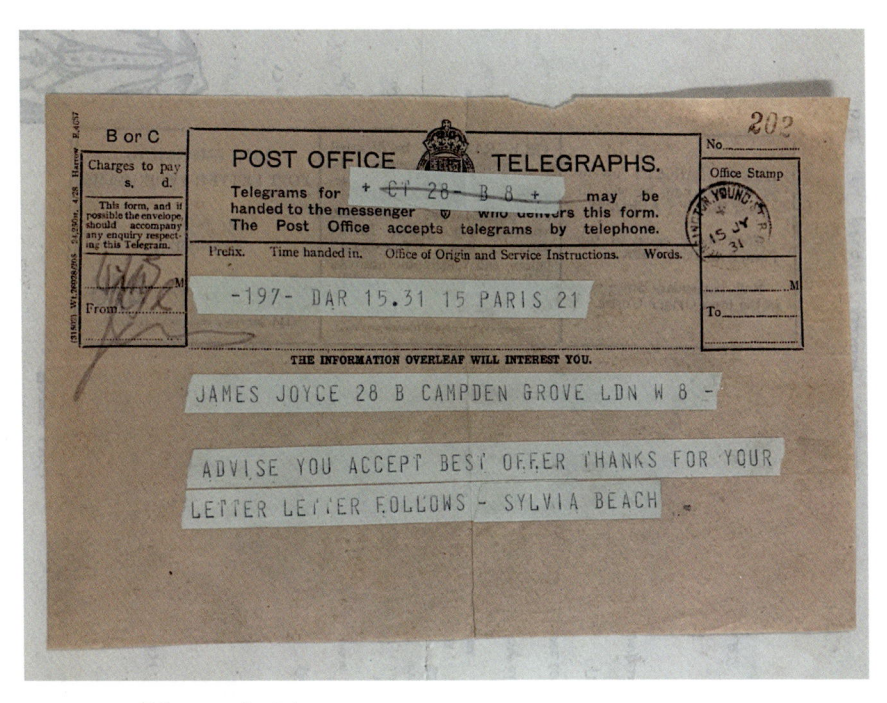

FIGURE 14 Telegram of 15 July 1931
© SYLVIA BEACH ESTATE

July 15, 1931
[postmark; telegram]

-197- DAR 15.31 15 PARIS 21

JAMES JOYCE 28B CAMPDEN GROVE LDN W 8 –

ADVISE YOU ACCEPT BEST OFFER THANKS FOR YOUR LETTER LETTER FOLLOWS – SYLVIA BEACH

>Telegram, 1 leaf, 1 side. ZJJF Jahnke.
>To JJ at 28b Campden Grove, London

[no date; ca. 16 July 1931]

P.S. I have just received Pinker's letter[1] enclosing the one from Miss Cunard's[2] friend.[3] Well, how the offers are pouring in!

Lucia wrote to Myrsine asking her to send Pinker an account of all the editions of Ulysses. I will send it as soon as I can. It takes time to look those things up.

I paid your garde meuble bill and gave the receipt to Georgio, asking him to let you know. It was a long time ago.

> AL, fragment, 1 leaf, 1 page, Sha&Co stationery. ZJJF Jahnke.
> Written below telephone number of Sha&Co: "Please notice that my telephone number was changed when the automatic was put in last spring".
> Dating: the letter refers to Joyce's letter of 13 July 1931, in which he wrote: "Another offer arrived for the U.S. publication of Ulysses but as I possess no rights in this book I sent it on to you via Pinker. It comes from a Mr. Herbert Rothschild." (*JJtoSB*, p. 173) Hence the date must be shortly after 15 July, the date of Pinker's letter to Beach.

1   The literary agent's letter is basically a cover letter, with no substantial communication. (Princeton).
2   Nancy Cunard (1896-1965). British shipping heiress, writer, poet and political activist. After World War I she moved to Paris and became involved in the Dadaist, Surrealist and Modernist movement. In 1927 she set up the Hours Press, which printed work by Ezra Pound, Norman Douglas, Laura Riding, and Samuel Beckett, among many others. https://norman.hrc.utexas.edu/fasearch/findingaid.cfm?eadid=00031&kw=cunard, accessed 7 September 2020, and Benstock, p. 389f.
3   Herbert L. Rothchild, or Rothschild (1881 or 1882-1935). Lawyer, book collector and patron of the arts, founder of the first movie theatres in San Francisco and owner of Herbert L. Rothschild Entertainment, Inc. (*The New York Times*, 17 September 1935, https://www.nytimes.com/1935/09/17/archives/herbert-l-rothchild-san-francisco-attorney-was-one-of-early-movie.html, accessed 7 September 2020).
    In his letter of 16 June 1931, Rothschild informed Nancy Cunard of an offer by Edwin Grabhorn of Grabhorn Press to publish *Ulysses* in America. Founded in San Francisco in 1919, the Grabhorn Press "became known for their well-produced, colorful and imaginative book designs as well as for their fine printing"; their books often became collectors' items. As Rothschild writes, he and Grabhorn were thinking of "a limited edition of possibly say two hundred copies in America of James Joyce's 'Ulysses'. The demand both for the Joyce book and for the Grabhorn imprint would in America be very great, and the one would enhance the other. Mr. Grabhorn would, of course, be willing to pay a substantial price to Mr. Joyce for the privilege of printing this book in America, and it suggested itself to me that you would probably be the best person in all this world to negotiate such a transaction." (Princeton) Nothing came of their idea for a deluxe edition.

July 17, 1931

Dear Mr Joyce,

I am sending you herewith a cheque for ten pounds. I have paid back the ten pounds that Myrsine loaned you (Frs 1284 counting the expenses of telegraphing the money). When I was away I told her to send you five pounds as soon as royalties to that amount came in, but there were very few copies of Ulysses sold during that time.[1] The last day or two sales have picked up a bit so I am able to refund Myrsine's loan and to send you ten pounds.

Your letter of the 13th has just been forwarded to me from Rocfoin. So Harpers has made an offer and gone the others one better – Hooray![2] that's one of the most old fashioned houses in America, the oldest, I think.[3]

Have you already accepted one of the others? Padraic Colum has just been in and when I showed him your letter he said: "That should be considered seriously". He is going to have a conversation with Molly,[4] he says, and will write to you what they think. He says Harpers has changed hands lately. A man named

---

[1] The poor sales refer to June. Beach's record book for 1931 lists 94 copies of *Ulysses* sold in June 1931 and 307 in August, with no figures for July (which are possibly included in the August sales). The lowest figures in 1931 were, as always, in the tourist low season, with 39 copies sold in November, followed by 57 in February. In all of 1931 Beach sold 1474 copies of *Ulysses*. (Princeton) See also letter of 15 November 1932, note 2.

[2] Beach had already answered Joyce's letter of the 13th in her 15 July letter from Rocfoin. She possibly mixed up dates here and is actually referring to another, missing letter, as Harper was not mentioned in Joyce's 13 July letter, but only in his letter of 19 July 1931: "Harper's now offer an advance of £750 of 15% royalties ..." (*JJtoSB*, p. 173) The "now", however, seems to suggest that Harper had been mentioned before, either in a missing letter or in oral communication.

In a letter to Giorgio and Helen Joyce, Joyce gave somewhat different figures: an advance of £500 from Harcourt Brace and £700 from Harper. (13 July 1931, ZJJF Jahnke).

[3] Probably the oldest to survive into Beach's time. Founded in New York in 1817 by James and John Harper, the publishing house J. & J. Harper exerted a great influence in letters and politics in the 19th century. Their first publishing venture was John Locke's *Essay on Human Understanding*. *Harper's Magazine* serialized many novels by leading American writers. By 1830, it was the largest publishing house in America. When the firm was joined by the two younger brothers, it changed its name to Harper & Brothers. Their authors included Melville, Twain and Henry James, whereas their few modernist writers, such as John Dos Passos, mostly appeared in their magazine. The company passed out of family hands in 1900. https://www.britannica.com/topic/Harper-brothers, accessed 22 November 2020.

[4] See letters of 25 August 1930, note 2, and of 25 April 1931, note 5.

Wells[5] (another of them) runs it, but although Colum would prefer Scribners[6] or Macmillans[7] for you, Harpers would probably be the best of the others. He thinks Harcourt[8] surer than the Viking,[9] but he says he has written you that. Hemingway[10] would give you good advice. If you haven't done anything definite yet shall I write to him? Georgio tells me <u>he</u> has advised you not to accept any offers for the present.

We are going to Rocfoin on Saturday to stay till the end of the month. I will arrange with Myrsine to send you any royalties there are.

---

5 There was indeed a change that year: Thomas Bucklin Wells (1875-1944) had "run it" up to May 1931, when he retired. Associated with Harper since 1899, Wells was the editor of *Harper's Magazine* from 1919 to 1931 and also functioned as general literary advisor and board-chairman of the book publishing branch. His successor as magazine editor was Lee Foster Hartman (Cf. http://content.time.com/time/subscriber/article/0,33009,803318,00.html, accessed 29 March 2021, and Chevalier, p. 375f.).

6 A New York publishing house founded in 1846 by Charles Scribner I and Isaac D. Baker, after whose death Baker and Scribner was renamed Charles Scribner and Company. Initially publishing theological books, morally uplifting titles with popular appeal and "no word unfit for a young girl's ear" (Malcolm Cowley), they changed to reprints and translations of British and continental European literary works. Charles Scribner II – who in 1905 also founded Princeton University Press – began to publish American authors such as Edith Wharton, Henry James, Hemingway and Scott Fitzgerald, which fundamentally changed their reputation as an old-fashioned firm. (Becket, pp. 412 and 416f.).

7 Macmillan and Company, London, founded in 1843 as a bookstore in Cambridge by two Scottish brothers, Daniel and Alexander Macmillan. After starting with textbooks, they soon also published novels as well as literary and scientific journals. In 1867 the firm expanded to the U.S. and some 20 years later the American branch began to publish its own books. Among their authors are Tennyson, Hardy, Lewis Carroll, Yeats, and Huxley, https://www.britannica.com/topic/Macmillan-Publishers-Ltd, accessed 22 November 2020.

8 Harcourt, Brace and Howe, New York, was founded in 1919 by two former publishing editors and a professor of English, who had been encouraged by Sinclair Lewis to launch their own firm. Lewis' novels were among their early bestsellers, which also comprised a wide variety of books, such as Maynard Keynes' *Economic Consequences of the Peace*, Carl Sandburg's Abraham Lincoln biography and Woolf's *Orlando*. When Howe left in 1921, the firm was renamed Harcourt, Brace and Company. The year they were negotiating *Finnegans Wake*, they started publishing Dos Passos' U.S.A. trilogy, and in 1932 they brought out their first T.S. Eliot title. Since 1970 the publisher has been known as Harcourt Brace Jovanovich. (Dzwonkoski, p. 180)

9 See letter of 27 May 1931, note 2.

10 See letter of 26 October 1926, note 1.

What a lot of press notices about you! That was a very good picture of you and Mrs Joyce in I forget which one of the papers.[11] There was also a notice in 'Les Nouvelles Littéraires'[12] and 'Paris Midi'.[13]

With best greetings to you all

yours sincerely
Sylvia Beach

> ALS, 1 leaf, 2 sides, Sha&Co stationery. ZJJF Jahnke.
> Last paragraph ("What a lot …") written in the left-hand margin, at a right angle from main body.
> To JJ at 28b Campden Grove, London

11 See letters of 8 July 1931, note 12, and of 21 July 1931, note 6.
12 *Les Nouvelles littéraires, artistiques et scientifiques: hebdomadaire d'information, de critique et de bibliographie*, a weekly journal of literature, art and sciences, founded in 1922 by the publishing house Librairie Larousse. Their very first issue of 21 October featured the review of a Contemporary English Novel study mentioning Joyce.

  The issue of 11 July 1931 contained a note on Joyce and Nora's marriage, giving legacy issues as its main purpose and mentioning Giorgio's own recent marriage as well as Lucia's dancing career. https://gallica.bnf.fr/ark:/12148/bpt6k6442357q.item, and https://gallica.bnf.fr/ark:/12148/bpt6k64520309/f2.item.r=Joyce, accessed 22 November 2020.

13 Founded in 1911 by the journalist and novelist Maurice De Waleffe, the prestigious *Paris Midi* was the only French daily newspaper at the time to appear at noon. It ceased publication in 1944.

  On 4 July 1931 the newspaper had a note on the marriage that after 27 years legalized "the happiest of conjugal existences" (original in French). https://data.bnf.fr/fr/12143381/maurice_de_waleffe/ and https://gallica.bnf.fr/ark:/12148/bpt6k4732066p/f5.image.r=Joyce, accessed 22 November 2020.

July 21, 1931

Rocfoin
par Maintenon
Eure et Loir

Dear Mr Joyce,
 We have just received your letter of the 18th.[1] It was addressed to Mademoiselle Monnier and began Dear Miss Beach. Harpers and the Viking are bidding higher and higher.[2] It's a good thing you waited. You seem to be the only writer whose affairs are prospering. I'm glad the publishers know what's what. It's a good idea for Faber to take over O.E.[3] I'll see just how many copies remain when I go back to Paris. Also will let Pinker[4] know all about the editions of Ulysses.
 I think you were right to sign up with the Viking Press if they bid highest. They will probably do a great deal better for you in the future than they have done in the past.
 They will advertise your new book very much so as to get back what they spent and your other works will all profit by the new regime. And after all they were your first publishers.[5] I would have liked Harcourt or Harpers better as publishers just the same.
 It was very funny about your re-marriage and the thing signing the Marry-your-aunt-Bill.[6] The pictures of you and Mrs Joyce are quite good. You

---

1 There is no extant letter of that date; Beach may be referring to that of the 19th.
2 Joyce wrote to Beach: "Harper's now offer advance of £750 of 15% royalties and Vikings £850 of 15% royalties including a signed edition on special paper of 150 copies. Pinker says Harpers is a good firm but their list is too big and that the Vikings are the only American firm which has weathered the recent storm well and that they have plenty of money (...) To revert to W i P there will be an English and an American contract both amounting to an advance of 15% of £1250 about 160,000 frs." (*JJtoSB*, 19 July 1931, p. 173)
3 *Our Exagmination*. See letter of 8 July 1931, note 8. "Sheets of [the Shakespeare and Company] edition were later sold to both Faber & Faber, London, and New Directions, Norfolk, Connecticut, who bound them with inserted title pages" (Slo + Ca, B.10, p. 78). Faber republished the collection in 1936, New Directions in 1939 (Deming 1977, p. 199, item 4906).
4 See letter of 27 May 1931, note 3.
5 Joyce's first American publication, *Dubliners* (1916), was actually not by Viking Press, but by Benjamin Huebsch, who back then had his own publishing firm, which later merged with Viking. With Joyce's loyalty being primarily to Huebsch, the contract with Viking for *Work in Progress* contained a clause providing that "if Huebsch left for another firm, he had an option for taking the contract with him". (Fitch, p. 319)
6 Joyce and Nora Barnacle got married on 4 July 1931, Joyce's father's birthday, legalizing their relationship after 27 years spent together. Joyce wrote to Beach that the strenuous part of

look young enough, both of you to be getting married for the first time and the bride is very pretty.

I have just received the copy of Eliot's letter[7] that Myrsine sent me with other things a week ago last Saturday. The envelope had been misdirected and went around the country and was returned to the rue de l'Odéon.

With best greetings

yours very sincerely
Sylvia Beach

I received your letter only this morning and I suppose you signed the contract with the Viking yesterday. So it is too late for me to veto it even I had wanted to.[8]

Mrs Crosby[9] wants to know whether she can do an edition de luxe of Chamber Music, at the Black Sun Press.

Adrienne says she approves of your decisions.

---

the wedding ceremony was when "the registrar refused to solemnise it, saying we should be divorced first." (*JJtoSB*, 19 July 1931, p. 174). Joyce had fabricated a story that he had already married Nora in Trieste in 1904, but that "in order to legalize his will he had to get married under English law." (Fitch, p. 317f.). As Beach wrote to her sister Holly, Joyce "thoroughly enjoyed the scandal created by the press". (qt. ibid.) "While I was signing the roll the King was signing the new law which the English call the Marry-your-Aunt Bill", Joyce went on in his 19 July letter to Beach. "His Majesty may soon have to sign another which might be called the Marry-your-Wife Bill."

"The Marriage (Prohibited Degrees of Relationship) Bill made legal the marriage of a man with his deceased wife's niece by marriage and of a woman with her deceased husband's nephew by marriage. It was passed by the House of Commons in May and by the House of Lords in July and received Royal Assent on 31 July 1931." (*Letters III*, note 2, p. 221). Ellmann mentions the London paper *Evening Standard*, which "carried on the front page a headline and a photograph of the newlyweds." (*JJII*, p. 638) And Joyce writes to Beach, "there are heaps more cuttings". (*JJtoSB*, 19 July 1931, p. 174). See preceding letter, notes 12f., and Joyce's account in a letter to Giorgio and Helen Joyce, 9 July 1931 (ZJJF Jahnke).

7   See letter of 8 July 1931, note 6.
8   Sic. Beach significantly failed to write "if", thus unwittingly turning the conditional into a statement of fact. Joyce had written, "[i]f you dislike or disapprove of the Vikings offer wire me so early on Monday as I must sign or decline that afternoon." (*JJtoSB*, 19 July 1931, p. 173-4). 21 July 1931 was a Tuesday. See also INTRODUCTION to the 1930s, p. 128f.
9   Caresse Crosby (1891-1970), American poet and wife of the poet Harry Crosby (1898-1929). In 1922, they went to Paris to escape the puritanism of their country, Harry turning into one of the most flamboyant of all American expatriates. Initially founded in 1928 to publish their own works, the Crosbys' Black Sun Press soon became noted for publishing modernist writers in limited deluxe editions. It was Hemingway who introduced the Crosbys to Joyce. Apart from *Tales Told of Shem and Shaun* (1929) the Black Sun Press published Joyce's *Collected Poems* (1936). (Slo + Ca A.36, p. 48, and A.44, p. 56f.; Kahn and Rood, p. 85ff.)

ALS, 1 leaf, 2 sides. On neutral paper. ZJJF Jahnke.
"I received your letter only this morning ..." written on top margin recto, above date and sender's address; "Mrs Crosby wants to know ..." written below date and sender's address; "Adrienne says ..." etc. written left of signature.
To JJ at 28b Campden Grove, London

August 6, 1931

Dear Mr Joyce,

I got your letter enclosing copy of Mr Monro's[1] letter to the Frankfürter Zeitung[2] this morning.[3] Ivan Goll[4] came to see me on Tuesday. He had come last week but I was away. He said he had had a correspondence with you[5] on the subject of the F.Z. affair and I understood he had agreed with you to put the matter entirely into the hands of the Rhein Verlag.[6] He said he himself could do nothing here and that the F.Z. representative here could do nothing. I asked him the representative's name and address but he got cross and didn't seem to want any of us to do anything about the matter here. I insisted on the representative's coming to see me so he said he would see him and send him around, but he didn't give me his address. He assured me that everything was to be left in the hands of Rhein Verlag. Georgio was in my shop at the same time and I suppose he has told you what Goll said. I had the impression that Goll didn't want to mix up in this affair and didn't want the F.Z. man here to come into it either. One reason is, I imagine, that he and his wife are getting ready to go to Challes-les-Eaux in Savoie for a cure for her. But I think he should attend to this just the same. He represents the Rhein Verlag here and should take action from this end. But he is very difficult to get hold of. I called him up at nine o'clock and he had already gone out, his wife said. I sent him a 'pneu'[7]

---

1 Originally Harriet Shaw Weaver's solicitors in London, Monro Saw & Company were by then also Joyce's legal representatives in England.
2 The *Frankfurter Zeitung*, founded in 1856 and banned by the Nazis in 1943, was a liberal German daily newspaper of high repute, particularly due to its *feuilleton*. After the war, in 1949, it was re-established as the *Frankfurter Allgemeine Zeitung*, still an influential newspaper.
3 On 30 July 1931, Monro Saw & Co. wrote a letter to the editor, inquiring about a short story, "Vielleicht ein Traum" ("Perchance to Dream") that the *Frankfurter Zeitung* had mistakenly published under Joyce's name earlier in July. "Our client has had no communication with you or with Madame Kafka and the text is not his. We invite you to inform us how your paper came into possession of this manuscript and what other explanations you have to offer." (Princeton). The story turned out to be by a young unknown British writer, Michael Joyce, rendered into German by the translator Irene Kafka. What was probably Kafka's and the F.Z. editor's accidental mistake greatly irritated Joyce, so much so that he drew on a number of people to protest on his behalf. Thus the incident turned into a full-blown affair. For a fuller account see INTRODUCTION to the 1930s, pp. 133-141.
4 See letter of 5 November 1926, note 3.
5 See *Letters III*, p. 224, for Joyce's letter of 30 July 1931 to Ivan Goll, which concludes: "*Perchance a Dream*, but certainly an outrage".
6 See letter of 16 September 1926, note 13, and note 10 below.
7 See letter of 24 July 1924, note 10.

last evening to come round to-day if possible about a translation of "Chamber Music" that a young German had just left with me. I would have sent it right on to you but the young fella said he was afraid to entrust it to the post. It wasn't his translation but was by a friend of his and this was the only copy or something and belonged to someone's mother (he spoke only German and a friend who interpreted into French knew almost no French). It's a beautiful MS. all in German script.[8]

Georgio has just been in. We are now convinced, both of us, that the Rhein Verlag is taking over the matter so as to get the damages that are rightfully yours. We must get the better of them if that is their game. The business must be handled through Messrs Monro, Saw & Co and I do hope it hasn't already been settled out of court by the Rhein Verlag, they pocketing a large sum for damages.

I supposed that if they were suing the F.Z. for damages it was for you. They have no right to anything themselves.[9] This was a case of making use of your name only and a very serious offence it is. But the Rhein Verlag doesn't come into it at all. Shall I write to Dr Brody[10] and say that your lawyers are doing

---

8   No such manuscript is known to exist. Neither is there a German translation of Joyce's first collection of poems *Chamber Music* (London: Elkin Mathews, 1907) by a translator named Schiller (see following letter of 11 August 1931). In fact, Joyce was at that time trying to arrange for a German translation of the poems. As he wrote to Beach in early September 1931: "... I asked [Brody] to get Felix Beran of Zurich to translate C.M." (*JJtoSB*, [no date], p. 179). The Austrian-Swiss poet Felix Beran (1868-1937), whom Joyce first met in Zurich during World War I, translated some poems from *Pomes Penyeach*, but none from *Chamber Music*. Eventually, only a few poems from *Chamber Music* were published in German during Joyce's lifetime, in a German anthology of British poetry, a journal, and a newspaper respectively: *Britanniens Neue Dichtung* (Münster 1923), ed. by Paul Selver, contained poem I, translated by Karl Arns. *Die Christliche Welt* (43/6, 1929) printed poem XXXII in Karl Thieme's translation, while the *Frankfurter Zeitung* (5 December 1930) published seven poems translated by Alastair [Baron Hans Henning Voigt]. (Slo + Ca, p. 115, and Füger, p. 430).

9   Rhein-Verlag, where Joyce's work had been appearing since 1926, had the exclusive rights on his works in German. This was the reason publisher Daniel Brody gave for inquiring at the *Frankfurter Zeitung* about their authorisation in this matter. (Cf. Daniel Brody to Hermann Broch, letter of 28 July 1931, in: Hack and Kleiss, column 225 [no pagination]).

10 Dr Daniel Brody (1883-1969), Joyce's German (Swiss) publisher, who took over Rhein-Verlag in 1929, when its registered office moved from Basel to Zurich and the operating office to Munich, where Brody was based (Hack and Kleiss, Appendix VI, column 1229f.). Born in Budapest into a family of newspaper publishers and printers, Brody had earned a law degree before he became the director of his uncle's firm. In 1918 he moved to Munich, where he changed to book publishing, joining in 1920 the prestigious Kurt Wolff publishing house, first publishers of writers like Franz Kafka and Franz Werfel. While it was Goll who had first discovered him for Rhein-Verlag, Joyce owed most of his early German

whatever is necessary and that I hope you will get a large sum from the paper for damages. I'm sorry I didn't know about all this sooner. I came back to my shop a week ago yesterday and was only away on Saturday and Sunday. I thought Georgio would have told you. I have seen him every day. Please let me know what replies you have from the F.Z. and whether you wrote to Dr Brody. With best greetings, yours sincerely

Sylvia Beach

Georgio asked me to tell you to be very careful not to accept a German cheque from any of these people just now. It might not be worth a penny.[11]

    I don't know what you mean by the question whether I disposed of a Ms that you gave me. I have never let go of a single crumb of any of your Mss. Please tell me what you are thinking of.

> ALS, 2 leaves, 4 pages, Sha&Co stationery. ZJJF Jahnke.
>
> "Georgio asked me to tell you ..." etc. written in top-left margin as well as on right of stationery logo on 1st leaf.
>
> To JJ at 28b Campden Grove, London, or The Lord Warden Hotel, Dover (where he went on 7 August).

    career to Brody. When he was looking for his own small press, Brody bought Rhein-Verlag for the sole purpose of "becom[ing] James Joyce's publisher," as he replied when asked about his choice from among several small publishing houses (Hack and Kleiss, Appendix IV, columns 1176-79).

[11] In the course of the German banking crisis 1931, the country's monetary system had virtually collapsed.

"SHAKESPEARE AND COMPANY"
— SYLVIA BEACH —
12, RUE DE L'ODÉON, 12
PARIS (VIe)

August 6   1931

Dear Mr Joyce,

I got your letter enclosing copy of Mr Monro's letter to the Frankfurter Zeitung this morning. Ivan Goll came to see me on Tuesday. He had come last week but I was away. He said he had had a correspondence with you on the subject of the F.Z. affair and I understood he had agreed with you to put the matter entirely into the hands of the Rhein Verlag. He said he himself could do nothing here and that the F.Z. representative here could do nothing. I asked him the representative's name and address but he got cross and didn't seem to want any of us to do anything about the matter here. I insisted on the representative's coming to see me so he said he would see him and send him

[margin notes:]
Georgio asked me to tell you to be very careful not to accept a german cheque from any of these people just now. It might not be worth a penny.

I don't know whether you mean by the question whether I have disposed of a MS that you gave me. I have never let go of a single Mss. Please tell me what you are thinking of.

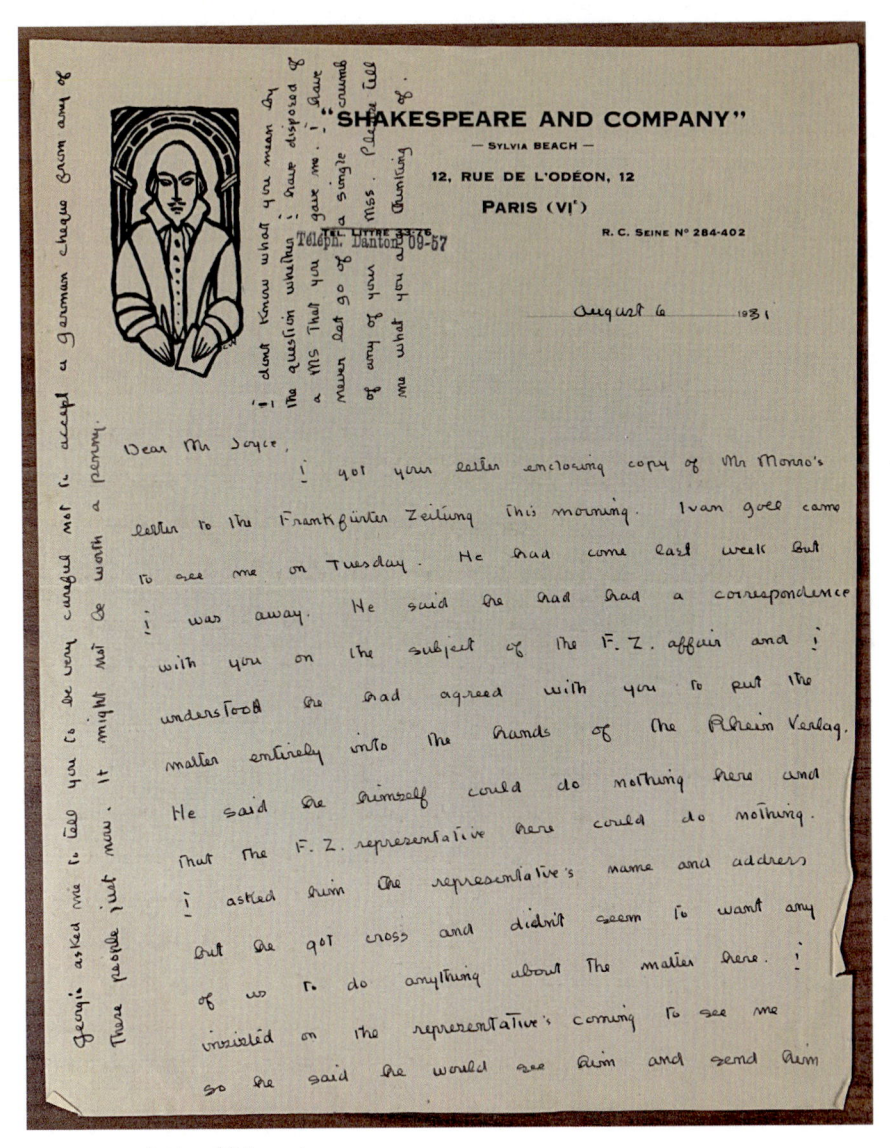

FIGURE 15   Letter of 6 August 1931
© SYLVIA BEACH ESTATE

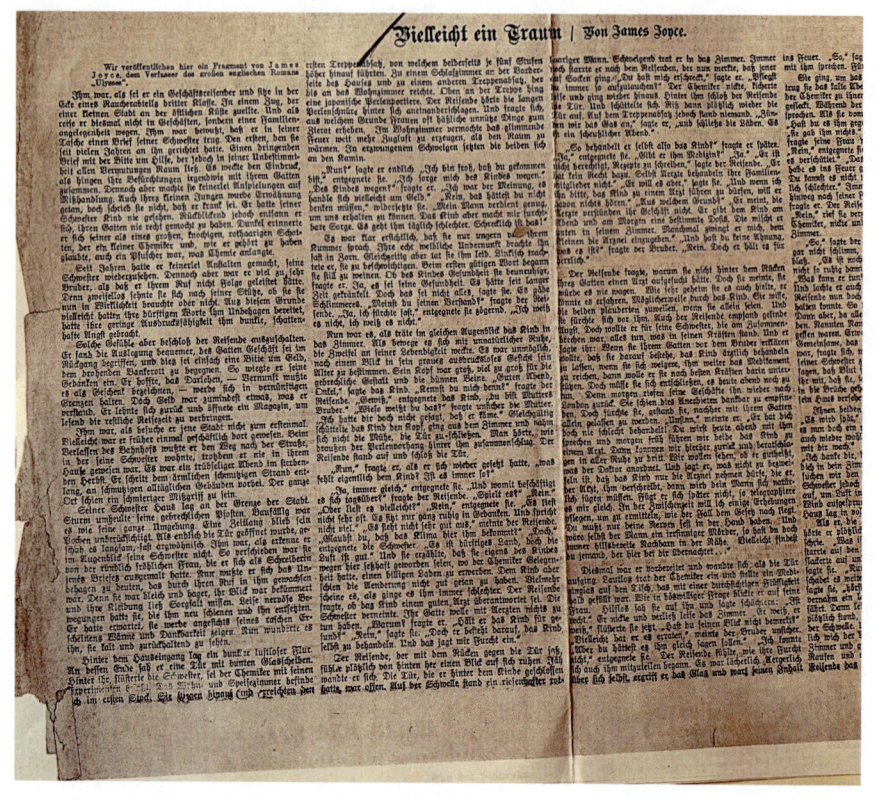

FIGURE 16 "Vielleicht ein Traum": a short story published under Joyce's name. *Frankfurter Zeitung*, 19 July 1931
COURTESY OF SYLVIA BEACH ESTATE

August 11, 1931

Dear Mr Joyce,

I will return to you tomorrow Dr Brody's letter.[1] When he found there was nothing to be got out of the affair for the Rhein Verlag[2] he wanted to drop it.[3] It's funny that the F.Z. doesn't even want to publish a rectification.[4] They all prefer to let it drop. Of course, as Brody says, it is well to be on good terms with such a fine paper, but I don't see why they should get off scot free after such an offense. I will write them a protest and also to Frau Kafka who must be crazy to do what she has done.[5] Colum[6] gave me the address of a journalist friend of his in Berlin: Hans Trausil,[7] Uhland Strasse 175, Gartenhaus 1, Berlin W 15. He says

---

1   Balancing between indignation and prudence, Brody writes that he has insistently asked the F.Z. to publish a rectification and is going to proceed against Irene Kafka, who he believes is the only one to blame in this affair. Advising Joyce to treat the newspaper with "special consideration" in view of their "consistent friendliness" to his work, he concludes by saying that after all, his legal advisor does not recommend to venture on a lawsuit. (Brody to Joyce, 30 July 1931. The English translation of this letter, which Beach mentions later in the present letter, is at Princeton.).
2   See letters of 16 September 1926, note 13, and of 6 August 1931, note 10.
3   However, in a letter written some days after Brody's, it was Beach who suggested to Brody that the Rhein-Verlag should let the matter drop: "Mr Goll ... agrees with me that the affair is entirely between Mr Joyce and the Frankfurter Zeitung and that it is quite unnecessary for the Rhein Verlag to come into it at all." (8 August, 1931, ZJJF Jahnke and Princeton. Cf. also Brody to Joyce, letter of 10 August 1931, ZJJF Jahnke).
4   Two days earlier, on 9 August, the F.Z. had in fact published a rectification of sorts, entitled "Michael and James".
5   See letter of 6 August 1931, note 3. It was Irene Kafka who had recommended the story for publication to the F.Z. She later claimed that it had been her secretary's mistake to ascribe the story to James Joyce (letter to Monro Saw & Co., 17 August 1931, Princeton). See also INTRODUCTION to the 1930s, pp. 134-39.
6   See note letter of 25 August 1930, note 2.
7   Hans Trausil (1890-1970). German poet, translator and editor. Among his translations is an anthology of Irish poetry in German, containing an introduction by Padraic Colum and a poem from Joyce's *Chamber Music*: "I hear an army charging upon the land" / "Ich höre eine Heerschar": *Irische Harfe. Gedichte vom achten bis ins zwanzigste Jahrhundert. Aus dem Gälischen und Anglo-Irischen übertragen von Hans Trausil*. Ebenhausen, Langewiesche-Brandt, 1957, reedited 1996.
    On 5 September 1931, Colum forwarded to Joyce a letter he had received from Trausil concerning the F.Z. affair, in which Trausil suggested that the Rhein-Verlag "insist upon a clear apology from the Frankfurter Zeitung, possibly in collaboration with the Irish minister, in case the paper continues its shabby attitude. Nothing undertaken privately will impress the Jewish journaille in this country." (August 30, 1931) To which Beach added in pencil: "This fellow holds Nazi views? SB" and in the left margin: "Colum's friend!!!" (Princeton)

he would be glad to do anything he could in the matter. And Colum is going to write to the Irish Minister in Berlin and ask him to send in a protest to the F.Z.[8] But he has to know what date this story appeared. I would like to know too. Goll[9] gave me the address of the correspondent here, but says he is away at present. Goll suddenly changed his tone and said of course this was not the Rhein Verlag's business.

I sent you the MS of the German translation of <u>Chamber Music</u>. The young friend of the translator told me he was writing to you. He had paid a visit to Gide and so maybe he is of that sect.[10] The translator, named Schiller,[11] is a young medical student, he says.

Mr Pollinger sent me a letter from Claude Kendall[12] who signs himself Aaron Sussmann.[13] He is quite put out. Myrsine says that in July a number of American Jewish book dealers came to the shop and said a great deal about how the sale of <u>Ulysses</u> was finished. They questioned her and she told them on the contrary it was selling very well, which was true. Sales are quite good this summer.[14] But they shrugged their shoulders and were as discouraging and pessimistic as they could be, she says. They are the people that are prowling around to see if they can lay their hands on <u>Ulysses</u>. Huebsch[15] came to

---

8   There is no evidence that Colum actually wrote such a letter.

9   See letter of 5 November 1926, note 3.

10   See letter of 23 June [?1924], note 1. "That sect" refers to André Gide's Marxism.

11   See letter of 6 August 1931, note 8.

12   The letter from Claude Kendall Publishers to Pollinger is a reply to Beach's demand of $25,000 for her rights on *Ulysses*. (See letter of 5 June 1931, note 4) They called the demand "absurd" and argued that Beach's refusal to allow an American edition was both against her own and Joyce's financial interests. The two pirated editions, expensive though they were, sold very well, without either of them deriving one penny of profit. Moreover, "A legitimate trade edition at from three to five dollars would have a splendid college sale". They withdrew the offer, only to renew it in the last paragraph, "if, at any time in the future, she changes her mind, or is persuaded by Mr. Joyce to do so." (Princeton) On Kendall see letter of 29 May 1931, notes 2 and 3.

13   Aaron Sussman, a former advertising agent, was collaborating with Kendall and he was writing here on behalf of Claude Kendall publishers. Sussman later had his own advertising company, Sussman and Sugar, Inc., which specialized in book advertising. Most notably he collaborated with Random House and designed for them the guide "How to Enjoy James Joyce's Great Novel *Ulysses*" printed to accompany their edition to help perplexed first readers. (Turner, p. 205f.).

14   As her record books for 1930-32 note, Beach had sold 133 copies of *Ulysses* in July 1931, while in the month she was writing this letter, she sold 307 copies, by far the largest figure that year (with a monthly average of 134 copies). (Princeton)

15   See letter of 6 June 1931, note 1. Huebsch had already sent a first proposal to both Joyce and Beach on 16 May 1931 (Fitch, pp. 316).

see me and was typical too. He said if the ban were removed it wouldn't sell any more at all in America.[16] Specially as everybody who should have a copy has a copy now, but that for your sake the most important was to have the stigma removed, the Viking Press would fix the courts beforehand so that the book would not be prosecuted, and prevent all publicity so that its publication would pass off quietly like any other book's, but to manage this they must feel that the rights belong to them to go ahead with a free hand and no expense. Huebsch was very sulky in his manners to me.

A young Englishman named Mason[17] who has been teaching in Germany is writing an interesting essay on you. He has a theory about the Joyce of Chamber Music and Ulysses[18] and is plunged in your work night and day he says, and he knows it well. He doesn't agree with Messrs Gilbert,[19] Colum, Curtius,[20] Gorman,[21] about some points, and modestly tells of some ideas of his own about you. I loaned him my set of Transition Work in Progress which he is reading very thoroughly. Perhaps you would like to see his essay if he gets it finished some time.[22] He is making an English translation of Dr Brody's letter for me and will bring it tomorrow. The Associated Press called up for a story about you. What about the F.Z. one? Shall I? They are to call up on Thursday again. I hope Mrs Joyce got the NeoLyse[23] I sent. With best greetings to her and yourself

---

16   In January 1934, just a month after the ban was lifted, Random House published the first legal American edition, which sold very well. See INTRODUCTION to the 1930s, note 4.
17   Eudo C.[Colecestra] Mason (1901-1969). He became one of Britain's most distinguished scholars of German literature. Specializing in German and English Romanticism, he also wrote two essays on Joyce in German (Lernout and Van Mierlo, p. 268), as well as an obituary of Joyce for a Basel newspaper, where he was teaching at the university during World War II. (*Sonntagsblatt der Basler Nachrichten*, 19 January 1941) Cf. Vogel, p. 175f.
18   On Mason's view of Joyce's works see his essay "James Joyce", in: Sühnel and Riesner, pp. 285-292.
19   See letter of 12 May 1931, note 10.
20   See letter of 2 November 1926, note 4.
21   See undated letter [after 14 June, before 22 July 1924], note 4.
22   Mason's essay on *Finnegans Wake* was to be published in the Swiss arts magazine DU, December 1948, and republished in Mason's study *Exzentrische Bahnen: Studien zum Dichterbewusstsein der Neuzeit*. Göttingen: Vandenhoeck und Ruprecht, 1963, pp. 284-92.
23   Joyce wrote to Beach on 9 August 1931: "Will you please ask anybody crossing to bring a box of *Neolyse* cachets. My wife has to take those and they cannot be had here." A lysis (French: *lyse*) therapy is indicated in the case of deep vein thrombosis in thigh or leg, for instance.

Sylvia Beach

Mr Pugh[24] sent me some beautiful photos of the Liffey and bridges and Dublin.

> ALS, 2 leaves, 4 sides, Sha&Co stationery. ZJJF Jahnke.
> "Mr Pugh sent me some beautiful photos of the Liffey and bridges and Dublin." written on the right of the stationery logo of recto 1.
> To JJ at Lord Warden Hotel, Dover

---

24   Thomas W. Pugh (1883-1968). A Dubliner from a family of old Dublin glassmakers, whom Joyce met in Paris and who "pleased him by knowing *Ulysses* and Dublin almost as intimately as he did himself." (*JJII*, p. 622) Pugh was also the first to walk through Dublin in the footsteps of Bloom and Stephen and to take pictures of Ulyssean locations.

By 1931, Pugh was one of the few Dubliners with whom Herbert Gorman was in regular contact for the second edition of his Joyce biography. Joyce would later ask Pugh for Dublin photographs to be published in the Random House pamphlet mentioned in note 13. (Joyce to Pugh, 6 August 1934, *Letters III*, pp. 313-14) Both Pugh and his family's products feature in *Finnegans Wake:* "Mind your pughs and keaoghs" (349.03) and "pughglasspanelfitted" (76.11f). (Gibbons, p. 192 and passim).

August 13, 1931

Dear Mr Joyce

You did quite right to refuse such a compromise as the one suggested by Mr Pinker's agent in Vienna.[1] Have they no representative in Germany who could attend to this thing properly for you? I enclose a letter from Brody[2] and the cutting from last Sunday's F.Z. that he has sent me. You have probably seen it already. From what I can make out of it the F.Z. is trying to laugh it off and I think if this is the reparation they are making – a cheap little story with "Michael and James" as the heading – it is disgraceful.[3] I am ordering this number of the paper from Hachette[4] and will send a copy to Georgio and ask him what he thinks of it. It's a pity he isn't here now to translate it for me, but I think I get the gist of it and it seems to me both 'fresh' and defiant. Is that right. But you will never get anything out them, I fear. From what people tell me and the attitude of the F.Z. itself there doesn't seem to be any hope of a case. But of course I don't know what the law is. Someone should represent you there and demand proofs of the existence of Michael Joyce and look into the matter. Georgio would have been the one but of course he can't get away just now. Do you know anyone?

Yours sincerely
Sylvia Beach

---

1 Ernst Hitschmann, Vienna, acting on behalf of Pinker's London agency. (Cf. Joyce's letter of 21 August 1931 to Giorgio and Helen Joyce, Jahnke). Hitschmann's "compromise" probably refers to Brody's suggestion "to get the F.Z. pay the Rhein-Verlag the fee they were going to pay Mme Kafka for her 'translation'", which Joyce mentioned in his letter to her, together with the letter he had received from Hitschmann. (*JJtoSB*, 12 August 1931, p. 175).

2 See letter of 6 August 1931, note 10. In his letter to Beach of 11 August 1931, Brody wrote about his continued efforts to get an apology from the *Frankfurter Zeitung* and "to let the true story out to everybody in the least interested in literary matters". As to the legal handling of the case, he was "perfectly happy with your suggestion to keep myself and the Rhein-Verlag out of all this." (Princeton).

3 "Michael und James" appeared in the F.Z. issue of 9 August 1931 (Princeton). An English translation of the article, which was made for Beach, is in zJJF Jahnke. Placing the blame for the mistake entirely on Irene Kafka, the newspaper argued that even a literary editor had no way of telling that the text was not Joyce's: "Perhaps it was an early work, perhaps it was a by-product, or perhaps a work written for self-relief in an hour of relaxation as Goethe turning from his 'Elective Affinities' wrought a story of a man of fifty ..." For further details see INTRODUCTION to the 1930s, p. 138f.

4 At the time, both a chain of bookstores and a publishing company, which grew out of the first bookshop established by Louis Hachette in 1826. https://www.hachette.com/fr/une-histoire-un-avenir/une-construction-patiente/, accessed 25 November 2020.

ALS, 1 leaf, 2 sides, Sha&Co stationery. ZJJF Jahnke.
Enclosures: letter from D. Brody to Beach and newspaper cutting, at Princeton
To JJ at Lord Warden Hotel, Dover
Dating: There are two letters of the same date. Since this letter opens with a comment on Joyce's letter of 12 August, which asks her to reply "by return", it is likely the first letter Beach wrote him that day, all the more so as she used to get her mail around 8.30 in the morning (see her letter of 15 July).

August 13, 1931

Dear Mr Joyce,
    I have just received the enclosed letter from Dr Brody.[1] I asked Goll[2] to come to see me and he read a copy I made of the article in the F.Z. which they suppose will make amends for what they have done. While Goll was here your wire came.[3] Goll agreed that the F.Z. was very flippant. I told him I wished to send them a letter which they must print on the front page stating that the story that they had printed was spurious but he said they would refuse outright to print any statement of mine on the subject. That it must come from you only – they would not dare to refuse your demand. Only your name would have any weight with them. But he said what good was it to put yourself on bad terms with them. I told him I didn't think you cared a damn about that, but that the F.Z. was certainly going to be very much disliked by you after this business. I am so indignant about their behaviour. I feel that it is the same as with Roth[4] and the other people. Nothing can be done against them. But Adrienne is going to help me with some letters to the 'Intran'[5] and 'Nouvelles Littéraires'[6] and I will tell the whole story to the Associated Press and everybody I see, and do all I can to expose the F.Z. I hope the other papers won't be afraid to mention it. We'll see.

Yours sincerely
Sylvia Beach

Did you ask Brody to represent you in the matter? when it happened?
    He speaks as though you had.[7]

    ALS, 1 leaf, 2 sides, Sha&Co stationery. zJJF Jahnke.
    "Did you ask Brody ..." written to the left of the salutation.
    Enclosure: copy of letter from D. Brody to Joyce, 12 August 1931, at zJJF Jahnke.
    To JJ at Lord Warden Hotel, Dover

1 See letter of 6 August 1931, note 10. The enclosed letter of 12 August was addressed to Joyce, with "a copy of this letter to Miss Beach in case you are perchance in Paris". Beach forwarded Brody's letter to Joyce in Dover, since the original was sent to his London address.
2 See letter of 5 November 1926, note 3.
3 "= NINETEENTH JULY ASK COLM FORWARD PAPER ALSO INFORM ASSOCIATED PRESS = JAMES JOYCE =" (*JJtoSB*, 13 August 1931, p. 175). The date refers to the appearance of the story "Vielleicht ein Traum" in the *Frankfurter Zeitung*.
4 See letters of 1 September 1926, note 4, and of 9 September 1926, note 2.
5 See letter of 1 May 1931, note 2.
6 See letter of 17 July 1931, note 12.
7 Neither of Brody's letters (to Beach and to Joyce respectively) gives that impression. Cf. note 2 to preceding letter.

August 17, 1931

Dear Mr Joyce,

We went away Friday night for the holiday – everything was closed on Saturday – and this morning I found your express letter of the 14th and the envelope which I am returning to you herewith to show you how it was open at one end when it came. A strip of paper had been pasted across it, was it by you, and this was cut open.

Madame Tisserand[1] knows nothing about it. Is someone in Dover spying on you?

I kept the letters until Colum[2] came in and showed them to him and gave him the F.Z. Nicholson's letter is satisfactory. Are you going to take his advice?[3] His friend Cyril Connolly[4] is in town just now. Adrienne is going to write to the Nouvelles Littéraires[5] in time for the next number and will ask Prévost (Jean)[6] who is now 'chef d'Informations' on the 'Intransigeant'[7] whether there is a chance of giving the affair publicity in the French papers. At present they are adopting an attitude of special friendliness towards Germany. The A.P.[8] didn't call up on Thursday. I waited to see if they would call up on

---

1 The concièrge at 12, rue de l'Odéon.
2 See letter of 25 August 1930, note 2.
3 Sir Harold Nicolson (1886-1968). British diplomat, biographer and author associated with the Bloomsbury group; husband of the writer Vita Sackville-West. Joyce's letter of 13 August 1931 to Beach apparently had among its enclosures a letter by Nicolson on the F.Z. issue (*JJtoSB*, 13 August 1931, p. 175f.). Ellmann mentions that in a letter to Joyce, Nicolson "urged him to demand apology on threat of suit" (*JJII*, p. 640). Nicolson's letter also dates from 13 August: at that time, mail posted before noon was delivered the same day within Britain (London to Dover, in this case).
4 Cyril Connolly (1903-1974). English novelist and literary critic, contributor to many major English newspapers, who in 1939 founded and edited *Horizon*, an influential magazine of contemporary literature. https://www.britannica.com/biography/Cyril-Connolly, accessed 25 November 2020.
5 See letter of 17 July 1931, note 12.
6 Jean Prévost (1901-1944), a man of many talents: novelist and boxing champion (who once fought a match with Hemingway), political activist and rugby player, essayist and journalist, who wrote on wide variety of subjects, such as literature, architecture, philosophy and cinema as well as history. Prévost had started at the *Intransigeant* as its *secrétaire de rédaction*. From 1924-1940 he was an editor of the *Nouvelle Revue Française* (*NRF*) and in 1925 he also joined Adrienne Monnier as an editorial partner in her literary review *Navire d'Argent* (Fitch, p. 188; Bluteau and Quellet, passim). For *NRF*, see letter of 22 February 1921, note 3; for *Navire d'Argent* see letter of 19 August 1926, note 1.
7 See letter of 1 May 1931, note 2.
8 Associated Press.

Friday and now I will try to get them to-day. From what H.N.[9] says the F.Z. is none too scrupulous. Will you take Nicholson's advice? Goll[10] said the F.Z. would never 'crawl down' and you could never win a suit against them but that doesn't seem to be H.N.'s opinion.

I hope you received the 'Revue des Deux Mondes'.[11] Please tell Mrs Joyce I was very much pleased to get a letter from her, and give her my love.[12]

Yours very sincerely
Sylvia Beach

> ALS, 1 leaf, 2 sides, Sha&Co stationery, ZJJF Jahnke.
> Enclosure: letter from Joyce, *JJtoSB*, p. 176.
> To JJ at Lord Warden Hotel, Dover

9   Harold Nicolson.
10 See letter of 5 November 1926, note 3.
11 See letter of 1 July 1931, note 6.
12 Nora Joyce's letter to Beach of 13 August 1931 is at Buffalo. The last of 6 extant letters that Nora wrote to her, it was the first in which she addresses Beach as Sylvia. In this letter, she thanked her for sending the Neolyse medication.

August 21, 1931

Dear Mr Joyce,

Yesterday I received your express letter or plutôt envelope (you wrote so many letters you used up all the stationery of the Lord Warden Hotel)[1] and today the Rheinverlag[2] and F.Z. letters etc[3] which I am returning to you herewith with the copy of certain passages in the Rheinverlag contract that you wanted. The question is: has the Rheinverlag anything whatever to do with the publication in a paper of a spurious work attributed to you? Does your name belong to the Rheinverlag? Adrienne has not done anything with the papers here yet because she wanted to see Prévost[4] about it. We dined at his house last evening – Soupault[5] was there and I told them everything and they both said they would occupy themselves with the business. Prévost asked me to give him the F.Z. with the story and their explanation so I am writing to Dr Brody to ask him to send me a number of copies. If I had had the cutting Brody sent me I would have given it immediately to Prévost but I sent it to you. He will try to get something into the 'Intran'.[6] He is 'chef d'informations' and on very good terms with Bailby.[7]

I sent for the United Press correspondent and he came to see me (last Monday) and promised to send out the "story".[8]

Thank you for the Shakespeare Cliff card.[9]

---

1 A hotel in Dover, where Joyce had stayed briefly in August 1930 and again from 7 to ca. 21 August 1931. In the 19th century, the Lord Warden was Dover's top hotel, which attracted a rich clientele. Among its guests were Louis Napoleon, Charles Dickens and William Makepiece Thackeray.
2 See letters of 16 September 1926, note 13, and of 6 August 1931, note 10.
3 The F.Z. *feuilleton* editors' letter to Ernst Hitschmann, Pinker's representative in Vienna, informed him of the rectification that had appeared in the newspaper on 9 August. See letter of 13 August 1931, note 3. For all letters on the *Frankfurter Zeitung* affair between the newspaper, Rhein-Verlag and Joyce (or his representatives), as well as other correspondence on the issue see APPENDIX C, Overview of Correspondence re F.Z. Affair.
4 See preceding letter, note 6.
5 See letter of 25 April 1931, note 2.
6 *L'Intransigeant*. See letter of 1 May 1931, note 2.
7 Léon Bailby (1867-1954). Editor-in-chief of *L'Intransigeant* from 1905-1932. Under his direction the newspaper became the first in France to introduce a daily literary section. https://www.lemonde.fr/archives/article/1954/01/20/leon-bailby-est-mort_2036370_1819218.html, accessed, 27 November 2020.
8 Beach gave an interview on the F.Z. affair to a Mr. Macmillan of the United Press of America.
9 The undated item no 183 (from August 1931) in *JJtoSB*, to which this letter is replying, was written on a picture postcard from Dover. A part of its white cliffs is named after Shakespeare (*King Lear*).

Thornton Wilder[10] asked news of you and your work. I showed Soupault your letter about Michael Joyce and the Blue Peter[11] and he was amused.

Yours very sincerely
Sylvia Beach

Gillet's article[12] is making a sensation here.

> ALS, 1 leaf, 2 sides, Sha&Co stationery. ZJJF Jahnke.
> "Gillet's article...." written diagonally on the right of the stationery logo, beneath the telephone number in the letter head.
> Enclosures: letter from the *Frankfurter Zeitung* to Ernst Hitschmann, ZJJF Jahnke and *Letters III*, p. 226, and letter from D. Brody to Joyce, ZJJF Jahnke. Rhein-Verlag extracts missing.
> To JJ at Lord Warden Hotel, Dover or 28b Campden Grove, London

10   Thornton Wilder (1897-1975). American playwright and novelist. He was a friend of Beach's, especially during his sojourns in Paris in the early 1920s and again in 1926. (*Sha&Co*, p. 111).
11   In his letter of 19 August 1931, Joyce wrote that finally Michael Joyce, the author of "Vielleicht ein Traum", had been tracked down: "He is a contributor to a monthly magazine called *The Blue Peter* (i.e. the flag ships hoist when about to sail). This is a magazine run by Bibby Cunard Ellerman etc lines to encourage tourists to book for advertised cruises etc." (*JJtoSB*, p. 177) According to her biographers, it was Harriet Weaver who eventually discovered Michael Joyce. (Lidderdale and Nicholson, p. 306).
12   See letter of 1 July 1931, notes 5 and 6.

August 22, 1931

Dear Mr Joyce,

Your express letter enclosing letters from Pinker[1] and Nicholson[2] and the F.Z.[3] came just now, and I am returning them to you herewith, also Georgio's,[4] and one I got from a Mr Watanabe enclosing a letter from his friends in Japan who are translating <u>Ulysses</u>.[5] I have replied that I have sent it on to you, and to come to see me. I don't know exactly what they mean to do – publish <u>Ulysses</u> privately or what. They should arrange with a regular publisher for a Japanese edition and he pay you something.[6] What news have you ever had of the <u>Portrait of the Artist</u> that someone was translating?[7] I would like to know what to tell Mr Watanabe when he comes to see me.

I hope you and Mrs Joyce had a good journey back to London and that you are feeling better after your dose of Dover.

With best greetings
Sylvia Beach

---

1 See letter of 27 May 1931, note 3. The letter is a very short cover letter to the letter from the F.Z., for which see note 3.
2 See letter of 17 August 1931, note 3.
3 The *Frankfurter Zeitung*. See letter of 6 August 1931, notes 2 and 3. There is only one extant letter from the newspaper around that date, which Beach apparently had returned to Joyce in her previous letter (see above, note 3). However, she may have failed to enclose it, or else this refers to another F.Z. letter now lost.
4 Giorgio's letter to his father, dating from 18 August 1931, is also mainly concerned with the F.Z. issue. Sharing Joyce's general mistrust of other people, he advises him to be "very careful and keep Rhein-Verlag away from this affair". (ZJJF Jahnke).
5 Kazuo Watanabe (1901-1975), a Japanese scholar of French literature who spent a few years in Paris, later to become a notable scholar and translator of Rabelais and Erasmus. (Eishiro Ito, personal communication, email 13 May 2020) He contacted Beach on behalf of friends in Tokyo, Sadamu Nagamatsu, Hitoshi Ito, and Hisanori Tsujino, who were working on a Japanese translation of *Ulysses* and who in their letter to Joyce asked for his permission to publish it. (Letter of 20 August 1931 from Watanabe to Beach and its enclosure, a letter of 20 June 1931 from the three Japanese translators to Joyce; Buffalo).
6 The way they put it in their letter, their intention was just "to distribute [the book] among our small literary circles." (ibid.) On 4 September 1931 Beach wrote to them on Joyce's behalf, asking them to draw up a contract with Joyce and to find a regular publishing house (Beach to Nagamatsu et al.; Buffalo).
7 The translation of *A Portrait* by Matsuji Ono and Tomio Yokobori, published by Sogensha, appeared in Japan in 1932 (Slo + Ca, D 87, p. 122).

Goll[8] is going to give another broadcasting performance on you at Salzburg[9] early in September. He must be annoyed to have this other affair[10] happen just now. Brody loaned his record[11] and it got broken it seems. Goll would like to have another for the Frankfurt broadcasting and to give to Brody afterward. He is in a great hurry so I told him I would give him one I have here and arrange with Mr Ogden about it.[12]

I suppose Goll should have one for himself too in return for his propaganda, although after his indifference in the F.Z. affair maybe he doesn't deserve it. He certainly doesn't.

I show all the letters on the F.Z. affair to Colum. Mary[13] told me the plot of Vielleicht ein Traum

Enclosures:[14]
1   Georgio's letter
2   Pinker
3   "
4   Frankfurter Zeitung
5   Watanabe
6   friends of Watanabe
7   card of Watanabe

ALS, 1 leaf, 2 sides, Sha&Co stationery. ZJJF Jahnke.
"I suppose Goll should have ..." written from top to bottom in left margin of last paragraph underneath Beach's signature; "I show all the letters ..." written recto

---

8   See letter of 5 November 1926, note 3.
9   It should read Frankfurt, which is what Beach originally wrote, but then crossed out and overwrote with Salzburg. See letter of 27 August 1931 for this second broadcasting.
    Goll had done a radio performance after a script by Goll and the German theatre director Kurt Hirschfeld, which was broadcast by Radio Berlin around 11 April 1931. Goll chose a "discussion contradictoire" rather than the lecture format, while it is uncertain whether the passages read were from Joyce's works in general (Goll's letter of 25 March 1931 to Beach, Princeton) or exclusively from *Ulysses* (Brody's letter of 11 April 1931 to Beach, and enclosure, Buffalo).
10 The *Frankfurter Zeitung* incident.
11 The recording of the last pages of "Anna Livia Plurabelle". See letter of 27 May 1931, note 9.
12 To this, Joyce replied that he gave one to Brody and that "he sent another to Frankfurt. Both are wasted. If they want a third let them buy it." (*JJtoSB*, 27 August 1931, p. 178).
13 See letters of 25 August 1930, note 2, and of 25 April 1931, note 5.
14 Beach's double mention of Pinker in the list may well be a mistake, with item 3 being Nicolson's letter, which Beach mentions in her letter but does not list in this note.

from bottom to top on right of stationery logo. Enclosures list written on small pale blue note paper, recto, Sha&Co stationery.

Enclosures: letter from G. Joyce (with addition by Helen Joyce and postscript by Lucia Joyce), letter from R. Pinker, letter from the *Frankfurter Zeitung*, at zJJF Jahnke (see note 3). Letters from K. Watanabe to Beach and from his friends S. Nagamatsu et al. to Joyce, at Buffalo. Watanabe card at Buffalo xx. Letter from Nicolson missing.

To JJ at 28b Campden Grove, London

August 26, 1931

Dear Mr Joyce,

the papers you sent to Prévost[1] came on Monday. Adrienne had invited him and the Soupaults[2] to dinner that evening so I gave him his parcel and showed them all the copy of Kafka's letter[3] you sent me and they were much interested, and astonished at such a thing having happened to a paper of good standing. Prévost said it was plain that in <u>Michael and James</u> they intended to be insulting.[4] They looked over the F.Z. and <u>Blue Peter</u>[5] carefully, both Prévost and Soupault, and Prévost took them away and promised to do what he could on the Intran. I hope Soupault will do something too. Dr Brody[6] has now sent me 3 copies of the F.Z. July 19 and August 9 issues.[7]

Bill Bird[8] is not in Paris. He is 'en voyage' and the maid thinks he will not be back before next Monday. I saw a journalist we used to know Paul Schinkman[9] – he used to be on the Chicago Tribune – and told him the story and everybody else I have seen lately and Gorman[10] who dropped in the other day looking as if he had been on a good long bat.

Adrienne is in bed with an awful cold and cough.

I have sold a great many shilling HCEs and ALPs this summer, and since Gillet's article[11] the French are buying them.

---

1   See letter of 17 August 1931, note 6.
2   See letter of 25 April 1931, note 2.
3   Probably the letter that the translator of Michael Joyce's story in the *Frankfurter Zeitung* sent to Joyce's London lawyers Monro Saw & Co. on 17 August 1931. In this letter, she declared once more that while it had been her new secretary who mistook Michael for James, thinking "that there could only exist one sole Joyce, the author of Ulysses", it was her own oversight as she checked her secretary's writing. Kafka again expressed her "deepest regrets" in this "painful affair". (Princeton).
4   While "Michael und James", the rectification eventually published upon Joyce's insistence, was hardly meant to be insulting, the F.Z. editors did not, in fact, express any apologies for the mishap and certainly did not argue in a defensive manner.
5   See letter of 21 August 1931, note 11.
6   See letter of 6 August 1931, note 10.
7   The issues with Michael Joyce's story "Vielleicht ein Traum" and with "Michael und James" respectively.
8   See letter of 1 August 1924, note 7.
9   Paul Alfred Shinkman (1897-1975). A foreign correspondent for the *Chicago Tribune* who reported from Europe from the 1920s to the 1950s. Memorable were his reports on Charles Lindbergh's Atlantic flight and Hitler's rise to power. (Rechcigl, no pagination) Shinkman's article in the *Quarterly Review* on the American writers in Paris suggests that he knew Sylvia Beach quite well.
10 See undated letter [after 14 June, before 22 July 1924], note 4.
11 See letter of 1 July 1931, notes 5 and 6.

With best greetings to Mrs Joyce and yourself
Sylvia Beach

> ALS, 1 leaf, 2 sides, Sha&Co stationery. ZJJF Jahnke.
> To JJ at 28b Campden Grove, London

August 27, 1931

Dear Mr Joyce,

I am sending you herewith an uncrossed cheque[1] on London for eighty pounds. I am glad you are going to take a holiday.[2] Will you please let me know if you got this cheque safely. The Colums[3] are leaving tomorrow for Dinard and he is then going to Ireland and hopes to see you when he goes through London in about ten days.

I am horrified at the United Press correspondent's story. Not a word of what I told him so carefully, and all that stuff raked up from their files about a typewriter, and the Lausanne invention a new detail.[4] And that's nothing to what poor Mrs Frank Harris[5] is going to read in the papers about her husband dying during an orgy in Monte Carlo. That's what the Associated Press informed me yesterday by telephone. And that he hadn't left a penny.

Ivan Goll[6] called me up last evening at 6.30 to get his ALP record[7] ready at once, packed in a wooden case, and he would call for it to give to a friend going to Berlin. So he rushed in and I gave it to him and he said a lady friend was going to take it by hand to Berlin and send it from there to Frankfurt by post. The radio Joyce evening is set for the 14th of Sept.[8] I supposed Ogden would give them another one. Goll insisted in that angry way he has – very menacing; but if Imhof now has taken the records[9] and you think I shouldn't

---

1   See letter of 5 November 1926, note 2.
2   Joyce and Nora spent the last few days of August 1931 in Salisbury, Wiltshire.
3   See letters of 25 August 1930, note 2, and of 25 April 1931, note 5.
4   Apparently the article ignored the *Frankfurter Zeitung* affair and instead reported on an impending eye operation in Lausanne. Beach's file of newspaper items on the F.Z. affair, while containing another short article on that entirely unrelated topic (see following letter, note 2), has no article that mentions a typewriter or Lausanne. (Princeton) In a letter of protest to the United Press of America, Beach again refers to both typewriter and Lausanne: see letter of 1 September 1931, note 3.
5   Nellie Harris (1887-1955), whom he had married in 1927, was Frank Harris' third wife. For the notorious rogue and womanizer see undated letter [after 14 June, before 22 July 1924], note 1.
6   See letter of 5 November 1926, note 3.
7   See letters of 22 August 1931 and of 27 May 1931, note 9.
8   Initially the ALP record was meant to be used in Goll's first radio programme of April 1931 (cf. Brody's letters to Beach, 2 and 8 April 1931, Buffalo). It is uncertain whether his second Joyce evening, this time with the ALP record, was ever broadcast on Frankfurt Radio.
9   Alfred Imhof of 110 New Oxford Street, London, gramophone and radio specialists, were the manufacturers of the "Anna Livia Plurabelle" record. As Ogden wrote to Beach on 27 November 1931, "Imhof has *not* taken over the record – except that by Mr Joyce's special request they have it on their lists and can try to push it." (Buffalo).

have given one to Goll (I probably shouldn't) I will pay for it myself. I showed him the correspondence from the F.Z. that Pinker sent me[10] and he said you ought to sue them.

Two Japs came yesterday about the Ulysses translation.[11] I told them to get an offer from the publisher, and that he must first bring out a "Portrait of the Artist as a Young Man". Do you remember who was translating that? He wrote several years ago, a professor at a university in Japan. The publishers of Ulysses ought to get hold of his translation first.[12] The united artists who wrote to you about Ulysses have been publishing fragments in their reviews which I am sending you.[13] One number is a special James Joyce number. The two who came yesterday and brought the reviews for you are not among the translators. Their speciality is French Literature. Their friends are waiting anxiously in Tokyo to hear whether they can have the rights for Ulysses. The translation is to be finished this fall.[14] I told the two Japs you had had another Japanese offer this summer and they exclaimed "a lival!"[15] They are going to write to their friends as soon as I hear from you.[16]

---

10 See letters of 21 August 1931, note 3, and 22 August 1931, notes 1 and 3.
11 Kazuo Watanabe and Taro Shibuya, scholars of French literature in Paris. They are both mentioned as intermediaries in the three Japanese translators' letter to Joyce, for which see letter of 22 August 1931, note 5.
12 To this, Joyce replied: "The question of *Portrait* may be waived in Japan." (August 1931, no exact date given; letter 180, *JJtoSB*, p. 177). A Japanese translation of *A Portrait* appeared in 1932.
13 In 1930, Nagamatsu and his colleagues began to serialize their Japanese translation in the literary magazine *Shi to Genjitsu* [*Poetry and Reality*]. (Ito, p. 198).
14 Their translation was published in two volumes in 1931-1934, by Dai Ichi Shobo, Tokyo (Slo + Ca, D 91, p. 123). It was the fourth translation of *Ulysses*, after the German, the French and the Czech.
15 The rival must have been Toyoichiro Nogami, who wrote Joyce a letter on 30 July 1931 (Buffalo). He, too, wrote on behalf of a whole team of translators, including himself, who had been working on a Japanese *Ulysses* since 1929. However, Nogami withdrew from the project and is not named among the six translators of the second Japanese translation, which in 1932-35 appeared in five volumes. (Ito, p. 198).
16 In his reply, Joyce wrote, "Japanese terms: Same as German but if they hold out you may reduce 25%. One half of advance of royalties payable at once when contract signed. Preference to the speedier Jap." (no date [August 1931], letter 180, *JJtoSB*, p. 177). "German terms" meaning the 12% royalties from the Rhein-Verlag (Crispi, p. 34). Apparently, the Japanese translators found Joyce's terms too expensive and hence chose another way. See letter of 30 August 1932, note 1.

That Mrs Emily Coleman is the author of a book called <u>The Shutter of Snow</u>,[17] her hallucinations when she was mad after childbirth. She was also secretary to Emma Goldman.[18]

With best wishes

Yours very sincerely
Sylvia Beach

Cheque for eighty pounds enclosed

> ALS, 2 leaves, 4 sides, Sha&Co stationery. ZJJF Jahnke.
> "Cheque for eighty pounds enclosed" written below date on recto 1.
> Enclosure: Japanese reviews missing
> To JJ at 28b Campden Grove, London

---

17 Emily Holmes Coleman (1899-1974). American born writer and poet, who in 1926 moved with her young son John to Paris, where she worked as society editor for the Paris *Tribune* (the European edition of the *Chicago Tribune*). She also contributed to *transition* and became acquainted with others who wrote for the magazine. A prolific writer and poet, she published a single novel, *The Shutter of Snow* (1930), which is based on her own experience of a postnatal psychosis after the birth of her son, and her subsequent internment in a mental hospital. Circulated widely among writers she exerted more influence by her personality than by her art. (Geddes, p. 71f.).

18 Emma Goldman (1869-1940), Lithuanian-born international anarchist, who in 1885 emigrated to the U.S., where she came into contact with socialist and anarchist groups. She was jailed several times for her agitations and after World War I, she was deported to the Soviet Union. Disillusioned with Revolutionary Russia, she went to live in Europe. Goldman played an important role in the development of anarchist political philosophy in the U.S. and in Europe. She spoke and wrote on "free love" and birth control, as well as contemporary drama, such as Ibsen, Strindberg, Shaw. These lectures were published in 1914 as *The Social Significance of the Modern Drama*. She was also published in *The Little Review*. https://www.britannica.com/biography/Emma-Goldman, accessed 27 November 2020.

August 28, 1931

Dear Mr Joyce,

I am sending you today's "Tribune" with a story about the F.Z. I didn't tell the press that you were going to bring suit but they took it for granted.[1] I saw a woman from the United Press yesterday who was sent to me to find out more about the affair. I showed her the clipping you had sent me[2] and said you were terribly displeased, and gave her all the information over again and she said she would see that something else were done. I told her there was no news about your eyes.[3] Also a man from Reuter's came and wanted to know about your eyes and I told him the same thing. He said he was commissioned to get a story about your new work and was it all right to tell him you had arranged with Faber and the Viking.[4] Maybe I shouldn't have. And today a man from the Chicago Tribune came to find out what you were doing in the F.Z. affair. His paper will print any further developments he says. I told him I knew nothing about any decision to sue the F.Z., and he is going to call up in a few days to know if I have heard anything. He wanted the name of your solicitors and address but I didn't give it. Shall I? All the newspaper correspondants are of the opinion that you have a good case against the F.Z. and that they are responsible and can't hide behind the Kafka lady.

I have sent you the Japanese reviews.[5] One number is dedicated to you and they seem to have done a good deal of "lifting" of your work not to speak of the articles on it.[6]

---

1 On Friday, 28 August 1931, the *Chicago Tribune*, Paris, featured a short article entitled "James Joyce To Sue German Newspaper For Use Of His Name". Among other things, it stated that Joyce intended to sue the *Frankfurter Zeitung* "for $5,000 damages for the appearance of an article under his name which he claims he did not write". (Princeton). Eventually Joyce was persuaded not to bring suit against the newspaper.
2 Probably the short article from the *Daily Telegraph*, "James Joyce's Sight", that appeared on 25 August 1931 as a result of Beach's interview with the United Press of America reporter. It mentions a forthcoming eye operation and how his impaired vision affected his work on *Work in Progress*, while ignoring the *Frankfurter Zeitung* issue. (Princeton).
3 There was talk of several further eye operations during those years, but they kept being postponed and were eventually considered too dangerous. The last eye operation Joyce underwent took place in Zurich on 15 May 1930, when Professor Vogt operated on his left eye for tertiary cataract. (See Lyons, pp. 198ff, and *JJII*, p. 623).
4 For the publishing houses, see letters of 27 May 1931, note 2, and of 9 May 1931, note 10.
5 See preceding letter, note 14.
6 Until February 1932, *Ulysses* was under copyright in Japan. See also Beach's letter to Léon of 30 August 1932, especially note 1 for the country's liberal copyright law. Among the numerous articles translated into Japanese without asking permission were several essays from *Our Exagmination* (*JJtoSB*, undated letter [mid-September 1931], p. 180).

Perhaps you have already gone away on your holiday. I hope you will have a good rest.

Yours sincerely
Sylvia Beach

> ALS, 1 leaf, 2 sides, Sha&Co stationery. ZJJF Jahnke.
> "Perhaps you have already gone ..." written in the lower left-hand margin.
> Enclosure: *Chicago Tribune* article, at Princeton.
> To JJ at 28b Campden Grove, London (from August 29: Salisbury, Wiltshire)

September 1, 1931

Dear Mr Joyce,

Thank you very much for the first printed pages of "Work in Progress".[1] It looks beautiful. I will give Georgio's and Helen's and Lucia's to their chauffeur the next time he is sent here for books, and Jolas'[2] copy I will send him as soon as they are back.

I enclose a copy of a letter I have sent to the United Press,[3] and am sending you last evening's 'Intran' with a small notice in it by Prévost.[4]

I have just had a nice letter from Gillet[5] who says he has had no news from you for a long time. He mentions a letter from George Moore[6] which he got on the subject of his article, evidently most unfavourable. Adrienne says Gillet's article[7] has had a great effect in France and is the most important for you since Larbaud's.[8]

---

1 These are sample page proofs for *Finnegans Wake* from Faber & Faber; by 1931, Joyce had started getting Book I ready for publication.
2 Eugene Jolas (1894-1952). American writer, poet, critic and translator, who grew up in Alsace-Lorraine and hence was fluent in three languages. Jolas and his wife Maria Jolas (1893-1987) were close friends of the Joyces in Paris and founders of the avant-garde literary magazine *transition*, which published instalments of *Work in Progress*. Eugene Jolas contributed an essay to *Our Exagmination*, entitled "The Revolution of the Language and James Joyce", and collaborated on the French translation of "Anna Livia Plurabelle". On *transition* see letter of 11 August 1927, note 3.
3 In her letter to the General Manager of the United Press of America in Paris Beach complains about "the silly stories" about Joyce's eyes that had appeared after her conversation with the UPA journalist and she reiterates the information she had given him on the F.Z. topic. "There was nothing in an account I gave Mr McMillan of the Frankfurter Zeitung affair that justified his going back to your office and writing that stuff about Mr Joyce using a big typewriter, and an operation on his eyes by a surgeon in Lausanne. When he asked me if there was any news on that subject I assured him there was none." (31 August 1931, ZJJF Jahnke). Joyce never consulted a surgeon in Lausanne and in fact, visited the city for the first time in February 1938. After Professor Vogt's successful operation on his left eye on 15 May 1930 in Zurich, there were plans for an operation on his right eye, which was postponed to spring 1931, but in the end never took place (Lyons, pp. 198-203).
4 See letter of 17 August 1931, note 6, and letter of 1 May 1931, note 2, for the newspaper. Prévost had published a few lines on Joyce as the "victime d'une curieuse homonymie dans la 'Gazette de Francfort'". (Princeton).
5 See letter of 1 July 1931, note 5.
6 See letter of 16 July 1924, note 12.
7 See letter of 1 July 1931, note 6.
8 See letter of 22 February 1921, note 2 (and for NRF note 3). Valery Larbaud's article "James Joyce" was published in *Nouvelle Revue Française*, xviii, April 1922. Based on a lecture he had given in December 1921, it discussed all of Joyce's works. Sections of it were translated as "The *Ulysses* of James Joyce" in *The Criterion*, no. 1, October 1922. (Deming 1970, p. 252).

But it doesn't interest you particularly, I imagine, with this Frankfurter Zeitung business[9] engrossing you at present. Adrienne says she has not been able to interest the French in it at all. She has told everybody she knows but without any result. She asked me to thank you for the page of "Work in Progress" you autographed for her.

Your portrait by Tuohy[10] arrived – Georgio warned me it was coming and asked me to keep it for him – and I have hung it above Wilde's[11] alongside in place of the clock which got broken of Mr W.S.[12]

With love to Mrs Joyce and best greetings to yourself
Sylvia Beach

> ALS, 1 leaf, 2 sides, Sha&Co stationery. ZJJF Jahnke.
>
> Enclosures: Beach's letter to the United Press of America, typed copy at ZJJF Jahnke; *L'Intransigeant* article, at Princeton.
>
> To JJ at 28b Campden Grove, London

9   See letter of 6 August 1931, note 3, and INTRODUCTION to the 1930s, pp. 133-41.
10 See letter of 13 July 1926, note 2.
11 Oscar Wilde (1854-1900). Irish playwright, critic and novelist. Princeton holds various portraits of Wilde.
12 The eponymous writer of Beach's bookstore.

September 5, 1931

Dear Mr Joyce,

I am so sorry to hear that you are not well. No wonder with all the cares you have had this summer and not even a rest in some place where you and Mrs Joyce could have had some good air and sunshine.

I am sending everything I have on the subject of the F.Z. affair[1] to Messrs Monro, Saw & Co,[2] that is, the correspondence between the Rhein Verlag[3] and the F.Z.[4] I have showed everything to everybody who has come in and they all agreed that you must bring suit for damages. By the way, does the Michael of the 'Blue Peter'[5] acknowledge authorship of "Vielleicht ein Traum".[6] I will send you the copies of the 'Intran' and the 'Chicago Tribune'[7] as soon as the Kiosque of the Carrefour de l'Odéon can get them for me. – and also copies to Borach, Brody, Goll and Curtius.[8] Here is a reply from The United Press. Will you please return it to me.

I have written to Mr Watanabe who represents his friends in Japan who are translating Ulysses,[9] to ask him for his written authorisation to publish the Ito article in an English review,[10] and will send it to you as soon as it arrives. Will you please read the enclosed copy of my letter to the translators giving the

---

1 See letter of 6 August 1931, note 3, and INTRODUCTION to the 1930s, pp. 133-41.
2 Joyce's London lawyers.
3 See letters of 16 September 1926, note 13, and of 6 August 1931, note 10.
4 There is no extant letter from Daniel Brody or Rhein-Verlag to the F.Z., but his letter to Joyce of 30 July 1931 mentions that "there have been many letters written to the F.Z. and also to Frau Kafka." (typed English translation of the original German letter; Princeton). See APPENDIX C, Overview of Correspondence re F.Z. Affair.
5 See letter of 21 August 1931, note 11.
6 See letter of 6 August 1931, note 3.
7 See preceding letter, note 4, and letter of 28 August 1931, note 1, respectively.
8 Georges Borach (1892-1934). One of Joyce's language pupils in Zurich during the First World War, with whom he became friendly. Joyce also got him involved in the F.Z. affair, asking him to write a letter of protest to the translator Irene Kafka (see Irene Kafka's letter of 17 August 1931 to Monro Saw & Co; Princeton). For Daniel Brody see letter of 6 August 1931, note 10; for Ivan Goll see letter of 5 November 1926, note 3; and for Ernst Robert Curtius see letter of 2 November 1926, note 4.
9 See letter of 22 August 1931, note 5. Beach's letters to Watanabe are at Buffalo.
10 Hitoshi Ito, one of the Japanese translators, who wrote an article about Joyce. Apparently the article satisfied Joyce, who had asked Beach to find out whether it was "merely expository" or "written from the Japanese viewpoint". (see letter 186 [early September 1931] and letter 188 [mid-September 1931], JJtoSB, p. 179f.). The article in question is probably "Concerning James Joyce's Method Ishiki no Nagare [Stream of Consciousness]", which appeared in the Japanese literary magazine Shi Genjitsu [Poetry and Reality] on 16 June 1930. (Eishiro Ito, personal communication, email 13 May 2020) It is uncertain

conditions,[11] and let me know if it is all right. You thought a sum outright would be best, but Soupault[12] advises a sum in advance <u>and</u> <u>further</u> <u>royalties</u>. He says it would be a great mistake to abandon all rights to royalties in the future – that the Japs have money. I will wait till I hear from you to send off my letter. Also will write to the professor[13] on the same lines.

I have been very busy, with no errand girl and no one to help me in the shop, otherwise I would have attended to the Japs some time ago. Myrsine[14] is not coming back to me. I decided to part with her for various reasons. One is that I cannot afford to keep her with business so bad. And she was not a great help to me. I could never rely on her. But the break was unpleasant. Adrienne has been advising me for several years to get rid of her.

Gorman came to see me yesterday. He is now working entirely on your biography and has abandoned Mary[15] for the time. He says that book on you ought to be ready by January[16] and the only thing that hampers him is that he is short of money. Mr Stanislaus Joyce is having all his documents copied in Trieste by an Englishman, at a shilling a thousand words; Pugh[17] has sent him some photos of Dublin; if he had a little money he would go to Dublin himself he says. I advised him to cable his publishers (of the book on Joyce) Farrar & Rhinehart,[18] to send him an advance, but he thinks they are getting tired of giving him advances. I suggested his picking up an elderly lady then. He seems to be working now and told me he was going over very carefully the stuff your brother had sent so far. He certainly looks more alert now, and cheerful.

---

whether the article was eventually published in English; neither Slocum and Cahoon nor Deming 1977 list any article in English by Ito.

11 Beach's letter of 4 September 1931 to Sadamu Nagamatsu, Hisanori Tsugino and Hitoshi Ito asked for "a royalty of 12% on the full price of all copies sold" with advance royalties on the first 5000 copies (Buffalo). See letter of 27 August 1931, note 16.

12 See letter of 25 April 1931, note 2.

13 Kazuo Watanabe.

14 See letter of 27 July 1922, note 3, and Fitch, p. 319f.

15 Herbert Gorman's historical novel *The Scottish Queen*, published in 1932. See undated letter [after 14 June, before 22 July 1924], note 4.

16 The expanded version of Gorman's biography, *James Joyce*, was eventually published in 1939.

17 Thomas W. Pugh (1883-1968). A Dubliner Joyce met in Paris, with whom Gorman occasionally collaborated. See letter of 11 August 1931, note 24.

18 A New York publishing company founded in 1929 by John Farrar, Stanley M. Rinehart and Frederick M. Rinehart. Formerly directors at Doubleday, Doran and Co., they took some fifty authors from their employer, among them the Rineharts' mother, Mary Roberts Rinehart, a popular and prolific mystery writer, who substantially contributed to their success. In 1945, the firm was renamed Rinehart & Company, after Farrar had left to form a new company with Roger W. Straus. (Gorman, pp. 135 and 138)

He said he wanted to see Georgio about reproducing Jack Yeats' picture of the Liffey[19] in his book.

I enclose a copy of my letter to Eliot about O.E.[20] This summer lots of young American students, Editors of reviews etc who worship you have visited my shop, bought Ulysses, H.C.E. A L P and even O E sometimes, and Frenchman since Gillet's article.[21]

Gilbert is in Pornic.[22] McAlmon[23] is back in Paris – Thérèse Fontaine's father-in-law[24] unfortunately for Gorman and his work, is dead – funeral today.

All this business is not very good for you when what you need now is a complete rest. I hope you will soon recover from that painful intestinal trouble and the eye ache. Yours very sincerely Sylvia Beach

> ALS, 2 leaves, 4 sides, Sha&Co stationery. ZJJF Jahnke.
> "All this business/Gilbert is in Pornic...." written perpendicular to the main body in the left-hand margin on verso of the second leaf.
> Enclosures: extant letters re F.Z. affair at Princeton, letter to S. Nagamatsu et al., at Buffalo, letter to T.S. Eliot, at Princeton.
> To JJ at 28b Campden Grove, London

19   Jack Butler Yeats (1971-1957). Irish painter, the youngest brother of William Butler Yeats. His picture "The Liffey Swim" (1923) is in the Yeats collection at the National Gallery of Ireland.
20   *Our Exagmination*, first published by Shakespeare and Company in 1929, was to be taken over by Faber & Faber, where T.S. Eliot was an editor. In her letter of 3 September 1931, Beach offers Eliot to sell the remaining 2000 copies of *Exagmination* at 7 Frs each, the price they cost her, including authors' royalties, and to transfer the rights to Faber & Faber. "[A]s you are going to have his 'Work in Progress', 'Our Exagmination' would be more in its place with you and would certainly have a much wider sale". (Copy of letter at Princeton. Beach noted in the margin, "there was no reply to this letter".) For *Our Exagmination* see letter of 8 July 1931, note 8.
21   See letter of 1 July 1931, notes 5-7.
22   See letter of 12 May 1931, note 10.
23   See undated letter [after 14 June, before 22 July 1924], note 2.
24   See letter of 8 July 1931, note 5. It seems that her husband Philippe Fontaine's father supported Joyce's biographer financially, as he was a patron of the arts and letters. http://www.annales.org/archives/x/fontaine.html, accessed 5 January 2020.

September 14, 1931

Dear Mrs Joyce

Miss Weaver[1] tells me that you are going to find a place in your luggage for the shawl that she has got for a friend of mine. That is very kind of you, but I am afraid it will be a nuisance for you and take up too much room. It is so hard to get everything packed. I know how it is, and what bores people are who ask you to take something of theirs. I thought perhaps this shawl would squash up small in a corner but I'm afraid it is going to be a bother all the same and you will curse me.

Miss Weaver says you are coming back in a fortnight, and Georgio told me ten days or so.[2] And she says you were quite fond of your flat and had arranged it beautifully. They seem to be as hard to find here as ever, and as dear. Georgio is having a lot of trouble with his, and he was just on the way to have a stern talk with his proprietor when I saw him on Friday. He looks very well after his stay at Montigny. Now that everyone is coming home from their holidays the weather has begun to improve but it is "too late" like the story of the man and the sharks.[3] Adrienne is recovering from a bad, longlasting cold. I am very busy without any help in my shop. I've given up the struggle to find an errand girl. They're no good. With love, yours affectionately

Sylvia

The Hemingways are here on their way home from Spain.[4]

>ALS, 1 leaf, 2 sides, Sha&Co stationery; "The Hemingways...." written in the left-hand margin. ZJJF Jahnke.
>To NBJ at 28b Campden Grove, London

1 See letter of 27 July 1922, note 2.
2 The Joyces returned from London either on 24 or 25 September. (Norburn, p. 150)
3 Reference unknown (while anachronistically evoking Hemingway's novel *The Old Man and the Sea*. A first short version was published in the magazine *Esquire* in April 1936. Hemingway may have told such stories among friends.).
4 See letter of 26 October 1926, note 1. Hemingway and his wife Pauline had sailed in May from Havana to Spain and stopped for two weeks in Paris before returning to the U.S. Beach and Hemingway talked at length about Roth's presumable latest piracy and he offered to seek help from his American lawyer. Joyce, however, "declined to have anything more to do with lawyers." (Joyce to Harriet Weaver, 1 Oct 1931, *Letters III*, p. 229).

September 28, 1931

Dear Mr Joyce,

    There is about seven thousand francs for you. If you will let me know how much you want to draw out I will send you a cheque. That is all that will come in for some time, I imagine.

Yours sincerely,
Sylvia Beach

        TLS, 1 leaf, 1 side, Sha&Co stationery. ZJJF Jahnke.
        To JJ at La Résidence, 4 avenue Pierre Premier de Serbie, Paris

November 10, 1931

Dear Mr Joyce

I am returning you herewith Mr Pinker's letter of the 6th.[1] As regards "Pomes Penyeach", I took out the American copyright of the book this summer[2] and I do not consider its publication in a volume with "Chamber Music" at all opportune at the present moment. The five thousand copies of my 1927 edition being now exhausted, I am arranging about a second edition[3] and would like to time it so as to coincide with the Oxford University Press edition.[4] Has the date of this been fixed?

Yours very sincerely

> TLCC, 1 leaf, 1 side. Buffalo.
> Enclosure missing.
> To JJ at 2 Avenue St Philibert, Passy, Paris

---

1 See note letter of 27 May 1931, note 3.
2 See letter of 25 April 1931, notes 6 and 7. The fifty American copies of *Pomes* had a notice, "Copyright 1931 by Sylvia Beach. Printed in the U.S.A." (Slo + Ca, A 25, p. 36f.).
3 The first edition of *Pomes Penyeach*, published by Shakespeare and Co contained the notice, "Copyright by James Joyce" (Slo + Ca, A 24, p. 35). By the time of this letter, as Joyce wrote to Harriet Weaver, Beach had the world rights to the book. (21 November 1931, *Letters III*, p. 234) However, nothing came of her plans for a second edition.
4 See letter of 25 April 1931, note 8. Faber & Faber also published the poems in March 1933. (Slo + Ca, A 28 and A 29, p. 39f.) For the deluxe edition with Lucia Joyce's *lettrines* see letter to Joyce of 28 September 1932, note 1.

February 2, 1932

Dear Mr Joyce,

It was very kind of you to offer me those handsome 'biches'[1] and the ten branches of lilac with a blue bow on the occasion of the tenth anniversary of your great Ulysses. It will always be a pleasure for me to see those 'biches' because they are very fine and particularly because they are a present from you.

With best wishes, yours very sincerely
Sylvia Beach

>   ALS, 1 leaf, 1 side, Sha&Co stationery. ZJJF Jahnke.
>   To JJ at 2 Avenue St Philibert, Passy, Paris

1   *Fr.* doe. In his *Paris Journal*, Stuart Gilbert writes concerning the 10th anniversary of *Ulysses* and Joyce's 50th birthday: "J.J. sent S.B. a present (clever move, though a little forced as it was his birthday) – two book supports, 'biches' from Brandt's shop." (p. 45).

February 4, 1932

Dear Monsieur Léon,[1]

In reply to your letter of 3rd inst.,[2] I made a present to Mr Joyce last December of my rights to ULYSSES, as far as an edition published in America was concerned. Some time later, on the 25th of January, Mr Colum told me that Mr Joyce was not satisfied with the contract between us for ULYSSES "because neither party was free to act without the consent of the other".[3] I replied that I supposed it resembled other contracts in that way, but, as I had already assured Mr Joyce in December, he might consider himself free from all obligation to me, and to dispose of ULYSSES to whomsoever and in whatever manner he pleased, without any question of indemnity to me.[4]

Of course I understand that Mr Joyce is anxious to have this assurance from me on paper, so I hereby agree to cancel the contract between us for ULYSSES, and to give up my claims to this work for future editions.

I do not think a new contract necessary.[5]

With regard to Mr Rosenfeld's letter,[6] will you please tell Mr Joyce that in my conversation with that gentleman, as I informed Mr Joyce immediately after it took place, I merely said that he could not be expected to pay the lawyers any more money, for they had not put a stop to the pirating of ULYSSES, that he could not afford to, the pirating having robbed him of the profits from the sale of the book. Anything else that Mr Rosenfeld wrote to Mr Levy[7] was his own idea, and I shall ask him to write another letter saying that when I saw a copy of his letter I did not approve of what he had said.[8] I quite understand

---

1 See letter of 25 August 1930, note 1, and INTRODUCTION to the 1930s p. 125.
2 In which Léon addressed the need, in Joyce's opinion, to revise the contract between them, the present one being "unworkable, ambiguous and not in conformity with French law". (Buffalo).
3 See "Memorandum of Agreement" of 9 December 1930, p. 147f., and also INTRODUCTION to the 1930s, p. 130.
4 For details see Fitch, p. 322f.
5 In his reply of 8 February 1932, Léon suggested to draw up a new contract regarding the continental rights to *Ulysses*, if she was willing to continue publishing it. (Fahy, p. 159) While it is unlikely that a formal agreement was set up, Beach continued to hold the continental rights until autumn 1932, when she sold them to the Albatross Press in Hamburg (Fitch, p. 335).
6 Henry L. Rosenfeld, an American lawyer based in Paris, whom Beach hired in connection with the lawsuit against the American piracy of *Ulysses*.
7 Louis S. Levy, of the New York law firm Chadbourne, Stanchfield, & Levy, which in 1927 filed Joyce's suit against Samuel Roth's piracy of *Ulysses*. (Fitch, p. 254).
8 As Léon wrote Beach on 3 February, Joyce took offence at Rosenfeld's letter to his New York lawyers, which made him believe Beach had given Rosenfeld the impression that Joyce was "in very poor circumstances and that even a tenth part of the money at present being made

that Mr Joyce is displeased at what he took to be an unauthorized step on my part.

Yours sincerely,
Sylvia Beach

> TLTSC, 2 leaves, 2 sides. Buffalo.
> To Paul Léon at 27, Rue Casimir Périer, Paris VII

---

on the pirated edition of *Ulysses* would be a godsend to him" so that he could take care of outstanding obligations, which he found "extremely prejudicial to his interests" in the American market. (Buffalo) Beach immediately wrote her letter of protest to rectify the misrepresentation of her statements. (Beach to Rosenfeld, no date [early February 1932], Buffalo XII).

There had been a disagreement between Joyce and Beach on who had to pay the fees due in the case against Roth. Her lawyer argued that Joyce was the owner of *Ulysses* until their contract in December 1930, upon which Joyce agreed to pay for the expenses (Fitch, p. 322), at least up to a certain point in time.

FIGURE 17 James Joyce and Paul Léon, 1934
BORIS LIPNITZKI © BORIS LIPNITZKI / ROGER-VIOLLET

February 9, 1932

Dear Monsieur Léon,

Will you please show the enclosed letter to Mr Joyce, and if he says it is all right, send it to Mr Rosenfeld as soon as possible.[1] No wonder Mr Joyce was not pleased with the letter to Mr Levy. I can well understand it.

Yours sincerely,
Sylvia Beach

>TLS, 1 leaf, 1 side, Sha&Co stationery. NLI Léon.
>Enclosures: 2 copies of Beach's letter to Rosenfeld and copy extracts from Rosenfeld's letter to Louis Levy dated 2 November 1931 and from Rosenfeld's covering note to Beach dated 9 January 1932, endorsed with pencilled notes in hand of Paul Léon. (Fahy, p. 160)
>To Paul Léon at 27 Rue Casimir Périer, Paris

1 In her (undated) letter to Rosenfeld Beach asks him to clarify to Louis Levy that her comments on the financial damages due to the piracy of *Ulysses* had been misinterpreted – and that she had "nothing whatsoever" to do with his suggestion that Joyce pay the lawyers' fees from his royalties. She states, in a somewhat ambiguous tone, that "knowing that any such arrangement would be absolutely unacceptable, it would never have occurred to me to suggest it." (Buffalo XII) See preceding letter, notes 6-8.

April 15, 1932   Shakespeare & Company
                                  12, rue de l'Odéon, Paris (VIe)

To James Joyce
For Ulysses royalties to date

Frs. 2329,68
Copies of 11th edition[1] sold: 3633
At 125 fr. 25%
31.25. Frs. 113.631,25[2]

Paid up to date
Sylvia Beach
Copies left of 11th edition: 347
The following copies have been given to
Mr Joyce 10
S.B. 10

    AD, on neutral paper. NLI Léon.
    to JJ at 2 Avenue St Philibert, Passy, Paris

---

1 The eleventh edition was the last to be printed for Shakespeare and Company, in May 1930.
2 The correct sum (i.e. 31.25 x 3633) would be 113.531,25.

May 11, 1932

Dear Mr Joyce,

To add to the information that I gave you on the telephone yesterday, the plates of which we spoke, or what they call the empreintes and the plombs[1] in French, are my property, and in case another publisher wanted to use them for a continental edition[2] he would be obliged to buy them from me, in the customary manner, at the price I paid the printer for them, according to his bill.

Yours sincerely,
Sylvia Beach

James Joyce, Esq.,
Hotel de Belmont,
30 Rue de Bassano,
Paris – 16

  TLS, 1 leaf, 1 side, on neutral paper. Princeton.
  To JJ at Hôtel Belmont, 28-30 rue Bassano, Paris

1 *Fr.* printing plates from hot lead (*plomb*) typesetting.
2 When Beach learned that in March Joyce had signed a contract with Random House for a first authorized American edition, she relinquished her plans for a 12th printing of *Ulysses*. Joyce still wanted her to bring out another impression "to keep the novel available and the cash flowing until the Random House edition was printed." (Fitch, p. 330) But Beach declared that she was not interested. See also INTRODUCTION to the 1930s, p. 130-32.

August 8, 1932

Dear Mr Joyce,
Miss Beach asked me to send you the enclosed letter from Warner Brothers, National Film.[1] I have also replied to them that their letter has been sent on to you and that they must apply to you for the screen rights.[2]
The address you wanted was under the gentleman's pen name

W.K. Magie[3]
Ticknock
Leighan Vale Road
Bournemouth

Yours sincerely
Jean Henley[4]

 ALS, 1 leaf, 1 side, Sha&Co stationery. NLI Léon.
 Enclosure: letter from Warner Brothers.
 To JJ at Carlton Elite Hotel, Zurich

1. That letter, in which Warner Brothers inquired about the price of the world film rights for *Ulysses*, is annotated in Joyce's hand: "Est-ce une plaisanterie? Qui sont ces gens là?" (*Fr.* Is this a hoax? Who are those people? Fahy, p. 160). Joyce was opposed to the idea of turning *Ulysses* into a film, as he considered it "irrealisable" (Léon to Ralph Pinker, 26 October 1932, *Letters III*, p. 263), and on a more private level, repeating the suspicion that the whole matter was "une blague" (*Fr.* a joke), he also had the answer to the above question: "some scoundrels want to pretend getting my permission, and that being refused, they will set out to disfigure my book", as he wrote in a letter to Giorgio (30 August 1932, ZJJF Jahnke; original in Italian). At the same time, however, Joyce "allowed Léon to keep the matter going, talked with Eisenstein about it, and did not discourage Stuart Gilbert from trying his hand at scenarios for *Ulysses*" (*JJII*, p. 654).
2. Apparently, it was not entirely clear whether Joyce's film rights to his own novel also extended to the United States. (Léon to Ralph Pinker, letter of 26 October 1932, *Letters III*, p. 263)
3. William Kirkpatrick Magee (1868-1961). Irish essayist and assistant librarian at the National Library of Ireland. Under his pen name, John Eglinton, he figures in the library chapter of *Ulysses*. His *Irish Literary Portraits* (1935) also contains an essay on Joyce. (*JJAtoZ*, p. 63)
4. Jean Henley (1910-1994), American art student who in 1932 and 1933 worked as Beach's part-time assistant. (Fitch, pp. 329 and 338).

August 18, 1932

Dear Monsieur Léon,

    As the doctor said I must entirely forget my work during my vacation, Miss Henley[1] did not forward my mail and I only saw your letter of July 14th yesterday when I returned.[2] The eleventh edition of ULYSSES is indeed nearly sold out, but, as I told Mr Joyce, I cannot risk reprinting it with an American edition pending. They would not have undertaken it over there if they had not had good reason to think it possible at present, and I hope for Mr Joyce's sake that all will go well. If, however, ULYSSES is suppressed in America, Mr Joyce may count on me to reprint it immediately here. We shall know this fall, I suppose. Meanwhile if ULYSSES is out of print for a while, everyone will quite understand the situation. A new edition would not take long to prepare and would go off all the better for having been unobtainable during the interval.

    I am sorry to hear such a bad account of Mr Joyce's eyes, but hope Dr. Vogt[3] will be able to make them well again. I hope Lucia is better now.[4]

Yours sincerely,
Sylvia Beach

    TLTSC, 1 leaf, 1 side. Buffalo.
    To Paul Léon at 27, Rue Casimir Périer, Paris VII

1 See preceding letter, note 4.
2 In that letter, Léon wrote that "the decision about a new – the twelfth – edition must be taken rather quickly." (Buffalo)
3 Professor Alfred Vogt (1849-1943), a Swiss ophthalmologist of international repute, whose operation in May 1930 saved Joyce from going blind and who continued to treat his eye problems.
4 After a nervous breakdown in April 1932 and several months in a clinic, Lucia spent the summer with the Jolases and a nurse in Austria (Vorarlberg).

August 30, 1932

Dear Monsieur Léon,

I enclose a letter that I have just received from the Japanese pirates of "Ulysses".[1] Will you please let Mr Joyce know and ask him what he would like me to do about it. They sent a cheque for 200 yen, which at about 5 francs a yen makes the measly sum of a thousand francs.[2] If Mr Joyce is not able to attend to the matter just now there is no hurry.

Yours sincerely,
Sylvia Beach

>   TLS, 1 leaf, 1 side, Sha&Co stationery. NLI Léon.
>   Enclosure: letter from S. Nagamatsu et al., at NLI Léon.
>   To Paul Léon at 27, Rue Casimir Périer, Paris VII

1 The team of the first of two Japanese translations of *Ulysses*, both in several volumes that had begun to appear in 1931 (and 1932 respectively). When in early 1932 Joyce heard that the translations were published in book form, he engaged a Japanese lawyer to take the case, since neither translation team had a contract with him. It turned out, however, that "there is a 10-year law limit to protect European copyright"; hence the Japanese, who considered Joyce's terms "exorbitant, waited till the 2 February jubileed by, and went ahead." (Joyce to Harriet Weaver, 8 June 1932, *Letters III*, p. 247) See also letter of 24 October 1932, note 2.
2 After Joyce's protests, Sadamu Nagamatsu, Hitoshi Ito and Hisanori Tsujino offered that sum for the Japanese rights to *Ulysses* in their letter of 5 August 1932. (Fahy, p. 224).

August 31, 1932

Dear Monsieur Léon,

Your letter of the 30th has come. I would, indeed, feel it very deeply if Mr Joyce thought it best to sever my connection with ULYSSES.[1] But in devoting myself to his work during the last ten years, combined with the exertions of running my shop, I have sacrificed my health to such an extent that my headaches, which the doctors agree are due to fatigue and mental strain, have not yet yielded to any treatment, and it is obvious that I must take care in the future if I am to continue to do any work at all. If I were hurried into printing a new edition of ULYSSES just at the present moment when the tourist season is over – and my books prove that sales depend largely on American visitors in the summer – without knowing something definite of the plans of Mr Joyce's publishers in America, there might be difficulties such as I have no longer, unfortunately, either the health or the courage to cope with. I am sure Mr Joyce will understand that my decision in this matter has not been taken lightly. To lose ULYSSES that I have always admired and loved above everything would be so painful to me that I cannot bear to think of it, but I must do what I think wisest, and Mr Joyce knows that he is quite free to take any step he considers best for his interests. There is nothing to stand in his way.

I enclose a statement of sales up to date.

> TL, draft with revisions and corrections, 1 leaf, 1 side. Buffalo.
> To Paul Léon at 27, Rue Casimir Périer, Paris VII

1 In his letter of 30 August, Léon took Beach's conditional agreement to publish a 12th impression – provided that no American edition be on the market – as an "unequivocal refusal to issue a further continental edition and that it would be up to [Joyce] to consider offering the book to another publisher." (Buffalo) At that time, Joyce and Léon were in fact already conducting negotiations. See INTRODUCTION to the 1930s, p. 131.

August 31, 1932

Statement of sales
Copies sold up to date: 3938[1]

Royalties on 3938 copies at 125 francs 25% 31.25
Frs. 123.062,50
Total of sums paid to James Joyce 119.716,80
Balance to credit of James Joyce today. Frs. 3345,70.

> TD, Sha&Co stationery. NLI Léon.
> Enclosure to preceding letter.
> To Paul Léon at 27, Rue Casimir Périer, Paris VII

---

1 The figure refers to the 11th edition, or rather impression, of *Ulysses*.

September 24, 1932

Dear Monsieur Léon,

    I am returning to you herewith Mr Yeats' letter to Mr Joyce.[1] Of course Mr Joyce has his reasons for not accepting, but it seems to me it would have done no harm to accept, and that it might have been the first step towards lifting the ban on "Ulysses".

    With regard to the copy of "Ulysses" that you saw marked "out of print" in a bookshop in the Rue de Castiglione, the booksellers are justified in saying that. I have announced to them that the edition is now exhausted except for a few copies (about 20) which I sell at the full price of 125 francs without discount to the trade. It may be some time before I can get rid of these copies at this price, and if Mr Joyce wishes to have the royalties on them paid without waiting, I will include them in the sum due to him for royalties up to date and send him a cheque at once. Adrienne Monnier tells me that it is quite customary for publishers to sell the last copies of an edition that is going out of print at full price only.

Yours sincerely,
Sylvia Beach

> TLTSC, 1 leaf, 1 side. Buffalo.
> Enclosure: letter from W.B Yeats, *Letters II*, p. 258f.
> To Paul Léon at 27, Rue Casimir Périer, Paris VII

---

1 In his letter of 2 September 1932, Yeats invited Joyce to join the Academy of Irish Letters recently founded by him and Bernard Shaw. A month later, Joyce declined, declaring "I see no reason why my name should have arisen at all in connection with such an academy." (qt. in *JJII*, p. 661).

September 28, 1932

James Joyce, Esq.,
Hotel Metropole,
Nice.

Dear Mr Joyce,
    I have sent you by telegram Frs. 4.500 to-day. Mr Léon wrote that you would like to have the balance of your royalties for the eleventh edition of "Ulysses". This sum is the balance. Within the next few days Mr Léon will receive a detailed account of all payments made to you and the copies of "Ulysses" sold every month since the eleventh edition appeared.
    I am looking forward to seeing Lucia's book.[1] Mr Kahane[2] has not showed it to me yet and I did not know it was out. I will call him up about it.

Yours sincerely
SYLVIA BEACH

>   TLTSCC, 1 leaf, 1 side, neutral paper. Buffalo.
>   To JJ at Hôtel Métropole, Nice, France

1 A small deluxe edition limited to 25 copies of *Pomes Penyeach*, plus an unspecified number of copies *hors commerce* (Paris: The Obelisk Press, 1932; London: Desmond Harmsworth Ltd., 1932). This edition is in facsimile of Joyce's handwriting, with initial letters designed and illuminated by Lucia Joyce (Slo + Ca, A 27, p. 38f.) Beach received a signed, unnumbered *hors commerce* copy, which is at Buffalo. (*JJtoSB*, letter of 26 September 1932, no. 198, note 2, p. 194)
    Joyce's main idea behind this edition was to give his artistically gifted, unstable daughter a sense of purpose and thus improve her spirits. The price of 1000 FF (between twice and four times as much as for a first edition of *Ulysses*, even considering the 10-year inflation) was partly meant to grant Lucia some material recognition (cf. also Joyce's letter to Harriet Weaver, 7 December 1931, *Letters I*, p. 308f., and *JJII*, p. 641).

2 See second letter of 2 May 1931, note 1.

September 28, 1932

Dear Monsieur Léon,

 I have sent Mr Joyce Frs. 4.500 by wire. I got your letter this afternoon, too late to go to the bank, and as you said Mr Joyce was in a hurry to have the balance of his royalties for the 11th edition of ULYSSES I thought that by telegram would be the quickest. This sum of Frs. 4.500 settles up the account between Mr Joyce and myself for the eleventh edition of ULYSSES.[1] In a day or two, as soon as I have time to copy the items from my books, I will send you an account of the sums paid to Mr Joyce and the sales.

Yours sincerely,
SYLVIA BEACH

  TLS, 1 leaf, 1 side, Sha&Co stationery. NLI Léon.
  To Paul Léon at 27, Rue Casimir Périer, Paris VII

---

1 The payment was the last business transaction between Joyce and Beach concerning her edition of *Ulysses*.

October 4, 1932

Dear Mr Joyce,

Lloyds Bank in Nice will pay you the equivalent of francs of the Pinker and New Republic cheques[1] that you sent me. The Pinker cheque for £ 12-10-2 at 88,50 comes to Frs. 1.106,95, the New Republic, $ 25.00 at 25,50, Frs. 637,50: total, Frs. 1744, 45, less three francs for expenses. So you will get one thousand seven hundred and forty-one forty five.

Yours sincerely

Oct 4 SB got 2 cheques from JJ. Had sum sent to him by Lloyds.

> TLCC, 1 leaf, 1 side. Buffalo.
> Postscript in Beach's hand.
> To JJ at Hôtel Métropole, Nice, France

1 See letter of 27 May 1931, note 3. *The New Republic*, founded in 1914, was one of the most influential progressive American weekly magazines (a monthly today). https://www.britannica.com/topic/The-New-Republic, accessed 9 December 2020. The November 10 issue of that year featured Joyce's poem "Ecce Puer".

October 24, 1932

Dear Mr Joyce

I am sending you the complete Chaucer that you were looking for,[1] a letter from Mr Okakura about the Japanese editions of ULYSSES and the articles that he sent,[2] and a letter from a Mr Daughtry asking for permission to quote from one of your poems in a book he is writing.[3] As Mr Léon takes charge of all your affairs, perhaps you would be so kind as to ask him to reply to these gentlemen. Although I shall always continue to be devoted to your work, Mr Joyce, I am sorry that I shall no longer be able to serve you personally. My time and energy are entirely absorbed in the problem of keeping my shop going in these bad times. Since most of the English and Americans have gone away, the library terms have to be revised for the French who, I hope, will take their place. From morning till night I am busy cataloguing and arranging the books and attending to all the rest of the work that is always accumulating on account of my headaches so often laying me up.

I want to thank you again for the sacrifice of a part of your royalties that you made in the arrangement with the Albatross for their publication of "Ulysses".[4]

---

1 Geoffrey Chaucer (ca. 1343-1400), the outstanding English poet before Shakespeare. In his letter of 23 October 1932, Joyce asked Beach to lend him a complete Chaucer, since his copy was locked up. "I want to read his poem *ABC* (every stanza begins with a letter of the alphabet) as Lucia has finished her 26 letters. A-Z. It is a translation from an old French poem." (*JJtoSB*, p. 185). After her illuminations for *Pomes Penyeach*, published in October 1931, Lucia Joyce started to work on the *lettrines* for Chaucer's poem. *A Chaucer A.B.C., being a Hymn to the Holy Virgin*, with a eulogizing preface by Louis Gillet, was published in 1936. See also letter of 28 September 1932 (to Joyce), note 1.

2 Professor Yoshisaburo Okakura of Tokyo (1868-1936), with whom Beach was corresponding about the legal position of the two ongoing Japanese translations that were both published in successive volumes. His letter of 2 October 1932 is about his dealings with the Japanese publishers (Fahy, p. 224). The articles are the principal criticisms of the Japanese translations which Beach had asked Okakura to send to Joyce (Letter of [?]May 1932, NLI Léon), and possibly also other Joyce criticism in Japanese. On the early Japanese criticism see Ito, pp. 196-99, and Slo + Ca, D. *Periodicals*, p. 123).

3 E.O. Daughtry wrote to Beach in October 1932 asking for permission to use verses from "Strings in the earth and air". Both his letter and the reply granting permission are at NLI Léon (Fahy, p. 228). A Dr. E.O. Daughtry is mentioned in an alumni magazine as the music master at the Reading Grammar School from 1913 until his death in 1943. http://www.oldredingensians.org.uk/pdfs/OldRed_Autumn_2011.pdf, accessed 9 December 2020.

4 This continental edition, the first authorized edition printed outside France, is usually known as the Odyssey Press edition. The Odyssey Press was a new imprint of the Albatross Press, specifically created for their publication of *Ulysses*, after publishing the same year an edition of *Dubliners* as the first volume in their Modern Continental Library. Founded in 1931 by the German publishers John Holroyd-Reece (né Johann Hermann Rieß) and Max

But I would have far preferred Mr Wegner's first proposition to give me 1% on your royalties which you would have received in full, my part being paid by the publishers.[5] If they saw fit to give me a little something on the sales I was naturally very glad, and Mr Wegner assured me that your royalties would not be affected by it. I regret that with the arrangement you made, it has come out of your own pocket. As it is done now, I will accept it, as I told you, but not for an indefinite period.[6] Only until they have paid me twenty thousand francs which I shall consider an indemnity for the plates that I had hoped to transfer to any publishers taking over "Ulysses"[7] and which otherwise are a dead loss. After that sum I shall instruct the Albatross to turn over my part to you. in the future. (sic)

Yours very sincerely
Sylvia Beach

> TLS, 2 leaves, 2 sides, Sha&Co stationery. NLI Léon.
> Enclosures: letters from O.E. Daughtry and Yoshisaburo Okakura, at NLI Léon. Articles missing.
> To JJ at Hôtel Lord Byron, Champs-Elysées, Paris

Christian Wegner, and funded with British money, the Albatross Press had its operational base in Hamburg and its editorial office in Paris, with Italian publisher Arnoldo Mondadori on its board. In a time of rising nationalism, their main purpose was to gain control over English-language books in continental Europe, the monopoly of which was held by the German publisher Tauchnitz (where *A Portrait of the Artist* had appeared in 1930). Besides *Ulysses*, Albatross would only publish one more book, *Lady Chatterley's Lover*, under their Odyssey Press imprint. (Wilson/Troy, n.p.)

Their low-price *Ulysses* edition, the first of four printings, was eventually published in December 1932. In their letter of 12 October 1932, Léon and M.C. Wegner of the Albatross Press informed Beach of their final agreement about the continental edition of *Ulysses*: At the particular request of Mr Joyce she was to be paid [20%] of the sum received by him at the signature of the contract, as well as [2,5%] of his royalties for five years. After that period, she would during her lifetime receive another 7,5% of Joyce's royalties (NLI Léon). Interestingly, they made two significant mistakes concerning Beach's shares: 25% instead of 20%, and 25% instead of 2,5%. In his report to Weaver, Joyce was to repeat the mistake of 25% (rather than 2,5%) royalties for Beach – the amount he had received from her. (Crispi, p. 50f.) On Joyce's "sacrifice" see letter of 8 November 1932, note 4.

5 Wegner's letter to Beach of 6 September 1932 (NLI Léon). This first offer of a proportional royalty to Beach had been made on Wegner's own initiative.
6 While in earlier negotiations (both her own and Joyce's on her behalf), Beach's royalties had been limited to five years, she was now after that period to receive during her lifetime another 7,5% of Joyce's royalties, as Léon and Wegner wrote in their 12 October letter.
7 The Albatross/Odyssey Press reset the entire text, with corrections by Stuart Gilbert. See INTRODUCTION to the 1930s, p. 132.

November 2, 1932

Dear Mr Joyce

We were in the country over all Saints' Day and I found your pneu[1] when I got back last night. Can you come Tomorrow Thursday? I will wait for you at the shop until 6.30 if that is convenient for you.

I laughed like anything over the "Rime of the Ancient Mariner".[2]

Yours sincerely,
Sylvia Beach

> ALS, 1 leaf, 1 side, Sha&Co stationery. NLI Léon.
> To JJ at Hôtel Lord Byron, Champs-Elysées, Paris

1 See letter of 24 July 1924, note 10. Joyce's telegram not extant.
2 "A Portrait of the Artist as an Ancient Mariner", a poem Joyce wrote in October 1932 making fun of various issues concerning *Ulysses*, such as the Japanese and American piracies or his new European publisher, while also paying tribute to Beach. He gave the manuscript to Beach, who noted in its margin: "referring to the Albatross Press edition of Ulysses". (Buffalo IV.B.11: Occasional Verses) The poem was published in *JJII*, p. 654f., and in *Poems and Shorter Writings*, p. 143f.

November 8, 1932

Dear Monsieur Léon,

In reply to your letter, "Pomes Penyeach" is nearly out of print.[1] There are only fifty copies left, but they do not go off very fast at this time of the year. As they are the last ones and a first edition of James Joyce, I have raised the price to twenty francs. Mr Joyce need not feel that his contract with me for "Pomes" binds him in any way. He would be right in thinking that it is now time for it to be brought out by his publishers in England and America who would be only too glad to have it in their catalogues, and I am not well placed here to handle it properly. I haven't the money to advertise it as they would do.[2]

With regard to Mr Joyce's kind arrangement with the Albatross for me,[3] that I accepted unconditionally at first, in thinking about it I felt that, as no indemnity was given to me when "Ulysses" was transferred to another publisher's, I could accept twenty thousand francs as an equivalent, at least, of the value of the plates, but considering that I am not going to be attending to Mr Joyce's affairs from now on, I would not care to take any more than that. Later, however, if he is as rich as he deserves to be, and has no particular need of the percentage of his Albatross royalties that he wanted me to have,[4] I will then gladly accept it.

Yours sincerely,
Sylvia Beach

    TLS, 1 leaf, 1 side, Sha&Co stationery. NLI Léon.
    To Paul Léon at 27, Rue Casimir Périer, Paris VII

---

1 Beach's second publication for Joyce (1927). While Slocum and Cahoon give no definite number of copies (A24, p. 35), Beach speaks of 5000 copies in her letter to Joyce of 10 November 1931.
2 In his letters of 31 October and 7 November 1932, Léon had asked Beach whether she considered another edition of *Pomes Penyeach* (NLI Léon and Buffalo). Faber & Faber published the poems in March 1933; in 1936, Black Sun Press (by then based in New York) published them for the first time in America, as part of Joyce's *Collected Poems* (after the noncommercial publication by Princeton University Press in 1931, for which see letter of 25 April 1931, notes 6 and 7). In 1937, Joyce's American publisher Viking published them as part of their *Collected Poems*. (Slo + Ca, A 44f., pp. 56 and 58)
3 See letter of 24 October, notes 4-7.
4 While it had been Joyce's initiative to increase Beach's share of his royalties to 2,5%, he chose not to tell her that he was "planning to have his royalties increased by that amount": he wanted Beach to believe that her royalty came from his share and not from the publisher. (Crispi, p. 46) Eventually, however, she learned that "it did not affect Joyce's royalties" (*Sha&Co*, p. 206)

November 15, 1932

Dear Monsieur Léon,

Your letter of the 14th has come. As Mr Joyce insists so kindly on my accepting his arrangements with the Albatross, I will do so, and thank him very much indeed. Only I do think he has been too generous in this matter.[1]

As for "Pomes Penyeach", of course I would like to have kept the remaining fifty copies to sell as Joyce firsts at twenty francs apeice. With this business depression[2] the thousand francs should not have come amiss. But as Mr Joyce does not wish it I will not insist.[3] I am sending him twenty five copies and am keeping the other twenty five to give away to friends from time to time.

Yours sincerely,
Sylvia Beach

I hope Mr Joyce has found his Ms.

> TLS, 1 leaf, 1 side, Sha&Co stationery. NLI Léon.
> Postscript in Beach's hand.
> To Paul Léon at 27, Rue Casimir Périer, Paris VII

1 Léon's wording in his letter reinforces the impression that Beach's share was at Joyce's own expense: he wished the "association between his royalties and the payment to [her]" to remain as had originally been arranged." (14 November 1932, NLI Léon).
2 The global economic depression, which began in the U.S. and lasted throughout the 1930s. It caused no violent crisis in France and in particular, the banking crisis was relatively mild. However, if it began more slowly and was less severe than in the other industrial countries, it lasted longer than elsewhere. (Hautcœur, pp. 39-42) But Beach's sales to a good part depended on overseas tourists, especially Americans.
3 In that letter Léon also informed Beach that Joyce was opposed to such an expensive price for the poems and wanted to buy the remaining 50 copies.

November 28, 1932

Dear Monsieur Léon,

In reply to your letter of the 24th which has just reached me, I would be very glad if you could take over Mr Joyce's affairs with his various publishers on the continent, and I will let him know at once that you are doing so.[1] Also if you will be so kind as to come around to my shop some day I will hand over the papers to you.

It is interesting to hear about the limited edition of ULYSSES that is about to appear.[2]

Yours sincerely,
Sylvia Beach

>TLS, 1 leaf, 1 side, Sha&Co stationery. NLI Léon.
>To Paul Léon at 27, Rue Casimir Périer, Paris VII

1 Joyce had Léon ask Beach whether she wished "to continue the administration of his accounts with his German and other publishers for the various translations of his works". (Léon to Beach, 24 November 1932, Buffalo)
2 In that same letter, Léon informed her of the limited edition of *Ulysses* to be published by The Albatross /Odyssey Press in 25 commercial copies and 10 *hors de commerce* copies on handmade paper, one of which was to be "specially printed for you at Mr Joyce's request." Cf. also Slo + Ca, A 20, p. 30.

February [?], 1933

Dear Mr Joyce,
  I still have the 200 yen cheque.

Yours very sincerely,
Sylvia Beach

>ALS, 1 leaf, 1 side, Sha&Co stationery. NLI Léon.
>To JJ at 42, rue Galilée, Paris

March 3, 1933

Dear Monsieur Léon,

In reply to your letter, the price of seven francs per copy of "Our Exagmination" that I quoted to Mr Eliot in 1931 was not exorbitant[1] but simply what it cost me, "including printing, paper and authors' royalties paid outright on publication".[2] At that time there were two thousand copies left, and I have sold about fifty and given away to students, professors, journalists and libraries quite a number since then, so there are now perhaps a hundred copies less. I have not had time to count them. It seems very likely that when Mr Joyce's new book comes out there will be a demand for "Our Exagmination", and I am waiting for that event to advertise it again. But now, at last, when the moment is coming and there may be a chance to sell these studies, it would be rather stupid to turn over all the remaining copies to some publisher for a mere song. However, if one of them has a reasonable offer to make I would be glad to hear of it.

With regard to "Ulysses", I asked the price I thought it is worth, but when this was refused I asked for an offer. None was made to me. Not of a penny, except Mr Huebsch[3] who suggested paying me a small royalty in the dim future, provided all the expenses of the case were paid.

Yours sincerely,
Sylvia Beach

  TLS, 1 leaf, 1 side, Sha&Co stationery. NLI Léon.
  To Paul Léon at 27 Rue Casimir Périer, Paris

1 Inquiring in his letter of 1 March "at what price per copy [Beach] would be willing to remainder" the essay collection, Léon remarked that he and Joyce expected the price she had set in negotiations with Eliot and Faber & Faber the previous year to be lowered to some reasonable level. "Exorbitant" was actually Léon's word (possibly at Joyce's instruction): he used it in reference to the price Beach had demanded for her *Ulysses* rights, while suggestively conflating her financial claims on the two Joyce titles. (NLI Léon and Princeton).
2 Beach is quoting from her letter to Eliot of 3 September 1931. (Princeton) See letter of 5 September 1931, note 20.
3 Benjamin Huebsch of Viking at some point in their negotiations suggested that Beach might take a portion of the royalties, an idea that Joyce opposed. (Fitch, p. 321)

March 20, 1933

Dear Monsieur Léon,

Here is the two hundred yen cheque that you asked me to send you, and I am sending you under separate cover a copy of "Our Exagmination",[1] and to Mr Joyce the prospectuses for "The Joyce Book".[2] And will you please tell him that I will look up the books he mentions,[3] but am wondering whether he hasn't got them put away somewhere himself.

Yours sincerely,
Sylvia Beach

>TLS, 1 leaf, 1 side, Sha&Co stationery. NLI Léon.
>To Paul Léon at 27, Rue Casimir Périer, Paris VII

1 See letter of 8 July 1931, note 8.
2 See letter of 25 April 1931, note 8.
3 Léon had asked her for the leather-bound manuscript copies of *Chamber Music* and *Pomes Penyeach*. His letter has a note in Beach's hand: "Joyce found these later. SB". (17 March 1933, NLI Léon).

March 31, 1933

Dear Monsieur Léon,
 If it is not too much trouble will you kindly send me an acknowledgement that you received from me the Japanese two hundred yen cheque for Mr Joyce.

Yours sincerely,
Sylvia Beach

>TLS, 1 leaf, 1 side, Sha&Co stationery. NLI Léon.
>To Paul Léon at 27, Rue Casimir Périer, Paris VII

April 14, 1933

Dear Mr Joyce,
   I have replied that I have handed their letter to you and that you will communicate with them.[1] Is that all right?
   Wishing you a happy Easter

Yours very sincerely
Sylvia Beach

> APCS, Sha&Co stationery. NLI Léon.
> Enclosure: letter from Sadamu Nagamatsu et al., at NLI Léon and Buffalo.
> To JJ at 42, rue Galilée, Paris.

---

1   On 5 February 1933 the Japanese translators Sadamu Nagamatsu, Hisanori Tsujino and Hitoshi Ito inquired about the cheque they had sent in August 1932. "Will Mr Joyce accept the 200 yen and permit them to continue with the translation of *Ulysses* into Japanese." (Summary in Fahy, p. 224) Beach's reply dates from 31 March 1933 (Buffalo). Joyce, however, enraged about the poor fee, returned the cheque to the translators. Cf. also letter of 30 August 1932, note 1.

Monsieur Paul Léon,
27 Rue Casimir Périer,
Paris.

May 8, 1933

Dear Monsieur Leon,
 A copy of Chaucer's poems in the Oxford edition containing the A.B.C. Hymn to the Virgin went off to Mr Reece[1] by express post this morning.
 I think Mr Joyce's account now stands as follows –

Chaucer Frs.	14,00
postage	7
last bill, balance due	7,50
	Frs. 28,50

Please thank Mr Joyce for his cheque for Frs. 70 of May 4 which Miss Weaver handed me.

Yours sincerely,
Sylvia Beach

  TLS, 1 leaf, 1 side, Sha&Co stationery. NLI Léon.
  To Paul Léon at 27, Rue Casimir Périer, Paris VII

---

1 John Holroyd-Reece (1897-1969), German-English publisher and co-founder of The Albatross Press. At Joyce's suggestion he interceded with the London publisher Burnes and Oates to publish Lucia's new set of *lettrines* as illuminations to the "Chaucer Alphabet". The book was eventually published in 1936 by the Obelisk Press. See letter of 24 October 1932, notes 1 and 4.

June 22, 1933

Dear Monsieur Léon,

I have written to Mr Tibor Lutter who wrote the enclosed letters[1] and told him that perhaps you would be so kind as to give him the information he wants about Mr Joyce.

Yours sincerely
Sylvia Beach

>ALS, 1 leaf, 1 side, Sha&Co stationery. NLI Léon.
>Enclosure: 1 letter from Lutter to Beach.
>To Paul Léon at 27 Rue Casimir Périer, Paris

---

1 Tibor Lutter (1910-1960), a Hungarian literary scholar. In his letter of 19 June, Lutter asked Beach to send him all Joyce books available and to grant him a brief exchange with Joyce or someone else about the author. Since Joyce was very little known in Hungary, he wrote, he could well be the first there to study and write about him "as frankly as possible". (NLI Léon) Interwar Hungary had an authoritarian conservative regime. By the 1950s, when Lutter was a professor in Budapest, his criticism had become "a good example of a dogmatic Marxist approach" to literature. (Katona, p. 117).

July 1, 1933

Dear Monsieur Leon,

I am sending you herewith a cheque for Mr Joyce for Frs. 410,00, equivalent of $20 which the Whitman Publishing Co.[1] has sent me for the right to include three of his poems in Miss Harriet Monroe's Anthology.[2]

Thank you very much for bringing me the book from Mr Joyce the other day. I forgot to ask him where to forward his letters in case any come here for him this summer, and you are perhaps going away. Will you please let me know?

Yours sincerely,
Sylvia Beach

> TLS, 1 leaf, 1 side, Sha&Co stationery. NLI Léon.
> To Paul Léon at 27, Rue Casimir Périer, Paris VII

1 Specializing in children's books, puzzles, and greeting cards, the American Whitman Publishing Company was hardly known as a literary publisher. https://whitman.com/about-us/history/, accessed 7 May 2020.
2 *A Book of Poems for Every Mood* (1933), edited by Harriet Monroe and Morton Dauwen Zabel, contained poems from the Renaissance to Joyce's time. https://picclick.com/POEMS-for-EVERY-MOOD-COMPILED-by-HARRIET-MONROE-323820509267.html#&gid=1&pid=8, accessed 7 May 2020. Harriet Monroe, founder of the American magazine *Poetry*, had already published a number of poems from *Pomes Penyeach* in her periodical.

August 7, 1933

Mr James Joyce
c/o Paul Léon
27 rue Casimir-Périer
Paris VII

Dear Sir,
   Miss Beach has asked me to send you the enclosed press cuttings.[1]

Sincerely yours,
p.p. Shakespeare and Company
Jane van Meter[2]

> TLS, 1 leaf, 1 side, Sha&Co stationery. ZJJF Jahnke.
> Enclosures: 2 press cuttings glued on at lower left-hand corner of letter.
> To JJ at Hôtel Richemond, Geneva (via Paul Léon)

---

1 Two short articles from unidentified American newspapers, entitled "Ulysses in Court. Plea to Permit Publication Will Be Argued July 25" and "Test set for Ulysses. Agreement Made for Single Judge to Pass on Book Seizure" respectively. After Joyce had signed the contract with Random House, Bennett Cerf attempted to bring the issue of the American ban on *Ulysses* to trial. By 18 July 1933, he reported that the book had indeed been seized and that a trial was scheduled for the autumn of 1933. "The government's suit for the confiscation of a copy of James Joyce's 'Ulysses' and a counter motion for its release will be decided on motion without trial before a single judge of the United States District Court, counsel for both sides agreed yesterday," as the latter article says.

2 Beach's American assistant for some time in the first half of the 1930s. "The first and only really professional assistant I ever had was Miss Jane van Meter, now Mrs. Charlton Hinman – her husband is a Shakespearean expert. I put an ad in the Paris Herald Tribune and Miss van Meter answered it. I could not wish anybody better luck than to have her as an assistant." (*Sha&Co*, p. 209).

December 9, 1933

Dear Mr Joyce,

Your telephone was not working when I tried to call you up. I wanted to congratulate you for the lifting of the ban on <u>Ulysses</u> in the United States.[1] I am so very glad of it. No more pirating, and what Harold Nicholson[2] at the Sorbonne last night called "the greatest modern work" will now be available to everyone. I am very happy over it.

The 'Herald', 'Tribune'[3] and 'Associated Press' called up a good deal on Thursday for your address, an interview with you and any comments you cared to make, but with no result of course. Mr Egbert Swenson[4] of the 'Trib' even came to the shop and was quite threatening. He went to see Wegner.[5]

Also I wanted to tell you what Harold Nicholson said in his lecture for the British Institute at the Sorbonne last evening. Almost the whole time he talked about your work, and with great emotion and enthusiasm.

Yours sincerely
Sylvia Beach

> ALS, 1 leaf, 2 sides, Sha&Co stationery. ZJJF Jahnke.
> To JJ at 42, rue Galilée, Paris

1 After more than twelve years, the ban was lifted on 6 December 1933 by Judge John M. Woolsey, the very day after Prohibition was repealed in the U.S. (Turner, p. 197) Arguing mainly along aesthetic lines and referring to the stream of consciousness technique with "its necessary implications" of "incidentally us[ing] certain words", he also presented Joyce as a literary sociologist, who "seeks to draw a true picture of the lower middle class in a European city" (Woolsey, pp. xi and xii). Woolsey famously concluded his judgment by stating: "... whilst in many places the effect of *Ulysses* on the reader undoubtedly is somewhat emetic, nowhere does it tend to be aphrodisiac. *Ulysses* may, therefore, be admitted into the United States." (ibid, p. xiv).

Before the final court decision, Woolsey also publicly took a stance against censorship: "I think things should take their chance on the market. Otherwise you have bootlegging, everybody sees about as much as though the traffic was openly permitted and the profits all go to persons illegally engaged." (*New York Times*, issue of 26 November 1933, Princeton)

Woolsey's decision in favour of *Ulysses* was included in the first Random House edition, which was published on 25 January 1934. Ironically, the novel's text was based on the corrupted version of Roth's pirated *Ulysses*. (Slo + Ca, A 21, p. 31).

2 See letter of 17 August 1931, note 3.
3 The *Chicago Herald* and the *New York Herald Tribune*.
4 Unknown.
5 Max Christian Wegner, co-founder and Paris representative of the Albatross Press, Hamburg. See also letter of 24 October 1932, note 4.

March 16, 1935

Dear Mr Joyce,
    Kahane[1] has given his consent so I am sending you <u>Miss Dorothy Pantling's</u>[2] two books for your signature.
    With many thanks

Yours sincerely
Sylvia Beach

    ALS, 1 leaf, 1 side, Sha&Co stationery. NLI Léon.
    To JJ at 42, rue Galilée, Paris

1 See second letter of 2 May 1931, note 1.
2 Identity unknown. In 1935, a Dorothy Pantling working as language teacher at the British Institute initiated the Institute's Seminar Library. She might be the actress Dorothy Pantling, who played Julia, with John Gielgud as Romeo, in a BBC radio production and who features in various poetry readings on BBC (Beck, p. 211, and https://books.google.be/books?id=s0 JYAAAAMAAJ&q=%22Dorothy+Pantling%22&dq=%22Dorothy+Pantling%22&hl=nl&sa =X&ved=0ahUKEwj344nihP_WAhUBohoKHUxpDs4Q6AEIRTAE, accessed 19 March 2020).

Sept 13 193[?]5   Les Déserts, Savoie

Dear Mr Léon,

I hope it is not too much trouble for you to forward the enclosed letter to Herbert Gorman.[1] I have not got his address and perhaps he has left the Vosges by this time and is now in Paris. But in case he has gone back to America I have put a 1.75 stamp on it. I would like to get in touch with him if possible.

Thank you so much!

Yours sincerely
Sylvia Beach

       APCS, picture overleaf of Chambéry, La Dent du Nivolet (1553m). NLI Léon.
       Dating: Fahy, p. 164
       To Paul Léon at 27 Rue Casimir Périer, Paris

1 See undated letter [after 14 July, before 22 July 1924], note 4.

December 5, 1935

Dear Mr Joyce,

Here is a copy of your <u>Daniele Defoe</u>.[1] I hope there are not too many mistakes. Paulhan[2] and Mr Henry Church[3] are anxious to have the honour of publishing it in <u>Mesures</u>[4] and Paulhan says if you would consent to have it translated into French the Italian text could be printed opposite.[5] Mr Church, who is an old friend of Pound[6] and subscribed to the first edition of 'Ulysses' would be very glad to have the pleasure of calling on you one day about the matter.

I enclose a letter from Factorevitch.[7]

Thank you so much for your cheque of November 26th for 60 frs.

---

1 In March 1912 Joyce delivered two lectures on Defoe and Blake at the Università Popolare Triestina, under the title "Verismo ed idealismo nella letteratura inglese (Daniele De Foe – William Blake)". The fair copy manuscripts used to be in Beach's library [Slo + Ca, E 11.x, p. 154f.] and are now at Buffalo. (VII.A.2.a.i. and VII.A.2.b.i.)
2 See letter of 13 June 1931, note 8, and note 4 below.
3 Henry Hall Church (1880-1947) and his Bavarian wife Barbara Church, a wealthy American couple living in a Le Corbusier-designed villa near Paris at the time. They were collectors of modern art and belonged to the literary circles around Beach, having been members of both her and Adrienne Monnier's library since 1927. The patron of several and the friend of many authors such as Wallace Stevens, Vladimir Nabokov and Robert Musil, Henry Church was also a writer in his own right. (Whelpton, p. 331, and Fitch, p. 349).
4 A French literary journal founded in January 1935, an offshoot of the *Nouvelle Revue Française*, managed by Adrienne Monnier (and Jane van Meter) and directed by Jean Paulhan, Henri Michaux, the philosopher Bernard Groethuysen, and the Italian poet Giuseppe Ungaretti. It was financed by Henry and Barbara Church. (Fitch, p. 349) *Mesures* soon began to publish translations of literature in English, such as works by W.H. Auden, Christopher Isherwood, E.M. Forster, Robert Frost.
5 Joyce's essay never appeared in *Mesures*. He made several unsuccessful attempts to publish the lecture, which was never published in his lifetime. In June 1913, he had submitted "Daniele Defoe, Part I" to Adolfo Orvieto, the editor of the Florence literary journal, *Il Marzocco* (cf. also del Greco Lobner). It first appeared in a Buffalo Studies volume on Defoe (1964) and in English translation in Joyce's *Occasional, Critical and Political Writings* under the title "Realism and Idealism in English Literature (Daniel Defoe – William Blake)".
6 See letter of 1 August 1924, note 6.
7 Not much is known about Factorevitch or Factorovitch (his first name possibly being Stuart), who acted as an assistant to Joyce in 1929. (Gilbert, p. 90) In a letter to Harriet Weaver Joyce explained what was Factorovitch's principal role: "He is a Russian (a bolshevik too and possibly a semi-official-one) but I don't mind as we never talk politics and he is most obliging but chiefly he represents a class of my readers which ought to have their say, i.e. the foreignborn admirers." (Letter of 28 May 1929, *SL*, p. 341).

I hope you and all your family are well and the 'Work in Progress' is being finished. There are a great many enquiries for it.

Yours very sincerely
Sylvia Beach

> ALS, 1 leaf, 1 side, Sha&Co stationery. ZJJF Jahnke.
> Enclosures missing.
> To JJ at 7 rue Edmond Valentin, Paris

SHAKESPEARE AND COMPANY
SYLVIA BEACH
12, RUE DE L'ODÉON — PARIS · VIᵉ

Téléphone:
Danton 09-57

Registre du Commerce
Seine 284.403

December 5th 1935

Dear Mr Joyce,
            Here is a copy of your Daniele Defoe. I hope there are not too many mistakes. Paulhan and Mr Henry Church are anxious to have the honour of publishing it in *Mesures* and Paulhan says if you would consent to have it translated into French the Italian text could be printed opposite. Mr Church, who is an old friend of Pound and subscribed to the first edition of 'Ulysses' would be very glad to have the pleasure of calling on you one day about the matter.
            I enclose a letter from Factorevitch.
            Thank you so much for your cheque of November 26th for 600 frs.
            I hope you and all your family are well and that 'Work in Progress' is being finished. There are a great many enquiries for it.
                        Yours very sincerely
                                    Sylvia Beach

FIGURE 18   Letter of 5 December 1935, Beach's new stationery
© SYLVIA BEACH ESTATE

February 28th, 1936

Dear Mr Joyce,

I am sending you under separate cover by registered post the eight copies of your 'De Honni-Soit à Mal-y-chance'[1] that the editors of 'Mesures' have had specially printed 'à part' for you. They admire it so much.

They are giving all eight of them to you, but have intimated that as a special favour, they would be glad if you would be very kind and sign one for Henry Church and one for Barbara his wife,[2] and one each for Jean Paulhan[3] and Germaine his wife. And your humble servants Adrienne Monnier & S B would each like one too if you saw fit.

Yours very sincerely
Sylvia Beach

    ALS, 1 leaf, 1 side, Sha&Co stationery. ZJJF Jahnke.
    To JJ at 7 rue Edmond Valentin, Paris

1 A translation of Joyce's essay "From a Banned Writer to a Banned Singer" by Armand Petitjean, reviewed by the author. It appeared in the French journal *Mesures*, II.1 (15 January 1936), pp. 91-99. There were 8 numbered and signed offprints. (Slo + Ca, D 34, p. 114).
2 See preceding letter, note 3.
3 See letter of 13 June 1931, note 8.

[August 3, 1936]

Dear Monsieur Léon

    Miss Beach sailed for America last week.[1] She will not be back until the middle of September.

    I enclose the receipt for the cheque you sent on July 31st 1936.

Yours sincerely
p.p. Shakespeare & Company
Margaret H. Newitt[2]

> ALS, 1 leaf, 1 side, Sha&Co stationery. NLI Léon.
> Dating: see enclosure below (receipt).
> To Paul Léon at 27 Rue Casimir Périer, Paris

Le 3 Août 1936
Reçu de Monsieur Léon
Le somme de frs 92555[3]
neuf cents vingt cinq francs
cinquante cinq centimes
par cheque no 3738514 Banque de France
Pour Miss Sylvia Beach
p.p. Shakespeare & Company
Margaret H. Newitt
(secretary)

> TDS, 1 leaf, 1 side, Sha&Co stationery. NLI Léon.
> Enclosure to preceding letter.
> Next to the signature, 3 fiscal stamps, each with a value of 25cts. and stamped "Received with thanks / Shakespeare and Company"
> To Paul Léon at 27 Rue Casimir Périer, Paris

---

1 This was Beach's first visit to America after 22 years, to celebrate her father's 84th birthday. (Fitch, p. 365).

2 Margaret Hope Newitt, an American student, who spoke fluent French, Beach's part-time secretary from 1936-37. (Fitch, p. 363).

3 The 2,5% royalties Beach received from the Odyssey Press edition of *Ulysses*.

July 2, 1937

<u>Vendredi, 2 Juillet 1937</u>
en soirée, à partir de 21h
les Amis de Shakespeare and Company fêteront la revue anglaise *Life and Letters Today*[1]
R.S.V.P Rafraîchissements

12, rue de l'Odéon, Paris (VIe)

> APC, 1 leaf, 1 side, Sha&Co stationery. ZJJF Jahnke.
> Not in Sylvia Beach's hand.
> To JJ at 7 rue Edmond Valentin, Paris

---

1 *Life and Letters Today* was an English literary magazine, owned and run by the poet, novelist, patron and critic Bryher (born Annie Winifred Ellerman), who had purchased it in 1935. The poet Robert Herring was its editor (http://www.imagists.org/hd/hdcmone.html, accessed 2 October 2020). On occasion of the Paris *Exposition Internationale*, which opened in June 1937, *Life and Letters Today* presented an all-French number, and Beach was in charge of the *Life and Letters* booth at the exposition. The formal reception she held in honour of Bryher and her magazine was to be the last gathering of the Friends of Shakespeare and Company (Fitch, p. 373).

March 6, 1939

Dear Mr Leon,
   Thank you very much for your cheque for Frs 596.18 for further royalties from the Albatross edition of Ulysses in 1936. Please thank Mr Joyce for me.

Yours sincerely
Sylvia Beach

>   APCS, Sha&Co stationery. NLI Léon.
>   To Paul Léon at 27 Rue Casimir Périer, Paris

APPENDIX A

Chronology of Major Events 1917-1941

FIGURE 19 Sylvia Beach at her bookshop, undated
PHOTOGRAPHER UNKNOWN. COURTESY OF SPECIAL COLLECTIONS, PRINCETON UNIVERSITY

1917	*March*	Sylvia Beach, a Paris resident for many years, first visits "La Maison des Amis des Livres", lending library and bookshop, and meets Adrienne Monnier.
1919	*January-July*	Sylvia and her sister Holly do post-war volunteer work in Serbia. Returns to Paris with plans to open a bookshop in London.
	November 19	"Shakespeare and Company" opens its doors at 8 rue Dupuytren, Paris.
1920	*July 11*	Sylvia Beach meets James Joyce at a party at André Spire's, a French writer, poet and friend of Adrienne.
	July 12	Joyce visits Beach at her bookshop.
	October	First (abortive) contract for a stage performance of *Exiles* in Paris. By July 1924 at least four attempts had failed.
1921	*February 21*	Margaret Anderson and Jane Heap, editors of *The Little Review*, where *Ulysses* had been serialized since April 1918, are convicted of publishing obscenity and fined $50 each. The publication of *Ulysses* in the English-speaking world becomes even less feasible.
	End of March	Beach offers Joyce to publish *Ulysses*.
	April 5	B.W. Huebsch declines to publish *Ulysses* after *The Little Review* court case.
	mid-April 1921	Beach signs a contract with Maurice Darantiere, master printer in Dijon, to print and publish *Ulysses*.
	July 27	Beach reopens her shop at 12, rue de l'Odéon. She moves in with Adrienne Monnier at 18, rue de l'Odéon.
	December 7	Valery Larbaud's *Ulysses* lecture and reading at Monnier's bookshop starts the French campaign for *Ulysses*.
1922	*February 2*	*Ulysses* is published by "Shakespeare and Company" in a first edition of 1,000 copies.
	August 18	Joyce meets Harriet Weaver for the first time, after she had supported him – anonymously in the beginning – ever since 1917.

	October	First English *Ulysses* edition (2,000 copies) published for the Egoist Press, London, by John Rodker, Paris. 500 copies were reportedly confiscated and burnt by British and American customs.
		By the end of the year, *Ulysses* has become "Shakespeare and Company's" bestseller, despite its high selling price.
1923	*January*	Second English edition published by John Rodker/Egoist Press, to replace the 500 destroyed ones. These were again confiscated by English customs authorities, but at least three copies survived.
1924	*November*	Phonograph record made of Joyce reading "Mr Taylor's Speech" from *Ulysses*.
1925	*February-March*	First performance of *Exiles* in English in New York (Neighborhood Playhouse)
	Sept 1925-Sept 1926	Five instalments of *Work in Progress* published in Samuel Roth's *Two Worlds*.
	October	A first version of "Anna Livia Plurabelle" in its original language published in Monnier's French journal *Navire d'Argent*.
1926	*July 1926-October 1927*	Twelve instalments of *Ulysses* published in Samuel Roth's *Two Worlds' Monthly* (unauthorized).
1927	*February 2*	International Letter of Protest, signed by 167 writers (among them Lady Gregory, Hemingway, D.H. Lawrence, Sean O'Casey, Virginia Woolf and Einstein), appears as a poster for display and as a pamphlet.
	April	International Letter of Protest published in *The Humanist*.
	April	First instalment of "Work in Progress" published in the first issue of Eugene Jolas's *transition*.
	April	Beach writes two letters to Joyce (one of them never sent off), telling him that she feels financially and emotionally exploited.

	June	Sylvia Beach's mother commits suicide; Beach lets her family believe that it was a heart failure.
	July 5	Joyce's *Pomes Penyeach* published by "Shakespeare and Company".
	October	First ever full translation of *Ulysses* – into German by Georg Goyert – appears in the Rhein-Verlag (Basel, Switzerland)
1928	*January 1928 to January 1930*	Joyce has five fragments of *Work in Progress* printed in America in order to prevent piracy.
	October 20	First edition of *Anna Livia Plurabelle* published in New York by Crosby Gaige.
1929	*February*	French translation of *Ulysses* by Auguste Morel published by "La Maison des Amis des Livres", Adrienne Monnier.
	End of May	*Our Exagmination Round his Factification for Incamination of Work in Progress*, by Samuel Beckett et al., published by "Shakespeare and Company".
	End of August	Another recording: Joyce reading the last pages of *Anna Livia Plurabelle*, at the Orthological Institute in London.
		In the U.S., Samuel Roth publishes a pirated edition of the 9th printing of *Ulysses* by "Shakespeare and Company".
1930	*January*	Second printing of the French *Ulysse* by Adrienne Monnier.
	May 15	Prof. Alfred Vogt successfully operates Joyce's eye in Zurich.
	June 12	Trade edition of *Anna Livia Plurabelle* published by Faber & Faber.
	June 30	Publication of *Haveth Childers Everywhere: Fragment from Work in Progress*, published by Henri Babou and Jack Kahane, Paris, and The Fountain Press, New York.
	June	Beach catches pneumonia, leaves Paris for 3 months.
	October	Third printing of the French *Ulysse* by Adrienne Monnier.
	December 9	Memorandum of Agreement between Beach and Joyce regarding the rights of publication of *Ulysses*.

1931	March 26	Adrienne Monnier organises a reading of the French *Anna Livia Plurabelle* at her bookshop.
	April 23	Joyce moves to London with Nora and Lucia.
	May 1	*Anna Livia Plurabelle*, translated into French by the seven translators known as the "Septuagint", appears in the *Nouvelle Revue Française*.
	May 2	With the help of her father, Beach secures the American copyright for *Pomes Penyeach*, a reaction to a young enthusiast's plans to print and sell the poems in America.
	May 8	Trade edition of *Haveth Childers Everywhere* published in Faber & Faber's *Criterion Miscellany* series.
	End of May	Benjamin Huebsch of Viking Press of New York is the first to make an offer for an American edition of *Ulysses*.
	mid-June	Rumours of another Roth piracy of *Ulysses* are circulating in New York.
	July 4	Joyce and Nora Barnacle get married in London.
	July	Joyce signs a contract for *Work in Progress* with Viking and Faber & Faber.
	July 19	The German *Frankfurter Zeitung* publishes as story by a Michael Joyce under James Joyce's name, marking the beginning of Joyce's campaign of litigation.
	early September	Beach dismisses her long-time employee Myrsine Moschos, "for economic and for other reasons".
	September 24	Joyce returns to Paris from London.
	November	The first edition of *Pomes Penyeach* is nearly sold out. Beach plans a second printing, which she does not pursue.
	December	Having failed to secure a contract in late summer, Japanese translators illegally publish a first volume of *Ulysses*.
	December 29	Death of Joyce's father.

1932	2 February	Joyce's daughter Lucia has a mental breakdown. She is institutionalized for a few days, the first of many times.
	February 4	In a letter to Paul Léon, Beach officially resigns as publisher of *Ulysses*. Léon's reply to her marks the beginning of his official role as Joyce's secretary and advisor.
	February 5	The first volume of a second Japanese translation of *Ulysses* is published: another piracy.
	February 15	Birth of Joyce's grandson, Stephen James Joyce, son of Giorgio and Helen Kastor Fleischmann Joyce.
	End of March	Joyce signs a contract with Random House for an American edition of *Ulysses*.
	August 8	Warner Brothers asks for *Ulysses* screen rights.
	End of September	Beach settles up the account between Joyce and herself for the 11th – and last – Shakespeare and Company edition.
	October	*Pomes Penyeach*, with illuminated initials by Lucia Joyce, published by The Obelisk Press, Paris, and Desmond Harmsworth, London.
	December 1	*Ulysses* first published on the continent outside France under the Albatross *ad-hoc* imprint 'The Odyssey Press', Hamburg, Paris, and Bologna.
1933	February 2	*The Joyce Book* published by The Sylvan Press and Oxford University Press, containing musical settings of the poems of *Pomes Penyeach* by 13 different composers.
	March 14	In spite of the severe rift in their relationship, Beach receives a first signed copy of the new English edition of *Pomes Penyeach* by Faber & Faber. With many of the American expatriates leaving Europe as a result of the economic crisis, Sylvia Beach's business suffers severely.
	December 6	In the US District Court trial "The United States v. One Book Called *Ulysses*" Judge John M. Woolsey lifts the American ban on *Ulysses*.

CHRONOLOGY OF MAJOR EVENTS 1917-1941

1934	*January 25*	First copies printed of authorized American edition of *Ulysses* published by Random House in New York. The edition proper follows in February.
	February 2	Beach and Monnier do not attend Joyce's birthday party and celebration of the US edition. Contacts with Joyce are at a minimum during the rest of the year.
	End of April	Sales of the American edition are at 35,000.
1935		Beach's problems this year are mainly financial. Efforts – with poor results – to sell manuscripts Joyce had given her as a present, in order to carry "Shakespeare and Company" through the depression.
1936	*February*	André Gide initiates a two-year series of readings for "Les Amis de Shakespeare and Company", founded to rescue Sylvia Beach's enterprise. As a paid-up member Joyce also attends.
	mid-July	For the first time in 22 years Beach visits the US and her family, returning mid-October.
	October	Beach contacts A.S.W. Rosenbach, the owner of the John Quinn *Ulysses* MS in New York, hoping to sell Joyce material – without success, however.
	October 3	First English edition, printed in England by John Lane | The Bodley Head, London.
	October	Beach moves out of the flat she shared with Monnier at 18, rue de l'Odéon, as Gisèle Freund had moved in in her absence. She now lives on her own, at no. 12, but maintains her friendship with Monnier.
1937		Business at the bookshop is meagre. Although there are still many customers who borrow books, only few people buy them.
	July	Holidays on Jersey, Beach starts writing her memoirs.
1938	*May*	Joyce's last formal visit to Beach and Monnier, at "Shakespeare and Company", to pose for publicity pictures for the publication of *Finnegans Wake*. The photographer is Gisèle Freund.
1939	*May*	Publication of *Finnegans Wake*. New York: The Viking Press; London: Faber & Faber.
1941	*December*	After America's entry into the war, Beach is forced to close her bookshop. It would never reopen during her lifetime.

APPENDIX B

Survey of Correspondence between Sylvia Beach and James Joyce or Paul Léon

1 Survey with Addresses

- "Paris" is not indicated with Joyce's private address unless he is staying at a hotel or a Résidence.
- Beach's much rarer travels/holidays are integrated into the column of her letters (marked in grey). Unless otherwise specified, Beach wrote her letters from Paris.
- Dates of Joyce's letters to Beach: with the help of the Buffalo catalogue and the Beach letters many approximations could be improved, or dates could be corrected as a result of evidence in her letters. *pm* = postmark.
Whenever a date was revised, the *JJtoSB* letter number is provided.

Beach to Joyce	Joyce's address	Joyce to Beach
	2 Nov-1 Dec	
	9, rue de l'Université	
3 Jan 1921	*1 Dec 1920-3 Jun 1921*	
	5, boulevard Raspail	
16 Feb 1921	|	n.d. [early 1921]
22 Feb 1921	|	
7 Apr 1921	|	
n.d. [10 Apr 1921]	|	9 April 1921
Cyprian Beach pp S. Beach	|	visiting card
[verso Joyce's visiting card]	|	
	|	13 Apr 1921
	|	16 May 1921
	?blvd Raspail / rue Card. Lemoine?	n.d. [Spring-Summer 1921?]
28 Jun 1921	*3 Jun-1 Oct*	
	71, rue du Cardinal Lemoine	

(cont.)

Beach to Joyce	Joyce's address	Joyce to Beach
n.d. [between 10 Jun and 27 Jul 1921]		
		n.d. [Jun to Sep?1921]
early Sep 1921 5 days at Hyères (Mediterranean coast)	*Jul-1 Oct 1921* 71, rue du Cardinal Lemoine	
	1 Oct 1921-17 Aug 1922 9, rue de l'Université	
		2 Feb 1922
		11 Feb 1922
		14 Mar 1922
		visiting card
		1 Apr 1922
		n.d. [? 1922]
		n.d. [after 13 May 1922]
27 Jul 1922 Statement of accounts		
n.d. [on/after 12 Aug 1922] Statement of accounts		
	18 Aug-15 Sep London Folkstone and Boulogne	
no evidence that SB took a vacation in August		29 Aug 1922
		5 Sep 1922
	18 Sep-11 or 12 Oct 9, rue de l'Université	n.d. [on/after 18 Sep 1922] *JJtoSB* no. 12
	13 Oct-12 Nov Nice	n.d., *pm* 13 Oct 1922 pc
		24 Oct 1922
		30 Oct 1922
		2 Nov 1922 telegram

(*cont.*)

Beach to Joyce	Joyce's address	Joyce to Beach
	12-14 Nov en route to Paris	
	14 Nov 1922-3 Apr 1923 26, Ave Charles Floquet	24 Dec 1922
	3-c. 12 Apr Neuilly, Maison de Santé (dental troubles)	
	12-25 Apr 26, Ave Charles Floquet	
	25 Apr-beginning of May Dr. Borsch's Clinique des Yeux	
	then back to 26 Ave Charles Floquet *until 18 Jun*	
	18-21 Jun Calais	
	21-29 Jun London	
	|	25 Jun 1923 pc
26 Jun 1923	|	
	|	28 Jun 1923 telegram
29 Jun 1923	*29 Jun-3 Aug* Bognor	
	|	12 Jul 1923
	|	n.d., *pm* 10-19 Jul 1923
	|	*JJtoSB* no. 211
	|	20 Jul 1923
27 Jul 1923	|	
	|	28 Jul 1923 telegram
	|	29 Jul 1923

(cont.)

Beach to Joyce	Joyce's address	Joyce to Beach
1923: no mention of a holiday in Fitch	*3-17 Aug* London *17 Aug-c. 3 Sep* Tours *3 Sep 1923-c. 7 Jul 1924* Paris Victoria Palace Hotel	
	|	n.d., *pm* 28 Aug 1923 pc
	|	*JJtoSB* no. 210
	|	15 Nov 192[?3]
	|	3 Feb 1924
	|	n.d., pm 27 Feb 1924
	|	n.d., probably before 8 April 1924
	|	*JJtoSB* no. 22
	|	n.d. [8 Apr 1924]
	|	*JJtoSB* no. 23
	|	12 Apr 1924
	|	16 Apr 1924
	|	19 Apr 1924
	|	n.d., *pm* 20 Apr 1924
	|	25 Apr 1924
	|	28 Apr 1924
	|	30 Apr 1924
	|	1 May 1924
12 Jun 1924	*10-c. 22 Jun* Dr. Borsch's Clinique des Yeux	
n.d. [after 14 Jun, before 22 Jul 1924] 23 Jun [?1924] 1 Jul 1924	| | | Paris Victoria Palace Hotel	
	|	4 Jul 1924

(*cont.*)

Beach to Joyce	Joyce's address	Joyce to Beach
	c. 7 Jul-18 Aug Saint-Malo	10 Jul 1924 pc
11 Jul 1924 holidays planned but deferred / cancelled because of father visiting		12 Jul 1924
		13 Jul 1924 pc
16 Jul 1924		
		17 Jul 1924
22 Jul 1924		
		23 Jul 1924
24 Jul 1924		
		25 Jul 1924
		28 Jul 1924 pc
29 Jul 1924		
1 Aug 1924		
		5 Aug 1924
7 Aug 1924 pc		
8 Aug 1924		8 Aug 1924 telegram
		12 Aug 1924 telegram
		12 Aug 1924 [wrongly dated 12 July 1924]
		JJtoSB no. 34
14 Aug 1924		
	Saint-Malo	17 Aug 1924
	Quimper	21 Aug 1924
		26 Aug 1924
		28 Aug 1924 telegram
	29 Aug-5 Sep Vannes	29 Aug 1924 telegram
		1 Sep 1924 pc

(*cont.*)

Beach to Joyce	Joyce's address	Joyce to Beach
	5-16 Sep Paris Victoria Palace Hotel	
	16-18 (or 19) Sep Calais	
	18 (or 19) Sep-c. 12 Oct London	
	|	n.d., pm 24 Sep 1924
	|	1 Oct 1924
	|	6 Oct 1924
	|	9 Oct 1924
	8, Avenue Charles Floquet	16 Oct 1924
	|	7 Nov 1924
	|	8 Nov 1924
n.d. [?20 Nov 1924]	|	
	|	21 Nov 1924
	28 Nov-c. 10 Dec Dr. Borsch's Clinique des Yeux	
	8, Avenue Charles Floquet	20 Dec 1924
	|	30 Dec 1924 pc
	|	31 Dec 1924
	|	*JJtoSB no 55*
29 Jan 1925	|	
	|	30 Jan 1925
	|	14 Feb 1925
	c. 15-25 Feb 1925 Dr. Borsch's Clinique des Yeux	
14 Mar 1925	8, Avenue Charles Floquet	n.d. [? Spring 1925]
	|	n.d. [? Spring 1925]
	|	14 Mar 1925
30 Mar 1925 pc	|	
	|	Easter [12 April] 1925

(*cont.*)

Beach to Joyce	Joyce's address	Joyce to Beach
	15-25 Apr Dr. Borsch's Clinique des Yeux *then up to mid-May at* 8, Ave Charles Floquet *second half of May* Paris, Victoria Palace Hôtel *from 1 Jun-21 Jul* 2 Square Robiac	
	|	5 Jul 1925
	|	n.d. [probably 11 Jul 1925]
	|	*JJtoSB* no. 61
	|	n.d. [? 14 Jul 1925]
	|	20 July 1925
	?Fécamp	n.d., *pm* 21-28 Jul 1925
		JJtoSB no. 64
	Fécamp	27 Jul 1925
	Rouen	28 Jul 1925 telegram
	|	29 Jul 1925
	|	[31 Jul] 1925
from 2-c. 20 Aug 1925 Les Déserts, Haute Savoie	travelling to Arcachon via Niort and Bordeaux	10 Aug 1925 pc
	11 Aug-c. 3 Sep Arcachon	14 Aug 1925 pc
	|	n.d. [20-29 Aug 1925]
	|	22 Aug 1925
	|	n.d., *pm* 25 Aug 1925 pc
	|	*JJtoSB* no. 72
	|	n.d., *pm* 28 Aug 1925 pc
	|	*JJtoSB* no. 73
	|	n.d. [23 Aug-3 Sep 1925]
	|	*JJtoSB* no. 74
	|	1 Sep 1925
	c. 3-5 Sep Bordeaux	4 Sep 1925 telegram

SURVEY OF CORRESPONDENCE BETWEEN BEACH AND JOYCE OR LÉON 289

(cont.)

Beach to Joyce	Joyce's address	Joyce to Beach
			5 Sep 1925 telegram
	5 Sep 1925-5 Aug 1926	
	2 Square Robiac	
			19 Oct 1925
	5-15 Dec	
	Dr. Borsch's Clinique des Yeux; unable to do any serious work for weeks	
	2 Square Robiac	[25 Dec] 1925
			29 Jan 192[6]
16 Feb 1926			
			14 Mar 1926
			Easter [4 Apr] 1926
22 May 1926			
	after 7 June operation on left eye (?Dr. Borsch)	
			19 June 1926
13 Jul 1926			
end of Jul 1926: one week at Boulogne; then move to Les Déserts until end of Aug	*c. 5 Aug-13 Sep* Ostend	n.d. *pm*: 6 Aug 1926 pc
n.d. [c. 10 Aug 1926]			
			10 Aug 1926 pc
12 Aug 1926			
19 Aug 1926 pc Myrsine Moschos pp SB			
			24 Aug 1926
			26 Aug 1926 telegram
c. 28 Aug 1926			
			29 Aug 1926 pc
1 Sep 1926			
			2 Sep 1926
9 Sep 1926			
10 Sep 1926 telegram			

(cont.)

Beach to Joyce	Joyce's address	Joyce to Beach
10 Sep 1926		
		11 Sep 1926
n.d. [before 16 Sep] pc		
		13 Sep 1926 telegram
16 Sep 1926	Ghent	16 Sep 1926 pc
		17 Sep 1926 telegram
	Antwerp	19 Sep 1926
		20 Sep 1926 telegram
	Brussels	22 Sep 1926
		23 Sep 1926
		JJtoSB no. 88
		n.d. [20-29 Sep 1926]
		26 Sep 1926
		n.d. [20-27 Sep 1926] pc
28 Sep 1926		*JJtoSB* no. 91
		29 Sep 1926 telegram
29 Sep 1926	*29 Sep 1926-4 Apr 1927*	
	2 Square Robiac	
22 Oct 1926		
25 Oct 1926		
26 Oct 1926		
2 Nov 1926		
5 Nov 1926		
		n.d. [after 5 Nov 1926]
		JJtoSB no. 92
24 Nov 1926		
24 Nov 1926 Statement of accounts		
29 Nov 1926		
n.d. Monday [? early Dec 1926]		
17 Dec 1926		
3 Jan 1927		
		n.d. [? late Jan 1927]
		30 Jan 192[7]
		n.d. [? Feb 1927]

(cont.)

Beach to Joyce	Joyce's address	Joyce to Beach
		n.d. [17 Feb 1927]
		17 Mar 1927
	4-c. 8 Apr London	5 Apr 1927 pc
	c. 8 Apr-21 May Square Robiac	n.d., pm 8 Apr 1927 pc
12 Apr 1927 [not sent]		
29 Apr 1927		
		n.d. [probably May 1927]
		JJtoSB no. 100
		n.d. [probably Spring 1927]
		n.d. [possibly Spring 1927]
		5 May 1927
		n.d. [probably May 1927]
		15 May 1927
		n.d. [?May 1927]
		n.d. [?May 1927]
		n.d. [probably May 1927]
	21 May-7 Jun The Hague	n.d., pm 24 May 1927 pc
		27 May 1927
		28 May 1927 pc
		n.d. [May-Jun 1927] pc
		4 Jun 1927 pc
		6 Jun 1927 telegram
		6 Jun 1927
	7-14 Jun Amsterdam	9 Jun 1927 telegram
		n.d., pm 9 Jun 1927
		n.d., pm 10 Jun 1927 pc
		14 Jun 1927 telegram
	14-20 Jun The Hague	16 Jun 1927 telegram
		[18 Jun] 1927
		JJtoSB no. 117

(cont.)

Beach to Joyce	Joyce's address	Joyce to Beach
		[18 Jun] 1927
		JJtoSB no. 118
	20-21 *Jun* Brussels	20 Jun 1927 telegram
	22 *Jun 1927-c. 21 Mar 1928* 2 Square Robiac	23 Jun 1927
		24 Jun 1927
		n.d. [late Jun ? 1927]
c. mid-Jul-mid-Aug 1927 Les Déserts		9 Jul 1927
		8 Aug 1927
11 Aug 1927 pc		
		14 Aug 1927
		n.d. [Sep 1927]
		27 Sep 1927
		1 October 1927
Autumn 1927 new car, to Rocfoin each Sunday, one trip also with Joyce; also a weekend in Normandy		n.d. [Oct ? 1927]
		n.d. [Oct ? 1927]
		JJtoSB no. 128
		n.d. [Nov ? 1927]
		[?19] Nov 1927
5 Dec 1927 Statement of accounts		
		11 Dec 1927
		JJtoSB no. 131
		1 Jan 1928
		20 Jan 1928
		n.d. [Feb ? 1928]
		14 Mar 1928
	Dieppe	22 Mar 1928 pc
		25 Mar 1928 pc
		27 Mar 1928 telegram

(cont.)

Beach to Joyce	Joyce's address	Joyce to Beach
	Rouen	28 Mar 1928
	1-c. 19 Apr	1 Apr 1928
	2 Square Robiac	
	c. 19 Apr	n.d., *pm* Dijon 19 [Apr
	leaves for Dijon, Lyon,	1928] pc
	Avignon, Toulon	
	|	20 Apr 1928 telegram
	Avignon	21 Apr 1928 pc
	|	23 Apr 1928 telegram
	23 Apr-7 May	23 Apr 1928 telegram
	Toulon	
	|	28 Apr 1928
	|	n.d. [23-29 Apr 1928]
		JJtoSB no. 142
	|	2 May 1928
	|	7 May 1928 telegram
	7-12 May	8 May 1928 telegram
	Avignon	
	|	8 May 1928
	|	10 May 1928
	|	12 May 1928 telegram
	12-17 May	13 May 1928 telegram
	Lyon	14 May 1928 telegram
	|	15 May 1928 telegram
	|	
	17 May-c. 14 Jul	
	2 Square Robiac	
	|	
mid-Jul to 13 Aug 1928	*17 Jul-22 Aug*	17 Jul 1928 pc
Les Déserts	Innsbruck	
	23 Jul-29 Aug	24 Jul 1928 pc
	Salzburg	
	|	30 Jul 1928 pc
30 Jul 1928 pc	|	
10 Aug [1928] pc	|	
n.d. [after 10 Aug 1928] pc	|	
18 Aug 1928	|	

(*cont.*)

Beach to Joyce	Joyce's address	Joyce to Beach
	29 Aug-3 Sep Munich	29 Aug 1928 telegram
	Stuttgart	3 Sep 1928 telegram
	3 Sep-4 Sep Strasbourg	3 Sep 1928 *JJtoSB* no. 149
	|	
	5-14 Sep Le Havre	n.d., *pm* 9 Sep 1928 pc
	|	14 Sep 1928 telegram
	14 Sep 1928-10 Jul 1929 2 Square Robiac *c. 7-18 Nov 1928*	
	3-c. 16 Dec 1928	[late Dec] 1928
	c. 4-c. 18 Feb 1929 (*with Nora* Maison de Santé)	
15 May 1929	2 Square Robiac	
June 1929 short holiday with Adrienne	| | |	
	10-c. 14 Jul London	10 Jul 1929 telegram 13 Jul 1929 telegram
?July/August 1929 Holiday at Les Déserts (10 days), Chambéry (medical treatment), and near Marseilles	*c. 14 Jul-14/15 Aug* Torquay | | |	n.d., *pm*: 16 Jul 1929 *JJtoSB* no. 151
	|	n.d. *pm* 22 Jul 1929 pc
6 Aug 1929 pc	|	
	|	12 Aug 1929 pc
	14/15-17 Aug Bristol	16 Aug 1929 pc
	17 Aug-19 Sep London	13 Sep 1929
	|	1929 note

(*cont.*)

Beach to Joyce	Joyce's address	Joyce to Beach
n.d. [1928/29] list Selections for Anthology		
	c. 19 Sep 1929-31 Mar 1930 2 Square Robiac	14 Mar 1930
	1-14 Apr 1930 Zurich consults Prof. Vogt	
	14-21 Apr Wiesbaden consults Dr. Pagenstecher	
	21 Apr-c. 13 May 2 Square Robiac	
	c. 13-14 May Zurich	
	c. 14 May-c. 5 Jun Zurich Prof. Vogt's Clinic	15 May 1930 telegram
	5-17 Jun Zurich	
	from 17 Jun 2 Square Robiac	
Jun-end of Aug 1930 SB with pneumonia > Rocfoin; later reconvalescing in Tours and Cévennes mountains		
24 Jun 1930 Statement of accounts	2 Square Robiac	
	2-18 Jul travels via London to Wales	
	18 Jul-1 Aug Llandudno	18 Jul 1930 pc
12 Aug 1930 pc	*1-c. 25 Aug* travelling in England	

(cont.)

Beach to Joyce	Joyce's address	Joyce to Beach
25 Aug 1930 to Paul Léon	*c. 25-29 Aug* 2 Square Robiac	
	c.29 Aug-c 11 Sep Etretat, Normandie	5 Sep 1930 pc
	|	11 Sep 1930 telegram
	c. 11 Sep 1930-11 Apr 1931 2 Square Robiac *except 23-27 Nov 1930* Zurich	
	|	
	2 Square Robiac	n.d. [probably Oct-Nov 1930]
	|	
9 Dec 1930 Memorandum of Agreement	|	
n.d. [end of 1930] list of English articles on *Ulysses*	|	
	11-19 Apr 1931 Paris: Hotel Powers	23 Apr 1931
	19-23 Apr Calais	
	23 Apr-7 (8) May London 74 Gloucester Place // Hotel Belgravia	25 Apr 1931
25 Apr 1931	|	
27 Apr 1931	|	
	|	29 Apr 1931
1 May 1931	|	
2 May 1931 (1)	|	
2 May 1931 (2)	|	
	|	5 May 1931
9 May 1931	*7 (or 8) May-7 Aug* London 28b Campden Grove	

(*cont.*)

Beach to Joyce	Joyce's address	Joyce to Beach
		10 May 1931
		n.d., *pm*: 11 May 1931
12 May 1931		
15 May 1931		
		18 May 1931
27 May 1931		
29 May 1931		
2 Jun 1931 pc		
		4 Jun 1931
5 Jun 1931		
6 Jun 1931		
		8 Jun 1931
		n.d. [9 Jun 1931]
10 Jun 1931		
		11 Jun 1931
13 Jun 1931		
19 Jun 1931		
		25 Jun 1931
? Jun-3 Jul 1931		
La Ferme des genets,		
Auberville s/Mer, Calvados		
1 Jul 1931 pc		
from 4 Jul-c. 1 Aug		
Rocfoin		
8 Jul 1931		
Myrsine Moschos pp SB		
12 Jul 1931		
		13 Jul 1931
15 Jul 1931 letter		
15 Jul 1931 telegram		
n.d. [c. 16 Jul 1931]		
17 Jul 1931		
		19 Jul 1931
21 Jul 1931		
6 Aug 1931		
		7 Aug 1931

(cont.)

Beach to Joyce	Joyce's address	Joyce to Beach
	7-c. 21 Aug Dover	
	|	9 Aug 1931
11 Aug 1931	|	
	|	12 Aug 1931
13 Aug 1931 (1)	|	
13 Aug 1931 (2)	|	13 Aug 1931 telegram
	|	n.d., *pm*: 13 Aug 1931
	|	14 Aug 1931
	|	16 Aug 1931
17 Aug 1931	|	
	|	19 Aug 1931
	|	*JJtoSB* no. 181
	|	n.d., *pm*: 20 Aug 1931 pc
	|	*JJtoSB* no. 182
	|	n.d., *pm*: 21 Aug 1931 pc
	|	*JJtoSB* no. 183
	|	n.d. [before 22 Aug 1931]
	|	*JJtoSB* no. 179
21 Aug 1931	*c. 21-29 Aug* London 28b Campden Grove	
22 Aug 1931	|	
26 Aug 1931	|	
27 Aug 1931	|	27 Aug 1931
	|	*JJtoSB* no. 184
	|	n.d. [after 27 Aug 1931]
	|	*JJtoSB* no. 180
28 Aug 1931	|	
	from 29 Aug, for 2-3 days Salisbury, Wiltshire	n.d., *pm* 31 Aug 1931 pc *JJtoSB* no. 185
1 Sep 1931	*c. 1-24 (or 25) Sep* London, 28b Campden Grove	

(cont.)

Beach to Joyce	Joyce's address	Joyce to Beach
		n.d. [before 5 Sep 1931]
		JJtoSB no. 188
5 Sep 1931		
		n.d. [early Sep 1931]
		JJtoSB no. 186
14 Sep 1931		
		n.d. [*pm*: 16 Sep 1931] pc
		JJtoSB no. 187
		20 Sep 1931
		JJtoSB no. 189
	24 (*or 25*) *Sep-c. 10 Oct*	27 Sep 1931
	Paris: La Résidence	*JJtoSB* no. 190
	4 avenue Pierre Premier	
	de Serbie	
28 Sep 1931		
10 Nov 1931	*c. 10 Oct 1931-17 Apr 1932*	
	2 avenue St Philibert	
		11 Nov 1931
		19 Dec 1931
2 Feb 1932		
		3 Feb 1932
		from Paul Léon
4 Feb 1932		
to Paul Léon		
		8 Feb 1932
		from Paul Léon
9 Feb 1932		
to Paul Léon		
		11 Feb 1932
		from Paul Léon
		9 Mar 1932
		from Paul Léon
		13 Mar 1932
		[28 Mar] 1932

(*cont.*)

Beach to Joyce	Joyce's address	Joyce to Beach
		3 Apr 1932
15 Apr 1932		
Statement of accounts		
	17 Apr	
	leaves 2 ave St Philibert intending to return to Campden Grove, London; but at Gare du Nord Lucia refuses to accompany her parents	
	17 Apr-c. 22 May	19 Apr 1932
	Paris: Hotel Belmont	from Paul Léon
11 May 1932		
	c. 22 May-3 Jul	
	2 avenue St Philibert	
	3-6 Jul	
	Feldkirch	
14 Jul-17 Aug 1932	*c. 6 Jul-c. 14 Aug*	14 Jul 1932
Les Déserts	Zurich	from Paul Léon
	Consultations Prof. Vogt	
8 Aug 1932		
Jean Henley pp S. Beach		
18 Aug 1932		
to Paul Léon		
30 Aug 1932	*c. 14 Aug-8 Sep*	30 Aug 1932
to Paul Léon	Feldkirch	from Paul Léon
31 Aug 1932		
to Paul Léon		
31 Aug 1932		
Statement of accounts		
		1 Sep 1932
		from Paul Léon
		3 Sep 1932
		6 Sep 1932
		from Paul Léon

(cont.)

Beach to Joyce	Joyce's address	Joyce to Beach
	8-c. 19 Sep Zurich Consultations Prof. Vogt	8 Sep 1932 pc
	|	19 Sep 1932 from Paul Léon
24 Sep 1932 to Paul Léon	*c. 19 Sep-19 Oct* Nice	
	|	26 Sep 1932
28 Sep 1932	|	
	|	27 Sep 1932 from Paul Léon
28 Sep 1932 to Paul Léon	|	28 Sep 1932 pc
	|	2 Oct 1932
4 Oct 1932	|	
	| | |	12 Oct 1932 from Paul Léon (and M.C. Wegner)
	19 Oct-mid-Nov Paris: Hotel Lord Byron, then briefly Hotel Lenox	
	|	n.d. [*pm*: 23 Oct 1932]
24 Oct 1932	|	
	| | |	30 Oct 1932 31 Oct 1932 from Paul Léon
2 Nov 1932	|	
	| |	7 Nov 1932 from Paul Léon
8 Nov 1932 to Paul Léon	| |	
	| |	14 Nov 1932 from Paul Léon
15 Nov 1932 to Paul Léon	| |	

(cont.)

Beach to Joyce	Joyce's address	Joyce to Beach
	mid-Nov-22 May 1933 42, rue Galilée	24 Nov 1932 from Paul Léon
28 Nov 1932 to Paul Léon Feb [?] 1933		
		1 Mar 1933 from Paul Léon
3 Mar 1933 to Paul Léon		
		17 Mar 1933 from Paul Léon
20 Mar 1933 to Paul Léon 31 Mar 1933 to Paul Léon		
		3 April 1933 from Paul Léon
14 April 1933		
		7 May 1933 from Paul Léon
8 May 1933		
	22 May-10 Jun Zurich Consultations Prof. Vogt	
22 June 1933 to Paul Léon	*10 Jun-4 Jul* 42, rue Galilée	
1 July 1933 to Paul Léon		
July and part of August 1933 Les Déserts	*4 Jul-end of Aug 1933* Evian-les-Bains, Geneva, Zurich, Nyon, Geneva	6 July 1933 from Paul Léon
7 August 1933 Jane van Meter pp Beach to Joyce via Paul Léon		
	42, rue Galilée	*pm* 2 Dec 1933

(*cont.*)

Beach to Joyce	Joyce's address	Joyce to Beach
9 Dec 1933		
		14 Mar 1934
	20 *Sep 1934-end of Jan 1935* Zurich	24 Dec 1934 pc
16 Mar 1935	*from 11 Feb 1935 to 15 April 1939 primarily* 7, rue Edmond Valentin	
13 Sep [193?5] pc Les Déserts to Paul Léon		
5 Dec 1935		
28 Feb 1936	7, rue Edmond Valentin	
24 Jul to mid-Oct 1936 visits the US		pm 27 Jul 1936
	Beaugency	31 Jul 1936 from Paul Léon
3 August 1936 Margaret H Newitt pp Sylvia Beach to Paul Léon		
		pm 22 Nov 1936
2 Jul 1937 pc *1 week in Jul 1937* holiday on Jersey	7, rue Edmond Valentin	
		25 Dec 1937
		25 Dec 1937
		[?1937]
		14 Mar 1938
	7, rue Edmond Valentin	3 Mar 1939 from Paul Léon
6 Mar 1939 pc to Paul Léon		
	St-Gérand	12 Feb 1940 pc
	Vichy	1 Jun 1940 pc
	St-Gérand	12 Dec 1940 pc (censored)
		11 no-date notes and cards

2   Visualization

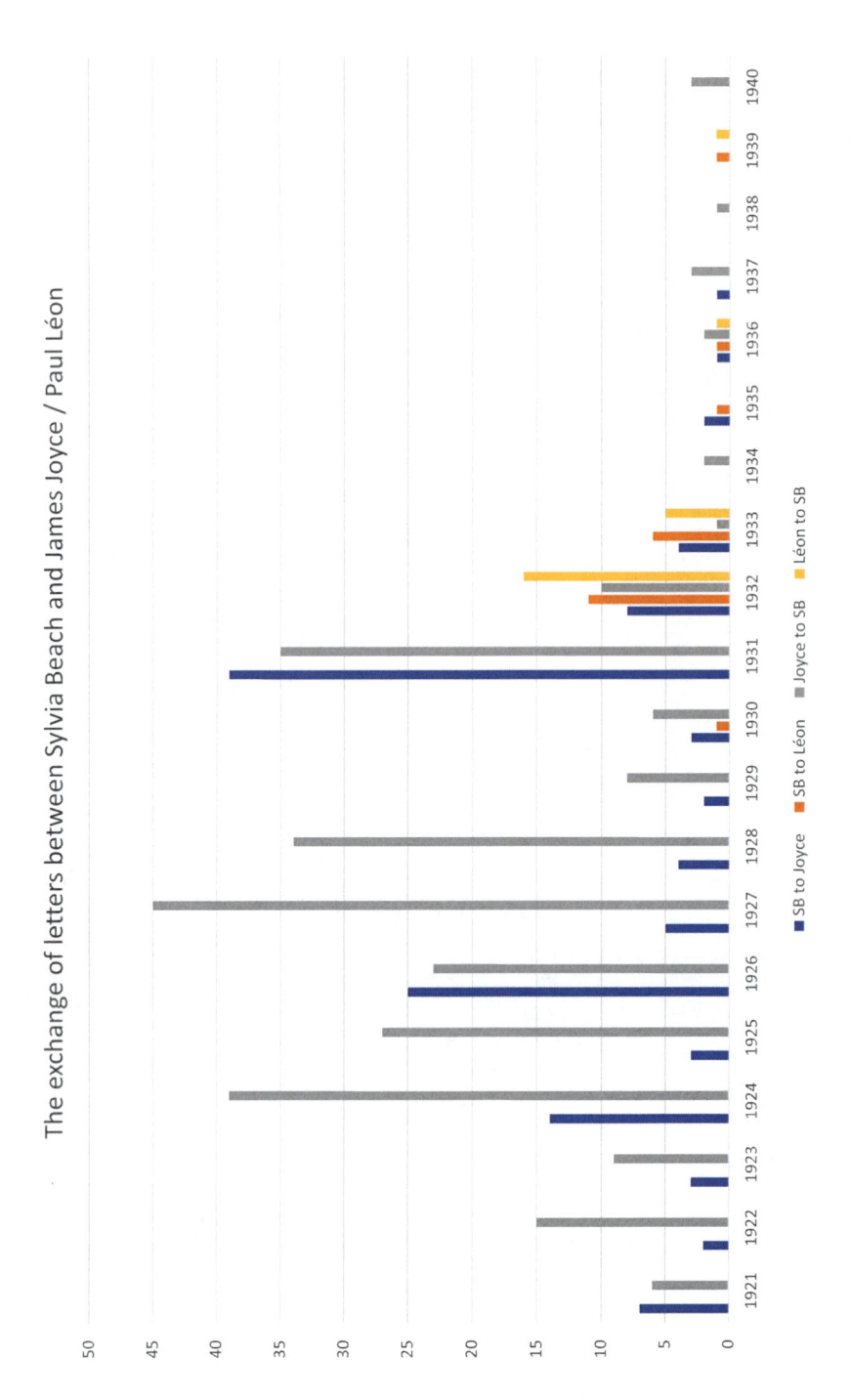

APPENDIX C

Survey of Correspondence re *Frankfurter Zeitung* Affair

This compilation is inevitably incomplete.

On 13 August, Joyce sent Beach his own intermediate count: "Have now sent off 36 letters and 11 wires on the F.Z. affair …" Up to that point, this survey lists the 15 letters and 3 telegrams by Joyce that could be located: hence at least 21 letters and 8 wires should be added to this count here, which could possibly be found at archives such as Monro Saw & Co.'s and that of various newspapers, as Joyce was looking for "energetic journalist[s] who could give the F.Z. affair the ventilation it needs" (Joyce to Eliot, 11 August 1931, *Letters I*, p. 306).

Of the "many letters written to the F.Z. and also to Frau Kafka", which Brody mentions in his 30 July letter to Joyce, only those that are specified in other letters are included in the overview, as are further letters that are not extant, but specifically referred to in other correspondence.

Date (all 1931)	Sender	Recipient
ca. 21 July	Daniel Brody	Joyce
25 July	Joyce	Giorgio Joyce
25 July (telegram)	Joyce	Daniel Brody
25 July	Brody	F.Z. / Irene Kafka
30 July	Joyce	Helen Joyce
30 July	Joyce	Daniel Brody
30 July	Joyce	Ivan Goll
30 July	Daniel Brody	Joyce
30 July	Monro Saw & Co.	F.Z.
31 July	Joyce	Georg Goyert
3 August	Joyce	Myrsine Moschos
5 August	Joyce	Daniel Brody
late July / early August	Daniel Brody	Sylvia Beach
late July / early August	Sylvia Beach	Daniel Brody
c. 5 August	Joyce	Sylvia Beach
c. 6 August	Daniel Brody	Joyce
6 August	Sylvia Beach	Joyce

(cont.)

Date (all 1931)	Sender	Recipient
7 August	Joyce	Sylvia Beach
8 August	Sylvia Beach	Daniel Brody
9 August	Joyce	Sylvia Beach
9 August	Joyce	Giorgio and Helen Joyce
c. 9 August	Joyce	Daniel Brody
10 August	Daniel Brody	Joyce
11 August	Daniel Brody	Sylvia Beach
11 August	Eudo C. Mason	Sylvia Beach
c. 11 August	Ernst Hitschmann (Ralph Pinker)	Joyce
11 August	Sylvia Beach	Joyce
11 August	Joyce	T.S. Eliot
11 August (telegram)	Joyce	Daniel Brody
c. 11 August (telegram)	Joyce	Ernst Hitschmann (Ralph Pinker)
12 August	Daniel Brody	Joyce
12 August	Joyce	Sylvia Beach
13 August	Harold Nicolson	Joyce
13 August	Sylvia Beach	Joyce
13 August (2nd letter)	Sylvia Beach	Joyce
13 August	Joyce	Sylvia Beach
13 August (telegram)	Joyce	Myrsine Moschos
13 August	Frankfurter Zeitung Redaktion	Ernst Hitschmann (Ralph Pinker)
13 August	Ralph Pinker	Joyce
14 August	Joyce	Sylvia Beach
15 August (telegram)	Joyce	Sylvia Beach
16 August	Joyce	Sylvia Beach
17 August	Sylvia Beach	Joyce
17 August	Irene Kafka	Monro Saw & Co.
mid-August	Georges Borach	Irene Kafka
mid-August	Irene Kafka	Georges Borach
mid-August	Irene Kafka	F.Z.
mid-August	Irene Kafka	Rhein-Verlag
mid-August	Padraic Colum	Hans Trausil

SURVEY OF CORRESPONDENCE RE FRANKFURTER ZEITUNG AFFAIR

(cont.)

Date (all 1931)	Sender	Recipient
c. mid-August	Monro Saw & Co.	F.Z.
18 August	Giorgio + Helen Joyce	Joyce
19 August	Joyce	Sylvia Beach
n.d., before 21 August (postcard)	Joyce	Sylvia Beach
21 August	Joyce	Giorgio and Helen Joyce
21 August	Sylvia Beach	Joyce
22 August	Joyce	Stanislaus Joyce
c. 20 August	Joyce	Jean Prévost
22 August	Sylvia Beach	Joyce
26 August	Sylvia Beach	Joyce
27 August	Joyce	T.S. Eliot
27 August	Sylvia Beach	Joyce
after 27 August (postcard)	Joyce	Sylvia Beach
28 August	Sylvia Beach	Joyce
30 August	Hans Trausil	Padraic Colum
31 August	Sylvia Beach	General Manager of United Press of America
1 September	Sylvia Beach	Joyce
3 September	Ralph Pinker	Michael Joyce
3 September	Michael Joyce	Joyce
5 September	Sylvia Beach	Joyce
5 September	Sylvia Beach	Monro Saw & Co.
5 September	Sylvia Beach	Georges Borach
5 September	Sylvia Beach	Daniel Brody
5 September	Sylvia Beach	Ivan Goll
5 September	Sylvia Beach	Ernst R. Curtius
5 September	Padraic Colum	Joyce
6 September	Joyce	Michael Joyce
8 September	Joyce	Michael Joyce
mid-September	Joyce	Sylvia Beach
mid-September	Monro Saw & Co.	Willi Rothschild, lawyer
17 September	Joyce	Ernst R. Curtius
19 September	Willi Rothschild, lawyer	Monro Saw & Co.
20 September	Joyce	Sylvia Beach

(*cont.*)

Date (all 1931)	Sender	Recipient
27 September	Joyce	Sylvia Beach
28 September	Ralph Pinker	Sylvia Beach
c. early October	Joyce	Monro Saw & Co.
2 October	Daniel Brody	Sylvia Beach
6 October	Monro Saw & Co.	Joyce
15 October	Joyce	T.S. Eliot

APPENDIX D

Joyce's Book Orders through Sylvia Beach

Title	Remarks
Arabian Nights Burton, Sir Richard. *The Book of The Thousand Nights and a Night* ... [Denver, Colorado: 1919]	Beach to Joyce 27 July 1922, note 3
Oxford Dictionary	Joyce to Beach, 30 October 1922 no further details
Vizetelly, Francis Horace. *English Speech and Literature.* New York and London: Funke Wagnalls, 1915. Fitzpatrick, Benedict. *Ireland and the Making of Britain.* New York and London: Funke Wagnalls, 1922. Davidson, John Morrison. *The New Book of Kings.* Boston: Roberts Brothers, 1884; London: The Modern Press, 1890. *The Complete Peerage of England, Scotland Ireland....* (8 vols) G.E.C. [i.e., George Edward Cokayne]. London: St. Catherines Press, 1910-59. Ed. Lord Howard de Walden [editor of vols 6-10, 13; Joyce ordered "8 vols, edited by Lord Howard de Waldon].	Joyce to Beach, 12 July 1923 See *JJtoSB*, letter 17, notes 2-5, p. 24
Young, Sir Charles. *Jim the Penman.*	Joyce to Beach, 17 July 1924 Beach to Joyce, 22 July 1924, note 3 Beach to Joyce, 1 Aug 1924
Kinane, Thomas H., R.C. Dean of Cashel, *S. Patrick, His Life, His Heroic Virtues.* Dublin: M.H. Gill & Son, 1889. Fleming, William Canon. *The Life of S. Patrick.* London R. & T. Washbourne, 1905. Fleming, William Canon. *Boulogne-sur-mer: St. Patricks native town.* London: R. & T. Washbourne, 1907.	Joyce to Beach, 25 July 1924 See *JJtoSB*, letter 38, note 2, p. 80

(cont.)

Title	Remarks
Luby, Thomas Clarke. *The Life and Times of Daniel O'Connell*. London: Cameron & Ferguson, 187?. Tone, Theobald Wolfe. *Life of Theobald Wolfe Tone* ... written by himself and continued by his son; edited by his son (Washington: Gales & Seaton, 1826)	*(cont.)* Joyce to Beach, 25 July 1924 See *JJtoSB*, letter 38, note 2, p. 80
Jullian, Camille. *De la Gaule à la France*; *Nos origines historiques*. Paris: Hachette, 1922. Bagnell Bury, John. *The Life of St. Patrick, and his Place in History* (London Macmillan & Co., Ltd., 1905). Perry, William James. *The Growth of Civilization* (London: Methuen, 1924) Boucicault, Dion. *The Shaughraun*. London: J. Dicks [1858?]; New York: Thitcher & Glasaeter [1875?]).	Joyce to Beach, 12 July [*recte* 12 Aug] 1924 See *JJtoSB*, letter 34, note 2, pp. 78-79.
The life of John Sims Reeves [?] Pearce, Charles E. *Sims Reeves. Fifty Years of Music in England*. London: Stanley Paul, 1924.	Joyce to Weaver, 5 March 1925 Beach to Joyce, 30 March 1925, note 1
Clodd, Edward. *Story of the Alphabet*. London: George Newnes, 1900. Pons, Emile. Swift: *Les années de Jeunesse et le « Conte du Tonneau »*. Strasbourg: Librairie Istra, 1925.	Joyce to Beach, 2 September 1926 See *JJtoSB*, letter 83, notes 2 and 3, p. 88

APPENDIX E

Currencies: Historical Values and Their Equivalent in 2020

Purchasing power of the old French franc, the dollar and the British pound, i.e. the purchasing power of FF 100 in 1921 would have been equivalent to € 114 in 2020.

	100 old franc are worth X € in 2020		100 US$ are worth X $ in 2020		1 UK£ is worth X £ in 2020
1920	100	1920	1,280	1920	46
1921	114	1921	1,430	1921	50
1922	114	1922	1,520	1922	58
1923	106	1923	1,500	1923	62
1924	94	1924	1,500	1924	62
1925	89	1925	1,460	1925	62
1926	66	1926	1,440	1926	63
1927	64	1927	1,470	1927	64
1928	64	1928	1,490	1928	64
1929	61	1929	1,490	1929	65
1930	59	1930	1,530	1930	67
1931	64	1931	1,680	1931	70
1932	69	1932	1,870	1932	71
1933	73	1933	1,970	1933	73
1934	73	1934	1,910	1934	73
1935	80	1935	1,860	1935	73
1936	76	1936	1,840	1936	72
1937	59	1937	1,770	1937	70
1938	53	1938	1,810	1938	69
1939	50	1939	1,840	1939	67
1940	42	1940	1,820	1940	57

SOURCES

1. FRANC FRANÇAIS ANCIEN – EURO 2020
Le convertisseur franc-euro mesure l'érosion monétaire due a l'inflation
https://www.insee.fr/fr/information/2417794

2. US DOLLAR
https://www.measuringworth.com

3. BRITISH POUND
https://www.bankofengland.co.uk/monetary-policy/inflation/inflation-calculator
All links accessed 2 March 2021.

Bibliography

Aguet, Joël. "Georges Pitoëff" and "Ludmilla Pitoëff". In: Andreas Kotte, ed. *Dictionnaire du théâtre en Suisse*. Vol 2. Zurich: Chronos Verlag, 2005. pp. 1413-1415.

anon. "Herbert L. Rothchild". In: *The New York Times*. New York, 17 September 1935.

Aslan, Odette. *Paris capitale mondiale du théâtre: Le Théâtre des Nations*. Paris: CNRS Editions, 2009.

Asselain, Jean-Charles, and Alain Plessis. "Exchange-Rate Policy and Macroeconomic Performance. A Comparison of French and Italian Experience between the Wars". In: Charles H. Feinstein, ed. *Banking Currency and Finance in Europe between the Wars*. Oxford: Clarendon, 1995. pp. 187-213.

Atherton, James S. *The Books at the Wake. A Study of Literary Allusions in James Joyce's "Finnegans Wake"*. 1959. Expanded and corrected ed. 1974. Mamaroneck, N.Y.: Paul Appel, 1974.

Aubert, Jacques, and Maria Jolas. "Accueils français à Joyce entre les deux guerres". In: *Joyce & Paris 1902.... 1920-1940.... 1975. Actes du cinquième symposium international James Joyce*. Ed. Jacques Aubert and Maria Jolas. Vol. I. Paris: Editions du C.N.R.S., 1979. pp. 37-58.

Basinski, Michael, ed. *Discovering James Joyce*. Exhibition Catalogue. The University at Buffalo Collection. Buffalo: The University at Buffalo, 2009.

Beach, Sylvia. *Shakespeare and Company*. New York: Harcourt Brace, 1959.

Beck, Alan. "John Gielgud – the longest radio career". In: *Studies in Theatre and Performance*, 20.3 (2000). p. 211. https://www.tandfonline.com/doi/abs/10.1080/14682761.2000.10807042?journalCode=rstp20, accessed 18 October 2018.

Becket, Margaret. "Charles Scribner's Sons". In: *Dictionary of Literary Biography, volume 49: American Literary Publishing Houses, 1838-1899*. Detroit: Gale Research Company, 1986. pp. 412-419.

Beckett, Samuel, et al. *Our Exagmination Round His Factification for Incamination of Work in Progress*. Paris: Shakespeare and Co., 1929. With contributions by Samuel Beckett, Marcel Brion, Frank Budgen, Stuart Gilbert, Eugene Jolas, Victor Llona, Robert McAlmon, Thomas McGreevy, Elliot Paul, John Rodker, Robert Sage, William Carlos Williams, and with letters of protest by G.V.L. Slingsby and Vladimir Dixon.

Benstock, Shari. *Women of the Left Bank, Paris 1900-1940*. Austin: University of Texas Press, 1986.

Bishop, Edward L. "The 'Garbled History' of the First-edition *Ulysses*". In: *Joyce Studies Annual* 9 (1998). pp. 3-36.

Bluteau, Emanuel, and François Quellet, eds. "Avant-Propos". In: *Jean Prévost, le multiple*. Rennes: Presses universitaires de Rennes, 2015. pp. 9-16.

Boyd, Ernest. "James Joyce". In: *Ireland's Literary Renaissance*. Revised edition. New York: Alfred A. Knopf, 1922. pp. 402-12.

Britzolakis, Christina. "Making Modernism Safe for Democracy. The Dial (1920-29)". In: *The Oxford Critical and Cultural History of Modernist Magazines*. Vol. II. North America 1894-1960. Ed. Peter Brooker and Andrew Thacker. Oxford: Oxford University Press, 2012. pp. 85-102.

Brockman, William S. "Jacob Schwartz – 'The Fly in the Honey'". In: *Joyce Studies Annual* 9 (1998). pp. 174-90.

Brockman, William S. "Learning to Be James Joyce's Contemporary? Richard Ellmann's Discovery and Transformation of Joyce's Letters and Manuscripts". In: *Journal of Modern Literature*. 22.2 (Winter 1998/99). pp. 253-63.

Brogniez, Laurence. Review of "Maxime Benoît-Jeannin, Georgette Leblanc (1869-1941). Biographie". In: *Textyles* 16 (1999). pp. 129-30. https://doi.org/10.4000/textyles.1229, accessed 8 December 2020.

Budgen, Frank. *James Joyce and the Making of "Ulysses"*. London: Oxford University Press, 1972.

Cap, Jean-Pierre. "Jean Schlumberger". In: *Dictionary of Literary Biography, volume 65: French Novelists, 1900-1930*. Detroit: Gale Research Company, 1988. pp. 293-297.

Carpenter, Humphrey. *A Serious Character. The Life of Ezra Pound*. London: Faber & Faber, 1988.

Cato, Bob, and Greg Vitiello. *Joyce Images*. Introduction by Anthony Burgess. New York and London: W.W. Norton, 1994.

Chevalier, Tracy, ed. *Encyclopedia of the Essay*. Chicago: Fitzroy Dearborn Publishers, 1997.

Colum, Mary and Padraic. *Our Friend James Joyce*. New York: Doubleday, 1958.

Crispi, Luca, and Sam Slote, eds. *How Joyce Wrote "Finnegans Wake". A Chapter-by-Chapter Genetic Guide*. Madison: University of Wisconsin Press, 2007.

Crispi, Luca. "A Commentary on James Joyce's National Library of Ireland 'Early Commonplace Book': 1903-1912 (MS 36,639/02/A)". *Genetic Joyce Studies* 9 (Spring 2009). https://www.geneticjoycestudies.org/articles/GJS9/GJS9_Crispi, accessed 9 December 2020.

Crispi, Luca. "Ulysses in the Marketplace: 1932". In: *Joyce Studies Annual* 20 (2012). pp. 29-65.

Danly, Susan. *Light, Air and Color: American Impressionist Paintings from the Collection of the Pennsylvania Academy of the Fine Arts*. Philadelphia: Pennsylvania Academy of the Fine Arts, 1990.

del Greco Lobner, Corinna. "D'Annunzian Reverberation in a Rejection Slip: Joyce and 'Daniele Defoe'". In: *Journal of Modern Literature* 22.2. pp. 395-99.

Deming, Robert H., ed. *James Joyce. The Critical Heritage*. Vol. 1. 1907-1927. London: Routledge & Kegan Paul, 1970.

Deming, Robert H. *A Bibliography of James Joyce Studies*. Second edition, revised and enlarged. Boston, Mass.: G.K. Hall, 1977.

Dokumentationsarchiv des österreichischen Widerstands. *Erkennungsdienstliche Kartei der Gestapo Wien*. https://www.doew.at/personensuche?firstname=Irene&lastname=Kafka&shoah=1&gestapo=1&politisch=1&spiegelgrund=1&lang=de, accessed 22 November 2019.

Dzwonkoski, Elizabeth. "Harcourt, Brace and Howe. Harcourt, Brace and Company. Harcourt, Brace and World. Harcourt Brace Jovanovich". In: *Dictionary of Literary Biography, volume 46: American Literary Publishing Houses, 1900-1980*. Detroit: Gale Research Company, 1986. pp. 180-183.

Ellmann, Richard. *James Joyce*. New and revised edition. 1982. Oxford and New York: Oxford UP, 1983.

Encyclopædia of Ireland. "Thomas Mac Greevy". Brian Lalor, general editor. Dublin: Gill and Macmillan, 2003. pp. 671-72.

Faerber, Thomas, and Markus Luchsinger. *Joyce in Zürich*. Zurich: Unionsverlag, 1988.

Fahy, Catherine, comp. *The James Joyce – Paul Léon Papers in the National Library of Ireland*. Dublin: National Library of Ireland, 1992.

Fargnoli, Nicholas A. and Michael P. Gillespie. *James Joyce A to Z. The Essential Reference to the Life and Work*. New York: Fact on File, 1995.

Fargnoli, Nicholas A., ed. *James Joyce. A Literary Reference*. New York: Checkmark Books, 2006.

Fitch, Noel Riley. *Sylvia Beach and the Lost Generation. A History of Literary Paris in the Twenties and Thirties*. New York: W.W. Norton, 1983.

Füger, Wilhelm, ed. *Kritisches Erbe. Dokumente zur Rezeption von James Joyce im deutschen Sprachraum zu Lebzeiten des Autors*. Amsterdam and Atlanta: Rodopi, 2000.

Geddes, Minna Besser. "Emily Holmes Coleman". In: *Dictionary of Literary Biography, volume 4: American Writers in Paris, 1920-1939*. Detroit: Gale Research Company, 1980. pp. 71-72.

Gertzman, Jay A. "Not Quite Honest: Samuel Roth's 'Unauthorized' *Ulysses* and the 1927 International Protest". In: *Joyce Studies Annual* 17 (2009). pp. 34-66.

Gertzman, Jay A. *Samuel Roth – Infamous Modernist*. Gainesville, FL: University Press of Florida, 2013.

Ghidetti, Enrico. *Italo Svevo: ein Bürger aus Triest*. Translated into German by Caroline Lüderssen. Frankfurt am Main: Cooperative Verlag, 2001.

Gibbons, Luke. "'Old Haunts': Joyce, the Republic, and Photographic Memory". In: Oona Frawley and Katherine O'Callaghan, eds. *Making Space in the Works of James Joyce*. New York: Syracuse University Press, 2014. pp. 187-201.

Gide, André. *Corydon, Quatre dialogues socratiques*. Nouvelle Edition. Editions de la Nouvelle Revue Française. Paris: Librairie Gallimard, 1924.

Gide, André. *Corydon*. Richard Howard, English transl. Urbana and Chicago: University of Illinois Press, 2001.

Gifford, Don, with Robert J. Seidman. *"Ulysses" Annotated. Notes for James Joyce's "Ulysses"*. Revised and expanded edition. Berkeley, Los Angeles and London: University of California Press, 1988.

Gifford, Paul, and Brian Stimpson. *Reading Paul Valéry. Universe in mind*. Cambridge: Cambridge University Press, 1998.

Gilbert, Stuart. *Reflections on James Joyce: Stuart Gilbert's Paris Journal*. Ed. Thomas F. Staley and Randolph Lewis. Austin/Texas: University of Texas Press, 1993.

Gillet, Louis. *Claybook for James Joyce*. Transl. and introd. by Georges Markow-Totevy. London and New York: Abelard-Schuman, 1958.

Gillies, Mary Ann. *The Professional Literary Agent in Britain 1880-1920*. Toronto: Toronto University Press, 2007.

Gorman, Deborah. "Farrar and Rinehart". In: *Dictionary of Literary Biography, volume 46: American Literary Publishing Houses, 1900-1980*. Detroit: Gale Research Company, 1986. pp. 135-138.

Groden, Michael. *"Ulysses" in Progress*. Princeton: Princeton University Press, 1977.

Hack, Bertold, und Marietta Kleiss, Hrsg. *Hermann Broch – Daniel Brody. Briefwechsel 1930-1951*. Frankfurt am Main: Buchhändler-Vereinigung GmbH, 1971.

Hautcœur, Pierre-Cyrille. "The Great Depression in France (1929-1936)". In: Glasner, David, ed. *Business Cycles and Depressions: An Encyclopedia*. New York: Garland, 1997. pp. 39-42.

Hayman, David, and Ira Nadel, "Joyce and the Family of Emile and Yva Fernandez: Solving a Minor Mystery" In: *James Joyce Quarterly* 25.1 (Fall 1987). pp. 49-57.

Herbert, Stacey. "A Draft for '*Ulysses* in Print: the Family Tree', an Installation for the Exhibition. James Joyce and *Ulysses* at the National Library of Ireland". In: *Genetic Joyce Studies*. Issue 4 (Spring 2004). https://www.geneticjoycestudies.org/articles/GJS4/GJS4_Herbert, accessed 15 May 2018.

Hogan, Robert, ed. *Dictionary of Irish Literature*. Revised and expanded ed. 2 vols. London: Aldwych Press, 1996.

Huculac, Matthew J. "The London Mercury (1919-39) and Other Moderns". In: Peter Brooker and Andrew Thacker, eds. *The Oxford Critical and Cultural History of Modernist Magazines. Volume I: Britain and Ireland 1880-1955*. pp. 240-261.

Ito, Eishiro. "'United States of Asia': James Joyce and Japan". In: *A Companion to James Joyce*. Richard Brown, ed. Malden MA and Oxford: Wiley-Blackwell, 2008. pp. 193-206.

James Joyce Archive Vol. 1. *Chamber Music, Pomes Penyeach & Occasional Verse. A Facsimile of Manuscripts, Typescripts, & Proofs*. Prefaced and arranged by A. Walton Litz. New York: Garland, 1978.

James Joyce Archive Vol. 28. *Finnegans Wake*. A Facsimile of Buffalo Notebook VI.A. Notebook VI.A. Danis Rose, ed. New York: Garland, 1978.

James Joyce Archive Vol. 53. *Finnegans Wake* Book II, Chapter 2. A Facsimile of Drafts, Typescripts, & Proofs. Danis Rose, ed. New York: Garland, 1978.

Jolas, Eugene, and Robert Sage, eds. *transition stories*. New York: Walter V. McKee, 1929.

Joyce, James. *Letters of James Joyce*. Vol. I, ed. by Stuart Gilbert. New York: Viking Press, 1957; reissued with corrections 1966. Vols. II and III, and *Selected Letters*, ed. by Richard Ellmann. New York: Viking Press, 1964 and 1975.

Joyce, James. *Letters to Sylvia Beach. 1921-1940*. ed. by Melissa Banta and Oscar A. Silverman. Bloomington: Indiana University Press, 1987.

Joyce, James. *Ulysses*. The Corrected Text. Ed. by Hans Walter Gabler, with Wolfhard Steppe and Claus Melchior. Harmondsworth: Penguin, 1986.

Joyce, James. *Ulysse*. Trans. Auguste Morel, Stuart Gilbert, Valery Larbaud. Paris: Gallimard, 1948.

Joyce, James. *Ulysse*. Trans. Tiphaine Samoyault, Patrick Drevet, Sylvie Doizelet, Bernard Hoepffner, Marie-Danièle Vors, Pascal Bataillard, Michel Cusin, Jacques Aubert, also editor. Paris: Gallimard, 2004.

Joyce, James. *Finnegans Wake*. London: Faber & Faber, and New York: Viking, 1939.

Joyce, James. "James Clarence Mangan". In: *The Critical Writings of James Joyce*. Ed. by Ellsworth Mason and Richard Ellmann. London: Faber & Faber, 1959. pp. 73-83.

Joyce, James. *Poems and Shorter Writings*. London: Faber & Faber, 1991.

Joyce, James [sic] [Michael Joyce]. "Vielleicht ein Traum". In: *Frankfurter Zeitung*, 19 July 1931. pp. 14-15.

Kahn, Sy M., and Karen L. Rood. "Harry and Caresse Crosby". In: *Dictionary of Literary Biography, volume 4: American Writers in Paris, 1920-1939*. Detroit: Gale Research Company, 1980. pp. 85-101.

Katona, Anna B. "Mark Twain's Reception in Hungary". In: *American Literary Realism, 1870-1910* 16, no. 1 (1983). pp. 107-20. www.jstor.org/stable/27746079, accessed 4 August 2020.

Kenner, Hugh. "Beaufoy's Masterpiece". In: *James Joyce Quarterly* 24.1 (Fall 1986). pp. 11-18.

Kugel, Adelaide. "'Wroth Wrackt Joyce': Samuel Roth and the 'not quite unauthorized' edition of *Ulysses*". In: *Joyce Studies Annual* 3 (1992). pp. 242-47.

Landuyt, Ingeborg. "Cain – Ham – (Shem) – Esau – Jim the Penman. *Chapter* I.7". In: Crispi & Slote, 2007. pp. 142-162.

Larbaud, Valery. *Lettres à Adrienne Monnier et à Sylvia Beach 1919-1933*. Ed. Maurice Saillet. Paris: IMEC Editions, 1991.

Larbaud, Valery, and Marcel Ray. *Correspondance 1899-1937*. Ed. Françoise Lioure. Vol. III. Paris: Editions Gallimard, 1980.

Laurent, François. "La création de la Revue Européenne et la collaborations de Valery Larbaud". In: Françoise Lioure et Auguste Dezalay, eds. *Valery Larbaud – Espaces et Temps de L'Humanisme*. Clermont-Ferrand: Université Blaise Pascal, Faculté des Lettres et Sciences humaines, 1995. pp. 163-170.

Lausberg, Heinrich, "Curtius, Ernst Robert". In: *Neue Deutsche Biographie* 3 (1957). pp. 447-448. https://www.deutsche-biographie.de/pnd118523058.html#ndbcontent, accessed 19 February 2018.

Lernout, Geert. "Singing Walking Gent: Sims Reeves in VI.B.13". In: *A Finnegans Wake Circular* 3 (Spring 1988). pp. 43-52.

Lernout, Geert, and Wim Van Mierlo, eds. *The Reception of James Joyce in Europe*. Vol. 1.: Germany, Northern and East Central Europe. London and New York: Thoemmes Continuum, 2004.

Lidderdale, Jane, and Mary Nicholson. *Dear Miss Weaver*. Harriet Shaw Weaver 1876-1961. London: Faber & Faber, 1970.

Lyons, J.B. *James Joyce and Medicine*. Dublin: The Dolmen Press, 1973.

Madison, Charles A. *From Irving to Irving. Author-Publisher Relations 1800-1974*. New York and London: R.R. Bowker Company, 1974.

Markow-Totevy, Georges. "Introduction". In: Louis Gillet, *Claybook for James Joyce*. pp. 13-25.

McCarthy, Patrick A. "Attempts at Narration in *Finnegans Wake*". In: *Genetic Joyce Studies* 5 (2005). https://www.geneticjoycestudies.org/articles/GJS5/GJS5McCarthy, 26 April 2020.

McCleery, Alistair. "The Reputation of the 1932 Odyssey Press Edition of *Ulysses*". In: *The Papers of the Bibliographical Society of America*, vol. 100, no. 1 (2006). pp. 89-103.

McCullough, Ann. "Joyce's Early Publishing History in America". In: Morris Beja, Philip Herring et al., eds. *James Joyce. The Centennial Symposium*. University of Illinois Press, 1986. pp. 184-192.

McDougall, Richard. *The Very Rich Hours of Adrienne Monnier*. An Intimate Portrait of the Literary and Artistic Life in Paris Between the Wars. New York: Charles Scribner & Sons, 1976.

Maman, Lill. "Sixteen Unpublished Letters by Emile Zola to Theodore Stanton". In: *The French Review*, 57.6 (May) 1984. pp. 802-9.

Martin, Paul. "'Mr Bloom and the Cyclops': Joyce and Antheil's Unfinished 'Opéra Mécanique'". In: *Bronze by Gold. The Music of Joyce*. Ed. Sebastian Knowles. Border Crossings 3. New York: Garland, 1999. pp. 91-106.

Mathews, Jackson, and Maurice Saillet, comp. *Hommages à Sylvia Beach (1887-1962)*. In: *Mercure de France*, vol. 349 (August-September 1963).

May, Derwent. *Critical Times: The History of the Times Literary Supplement*. London: Harper Collins, 2001.

Mercanton, Jacques. "The Hours of James Joyce". Transl. Lloyd C. Parks. In: Potts, pp. 206-252.

"Michael und James". In: *Frankfurter Zeitung*, 9 August 1931. p. 10.

"Michael and James". Typescript of a translation, with an autograph comment by Joyce. ZJJF Jahnke.

"Michael Joyce". Retirement notice. In: *The Old Lady*, September 1963 (Bank of England Archive, ref. no. E8/172). pp. 173-174.

Mitchell, Breon. *James Joyce and the German Novel: 1922-1933*. Athens, Ohio: Ohio University Press, 1976.

Monegal, Emir Rodriguez. *Jorge Luis Borges: A Literary Biography*, New York: Dutton Publishers, 1978.

Monnier, Adrienne. *The Very Rich Hours of Adrienne Monnier*. Trans. with introduction and commentaries by Richard McDougall. New York: Charles Scribner's, 1976.

Noël, Lucie. *James Joyce and Paul L. Léon. The Story of a Friendship*. New York: Gotham Book Mart, 1950.

Norburn, Roger. *A James Joyce Chronology*. Author Chronologies Series. Houndmills, Basingstoke: Palgrave Macmillan, 2004.

O'Neill, Patrick. *Polyglot Joyce – Fictions of Translation*. Toronto: University of Toronto Press, 2005.

Pearson, Neil. "A Very British Pornographer: The Life of Jack Kahane". In: *Obelisk: A History of Jack Kahane and the Obelisk Press*. 1st ed., Liverpool University Press, 2007. pp. 1-76.

Potts, Willard, ed. *Portraits of the Artist in Exile. Recollections of James Joyce by Europeans*. Seattle and London: University of Washington Press, 1979.

Pound/Joyce – The Letters of Ezra Pound to James Joyce with Pound's Essays on Joyce. Ed. Forrest Read. London: Faber & Faber, 1968.

Rabaté, Jean-Michel. "'Thank Maurice:' A note about Maurice Darantiere". In: *Joyce Studies Annual* 2 (Summer 1991). pp. 245-251.

Rechcigl, Miroslav. *Beyond the Sea of Beer. History of Immigration of Bohemians and Czechs to the New World and their Contributions*. Bloomington, Indiana: Author House, 2017. E-book, no pagination.

Saint-Amour, Paul K. "Soliloquy of Samuel Roth: A Paranormal Defense". In: *James Joyce Quarterly* 37.3-4 (2000). pp. 459-477.

Shinkman, Paul A. "The Regained Generation of American Writers: The American Writers, and Others, Who Were in Paris in the 1920s". In: *Quarterly Review*, vol. 66 (Spring 1960). pp. 206-213.

Shloss, Carol Loeb. *Lucia Joyce*. New York: Farrar, Straus and Giroux, 2003.

Sigler, Amanda. "Scandalous Reputations: Serializing *Ulysses* in *Two Worlds Monthly*". www.berfrois.com/2011/06/happy-bloomsday, accessed 21 February 2019.

Simmons, Ernest J. "In Memoriam Alexander Kaun". In: *Slavonic and East European Review. American Series* 3.3 (October 1944). pp. 137-9.

Slocum, John J., and Herbert Cahoon. *A Bibliography of James Joyce*. London: Rupert Hart-Davis, 1957.

Smythe, Colin. "Crosby Gaige and W.B. Yeats's *The Winding Stair* (1929)". In: Warwick Gould, ed. *Yeats Annual* 13 (1998) London: Macmillan. pp. 317-328.

Spanier, Sandra, and Miriam M. Mandel, eds. *The Letters of Ernest Hemingway: Volume 4, 1929-1931*. Cambridge: Cambridge University Press, 2018.

Spoo, Robert. "Samuel Roth: Discourteous Reprinter". In: *Dublin James Joyce Journal* 5 (2012). pp. 99-111.

Spoo, Robert. *Without Copyrights. Piracy, Publishing and the Public Domain*. New York: Oxford University Press, 2013.

Styan, J.L. *Modern Drama in Theory and Practice*. Vol. 2: Symbolism, Surrealism and the Absurd. Cambridge: Cambridge University Press, 1981.

Sühnel, Rudolf, and Dieter Riesner, eds. *Englische Dichter der Moderne*. Berlin: Erich Schmidt Verlag, 1971.

Swift, Jonathan. *Gulliver's Travels*. Ed. Peter Dixon and John Chalker. Harmondsworth: Penguin English Library, 1975.

Todorow, Almut. "'Wollten die Eintagsfliegen in den Rang höherer Insekten aufsteigen?' Die Feuilletonkonzeption der *Frankfurter Zeitung* während der Weimarer Republik im redaktionellen Selbstverständnis". In: *Deutsche Vierteljahresschrift für Literaturwissenschaft und Geistesgeschichte*. Vol. 62 (1988). pp. 697-740.

Tripmacker, Wolfgang. "Potsdamer Verlage in der Zeit der Weimarer Republik". In: *Leipziger Jahrbuch zur Buchgeschichte 1993*. Mark Lehmstedt and Lothar Poethe, eds. Wiesbaden: Harrassowitz, 1993.

Turner, Catherine. *Marketing Modernism. Between the Two World Wars*. Amherst and Boston: University of Massachusetts Press, 2003.

Van Hulle, Dirk. *James Joyce's "Work in Progress". Pre-Book Publications of "Finnegans Wake" Fragments*. London and New York: Routledge, 2016.

Van Mierlo, Wim. "The Subject Notebook: A Preliminary Analysis". In: *Genetic Joyce Studies* 7 (Spring 2007). https://www.geneticjoycestudies.org/articles/GJS7/GJS7 _MierloSubject, accessed 13 June 2020.

Vogel, Matthias. Postscript to the reprint of *Heinrich Füssli. Aphorismen über die Kunst*. Basel: Schwabe-Verlag, 2012 (originally published 1944, translated and edited by Eudo C. Mason). pp. 175-192.

Wadsworth, Percy Beaumont. "Visits with James Joyce". In: *James Joyce Quarterly* 1.4 (Summer 1964). pp. 14-18.

Walsh, Keri, ed. *The Letters of Sylvia Beach*. New York: Columbia University Press, 2010.

Welch, Robert, ed. *The Oxford Companion to Irish Literature*. Oxford: Oxford University Press, 1996.

Whelpton, Vivien. *Richard Aldington: Novelist, Biographer and Exile.* Cambridge: The Lutterworth Press, 2019.

Whitesitt, Linda, et al. "Antheil, George". In: *Grove Music Online. Oxford Music Online.* http://www.oxfordmusiconline.com/subscriber/article/grove/music/00997, accessed August 2020.

Whitton, David. *Stage Directors in Modern France.* 1987. Manchester University Press, 1989.

Wilson, Nicola. "Albatross". Summary of Michele K. Troy's book, *Strange Bird: The Albatross Press and the Third Reich.* 2017. https://modernistarchives.com/biblio/strange-bird-the-albatross-press-and-the-third-reich, accessed 12 September 2020.

Woolsey, John M. "The Monumental Decision of the United States District Court Rendered December 6, 1933, by Hon. John M. Woolsey Lifting the Ban on 'Ulysses'". In: James Joyce. *Ulysses.* New York: The Modern Library (published by Random House, Inc.), 1940. pp. xi-xiv.

Yared, Aida. "Joyce's Sources: Sir Richard F. Burton's *Terminal Essay* in *Finnegans Wake*". In: *Joyce Studies Annual* 11 (2000). pp. 124-166.

Index

Albatross Press / Odyssey Press   130-132,
    235*n*.5, 250-252*n*.2, 253-255*n*.2, 261*n*.1,
    265*n*.5, 272*n*.3, 274, 280
See also Ulysses, continental edition
    arrangement with Beach   131-132, 235*n*.5,
        250-251*n*.4, 253-254, 272*n*.3
    royalty payments   272*n*.3, 274
Anderson, Margaret   xv, 10, 12, 43, 50, 103,
    276
Anna Livia Plurabelle   151*n*.3, 161, 277-279
    ALP in Basic English   168*n*.9
    ALP in French   19*n*.3, 99*n*.3, 125, 134, 137,
        151*n*.3, 154*n*.1, 161*n*.3, 164, 173, 175*n*.3,
        180-181*n*.11, 226*n*.2, 279
    ALP reading at Monnier's
    See Joyce soirée
    ALP record   55*n*.9, 168, 175*n*.3, 177, 217,
        221, 278
    See also C.K. Ogden
    first edition (deluxe)   116*n*.4, 145n.2,
        160*n*.3
    Navire d'Argent   20*n*.2, 76*n*.1
    trade edition   181, 219, 230, 278
Antheil, Böske   186*n*.2
Antheil, George   xv, 97, 152*n*.8
Associated Press   207, 211-212, 221, 265

Babou, Henri   155, 160*n*.1, 161, 164, 166, 278
Beach, Cyprian (younger sister)   20, 22
Beach, Eleanor Orbison (mother)   xvi, 278
Beach, Holly (sister)   18*n*.2, 198*n*.6, 276
Beach, Sylvester (father)   xvi, 152*n*.7, 159,
    272*n*.1, 279
Beach, Sylvia
    assistants   *see* Cyprian Beach, Jean
        Henley, Myrsine Moschos, Margaret H.
        Newitt, Jane van Meter
    claims re American rights of
        Ulysses   127-129, 253, 257
    decision to publish *Ulysses*   xv-xvi, 4
    estrangement from Joyce   14-15, 107, 109,
        124, 126, 128-131, 133, 235, 277
    health issues   124, 168, 183, 242, 244, 250
    Les Déserts   37*n*.1, 72, 74*d*, 75*fig*.,78-80,
        113*fig*.

letters to JJ, story of   xvi-xviii
resigning as Joyce's administrator   250,
    255
resigning as publisher of *Ulysses*   130,
    235, 244
translating 2 missing pages of
    Ulysses   118
See also royalties, Shakespeare and
    Company
Beckett, Samuel   19*n*.3, 118*n*.12, 133, 169*n*.12,
    186*n*.5, 193*n*.2, 278
    French translation of ALP   154*n*.1
    Our Exagmination   187*n*.8
Beran, Felix   201*n*.8
Bernstein, Theodore (née Aline Frankau)
    62
Bertrand-Fontaine, Thérèse   186, 189, 230
Bird, William   xvi*n*.1, 57, 96, 219
Black Sun Press   xvi*n*.1, 160*n*.3, 198, 253*n*.2
Bloch-Savitzky, Ludmila   90*n*.9
Borach, Georges   137, 161*n*.3, 228, 306-307
Borsch, Louis, Dr. (ophtalmologist)   28,
    38*n*.1, 55, 58*n*.1+2, 284, 285, 287-289
Boyd, Ernest   53*n*.11, 56
Bradley, William A. and Jenny Serruys (The
    Bradleys)   105*n*.1, 109
See also Exiles, French translators
Brody, Daniel   135, 137-139, 161*n*.3, 201-202,
    205, 207, 209-211, 214-215, 217, 219,
    221*n*.8, 228, 305-308
See also Rhein-Verlag
Bryher (Annie Winifred Ellerman)   39*n*.2,
    104, 273*n*.1
Buchman, Alexander   152*n*.6+7, 159
Budgen, Frank   xvii, 7, 106*n*.1, 151*n*.4, 187*n*.8

Cape, Jonathan   5, 42, 51, 54, 107*n*.1
Carducci, Edgardo   78, 152*n*.8
Cerf, Bennett   *see* Random House
Chamber Music   72, 167, 175, 198, 207, 233
    German translation   201, 206
    inclusion of individual poems in other
        collections   70*n*.3, 91*n*.12, 152*n*.10,
        205*n*.7, 250*n*.3
    leather-bound manuscript   258*n*.3

INDEX

Chamson, André   174
Chaucer ABC   see Lucia Joyce
Chicago Tribune   48, 140, 187, 219, 223n.17-225, 228, 265
Chroniques du Jour   70n.1+4, 91
Church, Henry and Barbara   268, 271
Colum, Mary   123n.1, 136, 145, 151n.4+5, 161, 167, 186n.5, 194, 217, 221
Colum, Padraic   145n.2, 164, 167, 207, 221
  American rights for *Ulysses*   130, 235
  choice of publisher of American *Ulysses*   170, 173
  Frankfurter Zeitung affair   136, 205-206, 212, 217, 306-307
  "James Clarence Mangan"   145, 154n.5, 161n.6
  negotiations for book publication FW   194-195
Commerce   37n.8, 45n.1+4, 61
Connolly, Cyril   212
Copeau, Jacques   19n.3
See also *Exiles*
Criterion   54n.5-55n.7, 87n.6, 162n.10, 226n.8
  Criterion Miscellany   160n.2, 162n.9, 279
  Criterion Publications   54
Cronache d'Attualità   70
Crosby Gaige (publisher)   116, 145n.2, 154n.5, 160n.3, 278
Crosby, Caresse and Harry   xvi, 198-199
See also Black Sun Press
Cunard, Nancy   xvi, 193, 215
Curtis Brown (literary agency)   126-128, 170, 173, 175, 184-185, 189
Curtius, Ernst Robert   54n.1, 97, 98n.4, 136, 207, 228, 307

Daniel (Joyce's florist)   166
Dante Alighieri   103, 139, 185n.6
Darantiere, Maurice   4, 26n.3, 44, 69, 95n.1, 127n.2, 276
Davidson, Jo   51n.2
De Alvear, Elvira   181
Deluxe editions   xv, 187n.6, 193n.3, 198
See also *Anna Livia Plurabelle, Haveth Childers Everywhere, Joyce Book, Lucia Joyce, Pomes Penyeach, Tales Told of Shem and Shaun*

Dial   10, 48n.2, 54n.5, 74n.1, 78, 82, 84, 85, 87, 89n.2, 93n.4, 100n.3, 149
See also *Work in Progress*, Shaun
du Pasquier, Hélène   8-9n.18, 9n.19, 36n.3
See also *Exiles*, French translators
Dubliners   26n.3, 87n.8, 107, 120n.6, 131, 139, 167n.2, 175n.1, 197n.5, 250n.4
  French translation   5, 9n.19, 36, 90n.10, 78-79n.6
  German translation   99n.4
Dublin Review   149, 164
DuBos, Charles   36, 98n.4
Dujardin, Édouard   39-40, 46n.12, 50, 181
Duncan, Elizabeth   118
Duplaix, Georges   70n.3

Egoist   xv, 5, 12, 27n.2, 42n.1, 54, 57n.6, 97n.2, 277
  Egoist Press   51, 54n.6, 107n.1
Eliot, T.S.   40n.5, 54, 76n.1, 78n.3, 97-8n.4, 136-137, 139, 161n.3, 162n.9+10, 168, 177n.11, 187, 195n.8, 198, 230, 257, 305-308
Ellmann, Richard   xvii-xviii
Enemy   10, 89n.3, 110n.2
Establet, Antonin (proprietor of Paris restaurant)   171, 179-180
Evening Standard   138, 198n.6
Exchange rates   xxiii, 72n.3, 142, 172, 179, 311f.
Exiles   5-9, 46n.11, 120, 167n.2, 175n.1, 276, 277
  French translators   7n.9, 8-9, 34, 109
  German translation   6
  New York: Neighborhood Playhouse   9, 51, 62, 68n.2
  Paris attempts to stage *Exiles*   7-9, 34, 37, 52

Faber & Faber   54n.5, 129, 135-136, 160n.2, 162, 164, 168n.6, 181n.16, 187n.6+8, 190, 197, 224, 226n.1, 230n.20, 233n.4, 253n.2, 257n.1
Fargue, Léon-Paul   xv, 37, 45, 45n.1, 61n.5, 177n.11, 181n.17
Farrar and Rinehart   229
Fernandez, Yva   9n.19, 36, 78-9n.6
Finnegans Wake   xv, 11n.28, 28n.4, 48, 54n.5, 68n.1, 105n.2, 123n.1, 125, 143+144*figs.*, 167n.2, 185n.6, 207n.22, 226, 281

See also Anna Livia Plurabelle, Haveth Childers Everywhere, Tales told of Shem and Shaun, transition, Work in Progress
    Joyce's offer to Beach for publication   190
    negotiations for book publication   126, 129, 133, 136, 140, 190, 194-195, 197-198, 224
Flanner, Janet   xiii
Ford, Ford Madox   55*n*.9, 149, 178
Fountain Press   145*n*.3, 154*n*.5, 155*n*.7, 161*n*.6
See also James R. Wells
Frankfurter Zeitung affair   126, 133-141, 200-202, 204-207, 209, 211-219, 221*n*.4-222, 224, 226*n*.3-228, 230, 305-308
See also Giorgio Joyce
    Blue Peter   215, 219, 228
    Hitschmann, Ernst   209*n*.1, 214*n*.3-215, 306
    Joyce, Michael   135, 138*n*.20-139, 200*n*.3, 209, 215, 219*n*.3+7, 228, 307
    Kafka, Irene   133-139, 200*n*.3, 205, 209*n*.1+3, 219, 224, 228*n*.4+8, 305-306
    "Michael und James"   138-139, 205*n*.4, 209, 219
    "Vielleicht ein Traum"/ "Perchance to Dream"   134-135, 200*n*.3+5, 204*fig.*, 211*n*.3, 215*n*.11, 217, 219, 228

Galantière, Lewis   10, 80
Gallimard, Gaston   19*n*.3, 157*n*.14, 180, 181*n*.8
Gide, André   xv, 19*n*.3, 41, 45-47, 54*n*.1, 97-98*n*.4, 158, 161, 163, 177*n*.11, 206, 281
Gilbert, Stuart   116*n*.3, 126, 130, 150, 165*n*.10, 186*n*.5, 187*n*.8, 207, 230, 234*n*.1, 241*n*.1, 251*n*.7, 268*n*.7
    French *Ulysses* translation   19*n*.3, 20*n*.2, 117*n*.10, 118*n*.15, 132
    Ulysses Study   137, 165*n*.11, 268*n*.7
Gillet, Louis   xvii, xviii, 23*n*.2, 136, 184-185, 226
    "Du côté de chez Joyce" (essay on *Ulysses*)   184*n*.5
    "L'Extraordinaire Aventure de M. James Joyce"   185*n*.6
    "M. James Joyce et son Nouveau Roman"   136, 184-185*n*.6+7, 189-190, 215, 219, 226, 230

Preface to *A Chaucer A.B.C.*, with initial letters by Lucia Joyce   160*n*.1, 250*n*.1
Gogarty, Oliver St. John   162
Goll, Ivan   54*n*.1, 99, 135, 137-138, 154*n*.1, 201*n*.10
    Frankfurter Zeitung affair   135, 137, 200-201*n*.10, 205*n*.3-206, 211, 213, 222, 228, 305, 307
    French translation of ALP   99*n*.3, 154*n*.1
    radio performances on Joyce   153, 217, 221-222
Gorman, Herbert   10, 48, 80, 82, 162*n*.11, 168, 175, 207, 219, 267
    Joyce biography   40, 56*n*.3, 87, 117, 155*n*.12, 163, 175*n*.1, 177, 178*n*.14, 208*n*.24, 229-30
Goyert, Georg   10, 77, 80*n*.1, 135, 161, 278, 305
See also Ulysses, German translation
Grabhorn Press   129, 193*n*.3
Gregory, Lady Augusta   163, 277

Harcourt Brace and Company   190*n*.2, 194*n*.2-195, 197
Harper & Brothers   194-195, 197
Harris, Frank   39, 221
Haveth Childers Everywhere (H.C.E.)
    first edition (deluxe)   155, 160*n*.1, 278
    trade edition   160, 162*n*.9, 164, 166, 181, 219, 230, 279
Heap, Jane   43
See also Margaret Anderson
Hébertot, Jacques   *see Exiles*
Hemingway, Ernest   xiii, 42*n*.1, 96, 179, 186*n*.5, 195, 198*n*.9, 212*n*.6, 231, 277
Henley, Jean   241-242
Hoey, Patrick   76
Holroyd-Reece, John   250*n*.4, 261
See also Albatross Press
Huebsch, Benjamin   10, 26*n*.3-27*n*.2, 40*n*.4, 56*n*.3, 126-127, 167*n*.2, 175, 177*n*.10, 184, 186*n*.2, 197*n*.5, 206-207, 257, 276, 279
Hughes, Herbert   152*n*.8, 155*n*.7
See also Joyce Book, Pomes Penyeach

International Letter of Protest   *see Ulysses*, Paris edition

INDEX

Ito, Hitoshi, "Concerning James Joyce's Method *Ishiki no Nagare* [Stream of Consciousness]" 228*n*.10
For Ito *see also* Nagamatsu et al.

Jahnke, Hans E.   xi, xvi, xviii
  Bequest   xviii, 3, 126
Jaloux, Edmond   23, 104*n*.4
Jim the Penman   48
John, Augustus   162
Jolas, Eugene   110*n*.3, 123*n*.1, 181*n*.17, 226, 242*n*.4, 277
See also transition
  French translation of ALP   154*n*.1, 226*n*.2
  Our Exagmination   187*n*.8, 226*n*.2
Jolas, Maria   xvii-xviii, 125, 242*n*.4
Jouvet, Louis   8, 51
Joyce Book (Oxford Edition)   152*n*.8+10, 155*n*.7, 233, 258
Joyce, Charles   184, 189
Joyce, Eva Mary   177
Joyce, Giorgio   xviii, 31, 34, 78*n*.5, 116*n*.3, 117, 126, 137, 139, 155, 166, 168, 173, 177, 183, 193, 194*n*.2, 195, 196*n*.12, 198*n*.6, 226, 227, 230, 231, 241*n*.1, 280
  Frankfurter Zeitung affair   200-02, 209, 216, 217, 305-7
Joyce, Helen (Fleischmann)   139, 168, 173, 183, 194*n*.2, 198*n*.6, 209*n*.1, 218, 226, 280, 305-307
Joyce, James
  addresses   282-303
  about Sylvia Beach   xiv
  British authorities   52, 55, 58, 277
  eye operations   38, 124, 183*n*.2, 221*n*.4, 224*n*.2+3, 226*n*.3
  eye troubles   xxi, 5, 23, 25, 40, 61*n*.1, 90, 116, 230, 242, 278, 284-85, 287-89, 295, 300-302
  See also Louis Borsch and Alfred Vogt
  Flemish   78*n*.1, 79
  health problems   116, 187, 228, 230
  transition   110*n*.3, 185*n*.6
  wedding   *see* Nora Joyce
Joyce, Lucia   xviii, 20, 26, 32, 34*n*.2, 38, 61, 78, 88, 107, 116, 118*n*.16, 186*n*.5, 193, 196, 218, 226, 279, 300
  A Chaucer A.B.C.   160*n*.1, 250*n*.1, 261*n*.1

  dancing lessons   118*n*.16
  mental illness   124, 151*n*.5, 186*n*.5, 242*n*.4, 280
  Pomes Penyeach   160*n*.1, 233*n*.4, 247, 250*n*.1, 280
Joyce, Nora   xvii, xix, 14, 32, 34*n*.2, 107, 207, 213, 216, 221*n*.2, 228, 231, 279
  wedding   187*n*.12, 196*n*.12-198*n*.6
Joyce soirée   104*n*.4, 134, 168*n*.6, 175*n*.3, 181
Joyce, Stanislaus   xvii, xviii, 7, 46*n*.8, 98*n*.5, 99, 134, 139-140, 155, 158*n*.17, 177, 229, 307
Joyce, Stephen   xvii-xviii, 55, 280
Joyce, various works
  anthology (Mary Colum's plans)   151*n*.4, 161*n*.6
  Collected Poems   198*n*.9, 253*n*.2
  "Daniele Defoe"   268
  "De Honni-Soit à Mal-y-chance" ("From a Banned Writer to a Banned Singer")   271
  "Giacomo Giocondo"   100
  "James Clarence Mangan"   145, 154*n*.5, 161*n*.6
  "Rime of the Ancient Mariner"   252
  "A Muster from *WiP*"   *see transition stories*

Kafka, Irene   *see Frankfurter Zeitung* affair
Kahane, Jack   155*n*.7, 160*n*.1+2, 161, 164, 247, 266, 278
Kastor, Robert   130
Katz, Leslie   xiv
Kendall, Claude   126, 127, 129, 170, 173, 177*n*.10, 184*n*.4, 186*n*.2, 206
Knopf, Alfred A.   151-2, 161*n*.6, 167*n*.2

Larbaud, Valery   xv, 4, 9, 19, 22*n*.1, 23*n*.2, 37, 39-40, 45*n*.1, 46, 50, 50*n*.21, 53*n*.11, 56*n*.3, 90, 98*n*.4, 104, 120*n*.3, 226*n*.8
  Nouvelle Revue Française   19*n*.3, 56*n*.3, 226*n*.8
  supervising French translation of *Ulysses*   19*n*.2+3, 20*n*.2, 45*n*.4, 61*n*.5, 117*n*.10, 118*n*.15, 309
Latrasse, Marie   17
Lawrence, D.H.   39*n*.1, 82*n*.2, 167*n*.2, 170*n*.2, 173*n*.3, 175*n*.1, 277

Le Monde 161
League for Public Discussion 46
Leblanc, Georgette 103
Léon, Paul xvi-xvii, xix, xxi, 124, 125
    129-133, 145*n*.1, 151, 160*n*.2-161, 164, 187, 235*n*.2+5+8, 237*fig*., 241*n*.1+2, 242*n*.2, 244*n*.1, 247, 250-251*n*.4+6, 253*n*.2-254*n*.1+3, 255*n*.1+2, 257*n*.1, 258*n*.3, 272, 280
    French translation of ALP 125, 154*n*.1
    Léon Papers 125
    Noël, Lucie 125, 145*n*.1
Les Déserts *see* Sylvia Beach
Levy, Louis S. (lawyer) 235, 238
Lewis, Wyndham 10, 42*n*.1, 89*n*.2+3, 92*n*.1, 110*n*.2, 162*n*.10, 181
Lewisohn, Alice (and Irene) 51*n*.2, 62
Lewisohn, Ludwig 12, 96*n*.2
Linossier, Raymonde 18
L'Intransigeant 140*n*.22, 154, 211-212, 214, 219, 226-228
Little Review xv, 5, 12, 18*n*.1, 19*n*.2, 24*n*.13, 43*n*.4, 50*n*.23, 57*n*.6, 103*n*.1, 134, 223*n*.18, 276
London Mercury 135, 162
Lyons, James 77

MacLeish, Archibald xiii, 12*n*.30, 82*n*.2, 96, 159
Madame Tisserand (concièrge) 32, 35, 52, 212
"Mangan, James Clarence" *see* Joyce, various works
Mason, Eudo C. 207, 306
McAlmon, Robert xv, xvi*n*.1, 39, 50, 76, 95*n*.1, 97*n*.1, 155, 157*n*.13, 178, 181, 230
    Our Exagmination 187*n*.8
McGreevy, Thomas 117-118, 187
Mercure de France 24, 97
Mesures 78*n*.6, 268, 271
Monnier, Adrienne xvi-xvii, 18*n*.1+*n*.2, 20, 22, 23, 26*n*.3, 27, 37*n*.5, 53*n*.11, 72, 75*fig*., 122, 124, 156*fig*., 158, 182*fig*., 197, 246, 276-279, 281
    See also Anna Livia Plurabelle, French translation, *Commerce*, Joyce soirée, *Ulysses*, French translation
    family xvi, 74, 79, 97, 186*fig*.

Frankfurter Zeitung affair 136
La Maison des Amis des Livres xv, 19, 20*n*.2, 51, 118, 134, 174-175, 268, 276, 278
Rocfoin xix, 116, 186, 188*fig*., 190, 194, 195, 197
    see also Mesures and *Navire d'Argent*
Monroe, Harriet 263
Monro Saw & Company xvii, 135, 137, 200-201, 205*n*.5, 219*n*.3, 228, 305-307
Moore, George 39*n*.3, 46, 165, 226
Moore, Marianne 87*n*.5+6, 93, 162*n*.10
Morax, Victor 28*n*.5
Morel, Auguste 19*n*.3, 20*n*.2, 45*n*.1, 91*n*.12, 117*n*.10, 118, 165*n*.10, 278
Morris, Lloyd 87
Moschos, Myrsine xxi, 27, 49, 76, 100, 116*n*.3, 155*n*.8, 186*n*.1+2, 4+5, 187*n*.6+8, 188, 279, 305-306
    her sisters 49*n*.14, 58

Nagamatsu, Sadamu, and Hitoshi Ito, Hisanori Tsujino (Japanese translators) 133, 216*n*.5, 222*n*.13, 229*n*.11, 243*n*.2, 260*n*.1
See also Ulysses, Japanese translation
Navire d'Argent 20*n*.2, 76, 76*n*.2, 174*n*.8, 212*n*.6, 277
See also Adrienne Monnier
Neighborhood Playhouse *see Exiles*
Newitt, Margaret H. 272
New Republic 168, 249
New Statesman 120, 135
New York Herald (*Tribune*) 82*n*.2, 145*n*.1, 149, 187, 264*n*.2-265
Nicolson, Harold 138, 212-213, 216-217*n*.14, 265, 306
Nogami, Toyoichiro (translator) 222*n*.15
See also Ulysses, second Japanese translation
Nouvelle Revue Française 19, 23, 41*n*.1, 56*n*.3, 99*n*.3, 117*n*.10, 154*n*.1, 157, 161*n*.2+3, 164*n*.3, 173*n*.6, 180*n*.5+6, 181*n*.8, 185*n*.6, 212*n*.6, 226*n*.8, 268*n*.4, 279
Nouvelles Littéraires 104, 161*n*.5, 196, 211-212

Obelisk Press 160*n*.1, 247*n*.1, 261*n*.1, 313
O'Casey, Sean 136, 139, 277
Ogden, Charles Kay 161*n*.3, 168, 217, 221

INDEX 327

ALP record   *see Anna Livia Plurabelle*
Okakura, Yoshisaburo (lawyer)   133, 243*n*.1, 250*n*.2-251
See also Ulysses, Japanese translations
Our Exagmination (O.E.)   39*n*.2, 118*n*.12, 120*n*.4, 165*n*.10, 187*n*.8, 197*n*.3, 224*n*.6, 226*n*.2, 230*n*.20, 257-258, 278
Oxford edition   *see Joyce Book*

Paris Notebook (Joyce)   155*n*.6
Paulhan, Jean   180*n*.7-181, 268, 271
Pinker, Ralph   126-131, 135, 136, 167, 175, 184-185, 186*n*.2-187, 189, 193, 197, 209, 214*n*.3, 216-218, 222, 233, 241*n*.1+2, 249, 306-308
Piracy   12, 14, 278, 280
See also Ulysses, Pomes Penyeach, Samuel Roth
Pitoeff, Georges and Ludmilla   52
Pollinger, Lawrence (Curtis Brown agency)   127-129*n*.7, 131*n*.8, 170*n*.2+3, 173, 175, 177*n*.10, 184*n*.4-186*n*.2, 206
Pomes Penyeach   16, 147*n*.1, 233, 253-254, 258*n*.3, 278, 279, 280
  copyright   152*n*.6+7, 233, 253
  deluxe edition   *see* Lucia Joyce
  individual poems   152*n*.9, 201*n*.8, 263
  piracy, attempted   152, 159, 164
  set to music   *see Joyce Book*
Ponisovsky, Alex   125
Portrait of the Artist as a Young Man   5, 23, 26, 27, 42, 54, 57, 120, 167*n*.2+4, 175*n*.1, 251*n*.4
  translations
    French   39*n*.3, 90*n*.9
    German   99*n*.3
    Japanese   95*n*.2, 216*n*.7, 222*n*.12
Pound, Ezra   xv, 6, 11-12, 15, 18*n*.1, 24*n*.13, 43*n*.1, 57*n*.6+7, 78*n*.3, 97*n*.2+3, 100, 109, 138, 155*n*.12, 157*n*.13, 162*n*.10, 170*n*.2, 193*n*.2, 268
Prévost, Jean   212, 214, 219, 226, 307
Proust, Marcel   78, 135, 168*n*.5
Pugh, Thomas (Dublin photographs)   208, 229
Putman, Samuel   155*n*.13

Quinn, John   xvii, 11, 50, 57, 96, 107*n*.2, 147, 281

Random House   116*n*.4, 128*n*.4, 130-131, 206*n*.13, 207*n*.16, 208*n*.24, 240*n*.2, 264*n*.1, 265*n*.1, 280
See also Ulysses, American edition
  Bennett Cerf   116*n*.4, 127*n*.1, 130, 264*n*.1
Rascher Verlag   *see Exiles*
Records, unrealized
  Monnier's reading of French ALP translation   175, 180
  Work in Progress "four old men"   55-56, 62, 64
Revue des Deux Mondes   184*n*.5, 185*n*.6, 189*n*.2, 213
Revue Nouvelle   70, 78*n*.6, 173*n*.6
Rhein-Verlag   7, 88, 142, 201*n*.10
See also Daniel Brody
  Frankfurter Zeitung affair   135, 137-138, 200-202*n*.10, 205-206, 209*n*.1+2, 228, 306
  German translation of *Ulysses*   99, 172-174, 179, 214-216*n*.4, 222*n*.16, 278
Rocfoin   *see* Adrienne Monnier
Rodker, John   xvii, 27*n*.2, 187*n*.8, 277
Romains, Jules   xv, 51, 136
Rosenbach, A.S.W.   107, 281
Rosenfeld, Henry R. (lawyer)   235-236n.8, 238
Roth, Samuel (piracy)   5-6, 10-13, 80*n*.3+4, 82, 94, 96, 105*n*.2, 126-127, 129-130, 138, 140, 175*n*.5, 186*n*.2, 211, 231*n*.4, 235-236n.6-8, 238*n*.1, 252*n*.2, 265*n*.1, 277-280
  International letter of protest   5, 12-14, 82*n*.2, 96*n*.2, 104, 138, 277
Rothschild, Herbert (arts patron)   193*n*.3
Rothschild, Willi (lawyer)   140, 307
Royalties   xv-xvi, 42, 62*n*.8, 66, 69, 100, 102, 107, 109, 124, 126, 128, 129, 132, 140, 142, 151, 153, 166, 173, 186*n*.2, 190*n*.2, 194, 194*n*.2, 195, 197*n*.2, 222*n*.16, 229, 229*n*.11, 230*n*.20, 238*n*.1, 239, 245, 246-248, 257
  Beach, royalty payments   *see* Albatross Press
Rudge, Olga   97*n*.3

Sage, Robert   123*n*.1, 187*n*.8
Saillet, Maurice   xiv, 181
San Lazarro, Gualtieri   70
Satie, Eric   xv, 18*n*.1

Sato, Ken 95
Schaurek (-Joyce), Eileen 117, 177
Schlumberger, Jean (*Nouvelle Revue Française*) 19*n*.3, 173-174
Schwartz, Jacob 145-146*n*.3+5, 154*n*.5
Seldes, Gilbert 48
Serruys Bradley, Jenny 9
See also William Bradley
Shakespeare 39*n*.1, 52*n*.5, 135, 151, 184*n*.5, 185*n*.6, 214, 227, 250*n*.1
Shakespeare and Company
See also Our Exagmination, Pomes Penyeach, royalties, *Ulysses*
　bookshop xiii, xv, xviii, 3, 14, 20, 39, 98, 181, 186, 273, 276, 278, 280, 281
　literary patrons and friends xv, xvi, 18, 19, 23, 37*n*.8, 41, 51*n*.5, 57*n*.6+7, 80*n*.3, 98*n*.4, 109*n*.3, 151*n*.2, 165*n*.10, 174*n*.8, 181*n*.12, 184*n*.5, 186*n*.5, 212*n*.6, 226*n*.2
　publisher 12, 16, 26, 42, 102*n*.1, 187, 197, 230, 239*n*.1
　subscribers to lending library 17, 18*n*.2
Shaw, George Bernard 46, 46*n*.10
Sims Reeves, John 68
Sinclair, May 97*n*.2
Soupault, Philippe 118*n*.15, 136, 151, 154*n*.1+3, 157, 175*n*.3, 180, 181*n*.17, 214-215, 219, 229
Spire, André 181, 276
Stein, Gertrude xv, 104, 109*n*.3, 177*n*.11
Stephens, Cynthia and James 177, 187
Stream of consciousness 39*n*.3, 46*n*.12, 97*n*.2, 228*n*.10, 265*n*.1
Sullivan, John 78*n*.5
Sussman, Aaron 206
Symons, Arthur 40, 50

Tales Told of Shem and Shaun 160*n*.3, 168*n*.9, 198*n*.9
Téry, Simone 49*n*.16, 104*n*.4
Theatre Arts Magazine 68
This Quarter 48
Three Mountains Press xvi*n*.1, 91*n*.7, 96*n*.1
Times Literary Supplement 120, 150
Transatlantic Review 55, 87*n*.6, 178*n*.15
transition 5, 78*n*.3, 100-101*n*.4, 110, 116*n*.4, 118, 120, 143*n*.1, 168*n*.9, 175, 185*n*.6, 207, 223, 226*n*.2, 277

transition stories 123*n*.1
Trausil, Hans (journalist) 205, 306-307
Tuohy, Patrick 71, 227
Two Worlds 11, 82*n*.2, 277
Two Worlds Monthly 11, 13, 82*n*.2, 96*n*.4, 277

Ulysses
　American edition xvi, 14, 126-132, 136, 167, 170, 173*n*.4, 175*n*.1, 177*n*.10, 184-186*n*.2, 189*n*.4, 193, 206*n*.12-207*n*.16, 235, 240*n*.2, 242, 244*n*.1, 257, 264*n*.1
　See also Sylvia Beach, claims re American rights
　continental edition 126, 130-132, 235*n*.5, 240, 244*n*.1, 250*n*.4, 251*n*.4
　See also Albatross Press
　film rights, Warner Brothers 241
　French translation 5, 19*n*.2, 20*n*.2, 61*n*.5, 118*n*.14+15, 165*n*.10, 180*n*.6, 184*n*.5, 278
　See also Stuart Gilbert, Valery Larbaud
　　Penelope 45*n*.1+4, 48
　　Protée 19*n*.3
　German translation 10, 77*n*.6, 80, 99*n*.4, 136*n*.18, 142*n*.1, 255*n*.1, 278
　German rights 54, 201
　subscription brochure 142
　Japanese translation 95, 133, 216, 222, 224, 228-229, 243, 250*n*.2-252*n*.2, 259, 260*n*.1, 279
　See also Watanabe, and Nagamatsu et. al.
　second Japanese translation 222, 250*n*.2, 252*n*.2, 280
　Memorandum of Agreement 126, 130, 132, 147, 189*n*.4, 235, 236*n*.8
　Paris edition xv-xvi, 130, 169*n*.12, 248, 280
　　sales xvi, 15, 39*n*.1, 44, 49*n*.11, 62*n*.10, 88, 102, 109*n*.1, 111, 127, 128*n*.4, 142, 153, 180, 194*n*.1, 206, 239, 244, 245, 248
　　8th printing (2nd ed) 69, 102*n*.1
　　11th printing (last ed) xv-xvi, 130, 169*n*.12, 248, 280
　　12th printing of Paris edition (planned) xvi, 131, 235, 240*n*.2, 242*n*.2, 244
　　subscribers 5, 20, 23-25, 27

Piracy *see* Samuel Roth
record   5, 55-56, 64-65
reviews   149-150
translation rights requests   94, 95*n*.1, 222, 243*n*.1+2
U.S. ban   12, 39*n*.1, 54, 132, 207, 242, 246, 264*n*.1-265, 280
U.S. trial   1933 264*n*.1, 265*n*.1, 280, 321
United Press   214, 221, 224, 226-228, 307

Valéry, Paul   61*n*.5
Van Meter, Jane   264, 268*n*.4
Veneziani, Bruno   158
Vico, Giambattista   72
Viking Press   126, 129, 136, 140, 167, 170, 175*n*.1, 190*n*.2+3, 195, 197-198, 207, 224, 253*n*.2, 257*n*.3, 279
See also Benjamin Huebsch
Vogt, Alfred Dr. (ophthalmologist)   183*n*.2, 224*n*.3, 226*n*.3, 242, 278, 295, 300-302

Watanabe, Kazuo   216-218, 222*n*.11, 228-229*n*.13
  Shibuya, Taro   222*n*.11
Weaver, Harriet Shaw   xv, xvii, 5, 24*n*.13, 27, 46, 54, 72*n*.4, 107, 136, 166, 187, 200, 231, 261, 276
  as addressee   6*n*.5, 7, 7*n*.12, 9*n*.21, 10-11, 18*n*.4, 42, 43, 50*n*.23, 51*n*.2, 55*n*.9, 68*n*.1, 76*n*.2, 78*n*.3, 92*n*.3, 94*n*.1, 95*n*.1, 97*n*.1, 105*n*.2, 120, 127, 143, 151*n*.4, 154, 233*n*.3, 243*n*.1, 247*n*.1, 251, 268*n*.7, 343
  financial gift to Joyce   58*n*.1, 61
  FW (Book I.1)   106

FW (Book III.403-590) Shaun   90*n*.7, 112
Frankfurter Zeitung affair   135-136, 215*n*.11
  receives typescripts of *Work in Progress*   72*n*.5, 86*n*.1
Wegner, Christian   251, 265
See also Albatross Press
Wells, James R.   116*n*.4, 145*n*.3, 154, 161*n*.6
Wilder, Thornton   215
Williams, William Carlos   76, 187
Wilson, Edmund   168
Woolf, Virginia   120*n*.6, 177*n*. 11, 184*n*.5, 195*n*.8, 277
Woolsey, Judge John M.   265*n*.1, 280
See also Ulysses, U.S. ban
Work in Progress
  "A Muster from *Work in Progress*" (anthology)   123*n*.1
  Dublin, Georgia (Book I.1)   86, 87
  early publication plans for copyright reasons   105*n*.2
  Harriet Weaver's piece   106*n*.2
  Issy's alphabet   100-01*n*.4
  Mamalujo (Book II.4)   55*n*.9, 64*n*.2
  negotiations for book publication   *see Finnegans Wake*
  Questionnaire (Book I.6)   110
  Shaun (Book III)   72, 74*n*.1, 78*n*.3, 85*n*.1, 89*n*.2, 90*n*.7, 92, 112
  Triangle (Book II.2)   89*n*.1

Yeats, Jack B.   230
Yeats, William B.   6, 40*n*.5, 43, 46, 50*n*.21, 57*n*.6, 78*n*.3, 116*n*.4, 162-163, 168*n*.5, 195*n*.7, 246